Russian Research Center Studies / 72

The Classroom and the Chancellery

ALLEN SINEL

The Classroom and the Chancellery:

State Educational Reform in Russia

under Count Dmitry Tolstoi

Harvard University Press / Cambridge, Massachusetts
1973

To my wife and family

Preface

Scholars have too often neglected the accomplishments of the Russian autocracy's chief support, the conservative bureaucracy, to focus on the more exciting adventures of the revolutionary opposition. Yet, for most of the nineteenth century, tsarist ministers had a far greater impact on Russian society than did the young radicals. This study, in an attempt to redress the balance, examines the policies and achievements of the Russian Ministry of Education under the direction of Count Dmitry Tolstoi. Aside from a few minor modifications, the fundamental changes Tolstoi introduced in elementary, secondary, and higher education shaped the Russian school system until the first decade of the twentieth century. Not only was his program the most durable of the tsarist period, but it functioned at one of the crucial times in Russian history, the era of that country's emergence from a backward agrarian society toward a modern industrialized one. For these reasons alone, Tolstoi's reforms deserve the full treatment they have not as yet received. As one American expert on Russian education recently noted, "There is not even a serious study of such a central figure as Dmitrii Tolstoi." [1] Hopefully the present work will help fill this gap.

An analysis of Tolstoi and his policies serves a twofold purpose. In addition to providing a much-needed survey of the Russian educational system and its results in postreform Russia, it contributes to a more balanced assessment of one of tsardom's most important bureaucrats. Except for official and semiofficial histories of Russian education, like S. V. Rozhdestvensky, *Istoricheskii obzor deiatel'nosti Ministerstva Narodnogo Prosveshcheniia 1802–1902* (St. Petersburg, 1902) and V. V. Grigor'ev, *Istoricheskii ocherk russkoi shkoly* (Moscow, 1900), Tolstoi has never had a good press in Russia. Prerevolutionary and Soviet scholars have customarily denounced him in the most abusive language. He was for them the "Minister of Public Darkness," the symbol of all the evils in autocracy.[2] While many Western writers like William H. E. Johnson in *Russia's Educational Heritage* (Pittsburgh, 1950) have accepted these judgments without question, a few have not been so onesided. Nicholas Hans has argued that Tolstoi's policies logically followed rather than contradicted those of his "liberal" predecessor, A. V. Golovnin, but Hans overstates his case. Concentrating on pedagogical matters, he virtually ignores Tolstoi's demands for centralization and his repudiation of Golovnin's policy of local autonomy for schools.[3] More inclusive and closer to my own interpretation is Patrick Alston's description of Tolstoi as a "bureaucratic enlightener," but Alston, committed as he is to covering over two hundred years of Russian education, does not develop this thesis at length nor devote much space to Tolstoi's efforts in such important areas as university education, teacher training, and primary schooling.

My intention, of course, is not to whitewash Tolstoi, but to place his actions in what I feel is a fairer, more meaningful historical perspective. To do this, one must not repeat the errors of most of Tolstoi's critics and judge his reforms from one's own point of view regarding the appropriate development of the Russian state. Instead one must attempt the difficult feat of putting oneself in the minister's place, of considering his measures in the light of the serious problems facing the loyal tsarist official who sought in a period of rapid change to decide questions of vital state interest without altering the existing social or political order. Only then can one understand and appreciate the endeavors of Russia's able but conservative ministers. The specific challenge that confronted Tolstoi was to raise substantially the educational level of the Russian people while at the same time preventing his expanded and improved school system from equipping its charges with the intellectual weapons to threaten the autocracy. This perplexing dilemma and the ministry's vigorous efforts to resolve it constitute the underlying theme of the present study.

The monograph itself quite naturally falls into two major parts. The first, Chapters 1 to 3, provides the historical, political, biographical, and administrative context for the Tolstoi reforms. Chapter 1 defines the dilemma the promotion of education posed for the autocracy and focuses on the various solutions proposed by Tolstoi's predecessors. Chapter 2 analyzes the Russian political situation at Tolstoi's accession to office and the character and training of the new minister. Chapter 3 describes the nature and powers of the ministerial apparatus through which Tolstoi would have to work. The second section, Chapters 4 to 7, comprises the bulk of this study and examines in detail Tolstoi's transformation of Russian higher, secondary, and primary education in order to see just how well his department managed to resolve the dilemma of educational progress at each of the three basic levels of the school system. Receiving the most attention are the secondary schools; not only were they the "cornerstone" of Tolstoi's program, but their reorganization aroused the greatest public reaction.

While this work thoroughly examines the ministry's major institutions of learning, it makes no attempt to survey every aspect of Russian education. To do so would bury the reader under a massive catalogue of school descriptions and hence distract him from what should be his central concern — the ministry's endeavors to convert its educational system into a productive, loyal servitor of the Russian autocracy. Therefore private, female, and technical schools merit little attention; they enrolled a tiny proportion of the student population and involved the ministry only peripherally. Far more important were the military institutes and the schools in the Russian borderlands; but these too are not discussed, the former because Tolstoi had no control over them whatsoever, the latter because it would take a separate monograph to explore adequately the unique problems of educating the non-Russian nationalities and the great variety of projects introduced.

While the jurisdictional limits of the Tolstoi ministry thus generally offer a logical boundary to our investigations, its chronological limits (1866–1880) do not. Since the full significance of the Tolstoi reforms becomes clear only in relation to the policies of his predecessor, a comprehensive review of Golovnin's programs is necessary. Equally vital is an analysis of the university legislation of 1884. True, it did not appear until after Tolstoi left office, and significant changes in mood and personnel had occurred in the government; but the statute was basically the same plan he had submitted to the State Council in 1880, an integral part of his education reforms, and as such it deserves inclusion here.

I have received much help in producing this study, and it is a pleasure to acknowledge this assistance. Sir Isaiah Berlin first inspired my interest in nineteenth-century Russian history. John Bosher and Ivan Avakumovic reviewed early segments of the work and encouraged me to proceed. Richard Pipes not only guided the initial stages of my research but read all the major drafts of the manuscript. His advice was invaluable. I owe special thanks to my research assistants, Frank Leonard and Kay Orth, for checking obscure references and aiding me in compilation of the index. My greatest debt is to my wife, whose passion for clarity and proper English style never flagged and who thereby saved many a passage from obscurity.

I am also most grateful to the following institutions for their support: the University of British Columbia, whose research grants helped defray the travel and duplicating costs connected with my research; the Canada Council, whose generous leave fellowship enabled me to devote all my energies to revising the manuscript; Harvard University's Russian Research Center, which provided me with a pleasant environment in which to work; and the Intellectual Prospecting Fund at the University of British Columbia, which helped subvent the costs of publishing this book. The burdensome chore of typing and retyping the manuscript was done with great good humor by the secretaries of the Russian Research Center and of the History Department at the University of British Columbia and is certainly much appreciated. Finally, I should like to thank the editors of the *Slavic Review* for allowing me to use material from my article on Russian elementary education, which appeared in that journal in 1968.

On the matter of transliteration, I have used the Harvard College Library modification of the Library of Congress system, except that I have changed the *ii* at the end of proper names to *y*. In the case of pre-1918 orthography there has been an attempt to modernize the spellings.

It is impossible to end these prefatory remarks without commenting briefly on the relevance of my investigations to the recent educational crisis in the United States, particularly since student unrest played so important a part in the period under consideration. The dissimilarities between Russia a century ago and America today are too great, I think, to draw any conclusive lessons from Tolstoi's activities. However, certain weaknesses of the Tolstoi program do raise interesting questions about parallel developments in our own school system. For example, those who ignore or repress legitimate student grievances against the state or school, those who believe one can legislate student discontent out of existence, those who belittle the ability of teachers to manage their own affairs, and those whose method of instruction consists primarily in rote memorization would do well to recall the adverse effects of similar policies pursued in Russia during the 1860s and 1870s. The Russian experience thus may help discredit such facile or intolerant solutions to the educational problems of the present day. These problems in turn should increase our understanding of Tolstoi's predicament. When education appeared an unqualified good and students humbly attended lectures and then eagerly took up their appropriate roles in society, few comprehended the Russian ministry's suspicious attitude toward its charges. Now that education appears a definite threat to the established order and students have disrupted both campus and public life, one can at least better appreciate, though not necessarily approve of, the Tolstoi system.

Contents

The Classroom and the Chancellery

Few governments in nineteenth-century Europe so needed a vigorous school system and yet had more to fear from its products than the Russian. No longer a luxury for the rich or the special preserve of the church, education had become, in Tsar Alexander II's words, "a most important state concern because it guaranteed the future well-being of Russia." [1] It grew increasingly obvious during the century that if Russia were to safeguard her great-power status, she required a literate populace and an educated elite. Without a large skilled work force and competent bureaucrats, engineers, scientists, teachers, and other professionals, the emperors could not establish the efficient administrative apparatus, the industrialized economy, and the modern army essential for maintenance of their country's security.

But the schools were more than a source of technical personnel. Properly directed, they could strengthen Russia's internal stability. As an organ of propaganda, they could inculcate state-

approved beliefs and attack heretical or subversive views. As educator of the masses, they could wipe out the profound ignorance
which complicated the problem of reforming Russia's outmoded
political and social structure. As a civilizing force in the countryside, they could help unify the nation by narrowing the gap between the Europeanized intellectuals and the semi-Asiatic peasantry. Alexander had clearly not exaggerated education's role, for
the rapid spread of learning could greatly assist the transformation of Russia from an inchoate, vulnerable, underdeveloped land
into a cohesive, powerful, advanced state.

Despite its apparent benefits, many tsarist officials rightly considered popular enlightenment a mixed blessing. The success of
autocracy depended on its subjects' unquestioning devotion to the
throne and their unawareness of conditions elsewhere; education
could undermine these twin supports of faith and ignorance, since
its purpose was to improve the student's analytic and rational
faculties and to introduce him to the physical and intellectual
world surrounding him. Schools could thus both provide their
charges with the intellectual equipment to criticize existing society and demonstrate to them the shortcomings of their own situation by disseminating ideas from abroad.

While higher education because of its sophisticated curriculum
and teaching methods would most likely produce these dangerous
results, even elementary schooling could be a threat. The instructor might transmit the skepticism and Western radicalism he acquired at the upper levels of the education system to his own primary school classroom. Even if he did not, his pupils would still
emerge from the dark forests of illiteracy. Having taken these first
steps, they could more easily be made conscious of the inequities
in their position, of the evils within their country.

An expanding educational system could disrupt the political
tranquility of the regime by increasing the people's expectations
as well as their knowledge. With good schools everywhere the
state could give all segments of the population a chance to improve themselves. Such a policy broadened the scope of the state's
search for able personnel and thereby assured it of the sizable ed-

ucated elite it wanted; at the same time it placed the government in an unpleasant predicament. If it wholeheartedly pursued a program of "careers open to talent," it would not only bring into power new groups whose loyalty had not been proved by generations of previous service, but it would alienate those very classes it had traditionally relied on for support and trained assistance. On the other hand, if it did not guarantee the graduates of its schools upward mobility and an opportunity to use their newly obtained skills, it risked further frustrating its already discontented lower classes.

A formidable dilemma thus confronted the autocracy. The more it encouraged the spread of education, the more it endangered its own safety; for the intellectual weapons forged at school could as easily be used against the state as for it. When students today even in the comparatively liberal atmosphere of democratic societies often lead attacks upon the established order, how much more likely would they be to turn to revolt in the unenlightened and oppressive conditions of nineteenth-century Russia. The two-edged sword of education might strike down the autocracy instead of lopping off the Hydra-heads of illiteracy, technical backwardness, and bureaucratic incompetence. If the state were to survive, it must master the technique of blunting the dangerous side of the blade while sharpening the useful edge.

This complex task of honing fell to the Minister of Education. Elsewhere the clergy, local societies, and private individuals had played a vital part in advancing education; "in Russia," the *Zhurnal Ministerstva Narodnogo Prosveshcheniia* could boast in 1867, "the history of education is primarily a history of the government's efforts in this sphere," [2] and the minister was the official mainly accountable for the state's extensive activities in education. He thus occupied one of Russia's most strategic posts, because he alone was in a position to resolve the dilemma posed the autocracy by its insistent demand for well-trained subjects. The man who introduced the most comprehensive and, as it turned out, the most durable solution to the problem was Count Dmitry Tolstoi. This study will stress Tolstoi's attempts to establish a viable school system that would considerably improve Russian education and yet not jeopardize the position of the emperor and his government.

Although the same task had faced his predecessors, by the time Tolstoi took office in 1866 its successful completion had become a matter of national survival. The major threats to tsardom could easily be linked to the failings of its education program. Russia's defeat in the Crimean War and the recent spectacular victories of the well-equipped, well-trained Prussian army demonstrated the empire's vulnerability before the technologically superior Western nations. Russia could never hope to compete with these powers until it greatly improved and expanded its schools. Yet to do so seemed almost suicidal, for even the few universities and technical institutes that existed in Russia were already supplying the revolutionary movement with too many dedicated followers. The two-edged sword of education was clearly cutting both ways; and, just to make its handling more difficult, society for the first time was challenging state domination of school policy. The difficulty of Tolstoi's mission was outweighed only by its gravity.

The Liberal Statute of 1804

To explain Tolstoi's reforms fully, it is necessary to examine his precursors' efforts toward making education a loyal servitor of the state. There are two reasons for briefly indulging in this vice of most historians, the obligatory survey of the events preceding the period under investigation. First, the results of the previous ministers' activity — the schools, inspectorates, bureaus — were the raw materials with which Tolstoi would work. Second, a look at the past should put into clearer perspective for the modern reader, as it undoubtedly did for Tolstoi (himself a historian), both the dilemma created by promoting education in an autocracy and the possible answers to this dangerous paradox.

Since the time of Boris Godunov, tsars had demanded secular schooling for their subjects, but not until Alexander I did Russia achieve a comprehensive school network. While Peter I established the first technical schools, Elizabeth the first university, and Catherine II the first organized system of primary and secondary eduction,[3] Alexander integrated these tentative, incomplete measures into a coherent structure. That Alexander should accomplish this was quite understandable. Nourished on the theories of the Enlightenment, both he and his four young advisers, who comprised the famous Unofficial Committee, had confidence in education's ability to uplift and perfect the individual, thereby benefiting the state. They blamed the ignorance of the people and incompetence of officials for impeding the reform program they envisioned for their country. Consequently, education was one of the eight ministries introduced in 1802, with three of the four members of the Unofficial Committee serving on the ministry's major advisory body, the Central School Board *(glavnoe uchilishchnoe pravlenie),*[4] and, more important, a detailed statute on popular instruction was issued on 5 November 1804.

Reflecting its compilers' faith in the unqualified advantages of education, this school act was the most liberal of the nineteenth century. No fear of student unrest or of rapid social mobility prompted addition of the restrictive features so common to later decrees. Indicative of this trusting attitude toward schools were the powers given the university, the cornerstone of the new structure. Not only did it train scholars and prepare secondary school teachers, it supervised the state schools in its education district *(okrug),* the ministry's largest administrative unit.

Subordinate in theory to the district's curator *(popechitel'),* the university in fact enjoyed substantial autonomy, since the curator's duties as a member of the Central School Board kept him in St. Petersburg most of the time. A council of professors and adjuncts elected a rector, chose the faculty, and ran the university.[5] Moreover, as the district's chief executive organ, the university council designed course outlines for primary and secondary schools, confirmed teaching appointments, and nominated (subject to ministerial confirmation) gymnasium directors. The council's assistants in school administration — a university committee of six professors and the rector, the gymnasium directors responsible for the county *(uezdnye)* schools, and the county school principals *(smotriteli)* responsible for the parish schools — all came from within the educational system.[6] This self-contained, interlocking arrangement of inspection and decision-making sharply restricted the possibility of outside interference. It acknowledged the professional educator's authority in school matters — a reasonable principle because it respected the value of expert opinion, but one which succeeding tsarist governments would not accept.

Equally progressive ideas determined the scholastic programs of Russia's three school levels: the one-year parish school, the two-year county school, and the four-year gymnasium. Student welfare was the instructor's primary concern. Instead of the pedantic, authoritarian schoolmaster of the past, he must become his pupils' mentor and friend, for "teachers take the place of parents and therefore must take on the latter's feelings: gentleness, tenderness, patience and attentiveness to their [the students'] well-being."[7]

More important, the statute of 1804 sought to guarantee the fullest development of the pupils' potential. Borrowing extensively from Condorcet's proposals to the Assemblée Nationale in 1792, the ministry introduced the ladder system of education and a utilitarian curriculum. The ladder system, whereby the successful graduate could enter the institution immediately superior to the one he had finished, when combined with free tuition and the absence of nonacademic entrance restrictions, enabled students to acquire as much education as their capacities would allow. This was a most democratic arrangement for an autocratic state, since it in theory opened higher education and its privileges to all classes; but serfs of course needed their lord's permission to attend schools outside their village.[8] Those students who lacked the ability or inclination to work their way up the educational ladder still would benefit from attending class, for each school provided a complete and useful education conforming to the social position of the majority of its pupils. The parish school, for instance, included among its texts *A Short Manual on Agriculture, on Natural Phenomena, on the Composition of the Human Body, and in General on the Measures to Preserve Health*; the county school included a course in the "fundamental rules of technology relating to local conditions and industry"; and the gymnasium improved upon the rigid classical bias of

European secondary education by offering such practical subjects as statistics, political economy, technology, and commerce.[9]

Praiseworthy though they might be, Alexander's reforms had three substantial defects.

(1) The first prevented the ministry from extending its advanced program to all Russian educational institutions. In 1802 the emperor gave the new ministry "direct jurisdiction" over "all . . . schools, except those placed under the special protection of Her Majesty Maria Feodorovna and those entrusted by Our special order to other persons or departments."[10] Students could thus easily bypass the type of education the ministry thought good for them to attend the more narrowly conceived clerical seminaries, military academies, or noble boarding schools.

(2) The second flaw further limited the ministry's influence by leaving the parish schools a paper creation. Reluctant to interfere with the master-serf relationship and stingy with its own resources, the government made the village schools financially dependent on such unreliable groups as gentry, clergy, and peasant societies.[11] This lack of state support for elementary education minimized the democratic aspects of the 1804 legislation: without the bottom rung of the ladder in place, how could most of the lower classes begin their ascent? Both the ministry's restricted authority and its reliance on local organizations for elementary-school financing would blight the growth of education throughout the century.

(3) Shorter lived but more immediately damaging was the third failing: in its haste to bring enlightenment to Russia, St. Petersburg paid little attention to actual conditions within the country. Conservatives like N. M. Karamzin quite rightly criticized the government's measures for neglecting the peculiarities of the Russian situation, particularly the extensive illiteracy of the masses, the absence of a sizable educated class, and the underdeveloped state of Russian intellectual life.

Professors have been invited before there were students to hear them, and though many of these scholars are prominent, few are really useful; for the students begin but poorly acquainted with Latin, are unable to understand these foreign instructors, and are so few in number that the latter lose all desire to appear in class. The trouble is that we have built our universities on the German model, forgetting that circumstances in Russia are different. . . . In Russia there are no lovers of higher learning. The gentry perform service, while the merchants care only to obtain a thorough knowledge of mathematics or of foreign languages for purpose of trade. . . . The constructing and purchasing of buildings for universities, the founding of libraries, cabinets, and scholarly societies, and the calling of famous astronomers and philologists from abroad — all this is throwing dust in the eyes. What subjects are not being taught today at such places as Kharkov and Kazan! And this at a time when it takes the utmost effort in Moscow to find a teacher of Russian, when it is virtually impossible to find in the whole country a hundred men who know thoroughly the rules of orthography, when we lack a decent grammar, when imperial decrees make improper use of words.[12]

Both problems cited by Karamzin (the unsuitability of the teachers and the smallness and apathy of the potential student body) lessened the value of Alexander's reforms. The absence of a large academic community in Russia forced the new universities to hire foreign scholars with the unhappy results Karamzin so vividly described. At the other schools there were more native instructors, but they often lacked talent; for the teacher's low salary and inferior social position discouraged able people from entering the profession. While poor teaching may have kept some from the ministry's institutions, the indifference of those classes free to pursue education was the major factor. The lower orders considered schooling to be merely the acquiring of practical knowledge and withdrew their sons after they had learned the essentials of reading, writing, and arithmetic. The gentry, who could most easily afford higher education and on whom the government counted for trained officials, preferred the more exclusive and probably less difficult private institutions. That M. M. Speransky, dismayed by the ignorance still prevalent in the central bureaucracy,

wanted in 1809 to restrict high-level promotions in the civil service to those who had passed the university course or examinations
in fields relating to their branch of service demonstrated just how
unsuccessful the gymnasium and university were in attracting the
appropriate students. The extensive interdependence of the
schools transformed this shortage of good teachers and students
from a mere inconvenience into a crisis. Since a school at one level
relied on institutions at other levels for its pupils and instructors, a
serious deficiency at any rung jeopardized the entire system.[13]

These failures in implementation should not obscure the significance of Alexander's early reforms. They were an impressive
achievement, all the more remarkable because they were instituted at a time when that obvious result of free-thinking, the
French Revolution, still hung over Europe and when "enlightened" France was revoking the egalitarian, permissive policies of
the directory.[14] In addition to giving Russia the ministerial apparatus and the four-stage school network that would become dis-
tinctive features of its educational program, Alexander supported
the modern, progressive ideas of the ladder system and school autonomy, a policy that became the ideal of liberal educators for the
next hundred years. Not yet troubled by the possible dangerous
by-products of learning, the emperor had limited state control
over schools and had made these institutions a means of upward
mobility by opening them to anyone with talent and by explicitly
linking (in the Speransky Examination Act) government service
to educational qualifications, not social class. The shortcomings of
his measures did not stem from a fear of education, but from the
very backwardness and poverty he hoped education would help
eliminate.

Conservative Compromise Solutions, 1815–1848

Unfortunately for the development of Russia's schools, the first
decade of Alexander's reign marked the last time in the nineteenth century that the Russian state considered education an unqualified good. With the surge of conservative Russian nation-

alism after the victories of 1812, and the general religious revival and reaction against rationalism in full force, Russian ruling circles began turning against the existing school system — based as it was on foreign, particularly French, models. Instead of countering this opposition, Alexander (who had grown disillusioned with domestic affairs) actually strengthened it by entrusting the day-to-day management of his country to the notorious regimentarian Count A. A. Arakcheev. The government quickly unsheathed its first weapon in the struggle to keep education totally subservient to state interests. In 1817 Alexander joined the departments of religion and education into a single Ministry of Spiritual Affairs and Education under A. N. Golitsyn, the Procurator of the Holy Synod, expressly so "that Christian piety always form the basis of true education." [15] The stale air of outmoded religious study began to suffocate the free spirit of inquiry.

As they would for the rest of the century, the universities bore the brunt of the ministry's attack. The tradition of academic freedom, the sophisticated level of instruction, the breadth of the curriculum, and the maturity of the student body all made the university the institution most susceptible in the government's view to subversive influences. If Russian conservatives needed any proof of this, the recent activities of the German undergraduates (like the formation of a General German Student Union and the assassination of the writer Kotzebue) certainly provided it by demonstrating the political role university students could play. Fearing similar actions by Russian students, the ministry immediately conducted an investigation into reported unrest at Kazan University. The ensuing report by M. L. Magnitsky, prototype of the educational department's many obscurantist officials, proclaimed that the evils of unsupervised intellectual activity had now come to Russia; Kazan was a hotbed of sedition and heresy.

Faced with this apparent threat to national security, the autocracy turned to repression and control instead of seeking the causes of the disaffection. Although it rejected Magnitsky's drastic solution of closing the university, the government did in June 1819 appoint him curator of the Kazan district, with explicit orders to remove unreliable professors and to introduce Christian teachings into the university courses.[16] To save Russia from the misfortunes of Germany, where "the professors of godless universities imbue hapless youth with the subtle poison of skepticism and hatred of authority," Magnitsky sought to transform the faculty from scientists in search of truth into propagandists in service to the state. He called on professors to advocate the principles of Orthodoxy and autocracy and to adapt their views to the Scriptures, which alone form "the basis of all private and civic virtues." For example, courses in classics and history should praise the Christian elements of civilization and denigrate the pagan; those in political law should demonstrate "that the Monarch's sacred authority . . . comes down from God and that his legislation is the expression of the Highest will." [17]

Following Magnitsky's lead, other curators also disrupted Russian academic life. There were dismissals at Kharkov and Dorpat universities while in St. Petersburg, D. P. Runich, often called "Magnitsky's echo," persecuted professors for teaching "in a spirit contrary to Christianity and filling students with ideas which threatened public order and well-being." [18] Only Moscow University, probably because of its venerable position, generally escaped these reactionary measures.

The ministry's response to the actions of Magnitsky and his cohorts was ambivalent. On the one hand, it contributed to the oppressive atmosphere by giving its curators extraordinary powers. On the other hand, it blocked Magnitsky's attempts to translate his reforms at Kazan into a comprehensive university statute. No doubt ministry officials recognized the shortsightedness of the Magnitsky program. While useful in hindering the diffusion of radical doctrines, his tactics could ultimately destroy the university and thereby dry up a major source of the trained elite that Russia needed. The Kazan curator's answer to the dilemma of education was clearly no answer at all, yet it did set a dangerous precedent for future ministers. The impression that indoctrination, restrictions on academic freedom, and extensive state interference could combat the allegedly subversive tendencies of higher education would fade less quickly from the minds of Russian officials than the disastrous results such devices produced.

Where Magnitsky had endangered the entire educational system by his frontal assault on the universities, the young St. Petersburg curator, Count S. S. Uvarov, showed how one could improve the schools and still undermine the more radical features of Alexander's 1804 statute. Uvarov criticized the gymnasium's encyclopedic curriculum because it "included many subjects wholly incompatible with one another. . . . Political economy, commerce, finance, aesthetics, and philosophical analysis, the study of which requires a mature and trained intellect and is therefore usually left to the universities, have burdened the pupil's memory while not developing his intellectual powers." His solution, concentration on those subjects "which have been the basis of all education programs everywhere throughout history"—classics, mathematics, foreign languages — and the dropping of the less conventional courses in philosophy, commerce, political economy, and technology, became department policy in 1819.[19]

In the ministry's view the advantage of the revised curriculum was twofold: it better prepared students for the university and it helped counteract the democratic aspects of the ladder system. Indeed, elimination of the more practical subjects from its course marked the second step in the gymnasium's evolution from an accessible, diversified institution to an exclusive, specialized one. The first step had occurred on 1 February 1819 when the ministry received permission to charge tuition at its schools.[20] As a gymnasium education became too expensive and inapplicable for the poorer, less cultured groups, it would grow more attractive, so the government hoped, to the gentry, the class traditionally associated with the service privileges that now accompanied higher education.

It would be premature, however, to perceive in these measures a strict policy of class exclusiveness, especially since the government created numerous state stipends for those unable to afford gymnasium fees. The total repudiation of the lower strata's interest in higher education — like the terrorist campaigns of Magnitsky — was too myopic a policy for Golitsyn. Although he realized that the ladder system and the autonomous university could threaten the regime's political and social stability, he balked at destroying the liberal framework he had inherited. His successors would not be so hesitant.

The appointment on 15 May 1824 of Admiral A. S. Shishkov as Minister of Education, and the accession of Nicholas I soon afterward, accelerated the demolition of the edifice Alexander had built. Neither the youthful emperor, brought up to be a soldier, nor his minister, a patriotic defender of everything truly Russian, had the background to appreciate educational policies based on foreign models and on the Enlightenment's faith in the benefits of unlimited schooling. Dedicated to preserving traditional Russian institutions, Nicholas and Shishkov saw the rapid spread of learning as a threat to the old order — at best a mixed blessing, because "knowledge makes a bad person as dangerous as it makes a good one useful." [21] The uprising of army officers that greeted Nicholas on the very day of his taking the imperial oath underlined the urgency of the situation. Young intellectuals, many of whom had studied at Russia's best schools, were challenging the regime. Autocracy's century-long struggle with its educated elite had begun.

Nicholas and Shishkov immediately agreed on the tactics for combating education's two most dangerous offshoots: free thinking and social mobility. For both men vigorous moral instruction was the right antidote for the ideological poison drunk at school. Shishkov had warned his subordinates in September 1824 that young people "who lack reverence for God, devotion to the Emperor and the fatherland, love for justice and mankind and a sense of honor, will be infected by pseudo-philosophizing, flighty dreaming, puffed up pride and pernicious self-esteem." [22] Nicholas echoed this view in his manifesto announcing the execution of five Decembrists:

Let parents turn all their attention to the moral education of their children. The absence of firm principles . . . has produced this fanaticism which has aroused violent passions, this pernicious luxury of half-assimilated knowledge, this urge toward visionary extremes which starts by debasing morals and ends in perdition.[23]

Even with a model upbringing, the student whose education exceeded his place in society constituted a potential menace to the state. Frustration and despair, Nicholas predicted, would force this unlucky individual to "indulge in pernicious dreams and low passions," for the emperor like his minister believed that "knowledge is only useful when . . . it corresponds to a person's status." This concept was certainly not new. Frightened by the egalitarian ideas of the French Revolution, conservative officials everywhere worried that too much schooling might encourage the lower classes to rise above their proper sphere. As early as 1801, the French Minister J.-A. Chaptal had argued: "The principal goal of education ought to be to give everyone the knowledge necessary for him to fulfill the functions in society to which he is called." Twenty-six years later the Russian emperor advocated the same principle: "instruction should conform as closely as possible to the pupil's future so that each . . . acquires the knowledge which he needs to serve and better his lot [but] does not strive to raise himself way above the station allotted to him by the normal course of affairs." [24]

To achieve this aim, the education act of 1828 assigned each social class a specific school. Parish schools trained the "very lowest classes"; county schools gave the "children of merchants, artisans and other city inhabitants . . . that knowledge which according to their way of life could be most useful for them"; and gymnasiums established pensions to make it "most convenient for the gentry and local bureaucrats to educate their children." In an effort to enforce this simplistic arrangement, the ministry abolished the ladder system. The parish and county schools became blind alleys; they no longer prepared their pupils for secondary education but only for supplementary courses in trade, industry, and agriculture, the most suitable occupations, the government felt, for the lower classes. The gymnasium alone retained its dual purpose of providing a useful terminal education and of readying its graduates for further study. Since its expanded, seven-year course now offered both primary and secondary education to those passing an examination in the fundamentals of reading, writing, and arithmetic, the quickest path to higher education was to enter the gymnasium directly after a little private tutoring.[25] Although the gymnasium legally remained open to all classes except the serfs, its higher costs, and its new prolonged course, with as much as one-quarter to one-third of class time devoted to ancient languages, would restrict its appeal to the more politically reliable classes. The others would be shunted off to the cheaper, shorter, more practical education culs-de-sac, the county and parish schools.

While the ministry swiftly found a means of curtailing the school's role as a democratizing agent, it could not so quickly discover a safeguard against the subversive influences penetrating its institutions. Not only was it more difficult to rid the classroom of dangerous ideas than of unwanted students, it was unwise to use the ministry's strongest defense mechanism, rigorous suppression of faculty and students. This device, as the Magnitsky interlude had proved, endangered the whole school system. A far less destructive, but equally effective, policy was necessary, but such a program could only come from someone who combined a faith in the political status quo with an enthusiasm for the spread of learning. Neither Shishkov nor Nicholas was the type; Count Uvarov, who took over the ministry in 1833, was. As a scholar-essayist, president of the Academy of Sciences, founder of the Russian classical gymnasium, he appreciated the value of education; as a famous ideologist for autocracy, he feared education's latent threat to the existing government.

During his sixteen years in office Uvarov constantly sought to build a school network that would support rather than undermine Orthodoxy, autocracy, and nationality, the three pillars of the Russian state. To overcome the hazards of a vigorous educational program, he proposed the following three measures: seize complete control over school life, eliminate or de-emphasize politically dangerous subjects while instilling the desired moral and patriotic feelings, and reserve higher education for the most loyal and qualified classes. These were hardly new remedies, but Uvarov was the first minister to apply all three extensively and in conjunction with a serious campaign to improve Russian education. His protégé, Count Dmitry Tolstoi, would be the next.

Following the program outlined above, the ministry promptly set out to destroy the relative independence of Russia's educational institutions, the last remnant of Alexander's progressive legislation. It challenged the universities' jurisdiction over primary and secondary schools because, it argued, professors could not pursue their scholarly duties and at the same time properly supervise and direct other schools. Education had become too important to entrust to the teachers alone. Hence, by a decree of 25 June 1835, the curator and his ministry-appointed aides, the assistant curator and district inspector, took from the university council all authority over the educational district. State officials, selected by and solely responsible to the minister, now determined policy and controlled education in the provinces.[26]

Just a month after it relinquished its dominance over education in the district, the university also lost its autonomy. The new statute made the curator a powerful, locally based overseer of university affairs. He presided over the university's two major ruling bodies, the council and the board; appointed and directed the institution's inspectorate; and had the right to reprove negligent teachers and even initiate "legal measures to remove unreliable ones." While extending the curator's authority, the ministry curtailed that of the university council. It abolished the university court, transferred many council duties to the newly established and less representative university board, and interfered with the council's traditional privilege of faculty selection by permitting the Minister of Education to fill university chairs at his discretion.[27]

With the state more in control of its educational institutions, it proved to be easier to apply Uvarov's second remedy, that of student indoctrination and supervision. Although he recognized the school's propaganda potential, and indeed urged teachers to instill "devotion to the throne and obedience before authority," [28] Uvarov stressed the negative policy of avoiding harmful influences over the more positive one of inculcating the proper moral and political values. For example, the ministry considered the maintenance of discipline the "chief guarantee" of the university's well-being. It thus placed an inspector in every university "to keep an eye continually on the actions and thoughts of the students." To ensure that he performed this task well, the ministry paid the inspector more than most professors and allowed him to have as many as twelve assistants. The university also did not escape from the parade-ground atmosphere pervading Nicholas's Russia. Like soldiers, students wore uniforms, had swords, and won praise for the military virtues of obedience and orderly conduct.[29]

The relative sophistication of university students might explain the government's hesitation to proselytize vigorously among them in behalf of autocracy, Orthodoxy, and nationality. Gymnasium pupils lacked this maturity, yet here too the elimination of dangerous teachings remained the state's major concern. It therefore retained the 1828 course schedule, which assigned almost twice as much time to apolitical subjects like mathematics and classical and modern languages as it did to those with excellent didactic possibilities like religion, Russian literature, and history.[30] Subversive doctrines, the ministry undoubtedly felt, would be less likely to infiltrate a lesson on the ablative absolute than a discussion of parliamentary practices. Any subject that might introduce a student to contemporary problems or encourage him in the free exercise of his reason was especially suspect; it could awaken him to the evils of the present situation or give him too much confidence in his own mental powers. Consequently, in 1844, Uvarov cautioned the geography teacher to avoid in his statistics lessons "any judgments which have a close connection with the political sciences." Two years later he discontinued instruction in logic because its study provided "only abstract, obscure concepts which he [the student] later either forgot or used incorrectly."[31]

This failure to exploit the school's propaganda potential characterized Russian educational policy throughout the century. As long as it was chained to the static, outmoded concepts of autocracy, social immobility, and religious orthodoxy, the government could not produce an ideology capable of combating the dynamic theories of political liberty, social democracy, and economic equality flowing in from the West. Nor indeed did most bureaucrats attempt such a formulation. However, to attribute the school's meager role in indoctrination solely to the intellectual poverty and political myopia of the ruling circles is not sufficient. The great teacher shortage in Russia also played a part. Since the ministry needed every instructor it could find, it could not afford to be overly fastidious about each candidate's allegiances. Under these conditions it concentrated on developing an efficient system of state inspection and control rather than on devising a curriculum which loosely supervised, possibly unreliable teachers could manipulate to their own advantage. In education as elsewhere the government pursued a cautious, defensive strategy, one that might put off the day of defeat but would not lead to victory.

The shortcomings of the ministry's campaign to mold its students' minds made the success of Uvarov's third remedy, the exclusion of the lower classes from higher education, even more imperative. At least, the ministry could argue, the privileged orders — because of their secure position and their traditions of service and loyalty — would be less susceptible to the unsettling effects of education and thus less in need of indoctrination. Warning that an "excessive striving for further schooling might in some way shake the estate structure," Uvarov increased fees and entrance restrictions at institutes of higher learning. As he admitted in his circular of 2 June 1845, he was raising university and gymnasium charges "not so much to increase the finances of academic institutions as to keep youth's desire for education within limits harmonizing somewhat with [its] mode of life," since higher education was for the lower classes "a superfluous luxury which lifted these people from their proper station without advantages for them or the state." Those able to pay the tuition found a new roadblock in their path. A decree of 14 June 1845 required all members of the taxable population, except first-guild merchants, to obtain a certificate of release from their community before entering the gymnasium or university. Prospective students would not acquire this release easily, since their local society would hardly let them go unless they made satisfactory arrangements for their share of the communal tax obligation. While thus obstructing the nonnobles' path to the gymnasium, Uvarov sought to entice the gentry to these schools by setting up at well over half of them special dormitories or pensions for noble sons alone so that the young aristocrat from the provinces would have a place to reside worthy of his station.[32]

All these measures, Uvarov hoped, would keep the gymnasium primarily for the "children of the gentry and officialdom" and direct the middle class to the county schools. He was right. During his ministry the proportion of the gymnasium student body from the privileged orders stayed at almost 80 percent despite the growing demand of the lower classes for more education.[33]

If the conservative bureaucrat in Uvarov devised the three-point program to neutralize the disruptive forces education might create, the scholar in him stipulated that its implementation should not hinder the advancement of learning. The 1835 legislation may have curtailed the autonomy of the university, but it also substantially augmented the size and salaries of its faculty, thereby equipping it to handle the better-prepared students which the revised gymnasium curriculum and the more precise university entrance requirements would produce. Russia's research institutes benefited too from Uvarov's policies. Much of the 871,342 silver rubles he added to his budget from 1835 to 1848 went to strengthen the Academy of Sciences, to found an astronomical observatory at Pulkovo in 1838, and to build new libraries and museums.[34] His contribution to the gymnasiums was even more impressive. Years earlier he had adjusted their course to European standards; he now attacked their staffing problems. To obtain the best possible teachers, Uvarov raised wages, revitalized the Central Pedagogical Institute, and insisted upon the proper educational qualifications for all prospective instructors no matter how great the need for staff.[35] So successful were these measures that many like the pedagogue N. Kh. Vessel' considered the 1830s and 1840s "the gymnasium's best period."[36]

Uvarov's activities clearly reflected the complex task facing a dutiful Minister of Education. In order to raise the low level of Russian education without jeopardizing the security of the regime, he balanced beneficial policies like the search for competent teachers, the encouragement of research, and the preparation of suitable academic programs against deleterious ones like the extension of state controls, the constriction of curricula, and the limiting of access to higher schooling. Such uneasy compromises satisfied neither the proponents nor the critics of educational progress. According to the former, the ministry concentrated too much on the education of too few. Ignoring the illiteracy of the Russian masses, the ministry left elementary education to the Ministry of State Domains or the Holy Synod, although the former had no jurisdiction over privately owned peasants and the latter lacked the necessary teachers and pedagogical expertise. Even the expansion of secondary education suffered from Uvarov's greater concern for the quality than the quantity of schools, for the type than the numbers of students. In the decade 1836–1846 the number of gymnasiums increased only 12 percent from sixty-eight to seventy-six. True, enrollment rose 33 percent from 15,475 to 20,669 during the same period, but fell to 18,911 by 1848, the consequence of Uvarov's restrictive entrance requirements.[37]

Thus, on the one hand, Uvarov did not sufficiently promote the spread of education; on the other hand, he could not guarantee the loyalty of the elite he had trained. In fact, a small portion of this elite, disillusioned by the autocracy's failure to eliminate serfdom, censorship, and its other repressive features, had repudiated the government and decided to change Russian society from the outside rather than from within the system. At first, it relied on propaganda, disseminating its ideas through the famous "thick" journals and discussion circles of the 1840s; but later it would resort to revolutionary violence. While the state's intransigence toward reform nourished the growth of this radical intelligentsia, superficially at least it seemed that Uvarov was to blame; for had not almost all the intelligentsia studied at the ministry's schools?

The Reaction of Nicholas's Last Years

The revolutions of 1848 destroyed the Uvarov compromise. Frightened by the fall of his fellow monarchs, Nicholas became convinced that the revolution "is in its madness menacing our Russia."[38] Since Russia lacked the dissatisfied bourgeoisie and proletariat of the West, the emperor rightly viewed the highly educated as the most susceptible to the ideological poisons from abroad; he thus attacked the producers of this cultural minority, the gymnasiums and the universities. Not so easily panicked as his sovereign, Uvarov first tried to protect his creations. Only after both the university and the gymnasium underwent drastic revisions, only after he had totally lost his ruler's confidence for sponsoring a *Sovremennik* article defending the universities, only after he had suffered a stroke on 9 September 1849, did Uvarov finally leave his post on 20 October 1849.[39] It is important to stress the date of Uvarov's resignation because some recent writers associate Nicholas's suppression of education with the accession of Prince P. A. Shirinsky-Shikhmatov to the ministry,[40] when in fact the reaction was well under way by the time this "blind tool of his emperor's will" officially took over on 27 January 1850.

Like Magnitsky before him, Nicholas considered the universities his greatest threat, despite reassuring reports by the fall of 1848 that the "intellectual ferment had subsided." Dismissing Uvarov's suggestions for more religious instruction and stricter supervision of students as too irresolute to meet the crisis, the emperor forbade study and research abroad and then on 30 April 1849 restricted each university's enrollment, excluding state stipend holders and medical students, to three hundred.[41]

Not satisfied with reducing student numbers, Nicholas also wanted to exclude all lower-class elements. A decree of 26 January 1850 urged that university vacancies be reserved for those "who by birth or by fundamental state law had the right to enter government service [since those] . . . who are raised out of their natural environment by a university education, who do not possess in most cases any immovable property but who are full of daydreams about their capabilities and intelligence, very often grow restless and discontented with the present state of affairs, particularly if they do not find nourishment for their overexcited ambitions, or if they meet unexpected obstacles on the path to eminence." Too many, the decree continued, sought a university degree solely as a means to gain high civil service rank and thereby noble status.[42] So fearful had the government become of the university's subversive influence that it temporarily forgot its need for well-trained bureaucrats and even hoped that the nobility would reject the civil service in favor of an army career *"where a university education is not necessary."* [43]

This reactionary upsurge engulfed the faculty as well as their students. The last vestige of university autonomy disappeared as professors lost the right to elect their own officers and suffered harsh restrictions on their academic freedom. Now directly appointed by the ministry, the rector and deans were ordered to make sure through frequent class inspections and preliminary reviews of course outlines that lectures contained "nothing which contradicts the doctrines of the Orthodox church, the structure of the government or the spirit of our state institutions." Some subjects, however, were too dangerous to be taught at all. The ministry dropped philosophy from the curriculum to shield the young against the "seductive subtleties of recent philosophical systems" and abolished the course in European public law because "even in its most abbreviated form" it might "stimulate the students to consider unapproved topics." Research, too, was not immune from attack; according to an 1850 circular, no dissertation presented for an advanced degree could discuss principles opposing Russia's political system.[44] Russian universities would continue to experience much persecution during the nineteenth century, but these were their darkest days.

Uvarov's gymnasiums suffered less crude though equally severe modifications. The growing hostility in Western Europe toward classical schools reinforced similar views in Russian imperial circles. Many felt that Russia needed a more utilitarian secondary school and that the study of Greece and Rome, if not actually encouraging republican sentiments, did at least divert the student's attention from his own nationality. Such arguments appealed to Nicholas's pragmatic nature and to his lifelong distaste for the classics. He therefore demanded new academic plans which would prepare gymnasium graduates not just for the university but also for state service. The resulting lesson schedule of March 1849 allowed those not interested in the university to take instead of Latin and Greek more mathematics and Russian and a three-year course in Russian law. Once committed to this program, a student would find it difficult to enter the university because its admission requirements included knowledge of a classical language. Even the ministry had to admit that these revisions would probably reduce the number of gymnasium students going to a university.[45]

Still Nicholas was not satisfied, for he considered the existing Greek courses "completely superfluous"; and by May 1852 only nine gymnasiums continued to offer a full program in Greek and Latin. All the other schools had substituted jurisprudence and natural science for classics and gave university candidates a shortened four-year Latin course.[46] "Classical study," which, Uvarov had argued, "the most enlightened nations unanimously proclaimed the best means for . . . intellectual development," [47] had been replaced by a confused mélange of practical, professional, and general education.

Within fifty years Russian school policy had been turned on its head. In 1804 Alexander I had recognized only the benefits of education; his successor saw only its dangers. Where the older brother opened the ministry's institutions to everyone, sought a rapid expansion of higher education, and granted teachers considerable independence in running their schools, the younger one wanted the gymnasium and university reserved for the privileged classes, cut university enrollment, restricted the faculty's academic freedom, and destroyed its autonomous position. Nowhere was the political bankruptcy of the Nicholaian regime more evident than in its attitude toward education. In overreacting to the menace of a few intellectuals, it had ruined Uvarov's coherent, if limited, education system. All the emperor could replace it with was a series of short-sighted, repressive acts and a renewed emphasis on religious instruction. However, as the debacle of the Crimean War would demonstrate, Russia needed a literate populace, scientists, engineers, teachers, technicians, administrators — and not devout Christians.

A New Progressive Era in Educational Policy

The collapse of Nicholas's war machine in 1854–1855 shocked the Russian state out of its lethargy. Although the emperor had devoted most of his country's resources to strengthening the military, foreign armies now were threatening Russia for the first time since 1812. Trying to explain this paradox, ruling circles stressed the debilitating effects of their nation's backwardness. The problems facing Russia were indeed awesome. Unless she shook loose from the fetters of serfdom, modernized her traditional agrarian economy, stimulated industrial development, improved transport and communications, rooted out corruption and inefficiency in the bureaucracy, remodeled her huge standing army, introduced concepts of social justice, and increased her subjects' involvement in the state, she would face a constant danger of invasion from without and the probability of revolution from within. While he did not see all its ramifications, the new emperor, Alexander II, certainly realized the seriousness of Russia's predicament. He conquered his innate conservatism, indecision, and apathy long enough to launch his country's greatest reform movement of the century.

Any transformation of the Russian social and economic structure required an increase in the educational level of the population. Just as illiterate peasants could not run complex factory equipment, nor understand the intricate maneuvers of the modern army, nor easily handle the responsibilities of emancipation, neither could poorly trained technicians and administrators plot the correct path for economic growth, effectively command their nation's fighting forces, nor fully implement their sovereign's decrees. Consequently, the advancement of learning again became one of the tsar's urgent tasks. Alexander felt public education to be so important that within a year of his accession he demanded that the ministry's "academic institutions" be placed under his "personal supervision and charge." [48]

Despite the emperor's enthusiastic support of education, the ministry during the first six years of his reign produced no fundamental school reforms but merely repudiated Nicholas's more repressive actions. With four directors in seven years,[49] and with the tsar preoccupied with the impending liberation of the serfs, the ministry lacked the firm guidance necessary to implant a new school system on Russian soil. This irresolution at the center encouraged the development of two recent additions to the Russian educational scene: public participation in education and active student unrest. These two phenomena would plague school officials for the rest of the century.

The man who most stimulated society's interest in education was the famous surgeon of the Crimean War, Dr. N. I. Pirogov. His article, "Vital Questions," published by the Naval Ministry's journal *Morskii sbornik* in 1856, removed pedagogy, so one Russian educator claimed, from the special preserve of the expert and made it a pressing concern for the general literate public.[50] In simple language Pirogov explained that good schools were vital for national progress. Unlike the practical bureaucrat, however, he did not mean education's utilitarian purpose of preparing "financiers, soldiers, sailors and lawyers." Rather he wanted the schools to concentrate on developing the "inner man," on training all students regardless of class to "become human beings." Only after accomplishing this should the school consider vocational guidance.[51] The renown of its author, the official nature of its publication, and the directness of its prose guaranteed the article's humanitarian, democratic ideas the widest circulation and deepest effect. But Pirogov wanted not only the public's attention, but its energetic collaboration in educational matters. While curator of the Odessa district from 1856 to 1858, and of Kiev from 1858 to 1861, he consulted local groups on school policy, and, more important, aided the spread of the Sunday school movement in which masses of young idealists, usually students, brought literacy to working-class adults.[52]

Pirogov had not misjudged the public's mood. Emboldened by the relaxation of Nicholaian restrictions, caught up in the euphoria of the early days of Alexander's reign when, it seemed, great changes were in the offing, and eager to contribute in any way to its country's growth after thirty years of stagnation, Russian society enthusiastically pushed forward the cause of education. It supported the proliferation of pedagogical magazines including such influential journals as *Zhurnal dlia vospitaniia, Pedagogicheskii vestnik, Uchitel'*, and Leo Tolstoi's *Iasnaia Poliana*. It also championed the establishment of Sunday schools. Although the movement did not start until 1858 and soon suffered from government interference and the waning enthusiasm of both teachers and students, there were still over three hundred of these schools at the time of their proscription in 1862.[53]

This increasing public interest in education posed a new dilemma for the ministry. Limited in resources and personnel, it needed the money and pedagogical wisdom private individuals could provide, yet it feared they might use the schools for aims detrimental to the existing government. The ministry would have to tap the reservoir of public aid so as to ensure an adequate supply of water, but only in the channels dug by the state.

The potential hazards of private initiative in education must have appeared minor indeed when compared to the provocative behavior of university students. Between 1855 and 1859 the ministry had revitalized the universities, and for the first time students benefited more than their professors. While the faculty, it is true, regained their academic independence and could again offer the courses Nicholas had outlawed, they did not resume their rights of self-government, nor could they even elect their own rector and prorector until 31 May 1861.[54] Students, on the other hand, not only saw the hated enrollment quotas lifted and the restrictions on their activities eased, they also received at least unofficial encouragement to run their own affairs. As a result, undergraduate societies sprang up all over Russia and often furnished more of the student's education than did the classroom.[55]

The ministry soon rued its liberal impulses, for student disorders were becoming endemic to Russia's universities. The peculiarities of their life had made students one of the most volatile elements in Russia. Flattered by the public's new respect for the well educated, excited by the progressive trends of Russian politics, nurtured on the populist doctrines in the radical press, and cut off from most of the population by their education and close-knit corporate life, Russian students of the late 1850s — like today's undergraduate rebels — acquired an inflated sense of their own importance. This trait, then as now, was often accompanied by its natural partner, a contemptuous attitude toward authority, an attitude that the general ineffectualness displayed by local officials during demonstrations certainly did little to dispel. Young men so motivated would not tolerate any imperfections in the university system. They actively protested against bad teaching, against increased supervision, against limitations on student organizations, in fact against anything which they felt might spoil their university experience. Despite the existence of revolutionary student circles and the frightened claims of the Third Section, these demonstrations rarely assumed a political character.[56] Nevertheless, the emperor demanded that the ministry eliminate this unrest, for in an autocracy any disruption of the established order was considered an attack on the state.

The result of the government's deliberations was a typical example of tsardom's tendency to overreact to student unrest. It ignored the valid sources of discontent and resorted to the most unsubtle means of oppression. Disregarding the compromise solution proposed by the famous jurist K. D. Kavelin — that of placing student societies under faculty control — the ministry in May 1861 radically altered the student's position at the university.[57] Its plan was brutally simple. First, reestablish order by carefully supervising student activities on the school grounds, forbidding any outbursts during lectures and expelling all troublemakers. Second, undermine corporate feeling by abolishing uniforms, proscribing "the wearing of any type of insignia indicating nationality or membership in any association," and prohibiting meetings without official permission. Third, stiffen entrance requirements by conducting special final examinations at the gymnasiums and sharply curtailing financial assistance. To implement this repressive program Alexander turned to a military man. The reactionary Admiral E. P. Putiatin replaced the moderate, if irresolute, E. P. Kovalevsky as Minister of Education.

As usual, the government's despotic measures only exacerbated the situation. The students, who had quickly adjusted to the university's permissive environment, considered the new restraints on their activity an unacceptable reversal of official policy. Having tasted the fruits of liberty, they would not willingly accept the bread-and-water diet of rigid controls. Similarly provocative were the ministry's admissions restrictions. With the disappearance of enrollment quotas, many from the poorer classes sought a university education because it provided an excellent means to better their position. Life was precarious for these students; they could not afford tuition charges and often depended on the generosity of student societies for living expenses, but still they flocked to the universities. The 1861 decree, however, greatly reduced their chances for a higher education and hence a successful career, since it inhibited the charitable activities of student corporations and fixed the number of tuition exemptions granted by the university to two per province, a drastic decision when one realizes that Petersburg University had waived fees for 659 of its 1,019 students in 1859.[58] In the words of one student manifesto, the government had "thrown down the gauntlet." [59] The students replied with renewed demonstrations, particularly in St. Petersburg. Some faculty too refused to abide by the ministry's arbitrary rules; Kavelin and four of his Petersburg colleagues even resigned their posts in protest. Faced by both student and faculty rebellion, Alexander finally closed St. Petersburg University on 20 December 1861, an action that even Nicholas I had shied away from.[60]

Once more the ministry had gone too far in the suppression of its institutions. Not only did its activity threaten to bring higher education to a halt, but it introduced new tensions into an internal situation already turbulent because of the Emancipation Act's failings. The long-awaited liberation of the serfs of 19 February 1861 had disappointed peasants and intellectuals alike, for it gave the former serfs too little land while charging them too much for it. The peasants quite rightly felt themselves cheated by the settlement and expressed their anger in frequent outbursts of violence;[61] the educated elite grew disillusioned with the autocracy's ability to reform itself, and some again thought and preached revolution. If the government were to regain the support of enlightened public opinion, it would have to demonstrate its continued interest in improving Russian conditions, and in what better way than by repudiating the recent hostile actions against the universities. Thus, on 25 December 1861 it dismissed Admiral Putiatin, the man most closely associated with reaction. This would not be the last time Alexander II would sacrifice an Education Minister to the gods of public opinion.

Putiatin's successor, A. V. Golovnin, seemed an excellent choice to placate the government's critics. One journalist would even rank him among Alexander's "glorious appointments." [62] Although not an education expert, Golovnin had served on the Central School Board since 1859, possessed considerable administrative experience, and through his friendship with Grand Duke Constantine enjoyed a powerful position at court. Golovnin's intelligence,[63] managerial talents, and influential friends pleased Russian educators who had suffered under the four nonentities preceding him, and his well-known liberal proclivities lessened somewhat the anxieties of Russian literate society about tsardom's future direction. Even if one discounts the claims of some conservatives that Golovnin was a "red" who saw Russia's salvation only in a decisive break with the past,[64] it is clear that because of his role in reforming the Naval Ministry and in compiling the emancipation legislation, Golovnin was a prominent member of progressive government circles.

A truly formidable task awaited the new minister. In addition to his immediate assignment of quieting student unrest, he had to create from the wreckage of the Uvarov program, from the various projects left by his predecessors, and from the experience of Western Europe a viable education system that would meet the needs of a rapidly modernizing, but still underdeveloped country. With the "Great Reforms" of the 1860s Russia was entering a higher stage of development; but this advance placed increasing burdens on all government agencies and on few more than the Ministry of Education. Russia's revised law courts, its new organs of local self-government (the zemstvos), its growing industrial complex now stimulated by the vast labor force and market created by the freeing of the serfs, all required a constant supply of well-trained personnel from the ministry's schools. If the ministry were to fulfill this demand, it would have to repudiate its traditional restrictions on secondary and higher school admissions and seek other means to assure loyal graduating classes.

Elementary education offered an even greater challenge. When in 1861 the Emancipation Act explicitly asserted the state's responsibility for schooling the liberated peasantry, the ministry was totally unprepared. For years it had ignored primary education in the countryside, and it now lacked the administrative apparatus, the teachers, and especially the money to spread literacy among the immense and geographically diffuse agricultural population. Clearly the ministry needed assistance. The most logical source would be society at large, which had already shown its willingness to help and which by 1864 had in the zemstvos a proper governmental body to direct its energies. However, the extent of the zemstvos' contribution would cause anxiety within the education department. In return for their financial support the zemstvos quite naturally sought control over elementary schools and thus often infringed upon the ministry's powers in the provinces. Few tsarist officials would tolerate this threat to their authority.

Since his country's future depended so much on its schools, Golovnin felt he could not, as his precursors had done, formulate his policies in secret. Instead he widely publicized his proposed legislation, eagerly seeking advice from anyone either at home or abroad competent to judge pedagogical matters. Educated society debated matters like the university's corporate structure, the merits of a classical secondary education, and the role of the zemstvos in elementary schooling.[65] Although the final form of his education acts of 1863–1864 owed far more to the views of the ministry's consultative organs and especially to the wishes of the State Council than it did to the comments of private individuals, Golovnin had at least demonstrated his desire to adjust the methods of ministerial decision-making to the more advanced state of Russian public opinion.

Even if the ministry did not incorporate many of its suggestions, the public generally endorsed the overall direction of Golovnin's reforms.[66] As in Alexander I's early years, the spread and improvement of education became the ministry's primary concern. It was his duty, Golovnin explained, "to assist man in extending the limits of his knowledge and, especially, to disseminate this knowledge throughout our fatherland . . . the most urgent need of our time is . . . the proper and thorough education of the young generation from all estates." [67]

Accordingly, the new statutes disavowed the belief that one's schooling must conform to one's position in society and opened the university and gymnasium to "all classes and faiths." Yet Golovnin did not create equal educational opportunities for all. Russia still lacked a ladder system of schools; a classical education, though relatively unpopular with the lower orders, remained an essential prerequisite for university entrance; and substantial fees continued to make postprimary education a luxury the poor could not afford despite an increase in student financial assistance.[68] Without cheap or free higher education, gymnasium preparatory schools at the elementary level, and less rigid university admissions requirements, Russia would not have a truly democratic educational system.

More successful were Golovnin's efforts to raise the quality of Russian education by expanding academic programs and by improving teacher training. He eliminated the narrow utilitarian bias of the previous gymnasium curriculum, established an alternative form of secondary school — the realgymnasium — to satisfy the growing interest in natural sciences, encouraged greater specialization in the science faculties, and broadened the university's offerings by adding nineteen chairs to the forty-two set by the 1835 statute. To staff these enlarged university faculties, the ministry from 1862 to 1865 sent eighty-four young graduates abroad for further study.[69] The shortage of secondary and primary school teachers was no less pressing. In 1865 Golovnin introduced special university classes in pedagogy for future gymnasium instructors and set up supplementary education courses at the county schools to prepare elementary teachers. Since these and similar revitalization projects required heavy expenditures, Golovnin constantly demanded and got additional funds. In just five years his ministry's budget practically doubled from 3,657,764 rubles in 1861 to 7,066,150 rubles in 1866.[70]

Unlike his conservative predecessors, Golovnin had confidence in local enterprise and often left the implementation of his reforms to the schools themselves. Although nominally under the curator's jurisdiction, the university in fact became a self-governing institution. The professor corporation chose the rector and deans, hired new teachers, established its own court, and in general managed university business. Admittedly, most of the faculty's independence was subject to the minister's good will since he had to confirm many of their decisions, but the university had at least regained the important rights of initiative and election.[71]

The principle of school autonomy also prevailed in secondary and elementary education. At the gymnasium the pedagogical council, an assembly of all permanent faculty, enjoyed extensive authority over the school's academic, didactic *(vospitatel'nye)*, and financial affairs. At the elementary level special county and provincial school councils *(uchilishchnye sovety)*, staffed by representatives from the Ministries of Education and the Interior, from the Holy Synod and from the zemstvos, opened and closed schools, appointed teachers, and inspected primary schools, all without recourse to a higher power.[72] Golovnin had reversed the trend toward increased government interference and control. Despite his failure to reintroduce the ladder system, to release classical education's stranglehold on university entrance, and to grant college students freedom of organization, he had turned Russian education in a new direction. Encouragement and support now replaced restriction and repression.

Russian educational policy had come full circle. It had gone from the liberal plans of the Unofficial Committee in the early 1800s, which strove primarily for the advancement of learning, to the conservative program of Uvarov, which sought to combat the antistate tendencies stimulated by education and at the same time to improve the schools, to the reactionary tactics of Shirinsky-Shikhmatov, which actually caused the decline of Russian education, back to the essentially progressive statutes of Golovnin. The lesson to be learned by an observant minister from these reversals in policy was clear: autocracy would not long tolerate the shortcomings it saw in either the reactionary or liberal solutions to the dilemma of education, the former because it would not remedy

Russia's backward conditions, the latter because the educated elite it quickly produced often threatened the existing government. Only the conservative solution of seeking to nullify or prevent this elite's antagonism toward the state without greatly harming the progress of education — of achieving a balance, however precarious, between restraint and promotion — would endure.

CHAPTER 2 / The Shaping of a Bureaucrat

While the previous educational programs provided the general context within which Tolstoi would work, two other factors — the ominous events leading up to his appointment and the nature of his upbringing and training — more specifically determined the course of his reforms. The first would help define his overall strategy; the second, the tactics he would use to achieve his objectives. Since the situation in Russia at Tolstoi's accession is well known, it needs only brief treatment here. The bulk of this chapter will therefore concentrate on the much less researched topic, the schooling and early career of the new education minister.

Political Conditions at Tolstoi's Appointment

The direction of the Tolstoi ministry was set on 4 April 1866 when Dmitry Karakozov fired at the emperor as he returned from a walk in the Summer Garden. Alexander II escaped unharmed; his progressive policies did not. For conservative officials this assassination attempt proved just how much the liberal measures of the 1860s had jeopardized the autocracy. Instead of strengthening the state, they had encouraged divisive and disruptive activity like the peasant outbreaks right after the emancipation, the Polish rebellion of 1863, and now this unprecedented attack on the sovereign. Even the gentry, traditional servants of the tsar, had become too presumptuous: in 1865 the Moscow nobility had called for a general assembly to examine Russia's needs. The opponents of reform demanded an immediate retrenchment, and for once they had widespread support. Already frightened by the separatist tendencies of the Poles and shocked by the radicals' enthusiasm for the Polish cause, much of Russian society found the terrorist acts of the revolutionary movement intolerable and reaffirmed their devotion to the throne. As Iu. F. Samarin described the situation in Moscow on 12 April 1866: "Religious disbelief, nihilism, the impulse to political opposition, all had passed, all had dissolved." [1]

In such an atmosphere all liberal or even moderate ministers were suspect, but few more so than the Minister of Education A. V. Golovnin. He had closely associated himself with those advocating conciliatory gestures, not repressive acts, to quiet alienated groups within Russia like the Poles and university students. The continued unrest on the banks of the Vistula had convinced the emperor that this policy had failed in Poland; the Karakozov affair showed him that it had not succeeded in the field of education either. Golovnin's enemies, particularly the influential Moscow publicist M. N. Katkov, had argued that the present educational system, encouraging as it did school autonomy and an interest in the "materialist" natural sciences, would stimulate rather than prevent student disaffection. General M. N. Murav'ev's investigations into the assassination plot apparently corroborated Katkov's denunciations and discredited Golovnin. Not only had Karakozov studied at the ministry's institutions, but so too had most of his "co-conspirators." Worse yet, although Karakozov had demonstrated his unreliability during the Kazan disorders in 1861, the ministry still permitted him to reenter Kazan University and then transfer to Moscow, thus helping him corrupt Russian youth.

All too eager to generalize from this specific instance of the student as revolutionary, Murav'ev accused the education department of "flooding the country with destructive and pernicious forces" instead of producing "useful citizens." Permissiveness in education, he concluded, had facilitated the spread of radical teachings and encouraged the formation of those secret organizations which planned the emperor's death. That Katkov and Murav'ev, the two men most responsible — as propagandist and soldier respectively — for the brutal pacification of Poland, might have exaggerated the ministry's failings because they detested Golovnin's lenient attitude toward the Poles never troubled the tsar. Just ten days after Karakozov's shot he appointed a new Minister of Education, the Ober Procurator of the Holy Synod, Count Dmitry Tolstoi.[2]

Following his predecessor's example, Alexander naively hoped that increased religious and moral instruction would protect students from succumbing to the godless theories of radical agitators. No one seemed better suited to carry out this program than the secular head of the Orthodox church, especially since he had recently defended the clergy's role in education against Golovnin's attempts to place the church parish schools of southwest Russia under ministerial control. In the only dissenting opinion within the Committee of Ministers, Tolstoi praised the devoted service of the Orthodox priests.

> They have always been and will always be the sole protector of the orthodox-national spirit and the most reliable bulwark against every alien influence. . . . The fundamental principles supported by our church are immutable, and its servitors thus will always be undeniably superior to all other teachers of the people, who sometimes can be carried away by their own ideas which are not always useful to the state or government.[3]

"Fully sharing" this view, Alexander thought he had found the proper assistant to curb the subversive elements at the schools; Tolstoi became the first man since 1824 to hold the positions of procurator and education minister at the same time.

If the new minister had any doubts about his obligations, the imperial rescript of 13 May 1866 quickly dispelled them. It ordered him to "pursue the education of youth . . . in accordance with religious truths, with the fundamental principles of property rights and public order" and to "permit neither open nor veiled teaching of those destructive concepts which harm equally the moral and material well-being of the people." [4] Dutifully echoing his emperor's wishes, Tolstoi told his curators "to maintain authority and respect for law, to protect the rights of all and to bring up the young generation in an awareness of their religious and patriotic duties." As he grandiloquently concluded: "Let the remarkable words of our Monarch serve the education department as a permanent and steadfast guide in all its activities and undertakings; let these always be imprinted in the hearts of those who are entrusted with the sacred business of instruction *(vospitanie)*." [5]

The reaction which had swept Tolstoi into office clearly altered the ministry's priorities. Political considerations would once again override pedagogical ones; Tolstoi had to preserve "faith, morality, and the social order" before he could advance learning.

Education at Tsarskoe Selo

Such a plan of action required a loyal civil servant, not an educator, to carry it out — someone concerned with the security of his sovereign first, with the spread of learning second. Tolstoi seemed an ideal choice, for his schooling and subsequent career had prepared him more for the upper echelons of the bureaucracy than for the classroom or the lecture hall. Like so many tsarist officials, he had not studied at Russia's regular institutions, the gymnasium and university, but instead had attended the Imperial Lyceum at Tsarskoe Selo, a school created specifically to train young men for the civil service. It is particularly important to investigate Tolstoi's lyceum experience not only because it helped develop the future minister's skills, attitudes, and character, but because it provided him with his only first-hand knowledge of the process of education, a process he would later control.

Although no longer quite the idyllic institution Pushkin described,[6] the lyceum when Tolstoi entered in 1836 still occupied a unique position. Its exclusively aristocratic student body, its already hallowed traditions, its luxurious accommodations in a wing of the Imperial Palace, and its virtual elimination of the three major curses of Russian student life — insecurity, sickness, and poverty — set it apart from Russia's other higher schools. The guarantee of desirable posts in the Petersburg bureaucracy banished worries about the future; the hearty food, excellent sanitary conditions, constant physical exercise, and competent medical staff combined to keep everyone healthy; and the exorbitant fees of 2,000 rubles a year closed the lyceum to all but the recipients of full stipends and the sons of the very wealthy. Little wonder then that the lyceists enjoyed a sense of well-being and superiority. "From the first day," one alumnus claimed, "I was aware of a tremendous change for the better in my circumstances . . . everything filled me with a self-respect which I had never felt in the gymnasium." [7] Tolstoi would have echoed this opinion. As a scholarship boy from a poor provincial gentry family, fatherless since he was seven, he appreciated more than his rich classmates the advantages of being a lyceist and thus would seriously devote himself to the school's programs.

The lyceum's avowed purpose of training loyal, competent civil servants predetermined the nature of the school's six-year course. Utility was the key word. Students concentrated on foreign languages, the statesman's tool, and on the practical aspects of many subjects instead of pursuing a few in depth. Modern languages with German stressed most, followed by French and then English, received the greatest attention. One or two professors even taught courses like geography or fine arts in a foreign tongue. In addition to extensive language work the lyceum offered advanced instruction in religion, mathematics, Russian, physics, history, geography, diplomacy, political economy, statistics, juridical science, psychology, and moral philosophy.

Having to take at least eight major subjects a year along with drawing, penmanship, fencing, and gymnastics, no student could master all these disciplines; but he could learn their more immediately useful applications. Hence, problems involving weights and measures bulked large in math; Russian literature assignments included official proclamations, decrees, and manifestos; and, as might be expected, jurisprudence lessons examined the rights, duties, penalties, and rewards of the civil servant. Only if a student's chosen field of state service required an expertise which the lyceum could not provide, might he supplement this restricted academic fare by attending university lectures.[8] In general, however, school authorities considered each lyceist too important an investment in Russia's future to permit him to waste his time seeking knowledge for its own sake.

The lyceum clearly suffered scholastically from its professional bias. The proliferation of compulsory courses prevented students from attaining anything but a superficial understanding of the subjects covered. As one graduate justifiably complained: "A scholarly encyclopedism, it seems, was the god to which both the energy and time of the students were sacrificed."[9] Not only did the lyceum's once-over-lightly approach irritate the more dedicated students, it hardly attracted the best faculty available. The inability to focus only on their special area of research, combined with the possibility of having to teach in the first half or secondary school portion of the lyceum's six-year course and with the uneven preparation of their pupils, discouraged many serious scholars from coming to or remaining at the lyceum. While most instructors performed their duties competently, a number often lapsed into dry pedanticism; and only a few like I. P. Shul'gin, who left to become rector of St. Petersburg University, and his replacement I. A. Ivanovsky were outstanding.[10] The lyceum had rivaled the universities in excellence for the first decade of its existence; it no longer did so during Tolstoi's school years.

More concerned with the prospective bureaucrat's attitude than with his talent, the imperial government better equipped the lyceum to mold character than minds. As at its other institutions, the state relied heavily on the negative policy of discipline and control to protect students against harmful elements. A strict schedule prescribed the lyceist's activity from reveille at 6:00 A.M. to curfew at 10:00 P.M., allowing him little leisure for unapproved pastimes. To oversee the students and keep them at their chores, the school employed an inspector and twelve governors, or one supervisor for every eight boys. In Tolstoi's day the chief inspector, A. G. Obolensky, performed his feats of espionage so enthusiastically that all alumni recalled with horror his predilection for student informers and his constant searching through their belongings.[11]

The lyceum's isolated location simplified the inspectorate's job, for its charges could not leave the grounds easily. They even needed a special permit to visit their parents or relatives on holidays and received passes to Petersburg so rarely that they felt Pushkin's lines most appropriate: *Nam del mir chuzhbina,/ Otechestvo nam Tsarskoe Selo.* (For us worldly affairs were a foreign land,/ For us Tsarskoe Selo was our fatherland.) When a lyceist did get away from the regimented life of Tsarskoe Selo, he still did not escape annoying restrictions. School rules required that he wear full dress uniform at all times and avoid coffee shops, confectionery stores, gentry assemblies, and masquerades.[12] No other Russian student was so closely watched and regulated as the lyceist.

Not content with merely shutting out dangerous external influences, the lyceum in theory submitted its students to rigorous moral instruction in and outside the classroom. Here, if nowhere else, the government experimented with using the school as a propaganda device. Unlike those at most institutions, the lyceum's academic plans urged teachers to exploit their subjects' didactic possibilities. For instance, "the spirit of piety, love and devotion to the throne and fatherland should animate" the course in history; the presence of "moral lessons" determine the selection of literature assignments; and the problems of ethical behavior occupy classes in religion. Upon leaving the lecture hall, the lyceists faced other forms of indoctrination. They were often pages at court or escorts during royal balls, because frequent intercourse with the imperial household, it was hoped, would strengthen their attachment to the emperor and his service.[13]

Back on school grounds the omnipresent governors took over. Through conversation and personal example they were to develop all the essential qualities of the future bureaucrat: loyalty to the monarch, love of Russia, respect for authority, not to mention orderliness, honor, and humility. The governors, however, appeared more suited for enforcing regulations than for inculcating the desired values. Usually poorly educated foreigners, they lacked the subtlety to propagandize the relatively sophisticated lyceists. Only in Tolstoi's last two years at the lyceum did the director seek more qualified personnel for these important posts.[14]

The lyceum thus tried every device — from encouraging self-discipline to continual surveillance, from subtle persuasion to blatant propaganda — to guarantee the loyalty and integrity of its graduates. This program, the most extensive at any Russian institution, offered the future Minister of Education two valuable insights. On the one hand, it revealed how much was added to the effectiveness of moral instruction by isolation and a boarding-school atmosphere. On the other hand, it would demonstrate that no system of indoctrination was infallible, that the greatest proliferation of rules and supervisors could not prevent students from ignoring their preceptors and getting their ideas and attitudes from classmates and the outside world.

Indeed, their alma mater's traditions of schoolboy honor and liberalism often influenced the lyceists more than the faculty did. The lyceum's exclusive position, its secluded, intimate surroundings, and its many imposing school ceremonies produced an esprit de corps which its graduates retained the rest of their lives. New entrants quickly learned from the seniors that they must never betray the honor of the lyceum or their own class. Each class was, in fact, so solicitous about its reputation that it considered an insult to one an insult to all and broke off relations with any member who besmirched its name.

Tolstoi himself suffered under this code. During his final year at the lyceum he castigated a classmate for immoral behavior. Since the accused left school immediately thereafter, the lyceists blamed

Tolstoi for his expulsion and decided to ostracize the already unpopular young count. One student ignored the class's sentence, until Tolstoi allegedly told him that he "did not need anyone, but could make do without any contact with his companions." This partially self-imposed exile lasted the duration of the school year and exhibited, as an acquaintance pointed out, a "stubbornness . . . an inflexibility of conviction, a certain callousness" and, one might add, an indifference to popular regard which would characterize much of Tolstoi's later career.[15]

While approving the lyceists' loyalty to school and class, the inspectorate could not regard with equal joy their other major tradition, an enthusiasm for liberal causes. The lyceum's creation as part of the reform movement of Alexander I and Speransky and the role of two of its first graduates, V. K. Kiukhel'beker and I. I. Pushchin, in the Decembrist affair[16] gave the institute a certain progressive aura and encouraged "liberal" tendencies among its residents. They usually expressed these feelings by compiling clandestine satirical journals or reading controversial books and magazines.

To combat such unsanctioned activities, school officials suppressed student publications, punished the more outspoken pasquinaders, and placed the library under the inspector's personal jurisdiction. Undaunted, the lyceists continued to write and to subscribe to forward-looking contemporary journals like *Otechestvennye zapiski* and *Syn otechestva*. According to the future liberal leader of the Tver gentry, A. M. Unkovsky, who was dismissed in 1844 because of his own underground literary endeavors, "there was not a single foreign forbidden book which might not appear at the lyceum in the hands of fourteen- or fifteen-year-old boys." [17]

It would be wrong, however, to deduce from this that the lyceum was a hotbed of revolutionary fervor. True, the radical M. V. Petrashevsky may have studied Fourier's doctrines while a student in the late 1830s, but he antagonized rather than converted his classmates.[18] It was not the fanaticism of a Petrashevsky that prevailed at Tsarskoe Selo, but rather a combination of youth's ever-present distaste for authority and a nebulous form of genteel liberalism linked with the idealized figures of Pushkin and Alexander I. As one alumnus concluded, the lyceum "imbued all its graduates with a profound conviction that they were being educated 'for the common weal' . . . and has always remained true to the humanitarian ideas of its illustrious founder's reign." [19]

Its students' flirtations with radical doctrines notwithstanding, the lyceum ably fulfilled its purpose of providing trusted administrators for the government. Most lyceists became bureaucrats, not rebels, choosing the path of Gorchakov rather than of Kiukhel'beker. Among the lyceum's famous alumni were four successive Ministers of Education: A. V. Golovnin, Count D. A. Tolstoi, A. A. Saburov, and Baron A. P. Nikolai; three Ministers of Foreign Affairs: Prince A. M. Gorchakov, N. K. Giers, and A. B. Lobanov-Rostovsky; and such top-ranking officials as M. Kh. Reutern, M. A. Korf, and D. N. Zamiatnin. In fact, proclaimed Alexander II on the school's fiftieth anniversary, "there was not a department which, from the highest service ranks on down, did not employ individuals trained by the lyceum for honorable and useful labor." [20]

Tolstoi represented to the faculty the ideal product of the lyceum course. They awarded him a gold medal at graduation, because in their opinion he had most thoroughly acquired the moral outlook, patriotic feelings, and academic qualifications necessary for an efficient, knowledgeable, and loyal civil servant. Rarely would subsequent events prove lyceum professors to be so perspicacious. But the young count did not take away from the lyceum only the requisite skills and values. The lyceum's traditions as well as its official program of instruction left their mark on him; his early scholarly works sometimes displayed the vague Tsarskoe Selo humanitarianism, while his indifference to others and faith in his own convictions were undoubtedly strengthened by the social ostracism of his last year.

Although unique in organization and set apart from Russia's regular schools, the lyceum even offered him experiences especially useful to a future Minister of Education. It was at the lyceum that Tolstoi first saw the shortcomings of an encyclopedic, nonclassical curriculum and the political benefits of a rigidly controlled boarding-school atmosphere, lessons he never forgot. However, by attending the lyceum, he did miss two major features of the Uvarov educational system, the classical gymnasium and the vibrant intellectual life of the universities during the "magnificent decade." This lack of familiarity with the trials of secondary school Greek and Latin and with the idealism of college students may help explain Tolstoi's later inability to understand both the antipathy to his classical system and the causes of university disorders.

Early Bureaucratic Career

When Tolstoi graduated on 31 January 1843, the imperial bureaucracy beckoned invitingly. His diploma guaranteed him a position in the office of his choice, and his top standing gave him the rank of titular councilor, five grades above the base on the Russian fourteen-point civil service scale.[21] Displaying an early interest in educational policies, Tolstoi chose to serve first in the department of Her Imperial Majesty's Chancellery that had jurisdiction over girls' schools and charitable institutions. He thus followed in the footsteps of another lyceum gold-medal winner and his predecessor as Minister of Education, A. V. Golovnin, who had begun his career in the chancellery three years earlier.[22]

In 1847 Tolstoi transferred to the Ministry of the Interior. A special assistant in the Department of Spiritual Affairs, his tasks included a review of projects concerning the Jewish question; an investigation of the 1851 commission's findings on Moslem law, which led him to urge the political necessity of reducing the numbers of Mohammedan clergy; and the compilation of a detailed report on the non-Orthodox religions in Russia, the research for which no doubt provided the inspiration for his most famous monograph, *Le Catholicisme romain en Russie.* Unlike many of his colleagues, Tolstoi devoted almost all his attention to his duties; his work so impressed his superiors that in 1852 they promoted him, at the youthful age of twenty-nine, to vice director of the Department of Spiritual Affairs, and to director the next year.[23]

While on the fringes of the bureaucratic establishment during the first decade of his career, Tolstoi spent his next seven years at the heart of the reforming trend within the imperial government. In 1853 he became head of the Chancellery of the Naval Ministry. His superior, Grand Duke Constantine Nikolaevich, believed the administration would have to play a vital role in overcoming the debilitating effects of Russian backwardness, and hence he sought the best men available for his department. Indeed, he may well have dreamed, as the publicist V. P. Meshchersky contends, of creating a pleiad of youthful functionaries who would modernize the country.[24] Besides Golovnin and Tolstoi, M. Kh. Reutern (Minister of Finance 1862–1878), S. A. Greig (Minister of Finance 1878–1880), D. N. Nabokov (Minister of Justice 1878–1885), and State Council members Prince D. A. Obolensky and V. P. Mansurov also served in the Naval Ministry at this time. All except Golovnin entered the ministry between 1853 and 1855; all were comparatively young (Reutern, the oldest, was born in 1820); and all graduated from exclusive professional institutions, either the lyceum at Tsarskoe Selo or the School of Jurisprudence in St. Petersburg.[25] With the cream of junior officials in its employ, the naval department would soon become one of Russia's most advanced ministries. Once again, as at the lyceum, Tolstoi was part of a small, elite group being shaped to guarantee Russia's future.

Although an analysis of Constantine's policies lies beyond the scope of this study, a brief survey will suffice to indicate the progressive influences surrounding Tolstoi from 1853 to 1860. Intent upon improving his administrative apparatus, the Grand Duke surprised many contemporaries by demanding greater initiative as well as greater economy and efficiency from his subordinates. His famous statute of 1860 eliminated vast amounts of paper work by giving department heads and port directors considerable freedom of action, remedied fiscal confusion and waste by establishing a single budget and treasury for the entire ministry, and cut the ministry's staff from 391 in 1853 to 144 by removing redundant personnel and bureaus. In this way Constantine managed to reduce operating costs and at the same time expedite decision-

making. Viewing a streamlined bureaucracy as an essential prerequisite for his country's modernization, Alexander II urged
other ministers to follow his brother's example.[26]

This internal reorganization did not alone account for the
Naval Ministry's excellent reputation. Society undoubtedly was
more impressed with its advocacy of the humanitarian ideas prevalent in Russia after Nicholas's death. Constantine bettered the
conditions of the lower ranks, insisted on public discussion of ministerial proposals, and foreshadowed the judicial reforms of 1864
by introducing open trials in navy courts and protecting the rights
of the accused. The Naval Ministry even assisted the reform
movement in areas outside its own jurisdiction. For instance, its
journal, *Morskii sbornik*, published provocative articles on Russia's
needs and problems, and — more important — the Grand Duke
and some of his advisers like Golovnin, Reutern, and Obolensky
helped bring about the emancipation of the serfs.[27]

Tolstoi's position as director of the chancellery placed him in
the midst of his ministry's revitalization program. All orders, reports, and projects passed through his office. In addition to his
secretarial chores, he served on the pension committee, carried
out a survey of the Department of Naval Inspectors, prepared
new fiscal regulations for warships (which were not implemented
until 1873), and even had time for a brief study on the Admiralty
College published in 1855.[28] Thus, just at the period (1855–1860)
when the ruling circles in Petersburg were vigorously debating the
course of Russia's escape from the stagnation of the Nicholaian
era, Tolstoi held a high post in the ministry most closely associated with the progressive wing of the bureaucracy. However, his
constant exposure at the naval department to both the liberal
forces within the Russian government and the advantages of administrative decentralization apparently had little effect on Tolstoi; as will be shown later, the future minister would attack with
especial fervor the liberation of the serfs and the increase in the
powers of local collegiate organizations.

The Development of Tolstoi's Political Views

Although Tolstoi by the 1860s condemned rapid social reform and the principles of self-government, this does not mean that he entered the world a full-blown reactionary as his critics, outraged by his later career in the Ministry of the Interior, often imply. In fact, from the sketchy information available about the young count and from indirect evidence in his scholarly writings, it appears that Tolstoi wavered for some time before adopting his unpopular ideological stance. Two antithetical elements competed in his intellectual development. At school he breathed the progressive atmosphere of the lyceum; at home he inhaled the perfumed vapors of conservative Orthodoxy. Fatherless since seven, Tolstoi owed much of his early education to his father's cousin, Count Dmitry Nikolaevich Tolstoi. The latter epitomized the honorable, nationalistic, unquestioningly loyal, and extremely religious gentry servitor. So impressive was his devotion to emperor and patriarch that one subordinate claimed that it inspired him to return to Orthodoxy and made him "a genuine Russian in spite of [his] former cosmopolitanism." [29]

While the future minister's first monograph, a study of Russian financial institutions to 1796, reflects the influence of both school and family, the nebulous liberal humanitarianism of Tsarskoe Selo predominates. In this short, usually unanalytical description of Russian fiscal measures, the twenty-five-year-old Tolstoi advocated free trade and better treatment of the taxable population. Having demonstrated the harm state interference in domestic commerce had done the Russian economy, he then lauded the attempts by Boris Godunov and Alexis Mikhailovich to regulate the countless internal tariffs plaguing Russian merchants and proclaimed Elizabeth's removal of these duties in 1754 "one of the illustrious acts" of her reign. Tolstoi criticized the unjust as well as the restrictive aspects of tsarist economic policy. He favored a universal, equitable, and unoppressive taxation program — one that would require all estates, including the gentry and clergy, to pay taxes since they all received protection from the government. He even favored elected tax gatherers because they would be fairer than centrally appointed functionaries, a surprising sentiment considering his later violent distrust of private initiative.

This belief in humane taxation led Tolstoi to praise Ivan IV's entrusting revenue collection to certain local residents (*gubnye starosti*), for it "delivered [the people] from rapacious tsarist officials," and to condemn Peter's onerous poll tax, for it overlooked the vital axiom: "The welfare of the treasury is closely tied to the popular welfare, and the ruin of one means the ruin of the other." Only his naively nationalist conclusions specifically recall Tolstoi's conservative upbringing. He tempered his critique of Russia's "financial institutions" by insisting that they were organically necessary, "the products of . . . social needs and demands," and that they were definitely not so ruinous as those adopted in Western Europe.[30]

A look at Tolstoi's acquaintances of the period offers an even less precise view of his ideological allegiances than does an analysis of his scholarly work. During the 1840s and well into the 1850s he continued to frequent both liberal and conservative circles. On the one hand, his friendship with A. N. Pleshcheev, an idealistic poet who attended radical gatherings and later suffered arrest in connection with the Petrashevsky affair, was so close that the latter even dedicated a poem to him;[31] moreover, his professional colleagues for seven years were the progressive clique centered around the Grand Duke Constantine Nikolaevich. On the other hand, he enjoyed the patronage both of the famous conservative ideologue, S. S. Uvarov, now in retirement at his Moscow estate, and of a man constantly linked with the repression of Nicholas's later years, the archconservative Minister of the Interior D. G. Bibikov, whose daughter Tolstoi married in 1853.[32] Confused by the ambiguity of Tolstoi's early relationships, some contemporaries placed him in the liberal, others in the reactionary, camp; while his old enemy B. N. Chicherin accused him of opportunism, of adopting that outlook which would best advance his career.[33] Inconsistency, however, does not necessarily imply hypocrisy; and, until additional information becomes available, one must conclude that Tolstoi was still in the process of formulating his political beliefs.

The imminent introduction of those fundamental reforms so vigorously fought for by his co-workers at the Naval Ministry dispelled Tolstoi's indecision and brought out his right-wing proclivities. Frightened by radical changes which could undermine the regime he had been trained to protect and the very security of his class, Tolstoi attacked the core of the tsar's modernization program, the liberation of the serfs, in a vitriolic memorandum he sent the emperor in the winter of 1860. He particularly ridiculed the reformer's faith in the peasants' ability to meet their obligations and ironically concluded: "It would be more beneficial for the landowner to give the peasants their garden plot and one-third of the land free and to keep the remaining acreage: they [the landlords] will be ruined but at least to a lesser degree." Alexander angrily dismissed this critique as a lampoon revealing either the author's sinister intentions or his complete ignorance.[34]

Even after the serfs gained their freedom, Tolstoi continued his opposition. He used soldiers to force his peasants to pay their dues and bitterly fought his wife's former serfs and their liberal lawyers, led by A. M. Unkovsky, to keep large portions of the countess's estates. He summed up his feelings about the emancipation in a letter to his old patron Count Dmitry Nikolaevich Tolstoi, "Some hope that we will be left without income and Russia without bread. . . . How can one not thank the Editorial Commission!" [35] His own interests threatened, Tolstoi's concern for the poor as expressed in his 1848 monograph had disappeared.

Tolstoi's hostility to the emancipation placed him far outside the main currents of Russian political life, and he would find it increasingly difficult to serve in a bureaucracy committed to a massive reorganization of society. On 19 September 1860 he left the reform-minded naval department and first entered the ministry he would later dominate. For the next thirteen months he labored for the Central School Board, which, as the chief advisory body within the Ministry of Education, reviewed all major questions of school policy. Since the board was still gathering information for a comprehensive revision of the educational system left by Nicholas, Tolstoi had an excellent opportunity to study first hand the problems confronting Russia's schools, especially the now quite prevalent disruptions of university life.

Recognizing Tolstoi's administrative talent and political orthodoxy, the reactionary Minister Admiral Putiatin promoted him in November 1861 to head of the education department, the ministerial chancellery and treasury. But a month later Tolstoi resigned. Although Tolstoi did not explain his abrupt departure, it is more than coincidental that he quit the ministry the same day A. V. Golovnin took it over. Once again he would have had to work under a man intimately connected with the liberal attitudes and measures he detested, and this was more than he could bear. As one contemporary witness recalled, Tolstoi reacted violently to Golovnin's appointment. "He spoke against him [Golovnin] so fiercely and was so unrestrained in his expressions that during these exaggerated comments, I involuntarily thought: *Qui dit tant, ne dit rien.*" [36]

Alienated from the forces guiding Russia's emergence into a modern pluralistic state, Tolstoi could do little but withdraw from public life. He spent the years of busiest reform activity, 1862 to 1864, in semi-retirement, sitting on the Senate, acting as a trustee for two famous girls' schools (the Alexander and Catherine Institutes), and producing in 1863–1864 his two-volume study on the Catholics in Russia. [37]

While primarily a historical survey, not an ideological tract, Tolstoi's *Le Catholicisme romain en Russie*, which earned him a doctorate from Leipzig, reveals his complete conversion to the three tenets of official Russian conservatism: Orthodoxy, autocracy, and nationality. The anti-Roman prejudices of the author, undoubtedly intensified by the rebelliousness of the Catholic Poles, first strike the reader. Following the Slavophile thesis of Catholicism's spiritual bankruptcy, Tolstoi stressed the Latin church's pursuit of secular rather than godly aims. Its traditional role in worldly affairs and its doctrine of papal infallibility convinced him that the Catholic church was essentially a political institution whose pope owed his position "not so much to faith as to power" and whose priesthood was guided not by religion but by a "thirst for spiritual dominion." So wrapped up was the church in its strivings for self-aggrandizement that in Tolstoi's view it had forgotten God. Therefore, he concluded, the "whole Roman system was based on egoism, the Saviour and religion in the rear, the Pope and clergy in first place," and this egoism caused the corruption and downfall of the clergy. No longer in awe of their Maker, these "dissolute" priests "lived with concubines, begot children from them, forced people to pay for church rites, quarreled and even fought with their parishioners and whipped the peasants." [38]

Against this slanderous denunciation of Catholicism Tolstoi apposed a highly idealized description of the early Russian Orthodox church. Unlike their Latin counterparts, the Orthodox clergy in the pre-Petrine period "dreamed not of forceful ecclesiastical conquests but merely watched over the purity of their individual faith." Not only did they live a truly devout existence, they greatly assisted the development of the Moscovite nation. If invaders threatened, they rose en masse to repel them as had happened during the Time of Troubles (1598–1613) when "the Orthodox church preserved its teachings from armed Latin Catholicism and at the same time saved our nationality (*narodnost'*)" from the Poles. In peacetime, too, the church served the state but in a less obvious, more mystical way. The "imperceptible, but permanent close connection between secular and spiritual power . . . produced, maintained and strengthened the integrity and power of Russia. . . ." Tolstoi's nationalistic assertions, of course, conveniently ignored the widespread corruption among the Orthodox clergy and instances of church-state conflict like Ivan IV's execution of Metropolitan Philip. [39]

For Tolstoi Orthodoxy equaled nationality; the preservation of one meant the preservation of the other. This, he claimed, Russia's eighteenth-century rulers did not understand. They permitted and sometimes encouraged the decline of the church, thereby destroying the harmonious relations of tsar and patriarch which had protected the Russian state for centuries. They did not realize that by weakening their country's religious unity, they threatened its political unity as well. Catherine, for example, made the serious error of aiding Jesuit activity in Belorussia with disastrous results. The Jesuits "not only did not russify Belorussia but in fact

separated it from the state by catholicizing its inhabitants; . . .
they used education as a means for propaganda; . . . they were
the enemies of the state church. They destroyed their estates, oppressed their peasants, sowed dissension, carried out intrigues, and
when Russia was in danger, they fled or entered the ranks of the
enemy." [40] The moral was clear, particularly in the context of the
Polish demands for independence in 1863: a tolerant attitude toward alien beliefs could easily endanger the very existence of the
Russian state.

While not calling for the rehabilitation of the church to combat
divisive forces within his country, Tolstoi did insist upon full use
of autocratic power. In his opinion a ruler must never debase his
position by continually seeking compromises with his opponents.
He therefore condemned Alexander I for "attempting to reconcile
all tendencies, to satisfy, if possible, both sides. Such diplomacy in
administration," he argued, "gives birth to bewilderment, to
vagueness and debilitates authority." [41] It was not a sophisticated
doctrine Tolstoi preached — he was essentially a man of action,
not a philosopher — but its very simplicity pleased the emperor.
Frightened by society's increasing demands for freedom which accompanied his "Great Reforms," Alexander II could only rejoice
over an official who, "unlike so many other highly placed advisers, . . . contemplated no dilution of the central power, no loos-
ening of the unity of the empire." [42]

Bureaucrat and Scholar

This loyalty to crown and country, combined with the abilities
acquired from his practical lyceum education and early government career, strongly qualified Tolstoi to implement the restrictive programs that would follow the Karakozov affair. Having
spent almost all his life training for and working in state chancelleries, he had become the bureaucrat's bureaucrat. Not only was
he politically reliable, he was resolute, efficient, and coldly imper-
sonal. Even Chicherin, who hated Tolstoi, acknowledged the minister's strength of will, a characteristic clearly in evidence when

Tolstoi introduced his educational reforms despite tremendous opposition.[43]

Contemporaries marveled too at his managerial talents and industriousness. Meshchersky recalled that Tolstoi, although responsible for both the synod and the education ministry, held office hours just once a week, allowing each visitor two minutes to state his business. During Meshchersky's interview, Tolstoi's face expressed "attentiveness and an eager desire to shove out his petitioner." While not taking a single note, Tolstoi fulfilled Meshchersky's request within five days. The editor of *Grazhdanin* concluded that never before had he really understood the meaning of "times [sic] is money." [44]

The reluctance with which Tolstoi granted interviews and the curtness which he displayed during them reveals both his unwillingness to waste time in talk when a written report would be quicker and his dislike of social contacts. So cool was Tolstoi's manner that it frightened some subordinates. Academic Committee member N. N. Strakhov, for example, sighed "like a man suddenly delivered from great danger and troubles" after he successfully avoided a chance encounter with Tolstoi at a railroad station. "The task of conversing with him," Strakhov wrote, "seemed so difficult that up to this day I rejoice at the speed of my decision not to see [him]." Tolstoi would never use charm, warmth, or friendliness to achieve his ends. In fact, he told the university students of Odessa on 12 September 1867: "I do not want popularity, I despise the seeking for popularity (*populiarnichan'e*)." [45] His classmates at the lyceum would have agreed. These traits — steadfastness, administrative efficiency, indifference to public opinion — defined much of Tolstoi's personality and induced many to think him better suited for the Ministry of the Interior than the Ministry of Education.

However, these critics often ignored Tolstoi's extensive scholarly interests. In 1869 he assured the Second Session of Russian Naturalists: "Do not doubt that I, for my part, will continue to assist whole-heartedly everything which can promote the success of science, especially *Russian* science." He supported this contention by himself producing a significant array of monographs and articles. In addition to the two books already mentioned, he contributed numerous short pieces to historical journals like *Russkii arkhiv* and *Russkaia starina* and prepared longer studies on the Russian school system during the eighteenth century, on various aspects of Catherine's reign, and on the relations of the Lithuanian Metropolitan Josif toward the Uniates.[46]

Tolstoi was a noted bibliophile as well. His library housed in a uniquely constructed tower at his Riazan estate, contained forty thousand foreign books which represented "all fields of the serious literature in German, French, English, and Latin" but concentrated, as might be expected from his research activities, on education, non-Orthodox religions, and Catherine's era. The collection in Russian was equally impressive and included an excellent assortment of documents, particularly on Catherine II.[47] Thus Tolstoi's scholarly aspirations also formed an important part of his personality.

These two major aspects of the minister's character — the academic and the bureaucratic — well equipped him to perceive the dilemma facing Russian educational officials. Tolstoi the scholar appreciated the importance of learning, the joys of unfettered mental activity, the dangers of excessive interference in academic life. Tolstoi the loyal functionary acknowledged education's usefulness but wanted it closely controlled and directed because he distrusted its traditions of free inquiry, its potential threat to the status quo. Just as the political necessities of maintaining autocracy conflicted with and often hindered the free and rapid development of education in Russia, so too did Tolstoi's predominantly bureaucratic temperament clash with and often subdue his concern for scientific pursuits. It is in the context of this ambivalence in the personality of the Minister of Education as well as in the nature of education itself that Russian school policy after 1866 can best be understood.

CHAPTER 3 / The Ministry of Education:

Its Structure and Authority

Already nicked by the two-edged sword of education, the autocracy in 1866 called on Tolstoi to make this weapon safer to handle without destroying its usefulness for the state. Tolstoi willingly accepted the task, but argued that he would need to have the sword firmly in his grasp to dull the dangerous edge. Possessing the bureaucrat's distrust of individual initiative and faith in administrative decree, the new minister considered complete control over Russian education the essential precondition for successful reforms at all school levels. In his view, the liberalization within the education ministry under Golovnin, like the liberalization occurring in Russia after the Crimean War, encouraged rather than eliminated unrest. Thus, students and teachers, convinced of the ministry's weakness by its concessions, had increased their demands instead of thanking the department for their newly acquired rights.

A reversal of policy was not long in coming. Tolstoi's first major circular reiterated the emperor's urgent call after the Karakozov affair for total obedience from all government officials: "The primary duty of all who are in academic service must be the careful, assiduous and strict fulfillment of their obligations as prescribed by the general laws of the state and by the private orders of the ministry." [1] Centralization and subservience replaced local autonomy and open discussion as the guiding principles of the ministry. It would never occur to Tolstoi that it might be as difficult to wield the education sword when held too tightly as it was when held too loosely.

The process of gaining total dominion over the school system would be a complex one, for even autocratic Russia had many different loci of power with authority in educational matters. When Tolstoi took over the ministry, it had three major administrative centers — the chancelleries in St. Petersburg, the curators' offices in the district capitals, and the schools themselves, the last two considerably invigorated by his predecessor's program of decentralization. In addition to these elements within his own ministry, Tolstoi would also have to contend with a greatly stimulated public interest in schools and with the continued participation of other state agencies in the business of education.

Faced by such a variety of competitors, Tolstoi avoided subtleties and employed the most direct centralizing tactics. He strove to tighten his control over everything already under his jurisdiction, to emasculate those institutions he could not manipulate, to dominate previously independent bodies, and to prevent any outside interference in ministry affairs. These efforts to control educational policy form the leitmotiv of the Tolstoi era, a leitmotiv that will pervade the present chapter on the ministry's central apparatus and its relation to other parties involved in education, and later discussions on the ministry's schools as well.

Strengthening the Ministry's Central Departments

Ironically, Golovnin, who had encouraged local autonomy, actually left Tolstoi the administrative machinery necessary for the latter's centralizing intentions. Besides the usual clerical staff, Tolstoi had immediately subordinate to him two advisory bodies, the Ministerial Council and the Academic Committee; an influential monthly publication, the *Zhurnal*; and his personal representatives in the provinces, the curators.[2] To utilize these assistants effectively Tolstoi strove to ensure their loyalty and submission while adjusting their powers to fit the level of their reliability. He realized that he could not govern the schools of his ministry, let alone those of his competitors, without first becoming master in his own house.

Golovnin had made this task easier by abolishing the Central School Board in 1863. Seven years earlier Alexander II, disturbed by the chaos in Russian education, had given this institution substantial powers. Not only could it seek the emperor's support in its conflicts with the minister, it could also bypass normal government channels and submit its projects directly to the tsar for approval. While undoubtedly useful during the succession of weak ministers in the 1850s, the board's dominant position annoyed and hindered a more dynamic head like Golovnin. He therefore replaced the board by a regular Ministerial Council and an Academic Committee, both responsible solely to the minister. The council gave final review to all vital questions whether administrative, academic, or financial; the committee focused on scholastic matters like education statutes, teaching guides and programs, texts, and periodicals. There was now little chance that these two agencies would overstep their consultative role. The minister determined their agendas, unilaterally confirmed or vetoed all their major decisions, and in the case of his council even set the dates of its meetings.[3]

If his ministry employees hoped that Tolstoi's work for the synod would prevent him from closely supervising them, they would be disappointed. Tolstoi devoted most of his energy to his new post. As early as October 1866, one official complained: "Wrapped up in the affairs of the Ministry of Education, Count Dmitry Tolstoi does not have an opportunity to treat church business."[4] Even archbishops on essential business had difficulty seeing the procurator. This situation would continue until his resignation, for Tolstoi lacked religious fervor and in fact sometimes shocked contemporaries by his lax observance of Orthodox ritual and by his indifference to his holy office. A. V. Bogdanovich recalled that a few weeks after Tolstoi's death, "the Metropolitan called on me. He did not mourn Tolstoi but said that no one remembered when Tolstoi had last received the eucharist. While he was Procurator of the Holy Synod, Tolstoi never once entered Isaac Cathedral, never dropped into the synod chancellery where his uniform just hung on a stand." [5]

Even neglecting his duties as procurator, Tolstoi still might not have been able to run his department properly, had he not delegated some responsibility. Unlike Golovnin, who lightened his administrative burdens by broadening the authority of provincial agents, Tolstoi preferred to share his labors with his trusted and hand-picked assistant minister. Where Golovnin had generally left this position vacant, Tolstoi would elevate in turn two prominent curators, I. D. Delianov and Prince A. P. Shirinsky-Shikhmatov, to the job. Relieved by them of considerable paper work, of the need to attend many imperial commissions, and of such routine matters as the appointment of temporary teachers and the distribution of budget surpluses, Tolstoi would have sufficient time to oversee the workings of his Petersburg bureaus.[6]

Since neither his continual presence nor the departmental regulations of 1863 could stop the determined, recalcitrant employee from obstructing the ministerial will, Tolstoi quickly placed his own candidates in most key posts in a further effort to ensure the cooperation of his ministry's central organs. In the first five months of his term he appointed Delianov assistant minister and A. I. Georgievsky editor of the *Zhurnal*. By 1868 he had taken advantage of the unique provision allowing the expansion of the Ministerial Council beyond its permanent nucleus of the minister, Academic Committee head, and two imperial appointees to double its membership with his own nominees; at the same time he had placed three of his trusted pedagogical experts — Georgievsky, I. B. Shteinman, and N. Kh. Vessel' — on the Academic Committee. The installation of I. Girsh as director of the Department of Education in February 1869 completed this shakeup of the ministry's Petersburg personnel.[7]

Tolstoi had chosen his subordinates carefully; few ministers would have such devoted assistants as Delianov and Georgievsky. More clever than intelligent, the amiable Delianov preferred to temporize rather than face problems squarely; yet his loyalty to Tolstoi remained firm. Repudiating the ideas which had led him to defend university rights during his Petersburg curatorship in the 1860s, he helped direct the campaign against university autonomy that accompanied the student disturbances of the 1870s. Thus his selection as Minister of Education in 1882 horrified those like former War Minister D. A. Miliutin who hated the Tolstoi system. Miliutin called this appointment "a restoration of the ministry of Count Tolstoi which all Russia hated. The only difference between the former regime and the future one will be in the lining (*podkladka*); with Tolstoi the lining was bile; with Delianov it will be idiocy. Poor Russia!" [8]

While Delianov specialized in higher education, Georgievsky focused on the secondary schools. As a student at Moscow's historical-philological faculty, he had become a protégé of M. N. Katkov and P. M. Leont'ev, who later, E. M. Feoktistov suggests, persuaded Tolstoi to employ Georgievsky because they wanted a representative of their views at the ministry.[9] Whether or not Feoktistov is correct, this bright, diligent, but somewhat pedantic former history docent did press for Katkov's primary objective, the preponderance of classical studies in secondary education. As editor of the *Zhurnal*, member of the Ministerial Council, and president of the Academic Committee, Georgievsky played a large part in defining the new realschule and gymnasium and in defending these programs against their critics. Neither Tolstoi's dismissal nor eventual death lessened Georgievsky's faith in Tolstoi's policies. In fact, when the classical gymnasium appeared threatened in 1901, Georgievsky, then almost eighty, still proclaimed the 1871 statute "Russia's great step forward in education," and published a book-length attack on the proposed changes.[10]

With his central departments solidly under his command Tolstoi could begin to concentrate all authority over education in St. Petersburg. Once again the Golovnin legacy would prove surprisingly useful. In March 1865 Golovnin had strengthened the Academic Committee's control over schoolbooks by prohibiting the use in ministry institutions of any text which failed to receive the sanction of the Academic Committee or curator's council. Local officials would learn of these choices from a cumulative annual catalogue carried by the *Zhurnal*, the first one appearing just two months after promulgation of the decree.[11] Readily accepting this policy, Tolstoi would continue issuing comprehensive text lists throughout his term of office. This kept the Academic Committee quite busy. It usually met once a week, nine to ten months a year, scrutinizing two to five hundred books and periodicals annually.[12]

A series of administrative decisions supplemented the 1865 regulations and tightened the ministry's hold over the selection of texts. Tolstoi's hand-picked chairman of the Academic Committee, A. I. Georgievsky, attacked the curator councils' role in the examination of schoolbooks. Arguing that their irregular schedule of meetings and their lack of competent specialists hardly qualified them to review books intelligently or on time, Georgievsky succeeded in having more and more works sent directly to the Academic Committee for comment. Its endorsement became so important that publishers refused to print a text unless passed by the committee, for Tolstoi tolerated no deviations from the centrally compiled lists.[13]

Each new statute expressly limited a teacher's options to those texts approved by the ministry; and when some elementary instructors ignored these restrictions, a decree of 17 November 1879 ordered the inspector or school council to supervise personally the distribution of all primary schoolbooks. Even school libraries did not escape ministerial interference. Gymnasium faculty, for example, lost the privilege of stocking their school's collection in complete freedom after an investigation revealed the presence of many unsuitable and, from the ministry's view, harmful volumes.[14] Whether for library or classroom, all acquisitions now had to meet the ministry's standards of utility and political reliability.

An even more ambitious attempt to regulate Russian textbook literature was Tolstoi's campaign to acquire from the regular censorship bureau control over any elementary reader published for the masses (*narodnoe chtenie*). Disturbed by some populists' use of primers to spread antiautocratic sentiments in the mid-1860s, Tolstoi demanded his ministry review all such books even if they were not intended to be used in its schools. While the Minister of the Interior, P. A. Valuev, resented Tolstoi's meddling with his censorship powers, his successor, A. E. Timashev, who took over in March 1868, was more helpful. Affirming the education department's paramount interest in works geared to the beginning reader, Timashev ordered these books sent directly to the Academic Committee, where a special elementary text sector established on 19 May 1869 would judge their political, moral, and pedagogical qualities and periodically publish its findings in the *Zhurnal*. No longer would "subversive" primers face merely the hurried and often unpracticed eye of the local censor; all primary school texts now had to be approved by the new special sector.[15] By creating this subcommission of the Academic Committee, Tolstoi had strengthened the ministry's control apparatus and had extended its jurisdiction, at least in elementary education, beyond the confines of its own institutions.

The committee did not, however, employ its broad powers to strangle Russian pedagogical literature. Tolstoi wanted to control and direct education, not to stultify it. He therefore filled the committee with intellectuals: scholars like the famous Byzantinist V. G. Vasilevsky and the mathematician P. L. Chebyshev, experienced teachers like the director of Petersburg's Second Gymnasium V. Kh. Lemonius, pedagogues like the editor of *Sem'ia i shkola* Iu. I. Simashko, and literary figures like the critic N. N. Strakhov, the writer N. S. Leskov, and for a brief period the philosopher V. S. Solov'ev. Such an expert council seemed hardly likely to encourage harsh restrictions on texts. In fact, it publicly denied any desire to act as censor.[16]

The many ways it could endorse books provided a convenient legal excuse for the committee's indulgent attitude. It *recommended* works which deserved special attention, *approved* those which merely satisfied the requirements, and *allowed* those which were helpful despite definite inadequacies. Moreover, the criteria were far less strict for class reference (*uchebnye posobiia*) and library books than for basic texts (*uchebnye rukovodstva*). Most works could fit into one of these slots, but those in the "allowed" category had minimum marketability. From 1866 to 1877 the Academic Committee passed 1,549 of the 2,838 items submitted, or slightly over 55 percent — a high proportion considering their admittedly poor quality, and one which convinced Georgievsky that the committee had actually "misused" its authority.[17]

Primarily a supervisory institution, the committee did little to stimulate the preparation of better texts. Tolstoi merely continued Golovnin's program of schoolbook competitions, establishing in 1873 four annual prizes, totaling 5,000 rubles, for the best secondary and elementary school texts. The results were discouraging: over the next seven years the ministry made only six awards, two over the number allotted for a single year. Tolstoi begrudged even the small sums spent on these contests. For him the issuing of new, improved teaching materials remained secondary to the careful regulation of existing ones.[18] That properly compiled texts might not only raise the level of Russian schooling but also help to indoctrinate students did not concern Tolstoi so much as the possibility of subversive works appearing in the classroom because of the ineptness or disloyalty of local examiners. More interested in the exclusion of hostile values than in the inculcation of desired ones, Tolstoi emphasized the negative tactic, moderated somewhat by his employing expert personnel, of increased central control over textbook selection. This order of priorities would characterize the ministry's activities elsewhere and constituted a major weakness in the Tolstoi system, for it constantly placed the ministry on the defensive. As modern dictatorial states have realized, "the best defense is a good offense."

While the Academic Committee needed no more than minor adjustments to fit into the Tolstoi scheme, the *Zhurnal* would require a complete overhaul. Under Golovnin it had fallen from the ranks of Russia's leading educational magazines to the level of a compendium of largely undigested information. Golovnin had purposely humbled his own periodical because he did not want it to "compete with private publications, whose existence is necessary for the maturation of our pedagogical knowledge." The *Zhurnal* should merely "familiarize society with academic developments" everywhere by filling its pages with school reports and decrees, historical and statistical data on education, accounts of pedagogical activity abroad, and other similar articles.[19]

The *Zhurnal*'s restricted role pleased neither the academic nor the bureaucrat in Tolstoi. Accordingly, by the fall of 1866 he had replaced its editor and considerably broadened its program. Reflecting Tolstoi's personal commitment to research, the *Zhurnal* now devoted half its space to scholarly papers in all disciplines. More important, Tolstoi wanted his journal to snatch from the private sector he so distrusted the task of providing "scientific" direction for all teachers, and so he ordered it once again to examine in detail educational theory, techniques, and literature.[20] Its new format, which combined monographic studies, pedagogic treatises, and government pronouncements, made the *Zhurnal* one of the most significant and ambitious periodicals of nineteenth-century Russia.

The revised *Zhurnal* became another tool in the ministry's workshop of control devices, for its primary duty was to supply faculty with "a mass of truly beneficial reading" and to introduce more uniformity in Russian education. Undoubtedly, articles such as those by nationalist writers like M. P. Pogodin and K. N. Bestuzhev-Riumin provided the "beneficial reading" which, Tolstoi insisted, must "fortify their [the teachers'] minds with . . . the great principles and loyalties bequeathed us by history." [21] Subscribed to (often in multiple copies) by most state schools, the *Zhurnal* could act as a unifying force and combat deviations from centrally imposed programs by bringing the same definitive announcements to all employees. To dispel the ignorance of the obedient and to win over the recalcitrant, the ministry carefully defended its decisions in lead unsigned articles appearing in the "Contemporary Chronicle" section of the *Zhurnal*. Frequently, as in the case of the extensive editorials advocating the realschule and state control over elementary education, these articles came directly from Tolstoi himself. In less authoritative fashion the *Zhurnal* also advised local educators on a wide variety of pedagogical problems ranging from the proper instructional methods in virtually every subject to the appropriate behavior for the primary school inspector. After the entrenchment of the classical system in 1871–1872 it even added a special section for works on classical philology to help raise the low level of Latin and Greek studies in Russia and thereby improve instruction in these languages at the gymnasium.[22] Finally, the *Zhurnal* guided teachers and principals in selecting texts. Besides carrying the regular catalogues of approved books, it reserved an entire subsection for reviews of recent pedagogical literature. Tolstoi had transformed his official journal from an information bulletin into a multipurpose instrument for implementing ministerial policy.

Redefinition of the Curator's Powers

Although the strengthening of both the Academic Committee and the *Zhurnal* contributed to the centralization of authority, the most significant factor in this development was Tolstoi's reinterpretation of the curator's role. Taking advantage of Golovnin's willingness to delegate power, the curator, as the ministry's chief regional administrator, wielded considerable influence over his district before Tolstoi's appointment. The only internal check on his activity was his special council comprised of the deputy curator, the university rector, the district inspectors, and gymnasium directors and supplemented, if the curator so desired, by additional faculty representatives; but this council, like its ministerial prototype, could do no more than offer advice when asked. The curator called the meetings, retained sole right of initiative, and with the minister's support could overrule the council majority. The major external checks on the curator were those set by the ministry in its circulars and school statutes. Golovnin, however, arguing from his experience in the Naval Ministry that "many matters could be decided with greater benefit locally" than in St. Petersburg, had given his curators full responsibility for such essential features of academic life as promotion examinations, the distribution of courses, and the introduction of supplementary technical programs. The curators even controlled the careers of all primary and secondary school teachers and of some university personnel like docents and foreign-language lecturers. None of these could get a job, transfer, or be removed without the curator's permission.[23]

The school reforms of 1863–1864 further expanded this official's authority. Troubled by frequent student disorders, the ministry assigned the curator control over those institutions and regulations affecting the nonacademic side of student life. Without his approval the university could not grant financial assistance, issue codes for students or instructions for inspectors, or install professors elected to the university court. His influence over secondary schools also increased, for he now set entrance, promotion, and graduation examinations and resolved all conflicts between the gymnasium director and his council. Only in elementary education did the curator remain in the background, leaving the administration of primary schools to the newly created county school councils.[24] Thus, when Tolstoi took office, the curators had both the legal authority and the necessary support from St. Petersburg to become dynamic forces especially in higher and secondary education.

The existence of powerful, independent curators often far removed from the minister's watchful eye disturbed Tolstoi. Even if they did not use their privileges to introduce or permit measures which might undermine the school system and possibly the autocracy as well, they would undoubtedly pursue a variety of educational programs. Tolstoi feared this pluralistic approach: with his bureaucrat's trust in monolithic organizations, he considered deviations and nonconformity extremely dangerous; not only would such diversity confuse and hence unsettle the populace, it would also indicate an inherent weakness in the central authorities. These views compelled him to restrict the curators' prerogatives. Yet he could not reduce their powers too much because he needed strong representatives in the provinces to discourage local school officials from flaunting ministerial directives. Tolstoi wanted forceful curators, but only as executors of his commands. He therefore increased their supervisory responsibilities while curtailing their role in policy-making. They were there to control, not direct, education.

To make sure the curators fulfilled the goals set for them, Tolstoi carried out sweeping personnel changes, strengthened the inspection forces, and limited personal initiative by reserving all fundamental decisions for himself and the ministry's bureaus in St. Petersburg. Expecting some opposition from Golovnin's appointees about their humbler role, Tolstoi in his first three years either removed them entirely or transferred them to other districts, thereby destroying whatever power bases they had built up. Only P. D. Shestakov, who had impressed the new minister during the latter's 1866 visit to Kazan, kept his post.[25]

The vacancies generally went not to educators, but to administrators. Aside from exceptions like Petersburg University rector A. A. Voskresensky, who headed the Kharkov district (1867–1875), and Warsaw University rector P. A. Lavrovsky in Orenburg (1874–1880), most curators had little or no teaching experience. For example, Lieutenant General P. A. Antonovich in Kiev (1867–1880) had previously ruled the city of Odessa; P. K. Zherve in Dorpat (1869–1875) and Kharkov (1875–1879) had directed the Mikhailov county zemstvo board; and P. N. Batiushkov in Vilna (1869–1899) had managed the Chancellery of the Ober Procurator of the Holy Synod. By preferring state functionaries to pedagogues, Tolstoi had again placed plans for centralization above the demands of education. Ignorant of school problems, these curators would hardly provide local institutions with inspiring leadership, but they would be less likely to question the ministry's decrees or to allow unorthodox procedures. Tolstoi did not want and indeed would not tolerate another Pirogov.

His curators, Tolstoi hoped, would now concentrate on the supervision of education. So vital was this task that Tolstoi himself set the example of the personal inspection tours he wanted his curators to conduct. He would spend one month each year calling on schools, attending classes, and sometimes participating in the lessons. These personal appearances, the ministry idealistically asserted, would improve relations between the provinces and the capital and would establish mutual trust among "people of thought, people of science." Tolstoi's frequent spokesman, M. N. Katkov, went further and claimed that such trips assured proper guidance for teachers, dramatized the value of learning, and stimulated private financing of schools. Local authorities had a jaundiced, but probably more accurate, view of these visits. They felt themselves spied upon and acted accordingly. School buildings were cleaned; fresh uniforms appeared; students rehearsed the exercises to be given before the minister; tyrannical directors became mild and gracious; and at special dinners and receptions provincial dignitaries delivered adulatory speeches about Tolstoi's achievements.[26]

It would be wrong to conclude, however, that Tolstoi saw and heard only what his subordinates wished him to. True, his annual reports stressed the achievements of the ministry's program, but few ministers would tell their emperor otherwise or publicize their failings. Impervious to flattery, suspicious by nature, and conscientious in the extreme, Tolstoi was a most persistent and thorough inspector. To obtain information he even repressed his normal aloofness in favor of an informal chumminess. Hence the same man whom the sophisticated critic Strakhov fled from in fear could put a pupil at Orenburg sufficiently at ease to question him about his Kirghiz schoolmates. That his tours frequently produced tangible results best demonstrates Tolstoi's effectiveness. He based many requests for general reform on materials he gathered and promptly rectified specific local problems. Just months after his visits, one gymnasium lost its troublesome director, another no longer slighted the teaching of Russian, and the university in Odessa acquired its much-needed new building.[27] These ministerial excursions, then, were far more than cursory sight-seeing jaunts; their relative success must have constantly reinforced Tolstoi's faith in the value of surveillance.

Since their administrative burdens kept the minister and curators from reviewing most schools themselves, they had to rely on district inspectors to carry out investigations. Conceiving of these officials as ministerial policemen rather than as pedagogical advisers, Tolstoi ordered them to concentrate not on counseling teachers, but on observing how accurately faculty performed their duties. For Tolstoi the lax or disobedient instructor could do much harm because "students must get their examples of respect for law and devotion to the state" at school. The teacher who destroyed his pupil's belief in authority by flaunting "existing rules" was almost as dangerous as the one whose lectures threatened the essentials of faith and the moral and material well-being of the people. Therefore Tolstoi demanded that the inspector eliminate "every digression . . . from the course of study set up for each school." [28] The idea that instructors could achieve good results while ignoring ministerial pronouncements rarely occurred to the minister; he had a blind spot all too common in tsarist functionaries.

To guarantee that inspectors understood his narrow interpretation of their role, Tolstoi explicitly defined their obligations. They should merely be reconnaissance agents, checking on every aspect of school life from auditing procedures to instruction methods. The ministry told the inspector what areas to examine and exactly what to look for. The following brief excerpt from the section on moral education should indicate the meticulousness of the ministry's instructions. The inspector, for example, must discover "whether they [the faculty and staff] strictly observed that students punctually went to church on Sundays and holidays and showed the appropriate reverence during the service and in general whether they [the directors] were instilling in them [the students] a genuine religious feeling; whether the proper discipline was observed within the education institution, whether the students were trained to be clean and orderly . . . whether the rules of social propriety and courtesy, a love for labor and a serious attitude to their obligations were being instilled in them; . . . what rules existed concerning the supervision of students who lived in student apartments (*uchenicheskie kvartiry*) and also concerning the activities of the commuters and in general concerning the behavior of students outside the school."

Tolstoi even outlined the techniques the inspector should use in his espionage activity. His visits should be a "normal" not an "exceptional and extraordinary," occurrence and should take him into the classroom where he could watch lessons being given, into the teacher's study where he could privately confer with the instructor, and into the community where he could discover the relation of the faculty to society.[29] In theory the advice was sound, but in practice it demanded the impossible: inconspicuous, but omnipresent, invigilation.

Unfortunately for Tolstoi the effectiveness of the district inspectorate depended much more on its size than on his instructions. Unless the ministry's agents could visit schools often, they could not constitute a sufficient threat to prevent teachers from contravening ministerial decrees. Therefore Tolstoi sought to enlarge the inspectorate while reducing the amount of territory and the number of schools it covered. At his accession there were far too few inspectors — one in the Kiev district, two each in Moscow, Odessa, and Kazan, and three each in St. Petersburg and Vilna — to oversee the ministry's schools in their districts. To supplement this meager force, Tolstoi quickly sent an additional inspector to Kazan and to Moscow, insisted on personal surveys by the curators themselves, and filled the post of deputy curator which Golovnin had wanted abolished.[30] But what best lightened the inspector's burden was the creation of a separate organization to review elementary schools, the most numerous of all educational institutions.

Despite these efforts surveillance remained distinctly inadequate. The curator and his assistant provided little help because of their many other obligations, and even with primary schools excluded, district inspectors had too many institutions to observe. According to the ministry, elementary school inspectors should handle only 50 schools apiece. The district inspector would never enjoy such a favorable ratio, although he investigated more complex institutions and this undoubtedly took extra time. In 1874 the ratio of inspectors to schools was 1 to 57 in the Petersburg district, 1 to 71 in Moscow, 1 to 163 in Kharkov, 1 to 66 in Kazan, 1 to 42 in Vilna (not counting the 2,715 private Hebrew institutions also within their jurisdiction), 1 to 114 in Kiev (plus 93 Hebrew schools), and 1 to 44 in Odessa (plus 38 Hebrew schools).[31] The situation worsened after 1874. While schools continued their rapid growth, Tolstoi managed to get a mere two additional inspectors, both for the recently established Orenburg district. He had demanded another seven, but the Minister of Finance refused the less than 14,000 rubles needed annually.[32] The unsupervised teacher did not appear so dangerous to the government as he did to its minister.

Distances as well as numbers frustrated the inspector. Realizing this, the ministry in 1874 partitioned the huge Kazan territory of 572,000 square miles into two sections whose dimensions more closely conformed to those of the other districts. This division removed a serious weakness in the ministry's provincial administration, but it hardly solved the basic problem, since even average-size districts were too vast to be covered by the few inspectors allotted them. The staff in Petersburg, for example, faced an expanse considerably larger than Texas; that in Moscow a region almost equal to France. The comparatively small Kharkov district still exceeded California in area and had a single inspector.[33] Poor transportation facilities magnified these already immense distances. The autumnal rains, first wet snows, and vernal thaws made Russian roads virtually impassable in late fall and early spring, precisely when most schools were in session. While railways were affected least by climatic conditions, they did not offer a viable alternative to the carriage or sleigh, for Russia had only 13,860 miles of track by 1881. The absence of lines to Orenburg meant that the minister could not even reach all his district capitals by train.[34]

The logical solution to these transportation difficulties would be to divide every district into two or three sectors each with its own resident examiner. Although this procedure would obviously reduce the distances an inspector traveled, Tolstoi opposed its introduction because he wanted invigilators to concentrate on a particular type of school rather than on a region. The reason for the minister's unexpected support of a policy which would decrease an inspector's efficiency was his overriding concern for his classical secondary schools. He insisted that they have their own separate inspector and ruled in 1872 that each district inspectorate should include at least one classicist.[35] This plan precluded a territorial division of labors.

The final obstacle to intense school surveillance was the understaffed curator's having to load his inspectors with many supplementary assignments, the most time-consuming of which were publication of the district circular and participation on examining commissions. The chore of editing these comprehensive monthly circulars which carried anything of interest to the teacher from ministerial policy statements to pedagogical articles to résumés of school council meetings tied one investigator to the district capital, thereby keeping him from taking lengthy inspection trips.[36] In addition, inspectors represented the ministry at secondary school graduation examinations and usually presided over special examination committees which certified county and elementary school instructors and private tutors. These commissions found their obligations quite burdensome: the one in St. Petersburg met four times a week; the one in Moscow twice weekly from 1 September to 1 May.[37]

Hampered like most ministers by his country's difficult climate, meager resources, and legacy of underdeveloped provincial administration, Tolstoi failed to increase substantially the effectiveness of the district inspectorate. True, he did succeed in fully defining the inspectors' obligations, but his exhaustive instruction could not shorten the distances to be covered, take the place of missing inspectors, or free existing ones from their noninvigilatory duties. This inability to investigate thoroughly the activities of local officials and educators reinforced the minister's distrust of the autonomy granted them by his predecessor. It was dangerous enough, Tolstoi thought, to share one's powers with men one could govern; it was absolutely foolhardy to delegate authority to those one could not supervise. He would thus trample over the traditional prerogatives of the curators and teachers' councils, flattening private initiative in the process.

As succeeding chapters will show in detail, Tolstoi's reforms of the 1870s reserved all important judgments on school organization for the ministry's central apparatus. The gymnasium and realschule legislation of 1871–1872, for instance, empowered the education department to issue comprehensive decrees defining examination methods, disciplinary measures, and teaching programs at these institutions. Golovnin, it should be remembered, left testing procedures to the curator and student conduct to the individual pedagogical councils. Although he did publish directives on the gymnasium curriculum, these merely indicated the general scope of each subject and permitted "extreme diversity" in instruction. Over eight times longer than his predecessor's, Tolstoi's course outlines allowed no deviations whatsoever.

While focusing on secondary education, Tolstoi did not neglect the other schools under his jurisdiction. He compiled academic plans for female gymnasiums and fully delineated both the course of study and the internal administration of teachers' seminaries and institutes, municipal and model elementary schools. Only the primary education statute of 1874 did not explicitly assign the preparation of curricula to the ministry, but these schools rarely offered more than the proverbial "three R's" plus religion and had their own network of inspectors.

With the ministry itself now prescribing every essential aspect of school life, the curators lost their former creative role in education. One should not judge from this, however, that Tolstoi gave his curators little to do. On the contrary, just as he strengthened the ministry at the curators' expense, so too would the curators strengthen their office at the teachers' expense; for they obtained control over the previously autonomous universities and primary school councils. Whereas Golovnin had limited the curators to reviewing faculty decisions, the Tolstoi-inspired regulations of 1884 encouraged curator intervention in university affairs. The curators could convene the university's governing bodies, urge proposals concerning student supervision upon the rector, and unilaterally appoint deans of faculty. The gains in elementary education were still more impressive. Almost totally excluded from this field in the 1860s, the curators had by the mid-1870s acquired jurisdiction over such matters as the organization of refresher courses for grammar school teachers, the establishment of municipal schools, and the appointment of the director and inspector of primary institutions.

So vital did Tolstoi consider this expansion of the curators' responsibilities that in 1874 he demanded sizable increases in their budget and staff, but as usual the money was not forthcoming and the existing "desperate situation" remained unrectified until 27 January 1881.[38] While curtailing the curators' opportunities to formulate policy, Tolstoi had enlarged their administrative and supervisory powers. In this way he hoped to transform them from the senior education advisers Golovnin envisaged into the departmental henchmen he needed to enforce his will.

Tolstoi had thus greatly strengthened his ministerial authority. None of his predecessors had either the powers or the bureaucratic apparatus to influence school programs so directly or so extensively. Since education had become such a necessity and at the same time so serious a threat to internal stability, the minister thought that only with the tightest grip on the helm could he steer it in the proper channels. There were pedagogical as well as political advantages to this careful piloting. The Russian teacher certainly needed more guidance than his better prepared counterparts in the West, and the concentration of creative effort in St. Petersburg might produce plans superior to those compiled by local officials lacking the wealth of expertise Petersburg could draw on.

However, the disadvantages were no less clear. By advocating centralization Tolstoi not only discouraged instructors from seeking new solutions to educational problems, he also antagonized the Russian public which was growing used to having its opinions on school matters respected. It may well have been Tolstoi's fatal flaw that he willingly risked society's anger and the dangers inherent in perpetuating an outmoded system in order to maintain firm control over all his operations. One may say that this was the fatal flaw of the Russian autocracy too.

External Challenges to Ministry Policy

While unchallenged at the ministry, Tolstoi did not enjoy a free hand in Russian education. Other government institutions, financial considerations, and even the press would with varying degrees of success inhibit his actions. Russia's major consultative organs, the State Council and the Committee of Ministers, could review and, if necessary, suggest alterations in his measures. Although the council did, for example, substantially change his elementary school statute, Tolstoi generally found this procedural requirement more a nuisance than a barrier. As long as he had the confidence of his emperor, he could rely on the autocrat's prerogatives to get legislation past the opposition. He could either request Alexander to repudiate any unfavorable verdict from the council or avoid this body entirely by putting his project in the guise of a special report to the tsar which became law when imperially confirmed.[39] Tolstoi exploited both expedients, but never to better advantage than when Alexander II overruled the State Council's rejection of the ministry's secondary school acts.

However, after 1874 Tolstoi could no longer expect such assistance from the throne. Conservative bureaucrats like Tolstoi lost their most powerful leader at court, Count P. A. Shuvalov, who resigned in 1874, and their archenemy, the liberal War Minister D. A. Miliutin was becoming the most influential man in St. Petersburg. This increasingly unfavorable political climate in the government partly accounts for the ministry's failure to issue any major reforms during the last five years of Tolstoi's rule.

The passage of his legislation did not mean the end of outside interference, for these regulations came under the scrutiny of ad hoc commissions charged with examining the ministry's annual reports. Normally they limited their criticisms to minor and readily acceptable suggestions like raising the requirements for spiritual academy graduates desiring teaching posts at the gymnasium or obtaining better statistics about class sizes and gymnasium dropouts.[40] On at least one occasion the commission did dispute the fundamental principles of ministerial policy, but without result. Prince D. A. Obolensky, a member of the delegation entrusted with the 1872 report and an opponent of Tolstoi since their Naval Ministry days, attacked the classical system for producing fewer gymnasium graduates and hence reducing university enrollment. Receiving no support from his colleagues,[41]

Obolensky submitted an extensive memorandum to the emperor who, while condemning its "predominantly personal nature," sent it on to the Committee of Ministers. Upon hearing Tolstoi's rebuttal, the committee dismissed Obolensky's accusations notwithstanding their factual basis, and to vindicate his minister fully, Alexander immediately awarded him the Order of Alexander Nevsky.[42]

Far more difficult to overcome than these threats from within the government were the monetary restraints placed on Tolstoi's actions. Still recovering from the expenses of the Crimean War and the Polish pacification when Tolstoi took office, suffering from a highly unfavorable balance of payments, and incurring new debts during the Russo-Turkish War and the beginnings of state-induced industrialization, the government had few funds available for even so vital a service ministry as education. In Tolstoi's first full year at the ministry, the national debt ate up 19 percent of state expenditures, the War Ministry 30 percent, the Ministry of Finance 17 percent, and the Ministry of Education 1.6 percent. These proportions would barely fluctuate throughout Tolstoi's term. The debt, the war departments (including the Naval Ministry), and the Ministry of Finance continued to get over 70 percent of government funds, and this did not count the extraordinary sums granted for railroad building and for the military costs of the Balkan War. Although Tolstoi more than doubled his ministry's outlay from 7,037,000 rubles in 1867 to 16,861,000 rubles in 1880, he never obtained more than 2.7 percent of the state's normal expenditures. Only the synod, the Ministry of Foreign Affairs, and after 1874 the Ministry of the Imperial Palace consistently received less than he did.[43]

The emptiness of the imperial treasury inhibited Tolstoi in two ways. First, he could not adequately support all areas of education but had to devise a system of priorities. Following the policy initiated by Golovnin in his last budget, Tolstoi assigned secondary schools the largest slice of the ministry's pie, increasing it from 33.7 percent in 1866 to 41.6 percent in 1879. The other ministry favorites were the equally vital teacher preparatory schools, whose share increased from less than 1 percent in 1866 to over 8 percent in 1879. The universities lost most, dropping from a 25.5 percent portion in 1866 to 15.1 percent in 1879.[44] Not only did they need less capital for construction than the rapidly expanding gymnasiums and normal schools, but the ministry, like certain state legislatures today, no doubt hesitated to finance centers of antigovernment feeling. Second, lacking enough state funds for even his pet projects, Tolstoi had to use local communities, the newly created zemstvos, and other private donors, who would demand some influence over education in return for their generosity. Tolstoi would have to yield some degree of centralized control for the extra cash he required.

Although reluctant to make this sacrifice, Tolstoi would at times try to give the public the illusion that they were participating in ministry decisions. Proclaiming that education's success depended on a well-informed populace,[45] he did not exclusively pursue a policy of bureaucratic silence. Early in his career he would sometimes order the *Zhurnal* to give society advance notice of his plans, but this was mere tokenism. Most of the proposals Tolstoi chose to publicize much before their enactment were minor and uncontroversial, like those in 1867 to lift the standards of private schools, private tutors, and the Demidov Lyceum. The only major reform presented for public discussion was the municipal school legislation, which appeared in the May 1869 issue of the *Zhurnal.*

The contrast between Golovnin's and Tolstoi's attitude toward publicity remained all too obvious. Where Golovnin broadcast his designs in an earnest search for advice, Tolstoi — if he forewarned society about his schemes — generally did so not to consult popular opinion, but to justify measures already decided. For him the nature of Russian education was not an "open question." He therefore insisted on working in the shadow of imperial chancelleries and kept many of his most important policies from coming before the nation. So much secrecy, for instance, surrounded the compilation of the secondary and elementary school statutes that the ministry persecuted Academic Committee member A. S. Voronov for allegedly leaking information.[46] Public debate there could be, but only within carefully circumscribed boundaries.

In the ministry's view, the Russian press, particularly the

Petersburg threesome of *Golos, St. Peterburgskie vedomosti*, and *Vestnik Evropy*, frequently exceeded these limits. Having experienced a tremendous upsurge in numbers and prestige after 1855, Russian periodicals had indeed focused heavily on education, both because of its intrinsic importance and because of its wider social implications which could serve as a starting point for more general political discussions. While journalistic attacks could hardly block his projects, they did create difficulties for Tolstoi by encouraging public opposition to his measures and by giving support to his enemies within the government. In response to the press's assaults the ministry grew increasingly secretive, defended its policies in numerous *Zhurnal* articles, and called upon unofficial assistance from Katkov's *Moskovskie vedomosti*, which if anything denounced Tolstoi's antagonists more vitriolically than they condemned the ministry. For a brief period in 1871 it even used a temporary restraining order prohibiting collective representations in the press against the secondary school projects.[47]

Once his reforms were secure, Tolstoi took more direct action against his detractors. He transferred control over *St. Peterburgskie vedomosti* from the Academy of Sciences to the Ministry of Education in November 1874 and forced its editor, V. F. Korsh, to resign three years before his contract expired. Now administered by the Department of Education and edited by a ministry-appointed journalist, *St. Peterburgskie vedomosti* would no longer be in a position to attack Tolstoi's policies.[48] The independent periodicals proved harder to subdue, for Tolstoi still shied away from demanding harsh censorship restrictions. Indeed, he surprised everyone by not supporting the Minister of the Interior's move to repress the December 1879 issue of *Vestnik Evropy* for its vicious assault on the education ministry. However, the ever-intensifying revolutionary terrorism which culminated in the dynamiting of the Winter Palace on 5 February 1880 destroyed any trace of tolerance Tolstoi might have had. At his request the emperor specifically prohibited journals from discussing the educational system.[49] Unable to dominate the press, Tolstoi finally silenced it — a desperate measure which by no means resolved the problem the rapid development of public opinion would pose for tsarist bureaucrats like Tolstoi brought up in the tradition of being responsible to the autocrat, not to society.

Ministry Attempts to Broaden Its Authority

While the imperial government's system of internal review, the watchful eyes of the press, and especially the inadequacies of his budget all hindered Tolstoi's campaign to gain complete control over Russian education, the major obstacle was the great number of schools totally outside his authority. At his accession regional committees in the Polish provinces, Eastern Siberia, Turkestan, and the Caucasus ran the schools in their territories; and central departments like the Fourth Section, the synod, the Ministries of Finance, War, State Domains, and the Interior also had charge of many educational institutions. Such was the legacy of Alexander I's failure to define precisely in 1802 the education ministry's jurisdiction.

Tolstoi was highly successful in extending his power geographically. Since his centralizing plans perfectly suited the government's aims in Poland and relieved the overburdened governors of Eastern Siberia and Turkestan, they aroused little opposition. Frightened by the 1863 uprising in Poland, the tsar now considered any vestige of Polish autonomy a threat to Russian security and in 1867 gladly replaced the independent Polish education commission with the Warsaw curatorship, which was directly subordinate to the Ministry of Education. That same year Tolstoi established a central bureau in Eastern Siberia headed by the governor-general and his special assistant in pedagogical affairs, the chief inspector of schools. Formerly, provincial governors had administered the schools, but this arrangement, Tolstoi claimed, had prevented his ministry from either "correctly supervising education" or providing the "unified direction so necessary for its progress." [50] In Turkestan the minister faced a complicated situation because Russia's advancing armies controlled the area. Everything including educational policy fell within Governor-General K. P. von Kaufman's purview, but his preoccupation with more vital matters left local officials in charge of the schools. Using the familiar argument that without his department's guidance and supervision, education would not "correspond to the general needs of the state," Tolstoi persuaded the government and the War Ministry to put schools in Turkestan under the Ministry of Education, represented here, as in Siberia, by a chief inspector. Thus, by 1876, of the Russian borderlands the Caucasus district alone eluded the ministry's grasp.[51]

The ministry experienced the most trouble taking over institutions traditionally attached to other departments. In fact, it made just two major acquisitions, the elementary schools of the Ministry of State Domains and the Bashkir, Kirghiz, and Tatar schools in the east; and unique circumstances facilitated both takeovers. Under P. D. Kiselev the Ministry of State Domains had excelled in bringing education to the state peasants, but once the emancipation had removed these people from its immediate charge, it saw no reason to continue this expensive task. In 1867 its approximately 2,500 primary schools became the joint concern of the Ministry of Education and the zemstvos.[52]

In the case of the Bashkir, Tatar, and Kirghiz schools, political rather than administrative considerations prompted the ministry's actions. Tolstoi agreed with the Orenburg governor-general that the confusion produced by the proliferation of school officials from four ministries undermined the state's efforts to stop the Moslem religious teachers (the mullahs) from instilling their pupils with "hatred for everything Russian, wild superstition and fanaticism . . . ignorance, boundless laziness and a propensity for thievery. . . ." Only if the Ministry of Education exercised absolute and exclusive authority over native schools could these institutions "create among the non-Russians . . . a sense of citizenship (grazhdanstvennost'), bring them closer to the Russian population, and develop their spiritual and material forces." The State Council concurred and gave the ministry this authority in November 1874.[53]

These increases in the ministry's competence, however, did not affect Tolstoi's strongest competitors in the field of education: the Holy Synod, the Fourth Section of the Imperial Chancellery, and the Ministry of War. The first, of course, presented no threat because Tolstoi as Ober Procurator ruled the synod. The other two were independent organizations, and within months of his appointment Tolstoi discovered how jealously they guarded the schools under their command. Reports in 1866 that radicals were spreading revolutionary ideas among the masses through textbooks like I. A. Khudiakov's *Self-Teacher for Beginners in Reading and Writing*, which aimed at "changing the reader's entire outlook on the world," [54] prompted Tolstoi to challenge the autonomy of every ministry which had schools under its control. Supported by the Minister of the Interior, he demanded that no work unless passed by the censor and approved by the education department's Academic Committee could appear in the classroom of any school no matter what its affiliation. Other ministries could review for their own schools only technical books in their respective specialties. Tolstoi, for example, would leave studies on strategy and tactics to the War Ministry, on agricultural methods and forestry to the Ministry of State Domains. Circulated early in 1867, these proposals outraged both the Minister of War Miliutin and the Head of the Fourth Section, Prince P. G. Ol'denburgsky. They stressed the ability of their own education commissions to select appropriate texts and denied the need for uniform schoolbooks. They were right, and Alexander, now that the fear of insurrection after the Karakozov assassination attempt had dissipated, did not feel the matter sufficiently important to alienate Miliutin and Ol'denburgsky. He withheld his support, thus ending Tolstoi's initial attempt at centralization.[55]

Tolstoi accepted the Fourth Section's independence both because he could influence female education through his position on the Supreme Council for Girls' Schools and because the section's head, Prince Ol'denburgsky, generally endorsed the ministry's programs. His relations with the War Ministry were far thornier, for Miliutin, its chief, detested Tolstoi and his policies. Few cabinets would contain two such diametrically opposed individuals. On the one hand, Miliutin, troubled by social inequality, would argue that it was "necessary to toss aside all antiquated, obsolete privileges, to bid farewell once and for all to the rights of one caste over another." He backed his sovereign's efforts in this direction but felt they had not gone far enough. Anticipating the judgments of modern historians, Miliutin considered the absence of significant political concessions a major weakness of the "Great Reforms." "Our state structure," he wrote in 1879, "demands fundamental revisions . . . village self-government . . . local administration, district, provincial, central and higher institutions — all have outlived their time, all should receive new forms which would correspond to the great reforms completed in the sixties." Unfortunately, "the government . . . frightened by the daring appearance of socialist propaganda in recent years . . . thinks only of protective police measures." [56]

Miliutin was far-sighted enough to realize that political and social reform, not added repression, were the tactics the autocracy should employ against the revolutionary movement. Tolstoi, on the other hand, joined the proponents of a defensive but myopic strategy of retrenchment. He disapproved of emancipation, distrusted zemstvo initiative, and defended class divisions. Miliutin's new military service law, which allowed volunteers to receive an officer's commission on passing an examination, outraged him because it would destroy gentry prerogatives in the army and would attract to the officer corps "people desiring to acquire the rights of state service . . . in the cheapest way possible." [57]

That both men enjoyed the emperor's confidence underscored P. A. Valuev's complaint: "Everyone . . . around him [Alexander II] thought differently; he upheld a system of impossible diagonals." [58] By permitting such conflicting tendencies in his administration, the tsar sacrificed efficiency for increased autocratic power. With his enemies entrenched in the government, a minister would have to rely greatly on the emperor to achieve his ends, and he would never feel secure since the monarch changed sides all too frequently. One year, for example, he would support Tolstoi against Miliutin on secondary school reform; the next, Miliutin against Tolstoi on military legislation. This inconstancy not only made it difficult for subordinates but helped discredit the regime. Could educated society have much confidence in a government that often appeared to be pursuing contradictory aims?

What irritated Tolstoi more than Miliutin's progressive views was his control of an educational system that could rival his own ministry's. The war department possessed its own elementary, secondary, and higher schools, teacher preparatory institutes, pedagogical journal, academic committee, central school board — and it spent from four to over five million rubles a year on these institutions. Had Miliutin focused solely on military training, Tolstoi might have ignored the War Ministry's schools, but Miliutin did not do this. Instead, in 1863 he replaced the cadet corps by regular secondary schools called military gymnasiums but with little professional orientation; for he believed a general education vital for all future officers and considered the existing gymnasiums, still awaiting reorganization after Nicholas's destructive changes, unsuited for the task. Although Miliutin at first envisioned the eventual absorption of these institutions into the Ministry of Education, once Tolstoi took office, the personal and ideological hostility between the two men ruled out any talk of such a merger. Independently administered and emphasizing mathematics, science, and modern languages, the military gymnasiums plagued Tolstoi because they offered a practical alternative to the classical schools and thus, in Katkov's words, "flaunted the basis of our education legislation." [59] They proved to many that the Ministry of Education had no monopoly over correct pedagogical procedures and in so doing encouraged public opposition to the Tolstoi program.

Recognizing the power and skill of his opponent, Tolstoi did not challenge Miliutin's participation in secondary education directly. He tried rather to harass the war minister both by attacking his projects and by threatening his most vulnerable institution, the Medical-Surgical Academy in St. Petersburg. Not only did Tolstoi, often with assistance from conservative periodicals like *Moskovskie vedomosti, Russkii mir,* and *Grazhdanin,* continue to criticize openly the military gymnasiums, he also led the unsuccessful fight within the government against Miliutin's fundamental reforms in army service. He particularly opposed the possible democratization of the forces and claimed that the proposed education deferments would inundate the schools with uncommitted students. While more splenetic than imaginative or influential, Tolstoi's speeches did cause Miliutin considerable discomfort.[60]

No less disturbing was Tolstoi's attempt to wrest the Medical-Surgical Academy away from the War Ministry. Unlike the military gymnasiums, the academy seemed a reasonable target: its radical and sometimes riotous student body, its prior association with the education department, and the need of St. Petersburg University for a medical faculty all provided convenient pretexts for the ministry's takeover bid. But in Tolstoi's view the academy's primary failing was its lower entrance requirements. By accepting students without a classical diploma or its equivalent, it prevented Tolstoi's gymnasiums from being the exclusive pathway to university privileges. While Miliutin defended these admission concessions as the only means to get enough suitable candidates, Tolstoi quite rightly suspected him of using the academy to demonstrate the value of allowing graduates from nonclassical schools into university faculties.

Thus, in September 1873, Tolstoi demanded authority over the academy. The issue was a complex one, tied in as it was with the debates on the 1874 army reform, the classical-realist furor, the student disorders at the academy in the winter of 1874–1875, and the animosity of the two ministers. After twenty months of discussion in various subcommittees and in the imperial chambers, the Committee of Ministers finally decided for Miliutin, arguing that the academy's well-being outweighed the desire for uniformity in higher education and for a medical faculty at Petersburg University. Miliutin had not completely won, however, since he had to raise the academy's entrance standards to equal those at the universities.[61]

Tolstoi's bids to usurp the educational prerogatives of other bureaus had failed. He acquired only those schools that his competitors wanted to get rid of. It was in his efforts to extend his ministry's competence that Tolstoi's relatively weak position within the government was revealed. He never could muster enough forces on his own to challenge his fellow ministers' authority. He needed imperial support, but the emperor, who so vigorously shielded Tolstoi's measures from their opponents, proved equally conscientious in guarding other ministers from Tolstoi's assaults. Hence, much to Tolstoi's grief, Russia maintained her pluralistic approach to education. Even under the greatest centralizer in its history, the education department itself probably controlled less than half of Russia's schools. This situation seriously impeded the ministry's effectiveness, for the institutions outside its domain, especially the military schools, remained an eloquent reminder of an alternative and possibly less stringent system of education. Tolstoi could dominate his ministry, but not Russian education as a whole.

The diversity of the ministry's institutions of higher learning[1] and the specialized nature of their programs preclude any attempt to analyze here all aspects of Russian advanced education. Focusing primarily on the six universities under the 1863 statute, the present chapter (as succeeding ones) will stress the key problem facing Tolstoi: how to reconcile his country's need for a viable school system with the inherent dangers for autocracy of such a system. Nowhere would this dilemma be more acute than at the university, for its student body provided the technical elite the government sought and at the same time had from the late 1850s contributed greatly to Russia's instability by actively demonstrating for its rights and by joining the revolutionary movement in large numbers.

For Tolstoi the solution was simple, in conception if not in execution. Improve higher education by more teachers, better schools, extra funds for research; combat student unrest by stricter controls over faculty and more careful supervision and selection of students. Unfortunately, Tolstoi looked for his remedies on the surface, not diving below to discover either the basic causes of university disorders or the potential harmful effects of increased government interference on the quality of learning.

The Improvement of Higher Learning

A follower of Uvarov, not Magnitsky, Tolstoi conscientiously strove to raise the level of education. "I want Russia," he told a meeting of naturalists on 21 August 1869, "to be the equal of all other international powers not only in politics but also in learning." [2] Katkov, often the minister's spokesman, explained why. "Only learning *(nauki)* can improve our material means." The state that impeded the spread of learning, he warned, might "destroy itself." [3] Conservatives like Tolstoi and Katkov saw no less clearly than the progressives the importance of education for their country's future. They too recognized the danger of Russia's backwardness and the need for modernization — although, of course, within narrowly circumscribed limits. They too realized that only trained personnel could bring about this transformation and that for Russia to remain independent these experts must be produced at home, not come from abroad. The furtherance of higher education was no longer a luxury, but a matter of national security. The industrializing powers of the West had already defeated Russia once, in the Crimean War, and might easily do so again unless Russia emerged from her underdeveloped state.

While the university was supposed to supply the men who would transfigure Russia, it suffered itself from her centuries of backwardness. It would find the Russian academic class too small to furnish enough qualified lecturers. Statistics compiled by 1868 substantiated the rectors' complaints about the many empty professorial chairs, especially among the 89 added by Golovnin in 1863. Just 50 of the 114 teaching positions in the six historical-philological faculties governed by the 1863 statute were filled; the juridical faculties, which had to compete with the lures of private practice, listed yet fewer appointments, 43 of 114 posts occupied; and the situation was little better at Russia's four medical faculties at Moscow, Kiev, Kharkov, and Kazan, with 56 of 124 places taken. Although the physical-mathematical faculties with 80 of 114 positions staffed brightened the gloom somewhat, Russian universities still lacked half (244 of 487) the professors and docents required. Even after it counted junior instructors without advanced degrees, the ministry still had 196 teaching vacancies, an average of almost 33 per university.[4]

Disturbed by the teacher shortage, Tolstoi reassessed his predecessor's policy of sending Russia's future professors away to finish their studies. The results were not encouraging. Many graduates learned little from their years abroad, and of the seventy-seven that had come back, only thirty-six were lecturing at institutions of higher learning — hardly a fair return for the 400,000 rubles the ministry had invested from 1862 to 1866.[5] Blaming the program's failures on lax supervision, Tolstoi removed the rather permissive N. I. Pirogov as its foreign-based director, ordered participants to submit their quarterly statements to their former faculties as well as to the Academic Committee so that there would be a closer check on their scholastic achievements, and insisted that the university councils issue explicit instructions on the courses to take and the professors to consult. These measures might help make the candidate work for his 1,500-ruble annual stipend, but they certainly did not guarantee that he would enter the teaching profession upon his return. Tolstoi therefore accepted applications only from those who had seriously committed themselves to academic life either by having already undertaken advanced studies or by having completed at least two years of university teaching.[6] Yet even with these safeguards the ministry could not effectively control its students in Europe, nor could it unreservedly count on their services. Consequently, it sharply reduced the number of grants from Golovnin's average of twenty-three a year to eighteen in 1870 and nine in 1877.[7]

Under Tolstoi Russia would rely on native rather than foreign institutions to train its university teachers. In fact, by 1875–1877 the ministry supported 220 professorial candidates at Russian uni-

versities while sending only 32 away.[8] To attract promising graduates from the traditions of studying abroad, Tolstoi greatly expanded their opportunities at home. He opened scholarship funds
to future academics, created more junior positions (like that of
privatdozent) to give the candidates both classroom experience
and a modest salary during their dissertation work, and, most important, established in August 1868 thirty-six annual stipends
worth 600 rubles apiece and renewable for three years for those
"remaining at the university with the aim of preparing for a pro-
fessorship." Unlike Golovnin, however, Tolstoi insisted on some
assurance that his money would not be wasted. The presence of
faculty advisers and the obligation to write a special long paper
each semester, he hoped, would keep stipendiaries at the books.
The ruling that all students must teach two years for every year
on scholarship or repay their grant in full would definitely protect
the government's investment.[9]

The ministry's new scheme was most effective. It cost less, permitted stricter control over the participants, and eased the teacher
scarcity. By training scholars in Russia, Tolstoi saved 900 rubles
per award and shielded his charges from the potentially dangerous influences of both European political life and of the growing
community of radical Russian émigrés. While Russia's universities may have received instructors with somewhat narrower intellectual horizons, they too benefited from the ministry's program.
Its relative cheapness meant a far larger group of candidates and
hence, especially with the compulsory service requirements, more
lecturers. Between 1868 and 1875, for example, the number of
professors and docents at the historical-philological faculties rose
from 50 to 74; at the juridical faculties from 43 to 69; and at the
medical faculties from 56 to 110.[10] Many vacancies, of course, remained and would continue to exist until the late 1890s, but the
progress Tolstoi made was considerable.

The advancement of higher education demanded more schools
along with more teachers. Tolstoi, the *Zhurnal* claimed in 1876,
had answered this challenge by adding ten postsecondary institutions to the eight under his control in 1866. His achievement was
substantial, but not so sensational as the *Zhurnal* implied. The

ministry founded just three new schools: the Kazan Veterinary School, the Petersburg Historical-Philological Institute, and the Lyceum of the Tsarevich Nicholas, the last really the handiwork of Katkov. The other seven it merely raised from intermediate professional institutes to a position equivalent to that of the universities.[11] At the Demidov Lyceum, for example, the revisions of 1868 and 1874 eliminated the teaching of secondary school subjects, introduced the curriculum of the juridical faculties, lifted the government's yearly contribution by 31,463 rubles, and granted the underpaid lyceum faculty the salaries and rights of their university counterparts. Tolstoi's measures rescued the lyceum from extinction; its enrollment, which had dropped to 43 on 1 January 1866, reached 215 by 1874.[12] Similar increases in budget, academic standards, and staff privileges revitalized the Dorpat and Kharkov veterinary schools, the Lazarev Institute of Eastern Languages, and the Bezborodko Lyceum. Only with these improvements did the above places deserve to be listed as institutions of higher education, and in this sense Tolstoi did more than double their number in Russia.

Tolstoi also started work on the first Russian university in Siberia. The impetus came from Governor-General N. G. Kaznakov, who in 1876 warned that unless his region acquired a university, it would never have "a sufficient number of experienced, trained and conscientious personnel," and hence never be able to "make its natural resources productive."[13] These arguments coincided with the minister's own belief in the university's practical role in strengthening the Russian nation, but problems arose about locating and financing the proposed university. Kaznakov selected Omsk for security reasons; as a provincial capital relatively free of exiles, he felt it most suitable, that is safe, for students. A special investigating commission, on the other hand, preferred Tomsk because of its better facilities and climate, its larger Russian settlement, its greater economic potential, and its more generous offer of land to the university. Despite the intensification of student disorders during the late 1870s, the State Council at least in this instance did not panic. It placed the university's welfare above political expediency and in May 1878 decided in favor of Tomsk. Its own funds depleted by the Russo-Turkish War, the government called on the public to support the initial stages of construction. It responded generously, contributing over 362,000 rubles by 1879.[14] The treasury, however, ignoring Tolstoi's repeated requests for money, provided a mere 10,000 rubles in 1880 for a committee to supervise the building of this institution, which did not officially open until 25 February 1887 — seven years behind schedule.[15] Education still had low priority in the government's planning.

Although concerned most with schools, Tolstoi did not neglect Russia's major research centers: the Academy of Sciences, the central libraries, and the astronomical observatories. He improved the academy's facilities by granting an extra 17,000 rubles a year to its laboratories and museums and assured it a better staff by lifting the service rank of its positions one to four grades and by raising academicians' salaries to university levels.[16] Shocked that Russia's major libraries sometimes could not afford "even such books as every public library needs," Tolstoi doubled the Imperial Library's annual budget, raised that of the Moscow Public and Rumiantsev museums by 17,039 rubles a year, and gave these libraries the privilege of importing foreign books free of tariff and censorship requirements.[17] The Chief Physical Observatory in St. Petersburg and the Nicholas Central Astronomical Observatory in Pulkovo profited from similar additions to their operating expenses, pay scales, and staff.

Private attempts by Russian academics to further science also enjoyed ministerial support. In a significant departure from its usual practice the ministry aided many learned societies without insisting on any controls over their activity in return. Ranging from 2,500 to 6,000 rubles annually, these unconditional grants went to associations like the Imperial Archaeological Society and the Russian Historical Society and to various university groups. Furthermore, the ministry lifted both customs and censorship claims on books imported by the Russian Historical and Moscow Archaeological societies.[18]

National conferences proved more troublesome for the ministry. Tolstoi himself advocated them "as an excellent measure to uphold and strengthen the cultivation of . . . knowledge," [19] but the government was less enthusiastic. Fearing these meetings might develop into political forums or even into permanent pressure groups, it rejected any fixed schedule of conferences and required the consent of the Third Section, the Ministry of the Interior, and the local governor for all conclaves. Not satisfied with these restrictions, Justice Minister K. I. Pahlen demanded that the programs for every convention of jurists be reviewed by his and Tolstoi's ministries, that only commercial and civil law be discussed at the 1875 gatherings, and that the conference president be personally "answerable for every deviation . . . from the program." [20] The jurists did not assemble again that decade.

Less beleaguered were scholars solely responsible to the Ministry of Education. Given control over their agenda and proceedings, Russia's natural scientists and archaeologists held their first state-wide congresses, the former meeting six times, the latter four times during Tolstoi's ministry.

Within certain limits the minister had actively promoted higher education and scholarship in Russia. Students benefited from larger teaching staffs, greater opportunities for advanced training, the increase in institutions of university standard; professors from the growth of their faculties, the expansion of laboratory facilities, the improvements in research institutes, the encouragement of learned societies; and historians in particular from the ministry's role in collecting and publishing archival material through its own Archaeological Commission and its generous grants to Russian historical societies.[21] Admittedly, Tolstoi's contribution was quite prosaic. He concentrated on fiscal and administrative reform rather than on pedagogical innovation, but to many professors, jealous of their independence, this was just the minister they wanted, a man who would confine himself to doling out the cash. Unfortunately for them, the restiveness of their students would bring the ministry out of the bursar's office and ever closer to the lecture hall and faculty assembly.

A Decade of Modest Remedies for Student Unrest

If, as an academician, Tolstoi wanted higher education to flourish, as a conservative bureaucrat he dreaded the political awareness this training might produce; for Russian universities introduced students either publicly in the classroom or privately in the discussion circle to the progressive views of the age. While such an intellectual climate never pleased the autocracy, it became intolerable with the appearance of a revolutionary movement in Russia by the 1860s. For officials like Tolstoi the free interplay of ideas and the spirit of social criticism that prevailed at the universities heightened their students' susceptibility to the "foul machinations" of outside agitators. These firebrands focused on students, the Kazan curator P. D. Shestakov explained, because the latter's "natures so readily yielded to fanaticism." [22]

In a sense he was right, for radical theories and political disaffection had certainly unsettled the university community. Full of youthful idealism and liberated, often for the first time, from the physical and mental confines of family and school, Russian students were easily inspired by persuasive propagandists who promised them a more humanitarian and equitable world than the one they presently lived in. Their disillusionment with the government because it not only had failed to sustain its earlier reforming zeal but had begun to rely increasingly on repression, when combined with an inflated sense of their own importance derived primarily from their elite position, their isolation from the masses, and society's growing trust in the power of education, prompted them to demand immediate implementation of their newly acquired beliefs. Thus Franco Venturi considered the "going-to-the-people" escapade — the flocking of students in 1873 and 1874 into the countryside to convert the peasants to an agrarian communism based on the Russian commune — their answer "to the appeal of the . . . Populists." Statistics reveal the extent of this participation by postsecondary school students in subversive activity; they counted for 36 percent of those involved in the revolutionary movements of the 1870s.[23]

It would be wrong, however, to attribute student unrest, as the ministry generally did, solely to external forces. In fact, the revolutionaries themselves complained that the majority of the student body was either too apathetic or too frightened to undertake extreme political action.[24] Problems within the university rather than the attacks of professional agitators on the government usually sparked student outbreaks. The 1863 statute, which had granted autonomy to professors, gave little to the students. The two main grievances — penury and the prohibitions on corporate activity — remained. Attracted as much by the university's role in career placement as by its educational facilities, young Russians willingly underwent tremendous financial sacrifices to matriculate. Professors reported that never before had they seen students "so startlingly destitute on such a vast scale." This poverty, the Petersburg rector explained, could make a student's life grim. "He lives in small quarters often located on the outskirts of the city; he dines at the student canteen *(kukhmisterskaia)* on poor and unnourishing food; he goes on foot at all times of the year." [25]

With such widespread indigence the restrictions on the student's right of association became still less acceptable because the government was now not merely infringing on what many felt to be a fundamental freedom, it was depriving the needy of potential sources of aid like student treasuries, libraries, and fund-raising performances. The restoration of corporate privileges therefore would be a more effective rallying cry than any scheme for state reform.

Unwilling to admit the legitimacy of student grievances, Tolstoi blamed outside agents, unscrupulous teachers, and unmotivated students for university disorders and demanded tighter controls over college life. It was a short-sighted policy; for while it might help counteract revolutionary infiltration and the intrinsically liberal atmosphere of higher education, it would hardly correct those abuses within the university which drove many to illegal acts. Since students generally protested against specific annoyances like incompetent instruction, unfair punishments, or inadequate scholarship assistance, it is possible that a program which alleviated these problems might have placated much of the student body, thus turning them away from subversive influences. By responding primarily with increased repression, the minister could achieve brief successes, but he ran the risk of further alienating and politicizing the students. It would not take a frustrated student long to link his struggle for stipends and corporate privileges with the Russian people's need for a decent standard of living and the right of self-government.

Before criticizing Tolstoi too harshly, we should emphasize that the universities themselves under his supposedly liberal predecessor had instituted many of the rules which would later antagonize their students. The 1863 statute had entrusted university officials with most matters of discipline and student supervision. Normally assisted by his deputy and a secretary for student affairs, the inspector (or prorector, as inspectors chosen from the faculty were called) reviewed complaints, offered advice, and in general had "direct charge" over all students. The rector, deans, and inspector sitting as the university board judged student misdemeanors, while flagrant infractions came before a three-member court chaired by a professor from the juridical faculty. Everyone was subordinate to the university council. It selected the inspector (subject to ministerial approval), his staff, and the court, defined the inspector's duties, and compiled the regulations governing student behavior and the penalties for misconduct.[26] Since the curator merely confirmed these decisions, the ministry had little direct influence over measures of student control.

Students, however, benefited little from their university's relative independence. Although varying in severity from the harsh rules at Kazan to the moderate ones at St. Petersburg, the student regulations of the Golovnin era were hardly permissive. Some items were obvious formalities: students had to maintain order, obey the inspectorate, and report changes of address immediately. Others by their very pettiness insulted the student's *amour propre:* he could not applaud or hiss in lectures, smoke on school grounds, or leave the city without permission from the inspector or rector. More irksome yet were the restraints on collective activities like student organizations within the university, joint representations by petition or delegation, and the wearing of insignias and costumes of a society or nationality. While every university did not expressly forbid all these pursuits, only Moscow officially repudiated this policy by sanctioning certain student meetings. Equally strict punishment codes enforced the above rules; indeed, serious offenders faced anywhere from a year's rustication to permanent banishment from all universities.[27]

So stringent were the universities' disciplinary methods that the government did not consider changing them even after it discovered that students from higher educational institutes had dominated the revolutionary circles involved with the Karakozov assassination attempt. Instead it focused on improving the surveillance over students when outside the university.

A decree of 26 May 1867 demanded closer cooperation between police and school authorities and greater limitations on student extracurricular ventures. Dismayed by the police's ignorance about student affairs and by the ease with which Karakozov himself, despite his role in the 1861 disorders, could reenter Kazan University two years later and then transfer to Moscow, the government required education officials to provide the police with detailed information about all students and to circulate lists of those they had expelled. In addition, it put an end to the "concerts, spectacles, readings . . . and other public assemblies" held by students off university limits and prohibited local philanthropists from staging charity performances for indigent students without the school director's approval. These diversions, the May edict argued, cut into the time needed "to study and attend lectures regularly," but what the state really feared was the use of these gatherings for political purposes.[28]

Their grievances ignored, Russia's students remained a highly volatile group which the slightest spark could set off. The explosion was not long in coming. The dismissal of a Medical-Surgical Academy student in early 1869 ignited demonstrations in St. Petersburg for the right of free association and the abolition of police supervision.[29] As would be the case throughout the 1870s, the state responded by establishing an imperial investigating commission, this time comprising the Ministers of War, Education, State Domains, and Finance, the head of the Third Section, and the Petersburg Chief of Police.

The commission endorsed the disciplinary rules devised by the universities before Tolstoi's accession, but complained that these regulations were not uniformly applied. It thus reaffirmed the following as essential features of all student codes: subordination to school authorities; police jurisdiction over students; and the prohibition of corporate activity, including public assemblies, whether within or outside school grounds. It also extended the maximum penalties then operative to every institute of higher learning: discharge *(uvol'nenie)* for one year with permission to enter another school in a different city; dismissal *(udalenie)* for one or two years without the right to attend any institution during that period; and expulsion *(iskliuchenie)* for three years, after which time the student might renew his studies only with the approval of the department whose school he would enter and on the personal responsibility of the school's director.[30]

While still avoiding draconian measures like those in 1848 which might disrupt education, the government had tightened the restrictions on university students by insisting that the more lenient institutions strengthen the restraints placed on their charges. The confrontation politics of the university population had not succeeded, for the state met their challenge without a conciliatory gesture; but the battle had just begun.

Although it disavowed the policy of concession, the ministry did not rely solely on tighter controls and harsher deterrents to combat student unrest. Such negative tactics, it felt, would not correct certain deficiencies in the students themselves, which contributed no less than outside agitators to the disorders at the university. In Tolstoi's view too many candidates sought higher education "without adequate intellectual ability or motivation."[31] Interested solely in enjoying themselves or acquiring the service rank a university diploma would bring them and the guarantee it carried of a respectable position in the Russian bureaucracy, these men, the government argued, were basically frivolous and in their search for diversion they became easy prey for the revolutionaries. The solution was simple: direct all the student's energies to his studies so that he would better himself academically and have less time for unsanctioned extracurricular activities; and raise admissions standards so that the less able, less disciplined, and hence potentially troublesome, applicants could not get in.

This two-pronged attack must have pleased Tolstoi, since it offered the opportunity of improving education and at the same time of counteracting its harmful effects. In fact, until 1877 he concentrated more on lifting university standards than on expanding student restrictions. His program was useful in its elimination of the unprepared, practical in its attempt to exclude undesirable elements from the university, perceptive in its realization that the careerist or indeed anyone who found the university too difficult might take out his frustrations in demonstrating against his school, but naive in its belief that the diligent student would be too preoccupied not to notice or heed the disturbing circumstances of his and his classmates' lives.

To bring students back to the books, Tolstoi urged the introduction of modern pedagogical techniques. Anticipating the criticisms of today's students, he contemplated replacing lectures by the seminar system used so successfully in Germany. The research experience and the personal contacts with faculty that the seminar could provide, Tolstoi hoped, would stimulate the desire for learning far more than passively listening to a professor in an auditorium. Some universities like Moscow, Kazan, and St. Vladimir established seminar programs, but student "idleness," which Katkov called the great plague of college life, remained. Tolstoi then adopted less subtle devices. In 1872 he made attendance compulsory at all lectures, a step hardly consistent with his earlier preference for seminars. His order achieved little success because it did nothing to eliminate the causes of absenteeism: poor teaching, schedule conflicts, lithographed lecture notes, professorial indifference to monitor duties, and student poverty which forced many to work during class time. Universities continued to report poor attendance, especially in the historical-philological and juridical faculties where lecture courses prevailed.[32]

More fruitful were the ministry's revisions of entrance requirements. Acting on warnings received in 1866, Tolstoi first reviewed the position of auditor *(postoronnoe litso)*, because it offered, so some officials claimed, "dangerous elements" an easy path into the university. A good-conduct voucher and tuition money were all an auditor needed to attend classes; no one questioned his ability or seriousness of purpose. The ministry quickly remedied this situation. Believing only the socially respectable and the academically trained sincere in their quest for higher education, Tolstoi in May 1867 limited auditor privileges to the following three groups: those who had acquired an occupation or a definite status in society; those who had completed the classical gymnasium or its equivalent with satisfactory marks in religion, Russian, and either mathematics or Latin; those graduates of all other secondary schools who had passed a Latin examination. Persons in the last two categories had to qualify as regular students within a year or leave. Tolstoi hoped in this way to weed out the less committed and hence in his opinion more troublesome auditors.[33] The new regulations were effective; the proportion of auditors in the student body fell from 14 percent in 1864–1865 to a mere 5 percent in 1877–1878.[34]

With the auditor problem solved, the ministry turned to the general admissions policies established in 1863–1864. These too seemed quite lax. Most universities required only that candidates be at least seventeen and graduates of a classical gymnasium or its equivalent; just two set full qualifying examinations (*poverochnye ispytaniia*) for all aspirants. Disturbed by these loose standards, the ministry in a *Zhurnal* editorial of June 1868 demanded the introduction of entrance tests everywhere.[35]

Tolstoi received strong support for this policy from the special commission investigating the student disorders of 1869, for it also condemned the uncontrolled influx of people into higher education. Consequently, its regulations of 8 July 1869 advocated examinations for all first-year candidates and transfers and specifically requested that these tests be administered without the "least indulgence." That the committee insisted on a particularly rigorous screening for transfers, auditors, scholarship applicants, and previously expelled students and on conscientious character evaluations from gymnasium directors indicates the importance of political considerations in the committee's deliberations.[36] The itinerant, the poor, the unruly, if not actual subversives, were in the committee's eyes less stable and hence potentially unreliable students.

The entrance prerequisites instituted in 1869 would not succeed, however, unless rigidly enforced; and this the universities seemed unwilling to do. So few applicants failed and so many reports of excessive leniency reached the ministry that in 1871 it forbade university officials ever "to lower the norms in . . . [any] gymnasium course for those desiring admission." But only centrally administered tests would maintain the proper standards. Thus in 1871–1872 the ministry established state final examinations for gymnasium students as the primary entrance hurdle to the university. Whether graduates of public or private schools, within or outside the ministry's jurisdiction, candidates could now enter the university only upon passing the gymnasium final.[37]

At first the ministry freed the seminarians from this requirement, but soon this concession bothered Tolstoi — both because seminary graduates frequently displayed moral shortcomings and low academic achievements and because his critics quite logically demanded the extension of the seminary's special prerogatives to all other secondary schools. Tolstoi therefore abolished these privileges early in 1879.[38] The government had finally gained total control over university admissions; the gymnasium final — a series of tests compiled and regulated by the ministry — had become the sole university entrance examination.

Available enrollment statistics suggest some negative results of these measures. Seminarians (who, the ministry admitted, often lacked high intellectual and moral standards) would fill an increasing proportion of freshman classes during the seven years they enjoyed admissions concessions. An extreme example of what might happen occurred in Odessa where seminarians constituted 13 percent of the first-year university classes from 1867 to 1871 and 52 percent from 1873 to 1877.[39] Far more detrimental than the influx of seminarians was the sudden drop in university registration. The ministry itself announced that Russia's eight universities had 7,251 students on 1 January 1872, the last year under the old entrance system, but only 5,692 two years later. The addition of an eighth year to the gymnasium course partially explains this decline, since most of those who would have graduated in 1872 and gone on to the university now had to stay an extra year at the gymnasium; but the stricter examination rules also played their part and helped delay the return to the pre-1873 figures until 1877–1878. Enrollment then rose steadily to 9,859 in 1881 and 13,976 in 1894.[40] Nevertheless, Tolstoi's legislation had set back university expansion five years, something a backward country like Russia with its growing need for trained personnel could not afford.

For Tolstoi, however, the advantages of his plan offset any temporary fall in university attendance. In the first place, he argued, rigorous admissions standards would reduce the dropout rate by excluding the poorly prepared; and, in fact, the number of dropouts did decline from a high of 1,069 in 1871 to 778 in 1877 (still over 10 percent of the total student body). Even this slight decrease pleased the minister, for dropouts not only wasted the university's meager resources but they could form a disaffected group, deprived as they were of the privileges they had hoped to gain from a university diploma. Second, the revised admissions requirements indirectly aided the underpopulated historical-philological faculties without seriously depleting the other faculties. Since every university candidate now had to know Greek and Latin, the classical language prerequisites for liberal arts courses which had previously discouraged students would no longer create a problem. The historical-philological faculties' share of the student body rose from $5\frac{2}{3}$ percent in 1866 to over 10 percent in 1875, a modest but important increase because this faculty supplied so many gymnasium teachers in the humanities.[41]

Third and most significant, the new admissions policy made certain that the great majority of students would come from the classical gymnasium, the cornerstone of the Tolstoi system. This was the school the ministry best controlled and regulated; therefore it was the school whose products it felt it could trust the most. Given Tolstoi's priorities, his program was admirable. It provided universities with more carefully trained and screened applicants, curtailed somewhat the numbers of those who would not finish their studies, promised more instructors for the gymnasium, and all at the cost of a few lean years in university enrollment.

Concentrating on eliminating one potentially dangerous element from the university — the unmotivated or incompetent student — Tolstoi during his first decade in office generally neglected another equally dangerous element — the indigent student. The lower classes were flocking to the university because it offered them the most direct path up the social ladder, into government service and the more interesting professions of law and medicine. While the rich or well-born could rely on their wealth, their connections, and the special privileges they received from attending exclusive institutions like the Alexander Lyceum or the Page Corps, the not-so-favored had few alternatives but the university, particularly if they disliked the less prestigious world of business. Thus the career-oriented faculties of jurisprudence and medicine attracted the most students by far, and the proportion of the university population from the nonnoble estates mounted steadily from 33 percent in 1864 to 53 percent in 1881.[42] With more students from the lower classes, there was naturally more poverty at the university. In fact so indigent was the student body that one-third of it, an average of 2,000 people a year, enjoyed tuition exemptions; 40 to 60 percent of the students received some form of financial assistance.[43]

Since Tolstoi did not specifically exclude the poor from the university, he needed another means of protecting it from the restlessness of an impoverished student body. A rapid increase in scholarships would seem the most logical solution, but not for a department perpetually short of funds. Relying on private contributors and the university's own treasury to support the indigent, the ministry restricted itself to maintaining existing state fellowships, most of which were conditional on later service usually in secondary education and as a result drew few takers. It did so not only because it insisted on guaranteed dividends for its investments but also because it felt that excessive generosity would aggravate the situation by attracting even more poor students to the university. Consequently, at the six universities under the 1863 statute the number of stipends with service conditions — the form nearly all state grants took — rose just 0.6 percent from 516 in 1866 to 519 in 1874, while nonobligatory stipends, normally from private sources, increased 273 percent from 169 to 631, so that by 1875 the state provided only 122,845 of the 342,845 rubles awarded that year.[44]

To make matters worse, most available scholarships were too small. The highest average award, 247 rubles in 1877, barely guaranteed its recipient one hot meal a day and fell far beneath the 375 to 480 rubles most professors considered necessary for students to live decently during the academic year.[45] This made supplementary short-term grants all the more essential. Since the government withheld its own contributions and outlawed student organizations which might have collected additional funds, students depended on such uncertain sources as part-time employment and local charitable institutions to augment their meager incomes. Although the pay (except in the capitals) was low, tutoring remained the usual occupation; and at least so the rector of Petersburg University claimed: "those who gave lessons believed themselves lucky." [46]

Sympathetic Russians helped by supporting student canteens and trusteeships (popechitel'stva). The canteens offered cheap, if sometimes dreadful, food; the trusteeships, which were usually privately controlled and run by academics and interested citizens, distributed cash particularly to those ineligible for university loans or bursaries. First established in 1869 by the Kiev curator in response to the deaths of several destitute students, the trusteeships had spread to all six central universities and the Demidov Lyceum by 1875. From the limited data available it appears that the trusteeship grants were numerous but very modest. The Kazan association made 422 awards over three years at an average of 24 rubles per grant; the one in Kharkov, 386 awards in two years, about 26 rubles per grant.[47] These were stopgap measures that might alleviate individual cases but would hardly remedy the problem. Only massive state assistance could eradicate student financial difficulties, and this was never forthcoming.

The ministry's reaction to student poverty epitomizes its general attitude toward the possible subversion of the university during Tolstoi's first decade. Caught between its need for an educated elite and its fear of their political independence, it procrastinated, avoiding the extremes of repression and concession. It did not obstruct the university's generous scholarship programs or exclude the poor, neither did it expand its own role in granting stipends. Similarly, except for a circular in 1870 which made any criminal action, including those that had no connection with the university, sufficient cause for expulsion,[48] the ministry introduced no major new disciplinary measures, merely reinforcing the regulations compiled by the professors themselves under Golovnin. Rather, it emphasized the more positive policy of tightened admissions requirements which, if properly implemented, might raise academic standards as well as keep out potential troublemakers like the unmotivated, the unprepared, and the unruly.

On the other hand, Tolstoi certainly did not relax the existing prohibitions on student affairs. He mistakenly believed rigid control the only appropriate tactic in a situation so volatile that minor annoyances, a professor's incompetence, or an inspector's overzealousness could provoke serious disorders. Although the old unpopular rules remained, the ministry did seem relatively restrained in its fight against the radicalization of university students, particularly given their contribution to Russia's unstable internal conditions. They had, after all, called for revolution, spread "pernicious" doctrines among the peasantry, and even tried to kill the tsar. Nevertheless, the education department shied away from tyrannical laws like those Nicholas I instituted after 1848 with far less provocation.

Despite the huge student involvement in the "going-to-the-people" movement and the renewed university unrest in late 1874, the government apparently shared this moderate approach. The special conference of ministers which Alexander convened in 1874, under the chairmanship of Valuev, to investigate higher education preferred indirect academic restrictions to direct police action. While conceding the need for a stronger inspectorate, it generally opposed additional restraints; for these would incite, not pacify the students. Unfortunately, it did not extend this thesis to argue that existing prohibitions had already alienated the students. Disregarding legitimate student complaints, it proposed stiffer admissions and stipend requirements and the creation of examining commissions to rid the universities of careerists and others who lacked the material security or intellectual capacity necessary to withstand revolutionary agitators.[49] In short, the Valuev commission echoed the ministry's position.

The Increase in Repression after 1876

This compromise solution, however, which yielded little to students or government hard-liners, would not endure. As it became obvious that the massive arrests of young populists in 1874 had not destroyed the revolutionary movement, as the radicals grew bolder in their representations against authority and organized in March 1876 what Venturi called "the first political demonstration in the streets of St. Petersburg" in ten years[50] (a funeral procession to honor a fallen comrade who had died in prison), as the complications in the Balkans threatened to embroil Russia in another military adventure, tsardom could no longer tolerate a temporizing attitude toward university disorders. Faced with the continuing threat of insurrection at home and of war beyond its borders, the Russian state would have to eliminate all factors that weakened the country by creating dissension, and student unrest was one of them. Few denied the importance of calming Russia's institutes of higher learning; the problem was whether conciliatory or harsh measures would work better.

Still denying the validity of student grievances, the ministry chose repression. During the fall of 1876 Tolstoi's closest subordinates — Delianov, Georgievsky, and the new assistant minister, Shirinsky-Shikhmatov — led the fight for stricter student controls within the commission recently formed to review university legislation. In their opinion the university could "turn back unsettled minds to . . . the tranquility of study" only if it awarded fewer but more lucrative stipends and established an effective system of warding off undesirable influences and discouraging unruly conduct.[51] Accordingly, Georgievsky proposed the cessation of short-term grants *(edinovremennye posobiia)*, the reduction of tuition exemptions to 10 to 20 percent of enrollment, and the attachment of service obligations to every scholarship. The poor would then cause little trouble, for the few who came would have enough money and be committed to the state. Turning to the regulations on student affairs, the conservative faction of the committee not only advocated compulsory attendance and state-administered graduating examinations to keep students at their books, it also challenged professorial domination over university disciplinary procedures by seeking to abolish the university court and to free the inspector from the council's jurisdiction.[52] Delianov and company felt the university's collective bodies too inefficient and the faculty too indulgent to supervise students adequately.

These views found little favor either within or outside the commission. The commission majority, for example, wanted unconditional stipends, demanded more short-term grants, and even thought student corporations desirable in theory, although not yet appropriate for Russia. Such modest concessions would hardly satisfy the many professors throughout Russia in favor of immediately legalizing student associations, least of all the very progressive Petersburg University council. Incensed by the whipping of protesters that followed demonstrations against the excessive restrictions on student activity, the Petersburg council formed a special committee to investigate the matter. Its conclusions, signed by all but two professors and sent to the curator in December 1878, emphasized the apolitical character of the student body and blamed the government for the disorders. Pursuing a thesis employed today by their American counterparts when confronted with police brutality on the campus, the Petersburg professors argued that the state, by overreacting to university disturbances, only contributed to the students' radicalization. Therefore, they warned, peace would not return to the university while the authorities maintained their suspicious attitude toward students, their constant police surveillance, and their arbitrary system of administrative arrest. As the first tentative steps toward reform, the faculty urged that students receive the right of assembly outside the university and that the government treat demonstrators leniently.[53]

Two antithetical remedies for student discontent thus came before the ministry by the winter of 1878–1879. Given Tolstoi's faith in bureaucratic control and his distrust of local initiative, it is unlikely that he would ever have approved the Petersburg council's permissive approach to student demands and inconceivable that he would do so as Russia was entering the "crisis of autocracy," just when the failures in foreign and domestic policies were undermining the emperor's very throne. Externally, the mismanaged campaigns of the Russo-Turkish war in 1877–1878 had brutally exposed the weaknesses of the Russian military machine, while Russia's inability to preserve the fruits of its bloody victories in the face of European opposition at the Congress of Berlin further discredited the tsarist administration. Internally, the revolutionary movement had taken a violent turn to terrorism. Vera Zasulich's attempt to kill the Petersburg chief of police early in 1878 inspired a series of assassinations which included the governor of Kharkov and the head of the Third Section among the victims. Equally distressing was society's apparent sympathy for the radicals. The show trials staged by the Ministry of Justice in 1877 to dispel ignorance of the revolutionaries' fanatical aims — which, the government felt, largely accounted for "the deplorable indifference of well-intentioned elements of society" to radical propaganda[54] — had backfired, as the public rejoicing over Zasulich's acquittal vividly demonstrated.

Under such circumstances the Petersburg proposals for free student gatherings seemed to Tolstoi "positively harmful." He rebuked the university council and, to make sure it would not repeat its offensive submission, declared discussions about police supervision and similar matters beyond its legal competence. Few in official circles challenged this action; the threat of insurrection was too near. Even Miliutin attacked the Petersburg solution. In an argument reminiscent of the ministry's critique of faculty autonomy, he claimed that professors had not shielded their charges from dangerous influences but had rather "sought popularity among the students, and, by quarreling with one another, had lost all authority." [55]

The shots fired at the emperor by another former university student on 2 April 1879 destroyed any hope left the proponents of conciliation. His life once more in jeopardy, Alexander naturally could not appreciate these unproductive disputes on the student question. He instructed a special conference of ministers, chaired by Valuev and called to review all Russia's internal problems, to investigate the "spread of subversive ideas among the younger generation and to discover . . . measures to put an end to corruptive influences." After a cursory review of higher education, the conference unhesitatingly blamed the university's leniency for the disturbances. S. A. Greig, who had recently replaced the moderate Reutern as Minister of Finance, sang the old reactionary refrain about low tuition and plentiful grants filling the universities with those whose poverty made them most receptive to revolutionary agitation. Tolstoi's report was more sophisticated and all-inclusive. He attributed the unrest not to an abundance of needy students but to a general indifference to academic responsibilities, to inadequate controls over student financial assistance, and especially to professorial "autonomy in all matters." [56] Where a revised scholarship program would have answered Greig's criticisms, only a complete transformation of the Russian university would satisfy Tolstoi.

After heated debate the Committee of Ministers on 3 July 1879 accepted both the above analyses. Greig could applaud the committee's declaration that "the artificial stimulation of a desire for higher education [that is, scholarships] was positively harmful"; Tolstoi, its orders to finish his university statute quickly and to develop procedures for controlling university stipends. Only the emperor was unhappy. Prompted by M. T. Loris-Melikov, the powerful governor-general of Kharkov, he demanded immediate action, not tentative projects. In response the Valuev conference urged Tolstoi to remove incompetent inspectors and to free the inspectorate from the jurisdiction of the faculty, thereby repudiating a major feature of the 1863 legislation.[57] Tolstoi now had the mandate he wanted to tighten his authority over students and he reacted quickly by submitting new proposals to the committee within the month.

His plans met the government's stipulations for a restrictive scholarship policy and an effective inspectorate. Although Tolstoi did not, like Greig, intend to bar the indigent from higher education, he did want to keep stipends from going into the wrong hands. He therefore suggested that future awards depend on approval from the curator and inspector as well as from the faculty. To strengthen the inspectorate Tolstoi sought an increase in both its numbers and its independence of action. Disturbed by the failure of all but three universities to budget for assistant inspectors, he advocated empowering curators to use university operating funds temporarily for hiring additional inspectors. More important, he attacked the inspectors' subordination to university collegiate bodies. Not only did he fear that they might inhibit the inspector in his work, he also felt, as a confirmed believer in autocracy, that the council's democratic procedures made it incapable of inculcating the "spirit of order and discipline." On 31 July 1879 the Committee of Ministers ratified these general recommendations, leaving Tolstoi to fill in the details.[58]

Despite Alexander's demand for prompt action, the revised instruction did not appear until 5 November 1879. Ironically, the emperor's own emergency methods caused the delay. Just after escaping A. K. Solov'ev's shots, the tsar had delegated authority over all civil affairs to six "regional military dictators," the governors-general of Moscow, Kiev, Warsaw, Kharkov, Petersburg, and Odessa. Empowered to use any measure necessary, including administrative exile, to maintain the peace, these men would now control all schools "in matters relating to the preservation of order and public tranquility." In theory, then, they should sanction any change in the university inspectorate; and they insisted on their rights in defiance of Tolstoi's plan to consult only the easily accessible governor-general of Petersburg and the influential Loris-Melikov of Kharkov.[59] This was a serious tactical error, for it forced Tolstoi to introduce unpleasant reforms during the school term, thereby guaranteeing them the widest publicity and the worst reception.

This opposition was not surprising, for the November regulations replaced the faculty with the university administration and inspectorate as the major overseers of student life. Doubting the ability of academics (especially acting in an open forum like the university council) to discipline their charges, the ministry transferred the council's jurisdiction over punishments and stipends to the university board, a less representative body, largely composed of executive personnel — the deans and rector. The board also assumed the tasks of the now-defunct university court. It became the students' judge and jury, but even it could not officially interfere with the selection or activities of the inspector. He was directly responsible to the curator, who appointed him subject to approval from the governor-general and the minister.

Enjoying considerable independence and great power, the inspector became spy, policeman, and stipend supervisor all in one. Wanting full reports on each student, Tolstoi instructed his inspectors to compile conduct books *(konduitnie knigi)* from material gathered by meeting frequently with students at school, in their rooms, and during office hours held for those with special problems. The maintenance of order, of course, still occupied the inspector, and he now had an extraordinary weapon to back up his commands. He could place a student under arrest for up to a week. While not shirking the duties of informant and gendarme, the inspector was to focus his "particular attention" on the recipients of financial aid and prevent those "whose character and inclinations cannot serve as a good example" from retaining their bursaries. Indeed, scholarship holders were at the mercy of their inspector, for without his recommendation stipend applications could not go forward. He could even withhold part of an award already granted if he felt the student was squandering his money.[60] A vindictive, corrupt, or stupid inspector could terrorize the university population.

Making the inspector's increased authority still less bearable were the stricter student codes he would have to enforce. The

"Rules for Students" accompanying the November decree often resembled in their pettiness those set for gymnasium pupils in 1874. The education department treated college men like children and converted the lecture hall into a grammar school classroom. Students, for example, had to be properly dressed, arrive before their professor, and rise when university authorities entered or when answering a question. Once again the ministry singled out the poor student for its harshest restrictions. It transformed the giving of private lessons from a lifesaving job open to all into a privilege limited to those with unblemished records. Tutoring without a permit could mean expulsion, a risk the destitute would probably have to take.[61] These restrictions applied to normal conditions at the university. In case of disturbances, the ministry adopted at the urging of the Committee of Ministers a "no-holds-barred" policy. As Tolstoi explained to his curators on 29 October 1879: "When it is a matter of restoring order and discipline among the students you are empowered to use . . . all devices possible *even if they exceed the authority given you.*"[62]

It was one thing to issue such regulations, another to implement them. The ministry's usual fund shortages kept it from supplying the ideal ratio of one inspector to every 150 students. Yet Tolstoi managed to provide each inspector with at least three assistants. Much more difficult to counteract was the opposition his program encountered. If, as the Valuev commission complained, "almost all the more or less educated sector of the population" displayed "an outward indifference to the government's present fight against a relatively small number of subversives,"[63] it was unlikely that the universities would endorse Tolstoi's repressive measures. Moscow's professors called them "inopportune and out of step with the aspirations of Russian society"; St. Vladimir University overlooked the failure of all but ten of its 1,050 students to get their residence permits; St. Petersburg's rector flaunted the 1879 legislation by retaining command over the supposedly independent inspector. So distasteful were the inspector's new duties that many incumbents refused to accept them, and few qualified candidates applied for the post. In desperation Tolstoi urged the promotion of gymnasium inspectors to university positions, but, in what seemed like the proverbial "closing the barn door after the horse had gone," he warned against hiring military men since they would only anger instructors and students.[64]

Tolstoi could do little to overcome this hostility to his policies because he was beginning to lose the support of his government and emperor. As will be shown later, the state under the direction of Loris-Melikov was turning toward conciliation and placation of public opinion. By early 1880 it had disavowed the ministry's harsh solutions, and Tolstoi himself fell from office on 22 April 1880. For the moment, the university community had won.

In sum, Tolstoi's remedy for the disorders of 1878–1879 proved too bitter for the government to swallow. It tasted it, then spat it out. The basic ingredients of surveillance and restriction remained the same as in the 1860s, but he increased the dosage and added the element of scholarship controls to enhance the mixture's potency. The greatest change occurred in the manner of administration. Formerly, the autonomous professor corporation had charge of the patients, but the minister, no longer trusting the faculty to use the proper medicine in sufficient quantities, replaced them by his own agents, the university inspectors. While it assured a stricter fulfillment of the head doctor's orders, this measure, by removing the professors as attending physicians, left the ministry alone to bear the blame for malpractice.

A more serious error was the limited nature of the medicament prescribed. Shocked by the crisis in the country and the university, Tolstoi concentrated on eliminating the treacherous symptoms of the illness without carefully considering its underlying causes. A dose of concession, although it might not have saved those committed to the destruction of autocracy, might well have prevented the disease from spreading; yet this was not Tolstoi's diagnosis. His fear of an epidemic drove him to employ stringent purgatives to sick and healthy alike, purgatives which so irritated the constitutions of the latter that they became more rather than less susceptible to infection.

Tolstoi's successor, A. A. Saburov, with Miliutin's guidance, recognized these negative side effects and blamed his predecessor's oppressive remedies for the university's troubles. He proposed powerful tonics like the reestablishment of student corporate life, but the only balm he managed to apply was the repeal on 26 May 1881 of the 1879 legislation.[65] Three years later a new university statute would reaffirm Tolstoi's inadequate treatment of student unrest.

Toward a New University Statute

The fear of subversive elements being nurtured at the university drove Tolstoi to regulate closely the activities of faculty as well as students, but he would proceed at a much slower pace. Where restrictions on a student's freedom did not directly jeopardize and indeed might even assist his academic progress, similar infringements on a scholar's pursuits, Tolstoi realized, might hamper his research and teaching. He thus publicly defended the value of university autonomy which, he claimed in 1870, he had "painstakingly attempted to maintain." He was essentially correct. Tolstoi was in his own words a "constitutional monarch," seriously interfering in university administration only twice.[66]

Both these episodes involved the controversial procedures for rehiring professors after twenty-five years of service. To create room for younger faculty, Golovnin had insisted upon a two-thirds majority in the university council for the reappointment of such men. This law had merit, but it made it easy for ambitious junior instructors or personal enemies to block contract renewals at a time of severe teacher shortages. The plight of St. Vladimir's historical-philological faculty demonstrated the harm these regulations could do. Despite vacancies in ten of eleven chairs, the council refused to retain three senior lecturers. Disturbed by this unpardonable loss of faculty, Tolstoi in September 1868 reinstated two of the three men and six months later brought back Uvarov's system of having these reappointments depend on a simple majority.[67]

The second affair occurred at Moscow University where the rector's cavalier dismissal of an inquiry concerning the retention of a twenty-five-year man prompted the legal historian B. N. Chicherin to challenge the rector's authority, particularly his right to suppress minority opinions and to consult higher officials without previously conferring with the council. Although Tolstoi along with the council majority termed Chicherin's remarks "insulting," he did incorporate some of the jurist's demands in an 1868 decree defining the rector's prerogatives. The ministry reasserted the rector's traditional privileges as council chairman of setting agendas, of silencing rude members, and of rejecting proposals he felt outside the council's competence or contrary to existing statutes, but it by no means converted him into a dictator. The rector could no longer keep minority reports from his superiors nor bypass the council except in an emergency when convocation was impossible. Unfortunately for Moscow University, Chicherin did not stay around long enough to see his complaints heeded. He and four of his five supporters had resigned the preceding year.[68]

This tolerance for university autonomy was soon to disappear. Like many conservatives, Tolstoi had a low opinion of human nature and saw the university council as a battleground where professors selfishly fought for their own advancement but neglected the general welfare. The liberal dictum, "better the council select a poor professor than the Ministry of Education a good one," shocked Tolstoi, for it placed faculty rights above university well-being.[69] A proponent of authoritarian centralism, Tolstoi did not appreciate the professors' desire for self-government, especially since he had proof of their ineffectiveness: the conflicts at Moscow and St. Vladimir had indicated how badly the council met staffing problems; the reappearance of student outbreaks in 1869, how poorly they policed the university population.

Why did not the usually forceful Tolstoi act quickly on his beliefs? Katkov accused him of spending "too much time wavering and making up his mind," and the best recent historian of his policies concludes that he personally was "more interested in bringing civil service examinations . . . under ministerial control" than in ending university autonomy and that only the threat of losing his "grip on the ministry" goaded him into action.[70]

True, in comparison with Tolstoi's other legislation, the university revisions proceeded slowly. Twelve years of discussion preceded the new statute, but neither irresoluteness nor a concern for the university's independence satisfactorily explains Tolstoi's apparent procrastination because they contradict two basic features of the minister's character — the stubbornness which even his critics acknowledged and the hostility toward local initiative which underlay his entire ministerial career. Other more intricate reasons better account for the delays in university reform.

(1) Tolstoi, who had focused on secondary schools partly in the hope of assuring the university a properly prepared, loyal student body, would have been foolish to undertake a provocative transformation of the universities while there was the chance that the gymnasium legislation of 1871 would have resolved the university troubles.

(2) Once the continuation of student unrest after 1874 had made additional reforms necessary, the ministry no longer enjoyed the invulnerability necessary to introduce contentious regulations. The preparations for the Russo-Turkish War not only heightened the influence of Tolstoi's strongest opponent within the government, the war minister Dmitry Miliutin, they also distracted the emperor, whose support the ministry vitally needed, from internal affairs. Tolstoi could not risk defeat in the State Council just to please Katkov, especially since he and the Moscow publicist had increasingly grown apart in the years after the secondary school reforms.[71]

(3) University rehabilitation was too important for the education department to handle by itself. It was compelled to work with numerous outside experts and agencies: academic matters demanded the attention of men with greater competence than the ministry's professional bureaucrats; student revolutionary activity concerned the entire administration, particularly the Third Section, the Ministry of the Interior, and the special emergency commissions of Alexander's last years.

All these circumstances would prevent Tolstoi or indeed any minister from devising an instant answer to the "university question."

Only with the completion of his secondary school statutes did Tolstoi start on the universities. Following his normal procedure, he first sought in August 1872 faculty and curator opinions about the 1863 legislation. Although the curators attacked faculty autonomy, the overwhelmingly favorable response to the present system provided little excuse for ministerial interference.[72] The major result of the August circular was the public dialogue it stimulated on university structure. Within six months one of the few opponents of the Golovnin statute, N. A. Liubimov, professor of physics and long-time friend and biographer of Katkov, had published his dissenting views in Katkov's *Russkii vestnik*. Belittling the efficiency of university collegiate bodies, Liubimov wanted government participation in the selection of professors and the introduction of state graduation examinations. He thus went beyond criticizing the faculty's administrative talents to challenging their professional ability in choosing instructors and in evaluating students. His colleague at Moscow University, V. I. Ger'e (Guerrier), founder of the "Public Higher Courses for Women" in Moscow, soon rebutted these charges in M. M. Stasiulevich's *Vestnik Evropy*. For him the university's independence was the primary reason for its flourishing condition. The curtailment of these rights would destroy higher education. So began the repetitious polemic, most frequently conducted in *Moskovskie vedomosti, Russkii vestnik,* and *Vestnik Evropy*, on the merits of university autonomy.[73]

Since the debate itself lacked originality and played no significant role in the formulation of policy, it does not warrant treatment here; however, it should be noted that this controversy represented much more than a technical argument on university organization. It reflected the monumental conflict in Russian history between the proponents of a monolithic state with the central authorities always in control and the supporters of a pluralistic society with numerous areas reserved for local initiative. An assault on the university could be and certainly was construed by the liberals as an assault on the entire principle of self-government.

Despite the faculty's unqualified support, the Golovnin statute soon came under fire again. This time the university disturbances in 1874 and the extent of student complicity in the "going-to-the-people" movement turned much of the government against the existing university regulations. Blaming the disorders in part on the ineffectiveness of central controls over university affairs, the Valuev commission of 1874 suggested limitation of professorial autonomy and urged a thorough reappraisal of the 1863 legislation. It shared a conviction of many contemporary college trustees and state legislators that scholars are ill-suited for managerial duties and therefore should confine themselves to teaching and research. Acting on the commission's orders, Tolstoi on 21 April 1875 set up within his jurisdiction and under the chairmanship of his former assistant minister, I. D. Delianov, a special committee to assess the university program.[74]

Anticipating the outrage any curtailment of university privileges would produce, the education department officially proclaimed it was working only for the good of "science, scholarship, and pedagogy." This was not just propaganda, but it did hide the ministry's commitment to fundamentally restructuring the university as revealed in Delianov's instructions to his commission. He insisted that it not limit itself to such obvious obstacles to the advancement of learning as faculty irresponsibility and teacher shortages, but also examine such nonacademic problems as student demonstrations, the curators' ill-defined jurisdiction over higher education, and the debilitating effects of the frequent quarrels within university councils.[75] By so defining his committee's interests, Delianov made academic standards and university autonomy the focal points of his investigation; for nothing would have pleased Tolstoi more than a statute which improved the quality of university education and at the same time restricted the faculty's independence.

Before drafting any legislation, Delianov sought first-hand information about Russia's eight universities. On 20 September 1875, accompanied by five associates, he began a two-and-one-half-month inspection tour. Spending an average of seven or eight days at each university, the Delianov commission visited teaching facilities, attended faculty meetings, and held 454 private interviews of thirty to sixty minutes duration. Each university submitted its student regulations, lecture plans, examination rules, and whatever statistics it had recorded. The only serious opposition came from the Petersburg professors. They hoped to reaffirm their trust in their council by having it speak for them; and even when they met individually with the commission, they merely gave brief defenses of the present legislation.[76] The material gathered on this trip, supplemented by the responses to the circular of August 1872, would provide the basis for the ministry's discussions on university reorganization.

Although it obtained interesting data, the commission was not the most exhaustive, efficient, or impartial body. It neglected foreign developments and indeed devoted little time to those within Russia. A week was hardly sufficient for a thorough review of so complex an institution as a university. The commission might have argued that it concentrated on the interviews and that for these a few days were enough, but unfortunately it handled this investigatory technique badly too. Its questions often seemed less concerned with learning about the university than with testing out the ministry's projects on the professors; this gave the impression (probably correct) that St. Petersburg had prejudged the matter. Moreover, the absence of stenographic help increased the chance of inaccurate or subjective interview transcriptions. The probability of biased reporting was all too great, for Tolstoi and Delianov had placed on the committee only those closely associated with the ministry and its policies. There were the omnipresent Georgievsky, the Kiev assistant curator Novikov, and the 1863 statute's bitterest enemy, N. A. Liubimov. Even the two delegates from other departments had previously served Tolstoi. A. Gezen from the Ministry of the Interior had surveyed European technical education for Tolstoi in 1873, and professor V. M. Florinsky of the Medical-Surgical Academy had supported its transfer to the Ministry of Education.[77] Such a commission would not be sympathetic to antiadministration sentiments.

In contrast to the one-sidedness of Delianov's inspection team, the committee which began actual deliberations on the new legislation in September 1876 appeared quite representative of university interests. At the ministry's invitation the following joined the Delianov group: the Assistant Minister of Education; the director of the Demidov Lyceum; the rectors of all Russian-speaking universities except Kiev (whose head refused to come and sent his prorector instead); the former rector of Petersburg University and now Ministerial Council member, A. A. Voskresensky; a delegate from the Central Committee of Press Affairs, N. V. Varadinov; and professors K. A. Kossovich of Petersburg University and V. A. Kremlev of Kazan. The ministry had not packed its committee with reactionary lackeys as Chicherin claimed and Alston implies.[78] It appointed academics primarily, nine of whom held or had held top elective positions at their institutions and thus must have enjoyed the respect of most of their colleagues. Their experience protected the commission against ignorance; their personal success, which owed much to the present act's electoral provisions, guaranteed that law a fair hearing.

Although this commission would not author the final draft of the new statute, its proceedings deserve attention because they reveal the reasoning behind the minister's attempt at reform. Tolstoi did not participate in the sessions, but his three trusted subordinates (Georgievsky, Shirinsky-Shikhmatov, and Delianov) plus Katkov's henchman Liubimov ably presented the ministry's position; hence it is their views that interest us here. These four men, sometimes supported by the two bureaucrats from the Ministry of the Interior, Gezen and Varadinov, led the attack on the Golovnin statute but almost always formed the minority. The professional academics invariably rallied behind the existing arrangement — a further refutation, if one were needed, of Chicherin's comments about the committee's servility.

The university's program occupied the commission most. The autonomous council and faculty assembly controlled academic affairs: the former approved the calendar; the latter, lecture outlines and other curriculum matters. Only the subdivision of faculties, the transfer of professorial chairs, and the institution of compulsory subjects required the minister's confirmation. This independence, Georgievsky and his associates argued, had produced harmful consequences. With some insight they explained that many instructors had used the university's laissez-faire system to reduce teaching loads from the eight hours demanded by Uvarov to an average of four to five hours a week. Had the ministerial bloc concentrated on similar examples of faculty negligence, few would have doubted their concern for the university, but in their criticism of course offerings they displayed the essentially political motives of the ministry. They accused the faculty of emphasizing inappropriate and indeed potentially dangerous lecture series like the history of modern philosophy, which they characterized as the history of communist and socialist doctrines, at the expense of basic subjects like classical studies. They wanted to convert the historical-philological faculty into a supergymnasium where instead of the present 25 to 30 percent, over 50 percent of the lectures would be in the classics.[79] So structured, these faculties might raise contemporary problems less often in the classroom, but they certainly would not be better equipped to promote "science, scholarship, and pedagogy."

To ensure the proper distribution of courses in the future, the ministry demanded stricter controls over the curriculum. Drawing, as usual, on the German example, ministry spokesmen urged that Russia's faculties emulate those at Berlin University and submit in May for ministerial ratification the next year's lecture schedule and course synopses. In this way the government could correct any imbalance in the program and eliminate all suspicious-sounding subjects. As a final precaution, the ministry wanted faculties to investigate how carefully each instructor followed his outline. For Georgievsky, Varadinov, Gezen, and Liubimov these measures would not infringe upon academic freedom.

> To take it [academic freedom] away or to limit or restrict it by any . . . means, would seriously harm scholarship; but to regulate it in an intelligent and natural manner is absolutely necessary, for, otherwise, as the last thirteen years under the present university statute have shown, it [academic freedom] can readily turn into . . . complete arbitrariness.[80]

It was not a convincing thesis. What guarantee did teachers have that the ministry would not abuse its authority as much as the faculty allegedly had misused its autonomy, especially when the bloc's recommendations on the classics demonstrated to many what was meant by regulating in "an intelligent and natural manner?"

The arguments for state-run graduation examinations were somewhat more cogent. Since a university diploma did provide advantageous service prerogatives, the government had a legitimate interest in the methods which determined who received these rights. Existing procedures, however, left most important questions like the nature of the examination and the grading system to the universities themselves. The consequence was a great variation in standards which, so Georgievsky and Delianov explained, only state finals compiled by the ministry and conducted in part by nonuniversity personnel could eliminate. The government would award those who passed a certificate entitling them to the appropriate service rank, the university itself granting only the master's and doctorate. This arrangement, which recalled the German *Staatsexamen*, had obvious merits in addition to the equalization of service requirements.[81] Sheldon Rothblatt's description of the Cambridge University tripos in the mid-nineteenth century as a "useful device for controlling students" could apply equally well to the Russian state tests. "Success in the examination," Rothblatt contended, "required considerable advance preparation and cramming. . . . If a student were conscientious, if he needed the . . . financial reward that the tripos would bestow, if he crammed to the point of injuring his health — particularly in his last year — he would have little time for mischief." [82]

While burdening the students, the centrally administered test could relieve the professor, for it would reduce his examination duties and free him of the agonizing decision as to whether to jeopardize a student's career by maintaining high standards of grading. "Charitable considerations," one lecturer complained, "seriously interfere with the examination process." [83] These arguments did not impress the faculty because they saw the dangers of a state exam. It offered another means of checking on their performance and threatened their autonomy in academic matters. More important, the replacement of degrees by state vouchers symbolized the government's intention of directing university education toward the preparation of civil servants and not toward the pursuit of knowledge.

The ministerial bloc's distrust of the faculty also colored its views on university administration, for it stressed the reports of councils rent by factional strife in an effort to discredit the council's effectiveness. Georgievsky had earlier attacked the council's jurisdiction over the student body; he now criticized both its role in selecting professors and its relative independence from the curator. Angered by the leisurely hiring procedure of some universities, Georgievsky proposed the council have three months instead of the twelve provided in the 1863 statute to fill a vacancy before the minister could make his own appointment. While not as specific in their recommendations about the curator, the ministry spokesmen did insist that he should have a decisive influence in university affairs.[84]

Represented by Georgievsky and his friends, the Ministry of Education had challenged the fundamentals of university autonomy established in 1863. In every sphere of university life it demanded greater authority for itself and corresponding restrictions on faculty freedom. Ostensibly it did so because the university had proved incapable of running its own affairs; and indeed there were instances of incompetent instruction, of partiality shown during examinations, of petty feuds preventing the hiring of able teachers. But the ministry's major concern was not the university's scholastic well-being. It wanted most of all to transform this institution into a politically safe source of manpower for the state, and here as elsewhere increased control constituted its primary defense against the subversion of its schools.

Most professors naturally opposed the ministry's reasoning. Those on the commission, including the eight rectors, rightly considered such changes as ministerial confirmation of all course outlines and state-run final examinations antagonistic to the tradition of free inquiry and hence detrimental to teaching and research. Moreover, they were proud to be one of the few self-governing groups in autocratic Russia and did not intend to become a tool of the state. For them the central government must aid, not superintend, the university.[85] The demonstrations against Professor Liubimov after his return to Moscow University in late November 1876 revealed how strongly the university community shared the views of the academics on the Delianov commission. Fifty of his sixty-five students walked out; an extraordinary session of the university council censured him for his defamatory pamphlets; and thirty-five colleagues informed him in a collective letter that his use in a report to the government of inferior "lithographed lectures which the professors had not reviewed and the students themselves had rejected" had forced them out "of moral disgust to ask [him] to cease all relations with [them] except unavoidable official ones." [86]

Although similar reactions had not deterred Tolstoi from railroading through his secondary school projects five years earlier, this time he slackened his efforts. In 1871–1872 he had had the emperor's unconditional support, but Alexander, now preoccupied with Russia's poor showing in the Russo-Turkish War, was not prepared to outrage public opinion still further by advocating another unpopular educational reform. Only when serious student disturbances broke out in late 1878 and the tsar himself again became a target did Tolstoi think conditions right for introducing his legislation. The rapid passage by the Committee of Ministers in July 1879 of his controversial regulations on student affairs confirmed him in this judgment. On 6 February 1880, after eight years of preparation, he finally brought his revised university statute before the State Council. He could not have timed his presentation better. Just the day before, a revolutionary had blown up a room in the Winter Palace, killing eleven people and injuring fifty-six.

His project reflected only the minority view within the Delianov commission. It would emasculate the university council; increase the curator's powers; give the minister greater control over faculty appointments, examination procedures, and the curriculum; and reaffirm the 1879 legislation depriving the university's collegiate organs of jurisdiction over student activity. All that remained of the university's much-vaunted autonomy was the right to elect professors and a rector, and Tolstoi even requested the emperor to suspend this privilege temporarily.

Much to Tolstoi's surprise, his legislation no longer suited the government's mood. Under the influence of Loris-Melikov, who (less than a week after Tolstoi submitted his plans) had been given the task as chairman of the newly formed Supreme Executive Commission of restoring order to the country, Russia's ruling circles had begun to recognize the necessity of regaining the confidence of educated society. Instead of driving the uncommitted into the ranks of the insurrectionaries by further restrictions, the state should strive by concessions and by pinpoint attacks on the radicals to "detach the hesitant from the revolution." Since Tolstoi's university reform certainly did not fit into this scheme, the government rejected it and its sponsor.[87]

The Transformation of the Universities in 1884

Not until 23 August 1884, four years, three ministers of education, and one emperor later, did Russian universities get a new statute. Autocracy's flirtation with conciliatory policies did not survive Alexander II's assassination, for his son was no supporter of liberalization. The "progressives" like Loris-Melikov and Miliutin gave way to the archconservative K. P. Pobedonostsev and Tolstoi himself, who became Minister of the Interior in 1882. The belief in repression which dominated the thinking of the ruler and his intimate advisers guaranteed the revival of the 1880 university project a favorable reception at court, though not in the State Council. Despite the noticeable turn to the right in the government during the 1880s, the emperor would still have to overrule the council majority for the university regulations to become law.

While Tolstoi was no longer minister, this legislation, in content if not in implementation, should be considered part of his system. Not only did its provisions echo those of the minister's spokesmen on the Delianov commission and those in the 1880 draft, they also repeated such restrictive features as curator interference in council proceedings and state appointment of rectors, which Tolstoi had forced on Warsaw University in June 1869. Indeed, Tolstoi helped lead the defense of his former ministry's program.[88] In Katkov's words, with the 1884 university act the "careful ordering *(blagoustroistvo)* of scholastic affairs in Russia, which had concerned Count D. A. Tolstoi, has now achieved completion." [89]

The statute's primary purpose was political, not academic. It would, the ministry hoped, assure higher education the "proper superintendence and guidance" because it placed the university directly under the control of the ministry and its agents: the inspector, rector, and curator. As in 1879, the inspector acquired jurisdiction over all student activity within and outside the university. A ministerial appointee subordinate to the curator and rector, he owed no responsibility to the university's governing bodies. The rector grew more powerful too. Now the minister's appointed deputy instead of the professors' elected representative, his responsibilities went beyond personnel and curriculum matters to include the disbursement of funds, the determination of the size of entering classes, and the enforcement of rules for students and visitors. In 1863 the university was under the rector's "personal care *(blizhaishee popechenie)*"; now it was under his "direct management *(neposredstvennoe zavedyvanie)*." He had become the university's overseer rather than its protector. Equally striking was the curator's regaining the dominating position he had held in the days of Uvarov. He took over the faculty's right to nominate deans, personally supervised the fulfillment of all the ministry's decrees, and issued his own restrictions on student behavior. More important, he could easily meddle in the university's internal affairs since he could attend or convene the council, board, and faculty assembly whenever he chose.[90]

Some matters like the selection of faculty, the organization of student life, and the institution of teaching programs were too vital for even the ministry's trusted subordinates to handle. It would decide these questions itself. The minister controlled hiring policies: not only could he replace the council's candidates with other suitable men, he could on his own initiative fill professorial vacancies as soon as they appeared. In this way St. Petersburg would counteract the alleged sluggishness of the council's recruitment efforts and keep politically undesirable instructors out of the lecture hall. While the council still had some say in staffing decisions, it lost all influence over the compilation of the major codes affecting its students. The ministry would draft the instructions defining entrance standards, inspector duties, and student conduct.

Deprived of its authority in disciplinary actions, the faculty in theory could concentrate more on its lessons; but here too it experienced new restraints. Incorporating the earlier proposals by Georgievsky and Liubimov, the ministry insisted that professors obtain its approval for their course outlines and curriculum changes; and, to ensure the fulfillment of these plans, it required semiannual progress reports from the faculty and took charge of graduation examinations for everyone but advanced-degree aspirants. The ministry alone devised these tests and chose the commissions that administered them. Rarely before had Russian instructors faced so many checks on their performance and such a great threat to their academic freedom.[91]

Despite its commitment to centralization, the ministry did feel certain functions should be left to the university. However, lest the council use the few prerogatives not appropriated by St. Petersburg to reassert its claims to self-government, the ministry transferred most of the council's obligations to the university board. The latter in fact replaced the council as the university's major administrative organ, hardly a surprise since its members — the rector, inspectors, and deans — were all ministry appointees. Besides managing school finances, the board assumed the council's powers over the admission of auditors, the expulsion of students, and the distribution of stipends. It also became the university's court of appeal for student misdemeanors, but unlike the old court, which served under the council, the board answered only to the curator.[92]

The education department had stripped the council of its powers and turned the once-proud symbol of university autonomy into a travesty of its former self. Whereas previously the council had regulated every segment of university life, it now focused solely on scholastic concerns. Yet even here it did not determine policy, but merely sent its opinions to the ministry for confirmation. So little did the council have to do that the ministry omitted any reference to the monthly meetings insisted on by Golovnin and left the schedule to the rector's discretion. Reviewing the 1884 legislation, Delianov justifiably concluded that it had given his ministry "complete authority over both disciplinary and academic affairs at the university." By substituting "administrative centralism" for self-government, he had liberated professors from what Katkov called the "tyranny" of their colleagues only to place them under the despotism of the ministry.[93] The effects of this measure were felt outside the university walls because it demonstrated to all that the autocracy had ceased paying lip service to the idea of preserving the few areas of local government created during the "Great Reforms." The state would soon drag the zemstvos and city dumas along the same path toward stricter central controls.

While it stressed administrative reorganization, the university act did consider two other problems of higher education, teaching vacancies and student disorders. Retaining some interest in the quality of education despite its attacks on academic freedom, the state introduced numerous remedies for Russia's perennial faculty shortage. Some, like the increase in the ministry's authority over hiring, had questionable motives; others, like the attempts to discourage a professor's wasting his time and the university's money on small classes by making his salary depend in part on honoraria paid by his students, could, in Russia just as it already had in Germany, produce harmful results;[94] but a few would alleviate the situation. The universal adoption of a six-hour teaching load, although hardly overburdening the instructors, would at least guard against the shirking of pedagogical duties which the Delianov commission had discovered in 1875.

A more long-term solution to the staffing question was the elevation of the post of privatdozent to a training ground for professors on the German model. Faculties appointed at this rank only those who, if not recognized scholars, had either passed their master's examinations or taught at an institute of higher learning.

Serving a three-year term as privatdozent, the candidate would have time to complete his doctorate and would get the classroom experience necessary for most professorial positions.[95] This program admirably suited its purpose. The privatdozent obtained the financial support he needed during his graduate training; the university received a sizable influx of inexpensive but qualified young faculty; and the authorities gained an opportunity to investigate first-hand the future instructors' competence and political reliability.

The attitude toward student discontent was much less enlightened. Instead of offering concessions, the ministry brought in restrictions far more rigorous than those of the 1863 legislation, which had already angered students. Its statute reactivated the 1879 orders giving ministerial representatives rather than the faculty direct control over student activity. But the establishment of a loyal and efficient inspectorate did not exhaust the government's response to university unrest. As before, it sought to protect its institutions from two allegedly unstable elements — the indigent and the indifferent. The poor would find paying for their education harder, because the ministry abolished most temporary, unconditional grants and increased the university's basic fees by adding a 20-ruble charge (just 5 rubles below the average semester tuition) for taking the final examinations. Those lucky enough to win scholarships still could not rejoice, for harsh rules, devised specifically for stipend holders, regulated their lives. The unmotivated also experienced hardships. The new emphasis placed on written assignments, oral presentations, and the like made playing about difficult. So did the innovation of state graduation exams, since only by passing these tests could one acquire the service privileges formerly associated with the university degree.[96] Economically secure, carefully supervised, and busy students, the ministry hoped, would have less reason, less chance, and less time for demonstrations and other unsanctioned behavior.

The oppressive provisions of the 1884 law were not unique to Alexander III's Russia, for many European governments controlled course offerings, professorial nominations, and testing procedures. The situation was worst in France where "university instruction was carried out . . . under strict regulations laid down by the Ministry of Education. Attendance at lectures and exercises was compulsory; the courses of instruction were prescribed for each year; the state examinations had to be passed before the student could be promoted from one year to the next." [97]

While contemporaries like Matthew Arnold praised the "liberty of the German universities," there too the state still set certain final examinations, designated the teaching staff, and placed its own agents in every institution to check on the fulfillment of its ordinances.[98] Even in North America today, especially at public universities, the teaching staff often lacks much power. Boards of trustees, sometimes with no faculty representation, frequently appoint the president, deans, and department heads, determine fiscal policies, and jealously uphold their right to confirm most major faculty decisions. Obviously these similarities to foreign measures do not justify the harsh features of the 1884 statute. They do, however, show that the Russian ministry in its most reactionary university statute had not radically departed from accepted practices, that it was not so out of step as many believe with developments in more democratic societies.

Such considerations, of course, did not mollify the ministry's critics. They compared the reforms not with what went on elsewhere, but with what had been in Russia. They felt that Golovnin's legislation had set the proper direction, that his successors should merely reaffirm the privileges granted the faculty and extend these in some degree to the students. Tolstoi and his cohorts did just the opposite; they reversed the process toward liberalization and ushered in an era of rigorous control over university life. The education department had committed an act most galling to all but the very conservative; it had repudiated rights men had already won and cherished.

For the ministry this *volte-face* was essential no matter what the public thought. It believed that only a policy which destroyed the university's autonomous position, yet backed its academic pursuits, could pacify the universities without limiting their usefulness as educational institutions. At first, Tolstoi had concentrated on the second part of this program. He sought to improve higher education by reforming existing schools, aiding faculty, and supporting research activities. Even his initial answer to university disturbances — the tightening of admissions standards — had an academic justification. Soon, however, the increasing restlessness of the university population and its involvement with the revolutionary movement forced the ministry into more repressive actions which curtailed the university's independence.

This was a short-sighted decision. In the first place it alienated the faculty, the ministry's most essential ally. With few friends in the classroom, how could the government gain the loyalty of its students? Second and more important, this plan oversimplified the causes of student discontent. Admittedly, the Ministry of Education could not by itself transform Russian society, but it could at least alleviate grievances like the absence of corporate life, which drove many students into the streets.

Refusing to acknowledge the dangerous consequences of its own policies, the ministry blamed the infiltration of subversive influences and the incompetence of the university's democratic organs in disciplining their charges for all the troubles. Not only did Tolstoi misinterpret the reasons for student unrest, he overestimated the effectiveness of his weapons to combat it. Perpetual surveillance has proved a difficult if not hopeless task even with the advanced police methods of modern totalitarian states. How much less likely would be its success in the comparative inefficiency of Russia in the 1880s! One student of the time indeed claimed: "The university despite the new statute was so free in comparison to the gymnasium that we felt as if we had gone out into the fresh air." [99] Thus the abrogation of university self-rule would not nullify the threat posed autocracy by the products of higher education. The cycle of student disorders and government counterattacks would begin again in 1887 with the demonstrations at Moscow University.

CHAPTER 5 / The Entrenchment of the

Classical System in Secondary Education

Compared to the leisurely pace of the university reforms, the transformation of secondary education went at a brisk trot. Tolstoi had not been in office seven months before he challenged the gymnasium statute of 1864. Such haste was necessary because the secondary school represented for Tolstoi "the most crucial phase of the formal learning process." [1] Not only did it determine who would go on to university and hence indirectly into the higher levels of state service, but it provided the best opportunity for properly molding this future elite. Its course was long, its students still sufficiently malleable. Once they reached the university, they would be too cynical and independent to respond favorably to any manipulation of their minds and characters. Tolstoi felt that if he could organize the gymnasium correctly, he might indeed succeed in producing trained personnel who would serve but not question the existing administration. He would then be well on the way to resolving the dilemma created by Russia's need for rapid progress in education.

The key question, of course, was what should be the appropriate structure of secondary education. In Tolstoi's view the classics should predominate, for they alone guaranteed Russian students "serious" and "moral" rather than "superficial" and "materialistic" instruction. Only schools emphasizing Greek and Latin could *"create a new generation* . . . one trained to work at school and therefore able to work in life." [2] His sentiments echoed a faith in classical studies which had characterized the school systems of the nineteenth century. Throughout Europe educators had "maintained that a truly educated person should possess the traditional hallmarks of a liberal education, namely the classics." [3]

These subjects had retained their dominant position over the years because they suited both the demands of the pedagogue and the interests of those in power. For the teacher, classical studies had two advantages: the obvious one of introducing the student to the ancient world — the height of man's achievement and the foundation of the present civilization — and the less apparent one of offering the young brain the best exercise. According to the faculty psychology then in vogue, the mind contained separate parts like memory or reason which could be improved by constant use much the way a person's limbs were strengthened by physical exercise. The subjects requiring great intellectual discipline naturally developed the sharpest minds, and these were Latin, Greek, and mathematics, the most precise and logically ordered of secondary school courses.

For the proponent of political stability, a classical education could have two other benefits. First, it could curb education's tendency to encourage social mobility. As the primary path to higher learning, it would deter many of the lower classes from seeking a university education and thereby raising their social status. They could not spare either the money or the time for the gymnasium's expensive and protracted course, nor could they understand the value of its impractical curriculum. The poorer classes wanted an immediate return on investments in their children's education, and this the classical school did not provide. The "cultivated" classes alone could both appreciate and afford its program, and this meant that the elite education created would come from groups already in the upper echelons of society. Second, by engulfing them in the wonders of the past and in the intricacies of complex grammars, the classical gymnasium might isolate its select students from the new forces of the world outside and might shield them from dangerous philosophical by-products of scientific studies like materialism and nihilism which could undermine the basic values of the state. Such considerations combined with the triumphs of those countries that had adopted the classical system undoubtedly explain Tolstoi's enthusiasm for this type of education.

However, just as Tolstoi was entrenching the classical school in Russia, many educators, under the influence of the Industrial Revolution and the rapid advance of science and technology, were challenging the gymnasium's august position in Europe. The community's dependence on the factory owner, engineer, and scientist proclaimed to all the advantages of practical training over the useless memorization of dead languages. Even a humanist like Matthew Arnold believed "that the modern spirit will deprive Latin and Greek composition and verbal scholarship of their present [1868] universal and preponderant application in our secondary schools." [4]

Yet education officials waged a successful rearguard action against this attack upon the classics. Although schools offering little Greek or Latin by this time were common everywhere, they lacked prestige because they generally did not prepare students for their country's most illustrious education institution, the university. In Prussia, for instance, twenty-nine of thirty-eight university faculties opposed admitting graduates even of those *Realschulen* with Latin courses; in France, the government by 1864 had reinstituted the Greek prerequisite formerly waived for all entrants to the physical-mathematical faculties. Not until the end of the nineteenth century did nonclassical education gain widespread though grudging formal acceptance, the German *Realschule* achieving parity with the gymnasium in 1901. Nevertheless, that same year an English expert, after reviewing Prussian schools, concluded that "linguistic discipline" still prevailed.[5] This struggle over the nature of secondary education, complicated as in the West by the intermingling of pedagogical and political considerations, would also be fought out in Russia.

Ministerial Objections to the Golovnin Statute

On the surface it seemed that Tolstoi had little cause to attack his predecessor's policies. Had they not established the classical arrangement Tolstoi wanted? Not only did the 1864 legislation limit university entrance to graduates of the classical gymnasium, it also raised the classics' share of that gymnasium's curriculum to 31.5 percent, thus surpassing Russia's previous high of 28.7 percent under Uvarov.[6] Commendable though they might be, Golovnin's regulations had for Tolstoi two major weaknesses which could destroy the entire system. The first was the failure to distinguish sufficiently between the realgymnasiums and the classical ones; the second, the inadequacy of controls over school activity. The former would confuse the public about the respective merits of the two schools, thereby shaking their confidence in the supremacy of the classical course; the latter would encourage local independence, thereby depriving the gymnasium program of the necessary uniformity and coherence.[7]

Developments in secondary education after 1864 proved the minister's concern well-founded. The similarity between the real and classical gymnasiums had indeed damaged the ministry's case for the latter's superiority. Both institutions offered a seven-year course and taught the same subjects at the same level except for Latin and Greek. Even this distinction is overstated, because most gymnasiums lacked qualified instructors to teach Greek. The fundamental difference between these two schools was that one had Latin classes in all seven grades while the other replaced these with additional lessons primarily in modern languages and science.[8] By so ordering their curriculum, Golovnin did imply that the ministry considered its two secondary schools basically equal, an impression reinforced by his leaving the final decision on the type of gymnasium in a given area to local initiative. Instead of ending the classical-realist controversy, the Golovnin formula was so ambiguous that it encouraged the opponents of classical education to renew their struggle against the ministry's plans.

Some of the most telling arguments the ministry faced came from the famous pedagogue K. D. Ushinsky. His successes in education as inspector of the Smolnyi Institute, editor of the *Zhurnal*, and author of elementary textbooks, combined with his ability to raise the classical-realist polemic to the level of a serious pedagogical discussion, gave his views more weight than the usual vituperative attacks on the ministry's policies. In two *Golos* articles of 1867–1868 Ushinsky demonstrated the political, national, and educational shortcomings of the classical system. Instead of protecting students from radical theories, he argued, classical studies, if anything, had stimulated such thoughts; for *"the materialist point of view dominated the ancient world."*

Turning to his own country's needs, Ushinsky showed how the classical gymnasium was an imported luxury Russia could not afford. It did not produce the technical experts required by industry, government, and the zemstvos, nor did it provide its students with sufficient knowledge of Russia so that they could understand and resolve her problems. For Ushinsky the pedagogical values of the classics did not compensate for the above shortcomings; other subjects could develop the mind as well. In a passage recalling the rhapsodies of the classicists, he described the benefits of studying the natural sciences:

Drawing one closer to nature, they constantly fill the imagination with diverse impressions and forms; setting up numerous problems at every stage, they sharpen one's attentiveness and curiosity; demonstrating the most complex relations of phenomena, they increase one's powers of analysis and understanding; encouraging one to see immutable laws everywhere, they direct one's thoughts to theoretical and philosophical conclusions.

Such qualities of mind were just those the autocracy feared most.[9]

What bothered Tolstoi more than these journalistic sallies, which could easily be rebutted in Katkov's *Moskovskie vedomosti*, was the public's efforts to elevate the status of the realgymnasium. Stressing the apparent academic parity of the classical and real-gymnasium, many opposed the restriction of university entrance to those who concentrated on what *Golos* called "dead flesh in the form of classical languages." Support for opening the physical-mathematical and medical faculties to realgymnasium students came first from some members of Golovnin's own ministerial council and from the science faculties themselves. Then, in 1868–1869, several zemstvos challenged Tolstoi's authority by directly petitioning the government to admit realgymnasium graduates to the university. Tolstoi responded with a ruling from the Committee of Ministers on 26 May 1869 that such questions of education policy lay outside the zemstvo's competence.[10] This may have quieted the zemstvos, but it certainly did not resolve the issue. The realgymnasium still remained as a vivid reminder of a feasible alternative to a classical secondary education.

No less justified were the ministry's reservations about the 1864 statute's provisions for local initiative. An advocate of decentralization, Golovnin left most important matters to the individual gymnasium pedagogical council. Composed of the director as chairman, the inspector, and the entire permanent teaching staff, this body approved course outlines, compiled rules on student conduct, recommended examination procedures to the curator, and could resolve on its own initiative all scholastic or disciplinary questions not explicitly answered in the statute — provided, of course, that these decisions did not repudiate existing regulations. Since the ministry offered little specific guidance, the council in fact enjoyed great freedom in defining the curriculum. Golovnin, it is true, did publish a short description of gymnasium courses, but it merely suggested the major topics for each subject.[11]

This permissiveness encouraged the wide variety of teaching programs Tolstoi feared. The Academic Committee's survey of Russian language and literature courses in 1865 supported the numerous curator reports about the unevenness of gymnasium instruction. "Because of the lack of any clearly defined general principles of teaching, the programs . . . are extremely heterogeneous. . . . Not just the programs for the different districts but also those for gymnasiums in the same district, and even junior and senior classes at the same gymnasium do not agree with one another on the most essential pedagogical questions." [12] For Tolstoi this diversity, which he had personally observed at gymnasiums in the Moscow and Kazan districts, demonstrated how little guarantee the ministry had that its legislation would be carried out effectively. By November 1866 he had started work on a general syllabus which would "establish the proper uniformity in gymnasium teaching," leaving only the "petty" details to the pedagogical councils,[13] but these new academic plans would not appear until after the 1871 reform.

Thus, from his first days in office, Tolstoi began learning of his predecessor's "errors" in secondary education. If his subordinates' critiques were not persuasive enough, the minister also had the expert testimony of his closest advisers on the classical school, M. N. Katkov and P. M. Leont'ev. Exerting their influence through impassioned articles in *Moskovskie vedomosti* and through their agents at the ministry, A. I. Georgievsky and council member B. M. Markevich, the Moscow publicists demanded the prompt revision of Golovnin's statute.[14] Tolstoi responded quickly. On 5 October 1866 he sought his curators' views on the shortcomings in the present secondary school legislation. As summarized in the *Zhurnal*, the replies not only underscored the minister's two prime objections, the inadequate distinction between the classical and realgymnasium and the anarchy of existing teaching plans, but added further grievances to the list. Some of the curators focused on administrative matters like the pedagogical council's control over finances and student punishments, but others challenged the feasibility of the whole gymnasium program. To the latter a curriculum which had twelve major subjects plus writing and drawing was far too ambitious, particularly considering the gymnasium's low entrance requirements and short seven-year course. Under these conditions students would obtain at best a superficial knowledge of their courses. These criticisms were the excuse Tolstoi needed. Ignoring the few curators who supported Golovnin's policies, Tolstoi informed the emperor in 1867 that his inquiries had convinced him to undertake a thorough revision of the 1864 legislation.[15]

A Brief Interlude of Gymnasium Autonomy

While the ministry prepared its new statute, it generally left the conduct of school affairs to its curators and to the individual institutions themselves. Preferring to await the reform's completion rather than to introduce changes piecemeal, Tolstoi restricted himself to a few insignificant decrees and the publication of pedagogical advice in the *Zhurnal*. His rulings on the gymnasium's academic organization went no further than urging greater emphasis on Russian grammar or prescribing the proper system of Greek pronunciation.[16] The *Zhurnal* provided less authoritative but more extensive suggestions than these ministerial regulations. Available in all school libraries (each gymnasium had to subscribe for two copies),[17] it carried articles, often of high quality, on teaching virtually every gymnasium subject from physical education to natural science with, of course, particular attention paid the classics. Such indirect interference by the ministry would hardly disturb the faculty's freedom. No wonder then that one instructor judged "this time [1865–1870] . . . the gymnasium's best period . . . the teacher breathed freely, unencumbered by a mass of rules, circulars, instructions." [18] Consequently, this five-year span gives the historian, as it gave Tolstoi, a good opportunity to observe the effectiveness of local initiative in education.

With St. Petersburg so silent, many curators attempted to define gymnasium programs. They began issuing compulsory outlines for the major secondary school subjects. For example, the Kharkov curator distributed academic plans in Russian language and literature; his Moscow counterpart promulgated syllabi for history, mathematics, physics, cosmography, German, French, penmanship, and classics; the St. Petersburg curator even stipulated the number of written exercises for each subject per month.

These projects were often carefully assembled. In Kharkov twenty-two gymnasium personnel worked ten days with Russian literature professor P. A. Lavrovsky to draw up a conspectus for that district's Russian courses. The outpouring of plans in Moscow resulted from the labors of seven special commissions established by the curator's council in December 1868. Composed of gymnasium instructors and their university advisers, these committees decided on teaching methods, selected books for class and library use, and drafted comprehensive course outlines which, when approved by the council, became obligatory throughout the Moscow district.[19]

The responsibility for setting examination procedures fell on the curators as well. According to the 1864 statute, the curator's council should compile in consultation with the pedagogical councils of the district a special instruction on entrance, promotion, and graduation exams. Few such documents appeared until Tolstoi's warning in September 1866 that lenient testing standards were producing "superficial and conceited" students. Then within four months the Moscow and Petersburg curators issued district-wide examination codes. Both circulars entrusted the administration of tests to small faculty commissions, listed the fields to be covered, and established minimum requirements for promotion and graduation. Not all curators were so conscientious: the official in Kiev did not introduce his instruction until March 1869; his colleague in Odessa waited several months after this before he even ordered the preparation of his regulations.[20] Here was one of the dangerous aspects of decentralization. Not only did this process give the indifferent or indolent functionary additional obligations, it also made it easier for him to shirk them.

While the curators controlled academic affairs, each pedagogical council could itself settle questions of student conduct, discipline, and moral education. Aside from providing the inspector with two assistants called tutors (vospitateli), Golovnin's statute generally ignored the subject of student supervision. Recognizing the need for some official statement on student regulations, Golovnin turned to his curators for help and requested them to submit sample "Rules for Students." Of these the Petersburg project with its stress on mature teacher-pupil relations and its concern for the development of the student's personality was the most progressive and received the Academic Committee's recommendation as an example for all schools. However, in keeping with its reliance on local initiative, the ministry did not make adoption of the Petersburg rules compulsory. In fact, its only obligatory legislation on student deportment was an order making the gymnasium responsible for its students after school hours, particularly those who did unsatisfactory work or who did not live with their parents or guardians.[21] The latter formed a sizable group, since most smaller towns and villages did not have a gymnasium of their own. Since Tolstoi issued no major instructions in this area during his first five years in office, the gymnasium retained complete initiative over matters of discipline and punishment.

Consequently, student codes differed considerably from school to school. Some pedagogical councils, disregarding the sensible provisions of the Petersburg model, were despotic: pupils at Tambov gymnasium could be locked in a schoolroom for inattentiveness, those in Simferopol who did not live at home suffered under a six o'clock curfew, those in Smolensk faced expulsion for behaving improperly in public. Others were more indulgent and reasonable: the Novocherkassk council was so concerned with the causes of student misconduct that it did not frame a penal code but judged each case separately, the one at Ufa felt special instructions on student surveillance totally unwarranted. And a few were just desultory: in Voronezh and Samara gymnasium officials did not even begin work on guidelines for their charges until goaded by the curator.[22]

If the extreme variations in disciplinary measures and the slackness of certain pedagogical councils reveal the pitfalls of Golovnin's devolution of authority, the council's role in finding appropriate student mentors indicates the potential wisdom of this policy. The 1864 statute had ordered replacement of the often ignorant and regimentarian proctors *(nadzirateli)* by university-educated and pedagogically trained tutors, who would use persuasion and influence rather than fear and threats to guide their charges. However, it was so difficult to find college graduates for tutor's posts, especially by 1870 when every gymnasium finally received sufficient funds for the two tutors allotted it in the 1864 legislation, that the government temporarily permitted the retention of proctors and the selection of candidates without the necessary degrees.[23]

The old, unsatisfactory supervisory system remained, but some gymnasiums had devised a viable alternative to the tutorships, one which would not require increases in staff. Acting on their own, though in accordance with Tolstoi's wish that a teacher's duties include moral instruction and counseling, these schools established the post of class preceptor (klassnyi nastavnik), soon to become a basic feature of Tolstoi's secondary school reforms. At Taganrog gymnasium, for instance, each grade had its faculty adviser or class preceptor; he assisted the less successful pupils, observed the conduct, marks, and material needs of all students in that grade, and delivered monthly progress reports before the pedagogical council. It was a sensible, inexpensive arrangement, and those gymnasiums that adopted it won the ministry's praise.[24]

The results of this brief experiment in local initiative were uneven. As might be expected from the bureaucratic or military backgrounds of most curators, these officials would not always provide stimulating leadership nor concern themselves with compiling such vital parts of the gymnasium program as lesson plans or examination rules. This indifference pervaded some gymnasium councils too. They allowed courses to overlap or neglected their obligations to regulate student behavior. On the positive side, curriculum conferences like those in Moscow not only guaranteed expertly designed syllabi but also promoted the exchange of ideas so essential for the maintenance of quality teaching throughout the district. Furthermore, the creation of class preceptorships demonstrated that individual schools if left to themselves could furnish admirable solutions to the ministry's problems.

While a more liberal minister might have rejoiced over these signs of vitality in Russian education, Tolstoi saw mainly the diversity and laxity that he felt decentralization had produced. This observation enforced his desire to reestablish ministerial authority over schools. Viewing control as a "necessary appurtenance" of his system, he valued loyalty and obedience in his subordinates over originality and creativity. He thus risked alienating the more independent teachers in the hope that his ministry could again place secondary education on the proper path. With his country beset by subversive influences, Tolstoi wanted all instructors to look only to the ministry for direction.

Pushing Through the New Gymnasium Legislation

It would not, however, be a simple matter for the ministry to provide this guidance. Just as the liberal press including *Golos*, *Vestnik Evropy*, and *St. Peterburgskie vedomosti* battled with Katkov's *Moskovskie vedomosti* about the merits of classical versus real education, so too would many from the Petersburg bureaucracy struggle against the entrenchment of the classical system in Russia. Before Tolstoi could introduce any comprehensive changes, he would have to overcome or convert his and Katkov's opponents within the government. Although the major concern of this study is not the bureaucratic maneuvers surrounding the formulation of educational policies but the nature and implementation of these policies, it will be necessary to investigate the steps leading up to the 1871–1872 statutes because they reveal the broader political significance of the classical-realist debate and, in passing, offer some insight into the workings of the tsarist administration.

The first stages went smoothly because Tolstoi had restricted deliberations on the project to a committee of his handpicked council members and four invited outside experts. Three of these actually worked for the ministry: A. I. Georgievsky and P. L. Chebyshev on the Academic Committee and A. P. Serno-Solov'-evich as Petersburg assistant curator; the fourth was *plus royaliste que le roi*. He was Katkov's partner P. M. Leont'ev, the publisher of a special collection, *Propilei*, devoted to the classics and one of Russia's great champions of classical studies. In fact, the draft secondary school statute which the committee produced in March 1869 undoubtedly owed much to his work. Tolstoi had done a good job of packing his council, and the results showed it.[25]

The proposed law again reveals the ministry's attempt to better education while at the same time reducing its potential for producing disruptive elements. Most of the revisions suggested by Tolstoi could strengthen the gymnasium program and faculty and certainly marked no radical departure from Golovnin's legislation. These included preparatory classes and class preceptorships which already existed at several gymnasiums, eight instead of seven grades, greater concentration on major subjects, wage scales based on years of service, and a separate economic commission in charge of finances. Other revisions, however, like the ministry-devised lesson plans and testing procedures and the downgrading of the realgymnasium into a realschule, were more controversial. Presaging a new direction in Russian secondary education, they demonstrated the ministry's desire to protect pupils against subversive influences by rigidly controlling the gymnasium curriculum and to guarantee the students' seriousness of purpose by requiring all university candidates to pass through the rigors of the classics.

With the gymnasium statute completed, Tolstoi could begin work on his new realschule and on the problem of getting his plans through the State Council. Under Tolstoi's orders Ministerial Council member A. S. Voronov met with experts in science and technology to define the realschule's organization. Tolstoi probably believed that prior consultation with the parties interested in nonclassical education might forestall their attacks on his proposals. He made a serious tactical error, for Voronov shared the views of the anticlassicist writers for the St. Petersburg press. Criticizing the realschule's practical orientation, he advocated instead two separate but equal secondary schools, one specializing in the classics, the other in mathematics and natural sciences.[26] This solution would have undermined the privileged position of the classical gymnasium, just what Tolstoi's opponents wanted.

More successful were his efforts to build up support within the government for his reforms. Rather than immediately face a State Council known to be hostile to his project, Tolstoi followed a circuitous procedure. He first submitted his draft statute to a special interdepartmental board established at his request by the emperor in March 1870 to review the 1864 legislation. Here the classical faction predominated. In addition to the venerable chairman, S. G. Stroganov, who had fought for the reintroduction of the classics in 1864, the commission included four men from the Ministry of Education: Tolstoi himself; his council member A. P. Postel's; the director of the classically oriented Historical-Philological Institute, I. B. Shteinman; and the principal of the Petersburg Third Gymnasium, V. Kh. Lemonius. There were also two members from the central bureaucracy: Assistant Minister of the Interior A. G. Troitnitsky and State Secretary P. A. Valuev, who had earlier stressed the importance of a classical education for the civil service. By discussing his resolutions first in a friendly committee, Tolstoi hoped to win over the still-powerful Stroganov and to gain some sort of official endorsement for his program. This time he had judged correctly. The Stroganov commission unanimously backed the ministry's project in May 1870 and soon after rejected Voronov's counterproposals.[27]

Yet not until 27 February 1871, almost two years after the ministry had finished its draft legislation, did Tolstoi finally present the revised statute to the State Council. Despite Katkov's bullying, the minister had proceeded deliberately and with caution. Whether he did so from cowardice, as Feoktistov claimed, or from prudence it is impossible to ascertain. While those like Katkov, who wanted the reform adopted immediately, angrily attributed every delay to Tolstoi's irresolution,[28] a less impassioned observer could argue that a more precipitate introduction of so controversial a law would have been foolhardy. In any case the distinction between timidity and circumspection is too fine to be drawn from the available evidence. What is clear, however, is the force the State Council could exert within the government. Although the emperor could veto its decisions, it obviously wielded some power if only of a deterrent nature. Its opposition would cause difficulties even for a minister of Tolstoi's importance.

Anticipating the hostility his projects would produce, Tolstoi moved slowly and in great secrecy. Unlike his predecessor, he wanted no open discussions on education because he knew from experience what bitter attacks to expect from the press. He therefore censured his subordinate, A. S. Voronov, for supposedly leaking information on the changes in the gymnasiums and in fact did not publish his exact program until three months after setting it before the State Council. So covert were the minister's actions that even Katkov muttered.[29] This ministerial silence, however, did not prevent Russian journalists from continuing their vigorous campaign against the classical system. As a result, the Minister of the Interior, with Tolstoi's blessing, if not at his insistence, gained the emperor's approval early in the spring of 1871 for temporarily prohibiting the printing of collective representations against the ministry's policies. *Golos, St. Peterburgskie vedomosti,* and *Almanakh 1871* all felt the censor's heavy hand,[30] as the autocracy again exhibited that contempt for public opinion which would ultimately lead to its downfall.

While Tolstoi could ignore or silence his enemies outside the government, he would have to debate his opponents within the bureaucracy. Hence the brief accompanying his secondary school statutes reiterated the academic and political advantages of a classical education. Its pedagogical benefits were the traditional ones associated with faculty psychology. Tolstoi considered education mainly a process of developing mental discipline and the two ancient languages, because of their ordered yet complex structure, were the best subjects with which to exercise the brain. For him the arguments of the committee which established the classical gymnasium back in 1828 still held:

> First, it [the study of the classics] *teaches the mind to be attentive and diligent, to search for fundamental principles* and not to stop short at superficiality and easy imitation; secondly, *by its very difficulty . . . it trains one to be humble . . . and humility is . . . the primary requirement for any genuine education.*[31]

But the restoration of the classical system was more than a scholastic affair; it was a measure essential for the maintenance of state security. The destruction of the Uvarov gymnasium in 1849, Tolstoi claimed, had greatly contributed to the "materialism, nihilism, and most ruinous egotism which have so strongly seized our student youth." Echoing Katkov's tirades in *Moskovskie vedomosti*, Tolstoi emphasized classicism's effectiveness in combatting radical tendencies among the young. As he warned the State Council:

> The choice between a classical course and other academic programs as the basis for all higher education is not only a choice between serious and superficial teaching, but also a choice between moral and materialistic instruction and thus concerns all society. In fact, study . . . can either act upon all aspects of the human spirit, enriching and ennobling it (as does the study of the classical languages and their literature) or it can educate students one-sidedly and influence neither their moral nor their aesthetic development, but turn their attention prematurely and exclusively to political and social questions . . . the nature of the classical languages and also of much of mathematics is such that teachers can continually verify the students' knowledge of these subjects, . . . while they find it almost impossible to check their pupils' understanding of all other disciplines, and particularly of the natural sciences; and this explains both the growth of egotism and the formation of the most erroneous concepts.[32]

It logically followed from these assertions that the realgymnasium, since it offered just that sort of natural science curriculum which increased student pretensions and bred young materialists, could become a most dangerous institution. To prevent this and at the same time better meet the needs of society, Tolstoi proposed converting the realgymnasium into a more professionally oriented secondary school.[33] Scarcely hidden beneath these vague pronouncements was a simple political program: channel all students through courses which would not stimulate discussion of contemporary affairs nor encourage independent thought. A concentration either on the classics or on applied subjects seemed ideal for this purpose; the former would preoccupy the student with memorizing difficult grammar rules or translating from and into Greek and Latin, the latter with the solving of complex technical problems.

Although inconsistent and superficial, Tolstoi's contentions could be persuasive because of the Russian situation in 1871. True, the minister, like Katkov, misrepresented the nature of science courses and conveniently forgot that the classics provided an excellent source of republican ideas, but these lapses in argumentation did not outweigh the support given Tolstoi's accusations by events in Europe and at home. The publication and translation of Darwin's works showed how science could threaten the moral and religious foundations of a state; and, more important, the specter of revolution had materialized again. Not only had the government of France recently fallen, but Russian students, it appeared, had gone beyond the nihilistic poses of a Bazarov to join some form of international conspiratorial movement. Investigations conducted throughout 1870 revealed a link, however tenuous, between the university disorders of 1869 led by the science-trained students of the Medical-Surgical Academy, the followers of the infamous insurrectionist Sergei Nechaev, and the mysterious World Revolutionary Alliance. Indeed, the government was preparing its case against the ultraradical Nechaevtsy just as it was reviewing the secondary school reforms. The timing, if not the logic, of Tolstoi's presentation "could not have been better." [34]

Considering Tolstoi's measures too controversial to bring before the State Council without preliminary discussion, Alexander II on 8 March 1871 established a special conference *(osoboe prisutstvie)* to review the legislation. Chaired by S. G. Stroganov, the commission included the tsarevich, Tolstoi, and the following high-ranking officials: State Council President Grand Duke Constantine Nikolaevich, Fourth Section Head Prince P. G. Ol'denburgsky, War Minister D. A. Miliutin, Finance Minister M. Kh. Reutern, retired Education Ministers E. V. Putiatin and A. V. Golovnin, former Justice Minister V. N. Panin, former Minister of the Interior P. A. Valuev, Assistant Minister of the Interior A. G. Troitnitsky, Academy of Sciences President Admiral F. P. Litke, Second Section Head Prince S. N. Urusov, director of the State

Council's Financial Department K. V. Chevkin, and State Council member K. K. Grot.[35]

Conspicuously absent were those most affected by the deliberations — professional scholars and pedagogues who could attend sessions only at the conference's invitation — and the three men directly concerned with state security: the Third Section Head, the Minister of the Interior, and the Justice Minister. It seemed as if the government wanted to avoid challenges from both left and right. Yet the presence of such convinced opponents of Tolstoi as Miliutin and Golovnin guaranteed that the commission, despite its bureaucratic composition, would not be a rubber stamp.

Meeting five times in April, the committee produced the expected fireworks. Litke, Panin, Chevkin, Miliutin, Golovnin, and Grot immediately assaulted the classical school's privileged position. The bitterness of these attacks indicates that it was more than Tolstoi's educational reforms that angered Miliutin and company; the War Minister admitted as much in his unpublished memoirs. For him the victory of the classicist faction headed by Tolstoi and Katkov would signify a general return to the conservative policies of the past.[36] This association of classicism with retrogression, and realism with modernization, transformed the classical-realist dispute from a pedagogical discussion into a symbolic conflict about the nature of Russia's future.

With the outcome of these debates so significant, the realist party prepared its rebuttal with care. It first questioned Tolstoi's major thesis, the superiority of classical studies for scholastic and moral training. Insisting that the teacher, not the subject, was the decisive factor, it claimed that science courses could improve the student's capabilities as well as Greek and Latin. In the words of the Medical-Surgical Academy's director:

Science, if properly taught, harmoniously develops the young mind by its stress on synthesis and analysis, on inductions and conclusions . . . on working from simple to more important and difficult topics. Science, because it helps man to understand the immutable eternal laws of nature with all their inexhaustible variations, serves as the firmest and most diverse means for man's moral instruction. The methodical and scientific examination of each false deduction . . . produces truthfulness and steadfastness; [the comparison of] one's own fragile forces with the limitless, perfect, and eternal forces guiding . . . the universe makes the youthful soul receptive to religious faith.[37]

As for the classics' political usefulness, one need only recall that they formed the basis of French secondary education before the Revolution of 1789 to realize the weakness of this point.

Tolstoi's adversaries then appealed to common sense. Russia could not afford these squabbles about secondary education; its central task was to build more schools, to create more trained personnel. Miliutin and his cohorts concluded their presentation with a demand for an equal number of classical and realgymnasiums and the introduction of Latin at the realgymnasium so that its graduates might enter the university's science faculties. The realists' persuasive arguments, however, had little effect, for the majority of the commission (nine members) accepted the now-familiar case in favor of the classical system and thus approved the minister's program.[38]

On 15 May 1871 the projected statute accompanied by the conference's minority report at last came before the State Council. A fierce contretemps ensued. Tolstoi's antagonists within the Stroganov committee — Panin, Chevkin, Golovnin, and Miliutin — assailed his proposals, the latter so forcefully that the chairman, Grand Duke Constantine, frequently had to reprimand him. Undismayed, the minister defended his policy at length with vigorous support from Stroganov, who together with Katkov had brought the grand duke to Tolstoi's side. This time, however, the ministry did not prevail. Ignoring the recommendations of the two preliminary commissions and Tolstoi's backing from the royal family, the State Council decided twenty-nine to nineteen against restricting university entrance to graduates of the classical gymnasium.

The voting revealed few surprises. In general, the more progressive officials, those better attuned to public opinion and the needs of a modernizing country — men like Golovnin and Miliutin — opposed the reforms. The conservatives like Shuvalov or the tsarevich, who feared instability above all else, favored them. Yet the pattern was not perfect; classicism was not solely the cause of the right. Two proponents of the "Great Reforms," Grand Duke Constantine and D. N. Zamiatnin, sided with Tolstoi, while the archconservative Minister of the Interior joined Tolstoi's foes.[39]

The final decision now rested with the tsar. He received the council's minority and majority opinions, and the one he endorsed would become law. Not only did the minority report rehearse the usual arguments about the universally acknowledged supremacy of the classical curriculum in training students for all forms of higher study, it also played on the emperor's sense of self-importance. While admitting Tolstoi's program was unpopular, it blamed this not on its provisions but on public short-sightedness. "Most people," it asserted, "tend to value education for the external advantages it promises. They prefer the natural sciences and the modern languages which they feel are easier than the classics and which they mistakenly expect to have a more immediate benefit." Other European governments had not panicked in the face of a hostile society because they "considered it their sacred duty to protect the interests of the serious classical school and . . . to defend the universities against an influx of immature and unprepared students." [40]

The meaning was clear. Alexander must disregard public opinion and save Russian education by ruling that the classical gymnasium be the only preparatory school for the universities. This was simply a restatement of a major feature in Golovnin's widely accepted statute, but the State Council wanted to reverse its 1864 judgment. Its majority report found it unjust to close the university to students from the realgymnasiums and their equivalents and questioned the necessity of a Greek prerequisite in science faculties. It also pointed out the growing enthusiasm for scientific education in the West and stressed Russia's shortage of engineers, chemists, technicians, all products of nonclassical schools.[41]

However, these considerations could not overcome Alexander's fear of radical activity in the schools or the influence of his brother, the grand duke, and of the powerful Shuvalov. On 18

June 1871 the tsar upheld the minority view and ordered Tolstoi to incoporate into his new statute on the classical gymnasium the revisions vetoed by the State Council. Although postponing discussions on the realschule until fall, the emperor did rule that universities should definitely not admit realgymnasium graduates.[42] Tolstoi's adversaries had been robbed of victory.

The Gymnasium Statute of 1871

Promulgated on 30 July 1871, the gymnasium regulations epitomized for many the Tolstoi system: the sacrifice of all subjects but mathematics to the idol of classical studies. Greek and Latin increased their portion of weekly lesson hours from 31.5 percent under Golovnin to almost 41 percent, an impressive percentage but still below the 47 to 48 percent at Prussian and Saxon gymnasiums. This added emphasis on the classical languages left less time for all other subjects but mathematics. Even those with obvious propaganda possibilities like religion, Russian, and history suffered. Religion's and history's share of the curriculum each declined from about $7\frac{1}{2}$ to less than 6 percent, Russian's from 13 to 11 percent. Some subjects fared much worse: the useful course on the administrative and legal structure of the empire disappeared entirely, and the "materialistic" natural sciences no longer merited a separate course since, the ministry felt, their barest outlines were all students needed to know.[43] By thus focusing on the classics and mathematics, Tolstoi concluded, the gymnasium would "more easily" accomplish its purpose of preparing "intellectually mature students for the university and other higher educational institutions." [44]

There were indeed good pedagogical reasons for limiting a pupil's attention to a few subjects. In this way he would not disperse his energies but would instead reinforce skills he had already learned. However, concealed behind the above explanation was the wholly unacademic consideration of assuring the political reliability of gymnasium students. To attain this goal Tolstoi, like Uvarov, would depend more on the defensive tactic of shielding youth from harmful philosophies than on the positive one of inculcating state-approved virtues and beliefs. Hence he played down subjects with indoctrination potential because, while they might instill the proper values, he felt they would more likely provide a convenient channel for pernicious ideas to enter the classroom. An excess of lessons, Tolstoi claimed, had enabled instructors of Russian to waste time on "useless" and "sometimes positively harmful discourses" and their counterparts in history to expound general historical theories which "correspond neither to the students' intellectual maturity nor to the character of gymnasium teaching." [45]

Classical philology and mathematics suited his purposes far better. Their abstract nature would offer few excuses for extracurricular discussions; their complexity might keep pupils too busy to investigate the subversive views preached outside the school. When looked at in this light, Tolstoi's giving his students a greater concentration in Greek than even the Germans had — which he reasonably justified by stressing both the similarities between Greek and Russian and his country's cultural links with Byzantium — takes on a deeper significance.[46] As the more difficult of the two classical languages, it would envelop pupils longer in the intricacies of its highly inflected grammar. The weakness of this negative program was that the student, once subjected to radical doctrines, could draw on little he learned at school to combat them. Yet if his preoccupation with Greek syntax and quadratic equations postponed his contact with dangerous ideas until a less impressionable age, then Tolstoi would have achieved something. An older, more sophisticated mind, he could argue, would better resist the blandishments of revolutionaries.

More genuinely pedagogical motives underlay the ministry's lengthening the gymnasium course and raising entrance requirements. By adding an extra year to the senior class (to become a separate eighth grade in 1875), the new statute would give students sufficient time to master a difficult curriculum and would, Tolstoi asserted, help them mature intellectually and morally.[47] Lenient admissions tests as well as its short seven-year course had lowered academic standards at the Golovnin gymnasium. In fact, it was easier to enter the gymnasium than the far less demanding county schools. The 1871 regulations rectified this anomaly. Where formerly the ability to read and write, to add, subtract, and multiply, and to recite the major Orthodox prayers permitted one to enter the gymnasium, from 1871 candidates would also have to retell stories, write from dictation, read Church Slavonic, understand division, and relate important biblical events. The ministry increased requirements not to curtail enrollment but to obtain better students. Proof of this was its creation of two-year preparatory classes at the gymnasium for all eight- to ten-year-olds who could read, write, add, subtract, count to one hundred, and say their prayers.[48] Since these classes demanded less of applicants than did the prereform gymnasium, Tolstoi had actually relaxed admissions restrictions while simultaneously guaranteeing the gymnasium a steady supply of students who had undergone at least two years of properly supervised instruction.

Although concerned most with improving secondary education, these measures had their political usefulness. They might discourage applications from those whose scholastic deficiencies or financial insecurity would distract them from their studies and thereby render them perfect prey for outside agitators. The stiffer basic entrance standards or the two-year preparatory class hopefully would weed out the weaker students; and the extension of the gymnasium course from one to three years (depending on whether or not the preparatory class is counted) made this school more expensive and hence less attractive to the poorer segments of society.

Not only did the ministry reshape the gymnasium's academic program, it also altered the rights and duties of the teaching staff. These changes, like the course revisions, had the twofold purpose of advancing Russian education and preserving the loyalty of its products. However, where the curriculum modifications would only indirectly serve the latter aim, the reforms in school administration attacked the problem straight on by instituting strict controls over both students and faculty. It was these new provisions, not the adjustments in lesson hours or admissions requirements, that marked the fundamental departure from the previous legislation.

The clearest example of this policy reversal occurred with the restructuring of the pedagogical council. Formerly, this assembly of fulltime teachers determined the main features of the school's internal organization: teaching programs, examination methods, student rules. Such concessions to local autonomy, Tolstoi admitted, had worked in some countries, notably Germany and England, but Russia was not yet ready for so progressive a step. Its teachers could neither work effectively together nor devise their own academic plans. For Tolstoi the democratic composition of the pedagogical council encouraged "agitation and arid factional strife," and the freedom enjoyed by the individual instructor produced "serious pedagogic and didactic errors," culminating in intellectual chaos. Only extensive guidance from St. Petersburg, he argued, would eliminate these unfortunate consequences and give Russian education the necessary "uniformity and firmness." His ministry, therefore, must issue special examination rules, student penal codes, and detailed course outlines which, while not so complete as those in France or Belgium, would exactly delineate the aspects of every subject to be covered in each grade and thoroughly describe the areas requiring extra attention. Even relatively minor matters like the approval of conspectuses already based on ministerial instructions or the compilation of borrowing procedures for the school library were no longer left to the council's discretion.[49]

Changes in gymnasium administration further altered the council's position. The director's responsibility for his institution's affairs increased; a newly created economic committee composed of the director, the inspector, and three elected teachers relieved the pedagogical council of its fiscal concerns; topics affecting a single class or subject went before small ad hoc commissions chaired by the inspector, and not before the full council. Hence the council had more time for important questions — but fewer important questions to discuss. Where previously it had governed much of gymnasium life, it could now on its own authority simply select texts from ministry-approved lists and accept, promote, graduate, reward, and punish students. Tolstoi asserted that he had "not in the least diminished the significance of the pedagogical council." [50] He lied: he had destroyed its independence and its power.

Tolstoi gladly sacrificed local initiative to central domination. Distrusting both the competence and loyalty of his teachers, he reserved for his ministry all major decisions on the gymnasium's program, purpose, and organization. This action, in addition to providing the faculty with the comprehensive direction and coordinated syllabi it needed for good teaching, might also minimize the possible introduction of dangerous elements into the course. With proper methods outlined for them, Tolstoi believed, instructors would be less likely to adopt unsanctioned and thereby potentially harmful procedures. He, like most bureaucrats, mistakenly equated independent with subversive pursuits. That the proliferation of restrictions might inhibit pedagogical creativity or turn people against the ministry did not bother Tolstoi. The security of the empire, his first concern, demanded tight control over all educational institutions.

Students too faced stronger checks on their activity, for the 1871 statute substantially increased the size of the gymnasium inspectorate. Where Golovnin had called for two student overseers plus the director and inspector, his successor supplied seven: five class preceptors and two assistant class preceptors. Each grade would now have its own counselor to supervise its moral and scholastic development. The director took one class, appointed the inspector to another, and recommended to the curator those teachers giving the most lessons in their particular grade for the remaining posts. Because their subject outweighed all others, Greek and Latin instructors would be the logical candidates for preceptorships. Like the German *Ordinarius* after whom his position was patterned, the preceptor's duties went beyond student supervision to include informal sessions with parents and conferences with teachers about the proper distribution of assignments. For this he would receive an ample salary supplement of 200 rubles a year.[51]

The value of this reform naturally depended on whether the preceptor acted more like an adviser or a policeman, but its provisions would have one interesting side effect. By earmarking the preceptorship for classics instructors and then declaring this post "the best preparation for the office of director or inspector," [52] Tolstoi opened the way for classicists to dominate the faculty just as the subjects they taught dominated the curriculum.

While many would deny that the lack of "uniformity and firmness" had hampered Russian education, few would question the harmful effects of the teacher shortage. As will be shown later, Tolstoi's primary answer to this problem was the creation of normal schools, but his new statute did present two other possible remedies: the use of salary incentives and the addition of the director and inspector to the teaching force. The gymnasium's poor pay, an average of 900 rubles a year for a twelve-classroom-hour week, often deterred people from undertaking a pedagogical career. True, they might give additional lessons at the lower rate of 60 rubles an hour, but these classes greatly enlarged their course load; besides they were not always available.

Instead of eradicating this grievance by the direct if expensive means of raising wages, the ministry introduced more fringe benefits and a graduated pay scale. All teachers now received honoraria for their examination committee labors, free gymnasium tuition for their sons, and those in Russian and the classics at least 100 rubles extra a year to compensate for their heavy grading burdens. The revised salary formula provided less help for most instructors. They started at 750 rubles a year and only reached 900 rubles for the normal twelve-hour load after serving five years. However, each gymnasium could offer salaries of 1,250 and 1,500 rubles respectively to two senior teachers, chosen subject to curator approval on the basis of merit and continuous service in the same institution.[53]

Without actually expanding the gymnasium budget, this scheme may have induced the capable to stay, but it certainly did not attract young recruits. Basic salaries remained so low that many needed outside jobs or supplementary teaching assignments. From the ministry's point of view faculty poverty did have one advantage; it solidified the position of the gymnasium director. Since he distributed the extra class hours and influenced the selection of the two senior instructors, teachers who challenged his authority risked financial repercussions.

More fruitful and equally inexpensive was the ministry's increased utilization of gymnasium directors and inspectors. Following French and English models, Tolstoi required these officials to teach rather than, as previously, leaving it to their discretion. Such a policy, he explained, would restrict directorships to those with pedagogical experience, improve relations between the administration and the faculty, and bring students and instructors more directly under the supervision of the gymnasium authorities.[54] It was an intelligent arrangement, for it enabled the director and inspector to extend their control over school affairs while at the same time alleviating Russia's teacher shortage.

This search for cheap ways to resolve staffing problems reflected Tolstoi's general reluctance, given the straitened circumstances of the imperial treasury, to exceed the sums budgeted per gymnasium in 1864. Despite its year-longer course the new gymnasium cost the state only 60 rubles a year more than the old one.[55] Even with this careful economizing, the government could not afford the many schools Russia needed. Tolstoi turned to the public for help. His new statute encouraged local societies to contribute regularly by increasing their influence in school affairs. Their elected representative at the gymnasium, the honorary trustee *(pochetnyi popechitel')*, regained the privileges conferred by the 1828 legislation. Limited by Golovnin to fiscal matters, he could now review all questions and seek the curator's assistance if dissatisfied with the council's handling of his suggestions.[56] A conscientious trustee would provide both another check on gymnasium activity and an essential link between the school and the public.

The one feature of Golovnin's regulations that Tolstoi left alone was his unrestrictive admissions requirements. His gymnasium remained open to medically fit students of all social classes and religious beliefs. Although Tolstoi stiffened the entrance examination for the first grade, the preparatory classes made a gymnasium education more accessible than before to those with little prior instruction. Tolstoi also seemed slightly more generous than his predecessor with tuition scholarships. Like Golovnin he left fee scales to the pedagogical councils and authorized them to waive the charges, as in many German schools, for 10 percent of the student body and to employ some of the tuition money to aid outstanding poor pupils; but Tolstoi went still further. He declared preparatory class students, schoolteachers' sons, and deserving progymnasium graduates who had paid no tuition at their former school not subject to the 10-percent limit on tuition exemptions. Nothing in the 1871 statute thus specifically reserved the gymnasium for a particular social group. True, Tolstoi had earlier urged the use of the gymnasium pension to attract students from the gentry, but he did little to reinvigorate this institution except for removing the limitations placed on its size and on the age of its residents.[57] If Tolstoi wanted to exclude certain classes from his gymnasium, he relied on subtler devices like a difficult classical curriculum or a lengthy course of study to discourage them.

By strengthening the gymnasium's program, reaffirming its moral purpose, and reforming its administrative structure, Tolstoi boasted that he had given Russian education the "firm and solid basis it had long lacked." Although the minister exaggerated its advantages, the new statute did suit his avowed goal of producing loyal, competent candidates for the university and hence for government service. The overwhelming emphasis on abstract, traditional disciplines, especially the classics, would fully exercise the mind and, in Tolstoi's words, finally put Russia on that path "which has brought the other more advanced countries of Europe to the height of scientific and intellectual progress"; it might also draw the student's attention away from the contemporary problems of his society. The creation of class preceptorships better equipped the gymnasium for training "people who respect religion . . . and the law, who are true servants of the sovereign and the fatherland." [58] To ensure that each school carried out these scholastic and didactic obligations, the ministry destroyed the faculty's autonomy and determined every aspect of the gymnasium course itself. Like Uvarov before him, but with a heavier hand, Tolstoi relied on mental discipline, moral influence, and — most important — state control to combat education's negative effects.

The Introduction of the Realschule

With the gymnasium legislation in force Tolstoi returned to the controversial realschule project. Despite his earlier defeats within the State Council and the hostility of the press campaign against him, he did not yield to those who advocated the equality of scientific and classical education. His report presented to the State Council on 1 December 1871 still viewed the realschule as an intermediate institution, more advanced than any elementary school but less demanding than the gymnasium. Its basic task was not to promote scientific studies, but to meet the practical needs of the urban population.[59]

Once again the anticlassical camp rose in opposition. Seeing in the ministry's downgrading of nonclassical secondary education a general turn to the right in the government, the liberal Petersburg journals strove to reverse this trend by discrediting Tolstoi's policies and, by implication, everything he stood for. They too found the European experience an ideal support for their arguments. *Vestnik Evropy* may have overstated its case by characterizing "the recent history of schools in Europe" as "a series of victories and concessions to science," but it did have proof of a growing preference among foreign educators for modern languages and the natural sciences. Eager to link this popularity of nonclassical education with political success, Tolstoi's antagonists focused on developments in Prussia; for no other country could match its achievements. It had smashed the Austrian armies in 1866, crushed the French four years later, and united all of Germany under its banner by 1871.

This model of state power, the realists happily pointed out, possessed one of the most ambitious systems of nonclassical schools in Europe. The Prussian *Realschule* thus, with its nine-year course emphasizing mathematics, natural science, and Latin, and with its recently acquired privilege of sending its graduates to both arts and science divisions of the philosophical faculty, should become the prototype of the Russian realgymnasium. Elaborating on this theme, M. M. Stasiulevich published in the October and December 1871 issues of *Vestnik Evropy* so laudatory a defense of the Prussian *Realschule* that Katkov devoted eight lead articles in *Moskovskie vedomosti* to its refutation. The crux of Stasiulevich's thesis was that Tolstoi's professionally oriented realschule flaunted the example of the strongest nation of Europe which had made its *Realschule* of the first rank an institution of general education. As evidence he cited both the Prussian military service law which put the *Realschule* and the gymnasium in the same category and the *Realschule* statute which stated: "The *Realschule* . . . is not a *trade school*, but is concerned *as is the gymnasium with general education* . . . the gymnasium and the *Realschule* do not differ in principle." [60] Could backward Russia, Stasiulevich seemed to be asking his emperor, afford to disregard the educational wisdom of progressive and highly successful Prussia?

The ministry countered by showing how badly its critics had misinterpreted the German educational experience. In his 140-page first-hand report on the nonclassical schools of Central Europe, Georgievsky refuted the Russian realists' three major assertions: the superiority of the Prussian *Realschule*, the importance of its program for scientific studies, and the inappropriateness of technical courses in secondary schools. According to his survey published by the *Zhurnal* in December 1871, the Prussian *Realschule* was a failure. It so little conformed to society's needs that few students stayed the entire nine years. Even the *Realschule*'s right to send its graduates to a university had been overrated in Russia since these students faced strict limitations on what they could do with their degrees. As for the realists' other two points, Georgievsky insisted that the majority of pedagogues interviewed believed a classical education best for preparing students for higher technical institutes and approved the inclusion of practical or trade subjects in a realschule curriculum. The *Zhurnal*'s next issue featured I. B. Shteinman's résumé of the comments on the realschule project from educators in northern Germany, Baden, Württemberg, and Belgium. Their replies corroborated Georgievsky's conclusions.[61] These articles supplied the necessary support for the minister's own public statements. This time Tolstoi openly joined the battle, and he came well armed; for he had examined foreign legislation and had personally inspected the *Realschule* in Germany. Consequently, his 1 December brief to the State Council, which the *Zhurnal* immediately reproduced, provided a thorough justification of the ministry's policy.

Choosing his sources carefully, Tolstoi first deflated the reputation of the Prussian *Realschule* of the first rank. So unpopular had it become that many cities were converting existing *Realschulen* into gymnasiums and some states had prohibited the introduction of these institutions into their territories. German experts, Tolstoi declared, attributed the *Realschule*'s troubles to its impracticality: it devoted 15 percent of its curriculum to Latin but did not offer the college-entrance advantages of the classical gymnasium; it emphasized the sciences but did not furnish the concrete benefits of the technical school. Having earned the highest reduction in military obligations offered a secondary school pupil after only six years at the *Realschule*, its students had little reason to stay longer. Those who felt that the granting of the gymnasium's privileges to the *Realschule* would reduce the dropout rate were wrong, Tolstoi explained; they had ignored the wishes of the urban population who, one Prussian educator explained, "want their sons to finish their studies before they are eighteen so that the latter can help them from an early age." Since most students attending the *Realschule* sought "training for practical activity and not for state service," the correct solution for Tolstoi was to transform the *Realschule* into a shorter, more professional institution, and this was exactly what he proposed be done in Russia. His country, he concluded, must learn from Germany's mistakes. "One should not blindly imitate, but . . . one should extract from it [foreign experience] what is useful . . . , taking into special consideration the difference of educational needs and means in Russia." [62] He had rather cleverly flung one of his opponents' favorite arguments back into their faces.

Having ruled out the Prussian *Realschule* as a model, the minister then answered the demands of his government opponents for an eight-year realschule program broad enough to prepare all its students for higher education. Such a measure, Tolstoi warned, would only draw off students to a second-rate gymnasium which trained people less suitably than the classical gymnasium for any form of advanced study. Once more he quoted German academics: a Berlin gymnasium director, "The gymnasium must develop the scholarly, the *Realschule* the practical mind"; and the famous chemist Justus Liebig, "I have found that gymnasium graduates very quickly overtake graduates from polytechnical or industrial schools even in the natural sciences." It should be pointed out, however, that the minister's case was quite one-sided, for he never mentioned the many Prussian educators who stressed the excellence of a *Realschule* education.[63]

Academic considerations alone did not impel the ministry to establish a clear dichotomy between the gymnasium and realschule. In Tolstoi's scheme the realschule must attract one section of the population, the gymnasium another, and this could only be accomplished if their programs differed considerably. The realschule's short utilitarian course, designed for those who wished to finish school by age sixteen or seventeen or who found the gymnasium too difficult, he hoped would suit the desires of the middle class, thereby leaving the gymnasium for those classes traditionally associated with the privileges of university education and government service.

> If one wishes to spread nonclassical education as far as possible among the business *(promyshlennye)* classes, it is necessary . . . to adjust the realschule to their needs. Thus . . . the realschule course must not be too long since people who are almost exclusively concerned with practical everyday affairs nowhere seem inclined to prolonged study.[64]

Fearing any tear in the fabric of Russian society, Tolstoi wanted his schools to maintain social stability, not encourage upward mobility.

While refusing the realists' proposals for an eight-year copy of the Prussian *Realschule*, Tolstoi did offer them a compromise solution. He admitted that his original conception of the realschule as an institution preparing students only for "the various branches of industry and commerce" was too narrow. The revised statute, however, had eliminated this error, for it changed the realschule from a trade to an all-purpose school providing practical training and a "*general* education" opening the way to higher technical schools. Consequently, the number of realschule lessons on applied subjects dropped significantly, but Tolstoi refused to remove these courses entirely from the curriculum because, he insisted, they could temporarily replace the trade schools Russia lacked and because they "helped one better understand" the more theoretical sciences. This combined program of applied and general studies would enable the realschule to achieve two goals at once. Not only would it surpass its predecessor, the realgymnasium, in producing good candidates for further education, but it would still fill its country's urgent need for technical schools.[65]

Neither the minister's arguments nor his concessions moved the special conference which reviewed his project in February 1872, or the State Council which discussed it six weeks later. The majority in both bodies correctly assumed that Tolstoi, despite his talk about general education, considered the realschule primarily a professional school, decidedly beneath the gymnasium. They demanded an advanced realschule without applied courses that would concentrate on preparing its students for technical institutes. They defeated the ministry's statute by votes of nine to six and twenty-seven to nineteen respectively. This decision, the State Council minority complained, would intensify the classicist-realist debate and hinder economic progress. Any upgrading of the realschule, they argued, would encourage society to continue insisting on parity between classical and real education, thereby heightening the conflict over the nature of secondary schooling which had since 1849 rent the family, the school, and society itself. Russia could not afford such divisive tendencies. Less hypothetical and controversial was the minority's contention that the realschule would assist "the spread of technical knowledge . . . and as a result raise the level of our land's productivity." A developing nation lacking a large skilled labor force and about to enter the industrial revolution, Russia could certainly use a steady source of practically trained personnel. Once more, and this time with greater justification, the council's minority won out, for the emperor remained consistent in his support of the Education Ministry's policies.[66]

The realschule statute of 15 May 1872 reflected the ministry's two major principles of secondary education: the strict regulation of schools and the inferiority of real to classical studies. In its internal organization and its relations with St. Petersburg, the realschule closely resembled the gymnasium. Its regulations incorporated virtually all the important innovations of the 1871 reforms like the economic committees, graduated salary scales, and class preceptorships, and also placed the realschule faculty under the same ministerial controls as gymnasium instructors. The ministry defined scholastic plans, examination procedures, and punishment codes, allowing the pedagogical council little authority over school affairs.

Although sharing the gymnasium's administrative structure, the realschule had its own particular purpose and program. It "should offer," so article one declared, "a general education, though directed toward practical needs and the acquisition of technical knowledge." If this statement seems ambiguous, the remaining provisions of the 1872 statute would show that the ministry still conceived of the realschule as technically oriented. Where the realgymnasium had had a single curriculum which prepared students for "higher special schools," the realschule took many forms, most of which had a utilitarian character. Its first four classes all taught religion, Russian, mathematics, geography, history, penmanship, drawing (including mechanical drawing), and two foreign languages; its last two split into the basic *(osnovnoi)* sector which introduced courses in natural science, physics, chemistry, mechanics, and a commercial sector where bookkeeping and clerical tasks replaced chemistry and mechanics.

For the highly motivated students in the basic sector, realschule authorities could establish a supplementary grade with general, mechanical-technical, and chemical-technical divisions. The first stressed purely academic subjects and alone led to further schooling; the second stressed mechanics, modeling, surveying, and the like; the third, chemical technology and laboratory work. The combination of divisions or sectors each realschule had depended on local interests, a rare instance of Tolstoi's acknowledging the value of public initiative. Believing the gymnasium course ideal for any type of higher education, the ministry had organized its realschule so as to minimize its role as a preparatory school. Only one of its many permutations, the seven-year school with the basic sector and the first supplementary division, furnished a general education similar to that of the old realgymnasium and thus offered the broad training necessary for advanced study.[67]

Further emphasizing the primacy of the realschule's professional aims were the functions of its unique trusteeship *(popechitel'-stvo)* and the ministry's indifference to the first four realschule classes. Responsible for the school's well-being, the trusteeship comprised the mayor, the director, the honorary trustee, and five to ten private citizens nominated for ministerial confirmation by either the curator or by those supplying the money, if the school was publicly supported. In Tolstoi's view this committee would raise funds for the school and assure that it fit local conditions. Tolstoi would not guard the realschule so jealously as he did the gymnasium against deviations from ministerial plans. After all, the former sent pupils out into commerce or industry, whereas the latter prepared the nation's scholarly and bureaucratic elite. Thus the trusteeship could go beyond arranging excursions to surrounding factories or creating stipends for study at technical institutes to decide upon foreign language offerings and, with the curator's approval, needed improvements even in academic policy. But its major task for Tolstoi, and the one most indicative of the realschule's practical bent, was to find its graduates positions where they could use their specialized training.[68] That this training constituted the crux of the realschule program was also revealed by the ministry's approval of realschulen with only grades 5 and 6, the two that provided technical education. Directors could postpone introducing the lower classes, Tolstoi explained, for several other schools offered an equivalent general education.[69]

The circular of 31 July 1872 on the implementation of the realschule statute dispelled any doubts about the realschule's vocational nature. It first showed how misleading the official lesson plans were when they assigned applied courses such a small percentage of the curriculum: 2 and 6 percent in the six-year basic and commercial sectors respectively; less than 2 percent with the supplementary general class; and 12 percent with either the chemical-technical or mechanical-technical divisions. As the 1872 circular demonstrated, these figures included only the obviously technical subjects like bookkeeping or mechanical technology, but did not allow for practical orientation within the so-called general subjects, especially the drawing course which could occupy over one-fifth of the weekly lessons. For Tolstoi, "even in the real-schule's basic sector, instruction in mathematics and natural science and also in the graphic arts must be directed toward practical aims."

Second and more important, the circular specifically discouraged formation of the general supplementary division, the real-schule student's main pathway to further schooling. Curators instead should concentrate on the mechanical and chemical divisions because they, together with the commercial sector, "turn the realschule into the type of . . . polytechnic institute which has been so beneficial to trade and industry in Western Europe. . . . Only under these conditions can the government finally achieve its long-sought . . . aim — the greatest possible spread of technical knowledge. . . ." [70]

If Tolstoi's subordinates heeded his advice, the ministry would furnish two essentially different forms of secondary education. The realschule, its course shorter, more vocational than that of the realgymnasium, readied one for careers in business and industry. The gymnasium, its course longer, more heavily classical than its predecessor, opened the way to the university, government service, and the professions. By so dividing responsibilities, Tolstoi eliminated all confusion between real and classical education and at the same time provided a solution for Russia's shortage of skilled personnel. Where formerly the impractical realgymnasium or outmoded county school awaited those who could not handle the gymnasium's program, they now had the chance of acquiring a modern, serviceable, but not overly demanding secondary education. "Thanks to the realschule," the ministry claimed, "even mediocre students will receive useful training, and hopefully . . . not one bit of manpower will be lost to the country." [71]

The Sources of Tolstoi's Reforms

Like his other reforms, Tolstoi's secondary school legislation had numerous European precedents. In fact, despite the growing appreciation in the West for science-oriented curricula, it was Tolstoi and not his opponents who most closely followed European, particularly German, practices. Such vital components of his statute as the class preceptorship, the strong concentration on the classics, the privileged position of the gymnasium, the centrally compiled final examinations, and the very name realschule (*real'noe uchilishche*) mirrored German developments. Tolstoi proudly acknowledged his debt to Germany, frequently sending officials to inspect that country's schools and spending an extended period there himself. And why not, since contemporary pedagogues, impressed by the scholarship of the German university community and the successes of the literate German soldier, proclaimed that country's educational network the best in Europe. Later historians would be less enthusiastic; the Prussian system, one liberal German educator wrote, "was marked by an attitude of distrust on the part of the authorities towards the people and towards general education." [72] But this negative feature also suited Tolstoi's aims.

It would be wrong, however, to deduce from the above that the minister "simply translated from the German" as the philosopher and former gymnasium teacher V. V. Rozanov claimed. Significant differences did exist between Russia's schools and those of its powerful neighbor. Tolstoi's gymnasium treated the native language as a major not a minor subject, was a year shorter, and offered far more Greek, far less natural science than its Prussian counterpart. Even less dependent on the German experience was the new realschule. Tolstoi had declared the Prussian *Realschule* of both first and second ranks wrong for Russia: the former because it was too long, too impractical, and too similar to the gymnasium; the latter because it was too vocational and therefore lacked that concentration on basic subjects which "guarantees the success of every school." Tolstoi also repudiated the Prussian practice of letting instructors define their own courses, and like the French he issued obligatory teaching programs.[73] A nationalist historian himself, he saw the dangers in Russia's past subservience to the West and later (1884) would condemn eighteenth-century society for "taking from Europe only the externals and not the essence of education." [74]

Consequently, although he had remodeled Russian secondary schools along European lines, he had not, in his words, "blindly imitated" foreign institutions but had rather borrowed what he felt most appropriate for his country's particular conditions.[75] Some of his adjustments, like the shorter gymnasium or the multipurpose realschule, reflected a commendable effort to overcome the obstacles posed by Russia's meager educational budget and its lack of alternative types of secondary schools. Others, like tight ministerial controls over education, indicate the ministry's traditional, short-sighted response to Russia's unstable political situation.

Surprisingly few of Tolstoi's reforms came directly from the policies of his famous predecessor Uvarov, despite their earlier association. True, their programs were analogous in their emphasis on classical studies and the faculty's role as moral instructor. But in its specific features the Uvarov gymnasium, aside from the authoritative position of its honorary trustee, resembled Golovnin's school more than Tolstoi's. Both gymnasiums assigned approximately the same amount of time to Greek and Latin, an amount much below that allotted in the 1871 lesson plans; and the pedagogical councils of both schools had considerable initiative in matters which did not conflict with existing laws. Uvarov's decrees carried none of those provisions for strict supervision over school affairs that were so prevalent in Tolstoi's scheme.[76]

Far more important sources of the ministry's new legislation than either the German experience or the Uvarov tradition were the publishers of *Moskovskie vedomosti,* M. N. Katkov and P. M.

Leont'ev. Historians and contemporaries alike stressed their dominant influence. For scholars ranging from the liberal M. N. Kovalensky to the Soviet Sh. I. Ganelin to the North American Martin Katz, Katkov and Leont'ev were the "inspirers" of the secondary school reforms.[77] One of Tolstoi's curators insisted that the two publicists "actually directed educational policy," and he was seconded by A. V. Nikitenko, who called Tolstoi's relation with them that of pupil and teacher.[78] This was certainly the impression Katkov wanted to create. To Alexander III he complained: "I have exhausted both my strength and my credit with the soveriegn to support the minister"; to Feoktistov: "You know . . . how much energy it took to make of him [Tolstoi] a proper Minister of Education"; and to the journalist G. K. Gradovsky: "It is necessary to exhort and prop up Tolstoi . . . at every step. He has the same understanding of the classics as he has of Mars or Jupiter." [79]

Although these insults usually came from Katkov's friends or Tolstoi's enemies, they nevertheless contain a strong element of truth. With little training in either pedagogy or the classics, Tolstoi did rely on Katkov and Leont'ev in shaping the gymnasium curriculum. Not only had Leont'ev prepared a draft of the gymnasium statute, but many of the arguments Tolstoi used against the realists appeared first in *Moskovskie vedomosti*. Even before Tolstoi took office, Katkov had attacked the 1864 legislation, particularly its tendency to equate scientific *(real'nye)* with classical schools. The ministry, he insisted, must replace the ill-conceived realgymnasium with a professional school that would ready students for a definite occupation and give supplementary classes for those desiring advanced technical education. The result would be a bifurcated secondary school system with special privileges granted the classical gymnasium. He then provided the ministry with the appropriate defense for such measures. They were urgent, he warned, for an undue emphasis on *real* courses falsely agitates the mind. Classical studies alone furnished an "antidote" against this; on it "the fate of Russian civilization depended." As the essential prerequisite for university work, it "introduced the student to the life of mankind, . . . and harmoniously developed all his capabilities so that on reaching maturity, he could independently and successfully select his future field of endeavor." [80]

If the classical gymnasium were to fulfill this lofty purpose, it needed good faculty, more student advisers, and a better program. Katkov advocated graduated salary scales to attract instructors, the appointment of teacher-inspectors for every class to guide students more carefully, and a longer course, higher entrance requirements, and a greater concentration on the classics, especially Greek, to improve the curriculum. Since the secondary school legislation of 1871–1872 incorporated all the above proposals, *Moskovskie vedomosti* was really slapping itself on the back when it proclaimed that these revisions had finally made Russia "a full-fledged member of the family of educated peoples." [81]

However, the correlation between the minister's plans and the publicists' remarks does not prove, as Katkov and his cohorts asserted, that Tolstoi was merely the tool of the Moscow journalists. To be sure, they continually bullied him about their pet theories in education, but Katkov's later hostility toward Tolstoi indicates that the latter often acted more independently than Katkov liked. For example, the ministry's revisions of the realschule legislation yielded so much to the demands of the State Council that Katkov grumbled: "The compilers of the realschule project . . . completely lost sight of our great need for technicians." [82] His mutterings against the secrecy surrounding deliberations on the gymnasium statute further demonstrate that Tolstoi hardly consulted with Moscow at every moment.

Not only did the minister sometimes ignore the entreaties of Katkov and Leont'ev, but on his own initiative as Ober Procurator he set the precedent for a major feature of his reforms — the curtailment of local autonomy: school administration had rarely concerned the Moscow publishers. Early in 1867 Tolstoi fought against the rights of the clerical seminary's faculty-dominated board (*pravlenie*) to select texts, compile student regulations, define the inspector's duties, review teaching methods, and discuss possible changes in the statute. Although the resultant rules did not restrict the board so sharply as Tolstoi wished, they reduced faculty representation on it and placed the seminary directly under the bishop instead of under the more permissive spiritual academy. While less qualified than the academy's professors, the bishop would, the procurator hoped, be more effective in supervision, more intolerant of deviation, and more subservient to the synod than a group of scholars.[83] This undermining of the powers enjoyed by collegiate bodies became the theme of Tolstoi's career in the ministries of education and the interior.

Thus the Tolstoi-Katkov relationship was not simply one of leader and led. Gradovsky appeared the most astute of his contemporaries when he concluded: "They influenced one another. Katkov 'cultivated' the minister, and the minister worked through the publicist. . . ." It was a volatile but mutually beneficial alliance. Tolstoi needed Katkov's and Leont'ev's expertise and their favorable press; they in turn depended on the minister's authority within the government to carry through educational reform and protect their journalistic enterprises.[84]

This uneasy partnership produced from essentially European models a harsh but hardly reactionary solution to the dilemma created for the autocracy by the necessity of educating its population. In theory, the new secondary schools, now regulated by the ministry or its agents and not by semi-independent and therefore less trustworthy local organs, would furnish their country with a usefully trained populace without simultaneously stimulating their students to question, if not denounce, the status quo. To achieve this aim, Tolstoi sought both to improve the school system and to counter its potentially dangerous by-products. On the one hand, his ministry strengthened the gymnasium course, standardized curricula and examinations, and increased the educational alternatives open to society. On the other, it emphasized apolitical subjects, put students and faculty under closer supervision, and tried to channel those classes less traditionally associated with imperial service—and hence in its view less reliable—away from the privileges of the gymnasium and into the practical divisions of the realschule. Whether or not Tolstoi's statutes fulfilled their twofold purpose will be the subject of the next chapter.

Although relieved at the passage of the 1871–1872 reforms, Tolstoi could not yet rest content. His statute merely mapped out the appropriate route for Russian secondary education, but even the best designed road might crumble unless paved with the proper materials. The ministry therefore provided all the vital supplies — academic plans, examination rules, and student regulations — now left solely in its charge. It also assumed the responsibility for training the basic segment of the construction crews, the native and classical language instructors. In this way Tolstoi hoped to accomplish the difficult engineering feat of building a highway that would lead safely across the chasms of radical propaganda, democratic visions, and social concerns into the isolated valley of unhesitating service to tsar and country. Despite its control over the blueprints, materials, and workmen for this project, the ministry still had cause to worry. Would the type of road construction picked by the ministry fit Russia's harsh conditions as well as it did the West's milder ones? Would the traditional surface resist the poundings of new generations of student travelers? Would the guardrails protect against dangerous swerves from the chosen path? Would the laborers faithfully perform their tasks? To answer these questions it will be necessary first to examine the actual structure of the causeway and then to investigate how well it was used.

New Regulations on Courses, Examinations, and Conduct

The core substance for both the road's surface and the safety rails was the cement of the secondary school curriculum. Golovnin had given inadequate instructions about its mixing; Tolstoi would not repeat the error. The only acceptable procedure would be the ministry's. Its officials, together with experts from the Academic Committee and a few invited teachers, compiled detailed syllabi for all gymnasiums which took effect just a year after the new statute appeared. Within a month Tolstoi had distributed 1,200 copies of this circular and had ordered a larger second printing.[1]

Even though the ministry assured instructors that these directives "could in no way inhibit" their activity, it was not being honest. True, teachers might still draw up their own conspectuses, but they had little chance for originality. The ministry determined the appropriate pedagogical methods grade by grade and specifically defined every course's scope by describing in full its goals, the areas meriting extra attention, and the essential topics each class should cover. It became more explicit still about courses like Russian literature, natural science, or history whose subject matter, it felt, would most likely stimulate unwanted discussions of contemporary issues; these courses received extensive sample programs in addition to the material on classroom techniques and course content given to all subjects. Such elaborate instructions, Tolstoi made clear, were not for the teacher's "information *(svedenie)*" but for his "guidance *(rukovodstvo)*," and had to be followed. Curators must stop any digression from the official plan; faculty could only clarify, not alter, the ministry's instructions.[2]

While Tolstoi may have paid lip service to academic freedom, he now told teachers not only what to teach, but also how to teach it and what results to expect. This curtailment of faculty independence was primarily a political act aimed at preventing teachers from bringing into the school what the state felt to be subversive influences. As usual, Tolstoi did have reasonable pedagogical arguments to justify his restrictions. If left uncontrolled, he declared, instructors might overburden their students or distract them from other subjects. The future would show whether the ministry avoided the mistakes it attributed to the short-sightedness of the individual teacher.

The 1872 scholastic programs reaffirmed the ministry's narrow view of secondary education. Its quite traditional plans concentrated on providing the student with a firm grounding in the gymnasium's two major disciplines, languages and mathematics, instead of on arousing his creative abilities or his intellectual curiosity. In Tolstoi's scheme the main purpose of education was the disciplining of the mind, and lessons on vague themes like the meaning of literature or history, while more exciting than those in grammar or algebra, did not train the young intellect nearly so well. Where the latter because of their difficult but logically ordered subject matter demanded diligence and a good memory for success, the former because of their abstract nature and the absence of verifiable answers to the questions raised permitted pupils to get away with superficial glibness. These free-wheeling discussions could also, of course, readily serve as a pretext for the teacher and student to express their personal opinions about Russia's problems; and this the ministry could not tolerate, for it preferred to keep out dangerous ideas entirely rather than to refute them in the classroom. Nothing illustrates this formalistic and defensive attitude toward education better than Tolstoi's excessive concern with linguistic and arithmetic exercises and his neglect of the propaganda possibilities of the gymnasium curriculum.

According to ministry programs, indoctrination formed an essential aspect of only the religion and history courses, both minor subjects. The religion instructor should infuse students with the Christian spirit; the historian should develop patriotism and demonstrate the ultimate triumph of noble causes in the world. Even here Tolstoi hedged. Aware that the study of history could as easily discredit as sanctify the regime, he meticulously defined its scope. The 1872 circular gave the history course, despite its few lesson hours, more space than any other subject; its sample syllabus alone filled seventeen double-columned pages. It is obvious that Tolstoi feared history's political relevance more than he rejoiced in its propaganda value. For example, the history teacher was the only one whom the minister expressly warned against introducing concepts that might harm his pupil's moral development.

In addition, the teaching of contemporary events lost its former importance. Previously, the gymnasium's oldest students — those most interested in and capable of understanding their country's situation — studied the existing structure of the Russian government. They now had to turn to the remote past, to Greece and Rome, with much of their energy devoted to lengthy assignments from classical authors. The younger pupils took the modern history course, but it stopped rather early. The ministry listed the reigns of Louis XIV and Alexander I as the latest topics deserving special consideration in European and Russian history respectively. It thereby virtually excluded from these courses such impressive evidence of progressive forces at work as the French Revolution, the 1848 uprisings, and Alexander II's "Great Reforms." [3]

Further exemplifying this circumspect, intrinsically negative approach was the overwhelming emphasis on syntax and grammar in language instruction. The study of grammar, in fact, dominated classics courses in all grades. Formal grammar lessons occupied the lower classes; the no-less-tedious chore of rendering Russian into Greek or Latin prevailed at the senior levels. Even the summer offered upperclassmen no respite from their onerous translation tasks. Not only did they have assignments in the classics, they also had to paraphrase passages from Greek and Latin as part of their Russian language exercises. To be sure, there were sessions on classical literature, but they too stressed problems of translation and philology. Grammar held a similarly "prominent position" in the first four years of the Russian course. Although the senior classes were devoted to literary analysis, they met just twice a week and had limited aims. They were not to stimulate critical thinking, for this might produce an "absurd and harmful sense of self-importance *(samomnenie)*." Nor were they to demand originality in written lessons; clarity and grammatical perfection were sufficient. Modern language instructors also focused on the linguistic rather than the literary aspects of their subjects. If their students could read and write adequately in a foreign tongue, the course was a success.[4]

Since language classes filled 62 percent of the weekly lesson hours, a student, at least on paper, faced a dreary eight years. He would get little relief over the next two decades. Although the government did introduce a few minor modifications in response to the creation of a separate grade 8 in 1875, it would not fundamentally reform the curriculum until 1890 when it reduced the time spent on the classics and de-emphasized grammar lessons.[5]

In their format and general instructions the realschule academic plans of 12 May 1873 resembled those for the gymnasium. There were the same exhaustive descriptions of courses and teaching methods, the same admonitions against any deviation from the outlines, the same fixation on grammar in the realschule's language classes. However, in content these programs, as compiled by experts from the ministry, its Petersburg schools, and several technical institutes, often differed markedly from their gymnasium counterparts even for subjects offered by both schools. While the religion and geography courses were identical, many others included topics not given at the gymnasium. Chemistry classes examined the chemist's role in industry; French and German lessons covered technical terminology; history courses accented economic developments like the rise of the great Hansa and Italian trading cities; and drawing, an optional gymnasium subject, became so vital to the realschule program that Tolstoi insisted upon faithful observance of its official syllabus.[6] These curriculum adjustments again underscored the realschule's "*practical* direction."

The ministry's teaching programs seemed quite in keeping with the autocracy's desire for internal stability. Without downgrading the quality of education offered, Tolstoi sought to eliminate the two major factors he felt contributed most to student disaffection: the use of the classroom as a forum for radical doctrines and the flocking of students to institutions unsuited to their academic or social background. The stress on the mechanical aspects of language study and mathematics at the expense of more relevant and inspiring work in literary criticism and historical analysis would in theory lessen the possibility of the gymnasium course either stimulating political awareness or attracting those uninterested in or unfit for higher education. The latter group, it was hoped, would find the simpler, utilitarian realschule to its liking. It was a logical scheme but not a perfect one, for it had three serious disadvantages. It gave the students few ideological weapons to combat subversive ideas; it discouraged initiative and creativity; and it risked antagonizing the pupils by subjecting them to an excessively tedious curriculum.

To ensure the fulfillment of its academic plans, the ministry carefully regulated the means of evaluating pupils. While permitting every gymnasium to compile its own entrance and promotion tests, the December 1872 rules on examinations introduced rigid standards and reinforced the one-sidedness of the gymnasium course. On the five-point grading scale made compulsory throughout Russia, pupils needed for promotion an overall average of $2\frac{1}{2}$ in grades 1 and 2, of $2\frac{3}{4}$ in grades 3 and 4, of 3 in the rest. Students poor in languages and mathematics, the gymnasium's central disciplines, would never achieve these marks; for Tolstoi limited the subjects in most promotion examinations to only these two fields. Even in the two comprehensive written and oral tests, which covered the entire curricula of grades 1 to 4 and 5 to 6, respectively, he urged teachers to weight the classics and mathematics sections most heavily.[7]

Far more rigorous was the ministry's control over the graduation examination (*ispytanie zrelosti*, a literal translation of the German *Maturitätsprüfung* after which it was patterned). Leaving nothing to local initiative, Tolstoi had the curator prepare in secret a single test for his entire district. Even the examination's author, the curator, enjoyed little independence since the ministry delineated precisely the examination's format, scope, marking procedures, and standards. The test would be a grueling experience, very similar to its German equivalent. All students wrote a five-hour essay on a set theme, a five-hour paper in mathematics, and two three-hour ones on sight translations from and into Latin and Greek.[8] The last were the crucial papers, for failure here would prevent the candidate from finishing the examination.

If successful in the written section, a student could proceed to his orals. According to the ministerial circular, this examination should probe the student's ability to reason — to grasp the essentials of his subject, not his capacity to memorize — and therefore should focus on problem-solving in mathematics, sight translations from the classics, and general developments in Greek, Roman, and Russian history. Not satisfied with supplying instructors with the questions to ask, the ministry told them also how to grade. This was a complex process, as Tolstoi sought to establish impartial and uniform standards. He combated favoritism by weakening the individual teacher's influence over his pupils' final grades. The senior person in the discipline corrected the essays within his field; the entire examination commission, composed of the director, the inspector, the senior instructor, and two other teachers in the subject, actually marked the papers and conducted the oral; then the pedagogical council calculated the student's standing from his test performance and previous record. To prevent wide variations in standards from school to school, the ministry sent its own representatives to oversee the examinations and ordered them to report any faults directly to the curator.[9]

The gymnasium finals, Tolstoi argued, needed such supervision and guidance because they formed "the cornerstone of his academic reforms." Their strict implementation could guarantee the proper course of both secondary and university education. Based as they were on the official lesson plans, these tests would deter faculty from ignoring the ministry's instruction, especially its call for rigorous translation and grammar exercises, since these dominated the examination. Moreover, in its role as the university entrance examination for virtually all secondary school students, the gymnasium final benefited that institution by assuring it a well-screened student body.[10] It thus gave the state a means of controlling the type of preparatory training university students, the government functionaries of tomorrow, would receive.

The realschule again followed the gymnasium's lead. Its examinations were compiled and administered just like those at the classical school. Even the latter's emphasis on linguistic ability filtered in, as papers in modern languages featured prominently in the written tests. Of the changes necessitated by the realschule's different curriculum, the most significant were the rules governing entrance to the supplementary class; for they constituted a further attempt by the ministry to curtail the size of the realschule's nonvocational program. While the supplementary class's practical sectors, like the gymnasium's senior grades, required a 3 average for admittance, its general division, which alone readied students for advanced training, demanded a $3\frac{1}{2}$ average.[11] This uniquely high grade requirement, Tolstoi hoped, would discourage students from using the realschule instead of the preferred gymnasium as a pathway to the technical schools or would at the very least protect these institutions from mediocre realschule graduates.

Having specified the student's academic responsibilities, the ministry then considered his moral ones. Despite its general neglect of its schools' propaganda potential, the ministry did feel that they should mold the personality as well as train the mind. The 1871 statute did not explain how this would be done; it merely established class preceptorships and entrusted the pedagogical council with drafting a student penal code subject to ministerial confirmation. However, with the intensification of revolutionary activity and the proliferation of clandestine organizations that preceded the flocking "to the people" of young radicals in the spring and summer of 1874, the ministry could no longer maintain a passive approach toward character development. Hence a commission of all the inspectors from Petersburg's gymnasiums and progymnasiums produced under Georgievsky's guidance a lengthy document on student behavior which Tolstoi introduced at the gymnasiums on 27 April 1874 and extended to the realschulen five months later.[12]

Urging pupils to improve themselves "for the glory of your

Creator, for the comfort of your parents, for the benefit of your church and fatherland," this legislation prescribed their obligations to religion, schoolwork, faculty, and classmates. All Orthodox students must attend church faithfully and go to confession during Passion Week, but those of other creeds could worship as they pleased. Besides the usual statements on punctuality, attentiveness, obedience, and conscientiousness, the ministry also required pupils "to sit erect" throughout each lesson, to take down assignments in special notebooks, and to show their parents these notebooks daily. In dealing with his peers, the student should not fight, quarrel, or use improper language, but rather be "good-natured," assist his less studious friends, and oppose actions that might mar his school's reputation. Here was the Russian version of the Boy Scout Code. A student must be devout before his God, diligent for his teachers, respectful to his parents, and honorable and helpful among his classmates.

Although such platitudes could be found in almost any set of school regulations, other provisions of the 1874 rules specifically reflected Russia's tense political climate. Dismayed by the extent of student participation in subversive actions, Tolstoi saw every student as a potential revolutionary and treated him as such. He sought to limit the opportunities students would have to proselytize one another and to reduce their contacts with unreliable elements outside the school: the former by prohibiting students from forming societies and from bringing any books but texts into the buildings; the latter by declaring public places like clubs, coffee shops, taverns, billiard parlors, and, in many instances, theaters off limits and by proposing a rigid work schedule which would give pupils no time for frivolous pastimes during weekday nights.

While subjecting all students to these excessive restrictions, the ministry worried most about the out-of-town pupils who did not live at the pensions. Lacking any guidance from parents or relatives, these young men might easily yield to the temptations that abounded in the city. To keep this from happening, Tolstoi advocated housing these noncommuters in officially approved apartments *(uchenicheskie kvartiry)*, patterned after the pensions, cleansed of nonstudent occupants, and preferably managed by ministry personnel. Assigned in groups of fifteen to special tutors *(vospita-teli)*, the residents of these apartments faced compulsory prayers, a strict daily regimen, evening curfews, tight controls over their movements, and student monitors under explicit orders to keep out harmful influences. In part the need to protect youthful innocence from the corrupting forces of an alien city justified stern measures, but Tolstoi had another less lofty motive, the wish to insulate the young from all unsanctioned ideas. He would even make the possession of works not approved by school authorities a serious offense. With the establishment of these supervised apartments and of numerous restraints on a student's extracurricular interests, Tolstoi had done as much as possible to introduce the oppressive atmosphere of the boarding school at his ministry's regular secondary institutions.

An enlarged inspectorate and the threat of reprisals for rule infractions would ensure enforcement of this student code. The 1871 statute had increased the gymnasium's surveillance crew fourfold from the two tutors of the Golovnin era to six class preceptors and two assistant preceptors. These men now had in the punishments recommended by the ministry in April 1874 the weapons needed to back up their demands. The penalties ranged from reprimands delivered by the teacher to expulsion without right of transfer administered by the curator at the pedagogical council's request. The harsher the sentence, the higher the authority that pronounced it. Since these disciplinary actions were claimed to be essentially corrective, they must be just, fit the crime, and allow for such extenuating circumstances as the student's age, motivation, and previous behavior. Thus the code was rather benign in tone except for one medieval article which condoned incarceration for up to eight hours with black bread and water as the only rations.[13] Undoubtedly the strongest deterrent against bad behavior was the importance of deportment grades. A poor conduct record could hurt a student's chances for higher education and hence jeopardize his future. In fact, the edict on gymnasium final examinations insisted that pupils be judged first on "their moral maturity" and then on their intellectual achievements.[14]

The creation of so stringent a system entailed serious risk. By infringing on how students spent their leisure and by treating them like suspected criminals requiring police surveillance, the ministry might easily antagonize them, thereby undermining whatever good the school might have done.[15] The ministry recognized this danger, for its circular accompanying the April regulations urged the use of moral persuasion over repressive measures in the complex process of student upbringing. Stressing the educational influence of the teacher's personal example, the decree described the ideal pedagogue as the stern but not despotic taskmaster, who developed in his students orderly and conscientious work habits. The satisfaction his pupils would gain from fulfilling his precise and challenging assignments combined with the lessons they would learn from his own exact sense of responsibility would instill in them, the ministry optimistically concluded, "respect for law, . . . duty, . . . and [their] elders and comrades." School activities and lesson content could also serve the government's political purposes; faculty should direct morning prayers, classical history discussions, holiday celebrations in class, and indeed all subject matter to the creation of religious and patriotic sentiments.[16]

Thus the ministry did try to lessen the necessity for restrictive legislation by instituting a more active program of indoctrination, but its instructions were too vague and simplistic and the gymnasium's curriculum too linguistically oriented to guarantee satisfactory results. Policing the student body would remain Tolstoi's prime defense against subversion. Like a cautious doctor in the midst of what he believed to be an epidemic, Tolstoi preferred to rely on the tried method of quarantine instead of undertaking the search for an elusive vaccine. While he might in this way temporarily seal off the plague, he would never prevent its outbreak.

Teacher Preparation and the Implementation of the New Statutes

With the publication of these student regulations the ministry had completed the major legislative additions to its secondary school statutes. It had exhaustively described what its teachers must do, but such plans would be worthless unless meticulously carried out. For Tolstoi the slightest deviation would endanger his entire scheme. He viewed his department, like the monarchy in general, as a monolithic structure whose strength depended on its maintaining the firmest possible facade before society. The chinks caused by concessions or irregularities would shake the people's faith in the durability of the building; and without this confidence the government would labor in vain. Consequently, the ministry must resolutely implement every aspect of its revised laws. In this it had the emperor's backing. On 25 December 1873 he publicly reaffirmed his full support of the controversial gymnasium regulations, ordering "all other departments to render you [Tolstoi] unconditional assistance" in their execution.[17] The Russian autocracy had not yet learned the lesson of the reed and the oak: that a flexible program could better withstand buffetings than a rigid one.

Encouraging though it was, the imperial rescript could not provide the essential precondition for the reform's success — a competent, dedicated, loyal teaching force. If they did not have enough instructors, how could the schools perform their elaborate tasks? This question would plague Tolstoi throughout his ministry, for Russia, like most underdeveloped countries, would find staffing its expanding school network extremely difficult. The limited size of the educated class compared with the demand for highly trained personnel meant few capable candidates for the unremunerative and hardly prestigious post of gymnasium teacher. In 1870, for example, when schools had finally received the funds to hire the additional personnel called for in the 1864 statute, the number of vacancies left in all districts but Eastern Siberia reached 127, an average of over one per school. More distressing yet for the ministry, the gymnasium's basic subjects, the classics, lacked the most teachers: over $33\frac{1}{3}$ percent of the vacancies in 1870 were in Greek and Latin; almost 40 percent in 1872. In fact, seven gymnasiums that year still offered no Greek.[18] Obviously, the paucity of classicists could negate the advantages to be gained from a classical education.

The problem of numbers was not the only one. Since the ministry had never obtained the large, efficient district inspectorate necessary to check on its teachers' activity, it would have to rely on their conscientiousness for the accurate fulfillment of its plans. The system of teacher preparation the ministry adopted should therefore not merely turn out sufficient instructors, it should also ensure their devotion to the ministry's aims.

Less concerned than Tolstoi with producing submissive faculty, Golovnin had introduced a simple means of teacher training. In his scheme prospective instructors would have to take education courses in addition to their normal university degree program and then practice-teach at a gymnasium for a year before they could get a regular appointment. As a result, Russia's secondary schools would not only get university-trained faculty but would enjoy the benefits of a large number of apprentice instructors. Golovnin never implemented these proposals, for he left the ministry just one month after obtaining 300 scholarships at 360 rubles apiece to support those who would enter the plan outlined above.[19]

Despite its obvious advantages, Tolstoi quickly repudiated his predecessor's solution because in his view the university could not adequately train teachers or guarantee an emphasis on those subjects where the faculty shortage was the severest. Later contemporary accounts would bear out his charges. E. V. Beliavsky, an alumnus of the Moscow program, condemned the general quality of instruction; V. Smorodinov from Kiev complained: "The university regardless . . . of courses in pedagogy and didactics . . . did not offer any practical preparation for pedagogical activity."[20]

Disregarding in this instance both the German example and Katkov's advice, Tolstoi argued that special normal schools, not university seminars, alone could provide the proper concentration on education matters and the unified direction necessary for the training of gymnasium teachers. Accordingly, on 27 June 1867 he supplanted the pedagogical courses at the university by a historical-philological institute, loosely patterned after France's famous *Ecole normale supérieure*. Geared for graduates of the classical gymnasium or its equivalent, this institute's four-year curriculum would restrict itself to turning out history, classics, and Russian literature instructors since, Tolstoi asserted, these were the teachers Russia urgently needed.[21]

The institute became a vital feature of Tolstoi's system. It would fill in a shorter time and in a more professional manner than the universities the most pressing vacancies at the gymnasiums, and also it would furnish him with a means of controlling teacher preparation and hence with some assurance that new faculty would be both skilled and dutiful. Whereas the university's semiautonomous position had allowed little ministerial interference in teacher training, the institute's direct subordination to the minister encouraged his intrusions. He had to approve all decisions on essential matters like examination procedures, practice teaching programs, student obligations, and the rules of order within the faculty assembly. When unable to act himself, the minister could work through the institute director, whom he appointed without consulting the staff and awarded a salary higher than the rector's and equal to the district curator's as an indication of his importance. Together the minister and his agent, the director, would supervise all aspects of the institute's life, especially since the director for the institute's first five years was Tolstoi's friend and adviser on secondary education, I. B. Shteinman. Institute professors may have received the service rights of their university colleagues, but they certainly did not enjoy the same independence of action or predominant role in school administration.[22]

Exploiting its powers to the fullest, the ministry structured the institute to emphasize its vocational character and to protect its charges from subversive elements. The institute's narrow curriculum reflected the school's exclusively utilitarian aim. In their first two years the future teachers studied philosophy, religion, history, French, German, Russian and Slavonic literature, pedagogy, didactics, and especially Greek and Latin; for the classics and literature "formed the basis" of the institute's course. Not until their final two years did students go beyond this general approach, which must have recalled the gymnasium program they had just finished, to specialize in their field of interest. Yet even then they could not devote themselves to scholarly pursuits because they also had to focus on practice teaching in a gymnasium set up at the institute to give its pupils a constant opportunity to observe and apply the principles learned in class. This modest curriculum with its indifference to research, its concern for classroom techniques and, after 1874, its concentration on the classics and Russian in the two senior classes offered the uniform, practical orientation so frequently lacking in the university pedagogical courses, but it obviously could not reach the university's academic standards. Some critics therefore argued that the institute's products were unfit for work in the gymnasium's senior grades.[23] However, the limited nature of the institute's program perfectly suited the minister's goals. He wanted its graduates to know their subject and how to teach it, but not to acquire sufficient expertise to begin questioning the centrally compiled syllabi.

No less vital in Tolstoi's scheme than the institute's limited curriculum were its ambitious attempts at student control. Frightened by the damage a disloyal or corrupt instructor could do his pupils, Tolstoi made teacher candidates the most closely supervised student body in the country. All stipend holders, and these comprised the institute's entire enrollment, had to live at school because dormitories, so the minister contended, provided the best lodgings a poor youth might find in the capital. Although convincing on the surface, Tolstoi's arguments hid deeper political motives. In the light of his own lyceum experiences, he considered the boarding school the most effective means of inculcating desired values and of stopping the penetration of revolutionary propaganda. Its strict regimen, he believed, would accustom students to leading a "proper life" and develop self-discipline.

Consequently, each resident at the institute had to follow a rigid schedule which left little time for frivolity. It would be difficult to escape this regime. Highly qualified preceptors chosen only from those with university arts degrees or gymnasium teaching credentials were there to enforce the institute's program and to set a personal example of the religious, dutiful, patriotic instructor. The institute shielded its students from the dangerous influences so prevalent in the capital in the 1860s by restricting passes to leave the grounds and by prohibiting membership in clandestine organizations. If caught joining a secret society, whether subversive or not, a student faced expulsion, police surveillance, and permanent exclusion from all educational institutions. Tolstoi was taking no chances. Like the administrators at the *Ecole normale supérieure,* he "did not trust his young pedagogues" and demanded "vigilant control over their conduct and academic pursuits." [24]

Of course, one small school with an average class of twenty-five, no matter how perfect its structure, would not wipe out the instructor shortage. The ministry needed a network of these institutions, but unfortunately for Tolstoi they were the most expensive as well as the most desirable form of teacher preparation. Where the pedagogical courses had saved money by using the university's professors and physical plant, the institute required its own staff and facilities. Lacking the funds to create additional philological institutes *ab ovo,* Tolstoi decided on the clever expedient of transforming the crumbling Bezborodko Juridical Lyceum at Nezhin into a second normal school. His devastating account of the lyceum's failings — its transient faculty, dwindling enrollment, and superficial law course — and his convincing description of the greater need for teachers than for lawyers persuaded the State Council to override the defenders of the lyceum's traditional format and on 20 November 1874 to approve the school's reorganization.[25]

The new institute was a replica of the one in St. Petersburg, except that its faculty, since it worked much farther away from the ministry's watchful eye, enjoyed still less autonomy than its Petersburg counterpart. The education department exhaustively set down the duties of institute personnel, transferred the Petersburg school's harsh student code to Nezhin, and unilaterally determined grading procedures, promotion standards, and examination committee membership.[26]

Since an incompetent or frivolous student body could undermine even the most tightly regulated philological institute, Tolstoi sought to assure these schools of qualified applicants committed to teaching. He wanted university admissions standards for the institutes, but this, when combined with the institute's strict conduct rules and the low basic starting salaries and numerous ministerial restrictions that awaited the institute graduate, would make it difficult to attract sufficient candidates. Under such circumstances the ministry wisely concentrated its recruitment campaigns on the poorer gymnasium students, those who would best appreciate government financial assistance and be most likely to accept ill-paying posts.

Linking scholarships with service, the ministry offered a free institute education to all who agreed to teach for six years after graduation. Despite this guarantee on his investment, the plan did not completely satisfy Tolstoi because it drew more from the clerical seminaries than from the gymnasiums, and the seminarians, he complained, were badly trained and often displayed coarse moral traits. To remedy this enrollment imbalance, he urged that gymnasium directors "sell" the institute to capable language students from families who would not scoff at a teaching career. They should appeal to the pupil's conscience by stressing the academic profession's usefulness, to his scholarly interests by praising the caliber of instruction at the institute, to his common sense by noting the good jobs available upon graduation, and to his pocketbook by mentioning the comfortable grants and frequent travel allowances enjoyed by institute residents. In case these inducements should not work, the ministry set up twenty stipends in each of the Nezhin gymnasium's last four classes for those promising to enter the institutes. Exhibiting his characteristic fear of subversive elements, Tolstoi chose the Nezhin school over any in Petersburg since the former was far from the distracting influences of the capital. These recruitment policies, vigorous and sensible though they might have been, did not overcome the indifference of gymnasium graduates toward the institutes. The ministry was compelled to sanction admissions concessions to the less qualified but eager seminarians. Even after they had to take the difficult gymnasium final examination for university entrance, they still had only to pass a simple test in Russian, Greek, and

Latin to attend the institutes. It is not surprising, then, that from 1879 to 1881 the institutes accepted as many seminary as gymnasium applicants.[27]

The inferior preparation of some of their student body notwithstanding, the philological institutes remained one of Tolstoi's best solutions to the problems caused by promoting the spread of education in an autocracy. While not the most stimulating or liberal institutions, the government normal schools did furnish the necessary courses and practical experience for prospective gymnasium teachers. Not only did the two institutes produce approximately forty fully trained classics and Russian teachers a year,[28] they also preserved the latter's political reliability. Their narrow, utilitarian curriculum, boarding school controls, and mild program of indoctrination protected their pupils against dangerous views and thereby helped maintain their loyalty. Indeed, according to a recent Soviet study, no students from the philological institutes participated in the radical movements of the 1870s.[29] The Tolstoi normal school thus reduced both the number of empty staff positions and the possibility of harmful ideas infiltrating the educational system. The ministry had forged a powerful two-edged sword of its own, a sword it would wield most effectively in its battle against the menacing teacher shortages in elementary education.

Although they were the ministry's fundamental answer to the paucity of gymnasium instructors, the two institutes (with the Bezborodko one not graduating its first class until 1878) could not rectify the situation by themselves. Emergency measures were essential, and Tolstoi would have to allow universities to continue training gymnasium faculty by holding seminars on classroom techniques. Willingly accepting this task, the universities by 1869 offered from their regular scholarship funds over 130 stipends for prospective gymnasium instructors.[30] The ministry also opened gymnasium posts to graduates of the clerical academies who could pass a general test on gymnasium subjects and give two satisfactory trial lessons before a gymnasium director and a member of the historical-philological faculty.[31]

As these certification procedures indicate, Tolstoi — to his credit — did not let himself be panicked by the teacher shortage into hiring any available applicants. In fact, he introduced legislation in April 1868 and May 1870 to prevent the appointment of unsuitable faculty. All teaching candidates except those receiving pedagogical training at philological institutes, university seminars, or the like would not obtain accreditation unless they had proved their competence by scoring well in a university-administered written and oral examination in their chosen field and by successfully conducting several classes before the gymnasium director and another faculty member.[32]

Only in his sometimes desperate search for classicists to handle the expanded Greek and Latin courses did Tolstoi ignore his own sensible regulations on teacher certification. The sizable number of vacancies in the classics would force him as late as 1878 to make it easy for European graduates in these subjects to get gymnasium posts even if they had no practical experience.[33] This concession, however, was an exception, for Tolstoi still preferred a more structured and supervised system of obtaining foreign-trained classicists. Golovnin had felt the same way. In 1865 he had set up a program of bringing Slavic instructors in Greek or Latin to St. Petersburg for intensive Russian language study before they began work in the department's schools; but by 1871 this scheme no longer attracted many applicants. Since foreign students would not travel to Russia to complete their training, Tolstoi (on Georgievsky's advice) decided the ministry should go to them. In 1873 he asked Professor Ritschl of Leipzig University to establish a philological seminary there for prospective classics teachers from Russia and other countries. On full scholarship from the imperial treasury, these students spent three years attending university lectures, reviewing Greek, Latin, and pedagogy at the seminary, and learning Russian if it was not their native tongue. For each year in Leipzig they owed two years service to the ministry. The seminary would guarantee the state approximately twenty teachers a year for its annual 17,500-ruble investment. Tolstoi thought the expense justified because no school in Russia could provide so excellent a background in the classics.[34] The seminary had the added, though unpublicized, advantage of keeping a portion of Russia's future teachers away from the volatile atmosphere of the universities during the 1870s.

As a result of both Tolstoi's and Golovnin's policies, foreign classicists became a common feature at the Russian gymnasium. Unfortunately for the students, their unfamiliarity with the language and customs of their pupils would often nullify whatever expertise they might have acquired at the centers of classical learning outside Russia.

Regardless of the ministry's many-sided approach to teacher training, it still would have faced an insurmountable faculty shortage had it not been for the clever provision in the 1871 statute which required all gymnasium administrators to teach. By 1874 these officials were giving 2,302 weekly lessons, work that Tolstoi estimated would have otherwise necessitated 115 additional appointments.[35] To judge from the only available evidence (the ministry's incomplete statistics), the bringing of the director and inspector into the classroom — together with the institutes, Leipzig Seminary, and other programs of teacher preparation — did appreciably reduce the staffing crisis despite the increasing demand for instructors caused by the creation of new schools. The number of gymnasiums and progymnasiums rose from 167 on 1 January 1874 to 206 just four years later, but the number of empty posts actually fell 13 percent from 157 to 137 — a substantial figure, yet far below the average of over one per school recorded in 1870. Particularly gratifying to Tolstoi must have been the 25-percent decline in vacancies in the classics from 68 to 51 during the same period. However, the best indication of the ministry's success occurred in 1881 when, with its two institutes and foreign seminary now fully functioning, it reported that there were not enough positions for all the graduates of the Petersburg philological institute.[36]

It would be no easier to find technical and language experts for the realschule than to acquire classicists for the gymnasium. Nevertheless, the ministry would not expend the same effort on this problem, a further demonstration of the realschule's secondary importance. Once the finance department refused the 44,000 rubles Tolstoi requested for a special normal school at Petersburg

University to train modern language instructors, he limited himself to setting up stipends at Russian and foreign institutions for prospective teachers of mathematics, chemical technology, and commerce who agreed to serve six years in the ministry's schools. This restricted scholarship scheme could only slightly ameliorate conditions at the understaffed realschulen. Tolstoi reported 38 vacancies at 30 realschulen in 1874, 60 vacancies at 67 realschulen in 1878.[37]

According to the ministry's annual reports at least, the teacher shortage did not greatly hinder the implementation of the 1871–1872 legislation. Most gymnasiums immediately adopted the proposals for a preparatory class and an eighth grade. No less quickly did directors and inspectors accept their teaching obligations: only nine in 1872 did not give courses. Sometimes it took the ministry a little longer to achieve success. The universal installation of the full Greek program was impossible at first, but by 1875 only eight schools did not offer the proper amount of Greek instruction. Similarly, the deviations from the central academic plans, which the curators had criticized initially, all but disappeared after 1876.[38] Equally encouraging were the results at the realschulen. By 1877, Tolstoi asserted, the ministry's syllabi prevailed everywhere, and 25 of the 67 realschulen had already established supplementary divisions.[39]

The introduction of a few essential innovations, however, like the uniform penal code and the standardized final examination, proved troublesome and revealed the ineffectiveness of the ministry's control apparatus. In 1875 the curators complained that disciplinary actions varied considerably even from gymnasium to gymnasium. But there was little Tolstoi could do except rebuke the wayward, for he lacked the omnipresent inspection force to discourage instructors from ignoring his decrees.[40] Irregularities also plagued the final examinations. During the first year under the new regulations only one district established a single test for all schools, and few commissions maintained strict grading standards. As late as 1874 important regulations like giving the examination on the same day or the submission of satisfactory papers to the curator's council for review were widely disregarded. Conditions soon improved markedly, so that cases of excessive leniency and procedural infractions were the exception rather than the rule. Yet Tolstoi saw no hope of their complete elimination until his ministry acquired sufficient personnel to police the examinations thoroughly.[41] Regardless of his impressive efforts at centralization, Tolstoi like every other tsarist minister was extremely dependent on the conscientiousness of his local officials.

While the ministry could attribute the temporary misapplication of its student and examination regulations to unintentional errors in interpretation, it had to admit that the faculty purposely obstructed the institution of class preceptorships. Many teachers refused to serve or quickly resigned their posts; thus the number of preceptors actually declined from 675 in 1873 to 660 the next year despite the increase in schools. The ministry offered no reasons for this phenomenon, but one can speculate that the more liberal instructors did not want to play gendarme and the more practical thought it less onerous to earn the 160 rubles paid class preceptors by giving additional lessons. This resistance from the faculty may well explain why the ministry adopted so moderate a tone in its advice to preceptors, even though the decree appeared in August 1877, just when the revolutionary movement had broken out with renewed vigor. Like the locally compiled preceptor instructions already in use, the ministerial circular played down the preceptor's inquisitorial functions and stressed his role as moral tutor, student benefactor, and information officer. In his first guise he should instill feelings of duty, honor, respect for law, and devotion to emperor and fatherland; in the second he should assist the slow or ill, inspect gymnasium sanitary conditions, and protect his charges against the unfair demands of their teachers; in the third he should broadcast examination and discipline regulations, tell students what books from the school library to read, and report to gymnasium authorities and parents on each pupil's attendance, conduct, and intellectual progress.[42] If preceptors followed this advice, and Tolstoi proclaimed in his 1877 report that they did, they would indeed perform a useful service for both students and faculty. His judgment, based on the first few months of the instruction's operation, was premature; Delianov would later condemn many preceptors for not fulfilling their obligations.[43]

These difficulties with the preceptorships notwithstanding, Tolstoi insisted that he had successfully completed his reforms of secondary education by his last years at the ministry. Employing the statistics gathered annually by his curators, the minister could show that with the exception of the preceptorships, which in 1877 still had 131 vacancies,[44] the major provisions of his statutes had gained nearly universal acceptance. Moreover, each year the ministry learned of fewer deviations from its teaching programs, examination rules, and discipline regulations. Even the teacher shortage was abating.

Undoubtedly most pleasing to the minister was the entrenchment of classical studies. Not only did they dominate the curriculum and the examinations, they also indirectly determined the composition of the gymnasium's top managerial staff. Over half the class preceptors (590 of 1,090 in 1877) were classics instructors, a consequence of the ministry's reserving these posts for those giving the most lessons in a particular grade. More important, the ministry usually appointed directors and inspectors from the classicists' ranks too because, it felt, the administrators of a classical gymnasium should know the classics. As a result of these efforts, 103 of 144 directors and 105 of 167 inspectors taught at least one classical language by 1877. So predominant were Greek and Latin instructors in gymnasium administration that the emperor, upon Tolstoi's dismissal, would order a fairer distribution of offices among faculty in other disciplines.[45] The Tolstoi system was thus in full bloom, but what would be its fruits? To answer this question, one must compare the ministry's descriptions of its crop with those of the students and teachers who tasted it.

The Achievements and Failures of the Ministry's Reforms

No aspect of Tolstoi's program was expected to produce greater benefits than its overwhelming classical bias. For ministry spokes-

men a curriculum so organized would best train the young mind:
the memorization of grammar rules, the translation from and into
Greek and Latin would develop the student's powers of retention
and concentration, his "perspicacity, cleverness, and wisdom";
the study of classical literature would stimulate his imagination,
his moral and aesthetic sensibilities.[46] Every facet of the intellect
would benefit.

However, for many Russians from all sectors of society, the
gymnasium course was a physically exhausting, mentally stulti-
fying experience, not the productive adventure in learning the
ministry described. Russian language instructor N. D. Bogatinov,
for example, attacked the gymnasium's "insufferably heavy and
excessive demands"; classical scholar V. I. Modestov claimed the
pupil's long hours of study impaired his health; even the government warned Tolstoi against overburdening the students. So oppressive was the work load that students habitually cheated by
copying the papers of their brighter colleagues. While the academic plans with their emphasis on written assignments and frequent tests left students little free time, the ministry was not alone
to blame since, then as now, teachers often became overzealous
taskmasters.[47]

Unfortunately for the diligent, their classics lessons rarely com-
pensated them for their labors. Few could recall their gymnasium
careers without noting the dry, formalistic approach to the classical languages. I "cruelly suffered from lifeless teaching," wrote
one student; my instructors "treated grammar as if it were the
catechism." Another elaborated: "Day after day for eight years
they forced us to cram Latin and Greek grammar, conjugations,
declensions, exceptions, irregular verbs; but during those eight
years they did not succeed in explaining to us . . . the greatness of
Rome, the beauty of Greek culture." [48]

The prevalence of such complaints demonstrated better than
any curator report the widespread implementation of the ministry's syllabi. Although it is true that any program centered on the
classical languages could easily bore young students, as generations of English schoolboys will attest, and there was much dreary
Latin and Greek instruction in Russia before Tolstoi's legislation,

his course outlines and circulars did seem particularly well-suited to producing the uninspired teaching so frequently mentioned by students at the Tolstoi gymnasium. In addition to stressing the importance of intrinsically dull lessons in grammar and syntax, these decrees discouraged experimental techniques and other forms of teacher initiative. Tolstoi's directives, one instructor argued, had transformed the educator into a tradesman. "The destruction of pedagogy began," a second asserted, in 1871 when "the ministry wished to determine . . . every step taken by the teacher." [49]

Of course, some faculty did disobey the official instructions and thus managed to excite their pupils: take, for instance, P. N. Miliukov's classics teacher whose discussions of Greek moral philosophy left "far behind the police barriers of . . . Count Dmitry Andreevich [Tolstoi]" or the future Marxist V. A. Posse's religion instructor who defied the approved syllabus in his efforts to reconcile science and religion.[50] But both ministerial sources and student memoirs in an unprecedented show of unanimity agree that such teachers were rare; most followed the dictates of St. Petersburg.

There is no facile explanation for this wholesale adoption of the ministry's curriculum. Some may have feared the censure they would incur if their unorthodox approaches were discovered, but the handful of overworked inspectors per district posed no serious threat to the careful, if insubordinate, instructor. More likely, many teachers — especially the lazy, incompetent, or insecure — used the prescribed conspectuses because these programs freed them from the laborious task of compiling their own and then of justifying before the pedagogical council the revisions they had made.

Non-Russian classicists, one functionary pointed out, adhered most closely to Tolstoi's instructions. As foreigners, they often lacked the self-assurance and the necessary fluency in Russian to go beyond philological questions to theoretical discussions of classical literature. Contemporary reports supported this thesis. Miliukov learned Latin from a German who barely knew Russian. Even in far-off Orenburg the classics instructors were German or

Czech "as lifeless and alien as the languages they taught," for Tolstoi's and Golovnin's recruitment campaigns abroad had made these foreigners a prominent feature of Russia's gymnasiums everywhere. As Beliavsky ironically commented, the appointment of a Galician Greek teacher and a Czech Latin teacher had provided his school with the ideal faculty.[51]

This combination of narrowly conceived course outlines and competently trained, but frequently ungifted, unadventurous, or overly constrained teachers was deadly. It would often produce that oppressive intellectual atmosphere which outraged the gymnasium student body and the public at large and helped generate an intense hostility toward the minister. For one student, in fact, the school had become an institution of pure evil. It "just sought to take away all happiness, . . . to quell every passion, to tear out by the roots all shoots of independence, or individuality, to annihilate all interest in knowledge." While less dramatic in their indictment of the gymnasium, Tolstoi's opponents generally echoed this description and considered the grammar-oriented classics lessons most at fault. Such opinions reflected no particular political persuasion. The radical populists and the liberal backers of *Vestnik Evropy* could all agree with the aging, conservative nationalist M. P. Pogodin when he wrote in 1875:

> Our system . . . fails to satisfy innate curiosity, provokes no questions, . . . [encourages] the most intolerable pedagogical methods, . . . [and therefore] must inevitably *blunt* the mental capabilities of the majority, must shrivel the heart, discourage action, and produce a general loathing for study.[52]

Before we Americans self-righteously join Tolstoi's critics in condemning his policies, we should at least be aware that Pogodin's charges read like those leveled by progressive educators against our own school system[53] with all its local autonomy, academic freedom, and advanced teaching methods. The parallel of course is not a perfect one, but it is sobering.

These complaints did not cause the minister to doubt his policies. Although one of his chief defenders, the Kazan curator Shestakov, insisted that Tolstoi worried over the classical system's adverse effects, especially after Modestov's harsh attack appeared in *Golos* during 1879, Tolstoi certainly did not show his concern publicly. He never modified his programs, and Modestov lost his post at the synod's St. Petersburg Spiritual Academy — not the usual reward for one who has unsealed a minister's eyes.[54]

Indeed, from Tolstoi's point of view the reports of student unhappiness were not necessarily disquieting. After all, the ministry wanted its gymnasiums to develop mental discipline, not to cater to the adolescent wishes of the student body, and the training of the intellect (like that of the athlete's body) was not always a joyous experience. Had not the great Pestalozzi once said that "all learning is accompanied by pain." For educators like Tolstoi both then and today, school should be hard work, because unoccupied pupils can easily get into trouble. Too much leisure was particularly dangerous in Tolstoi's Russia, where the opportunities for mischief included participation in revolutionary activity. By exercising the mind to near-exhaustion, the instructor would not only increase the student's intellectual powers but leave him little mental energy for extracurricular pursuits.

While such arguments, despite their cold-blooded mechanistic approach to the student, do contain some truth and have motivated many teachers, they would not convince Tolstoi's critics that the 1871 statute had, in the ministry's words, astonished its foes by its outstanding successes.[55] To substantiate his achievements, Tolstoi relied not on controversial theories of education but on allegedly impartial statistics. For example, he declared, "the ever-expanding financial assistance" given his secondary schools by society demonstrated their popularity. Between 1871 and 1881 zemstvo grants to these schools rose threefold, city grants eightfold. Although the government remained the major financier of secondary education, public organizations by 1877 supplied an impressive 940,000 rubles annually. They helped finance 51 percent of the gymnasiums and 83 percent of the realschulen founded during Tolstoi's initial decade in office.[56]

The Russian public had certainly not repudiated the Tolstoi system by closing its pocketbooks, yet the ministry's case does demand qualification. First, many private contributions went to the realschulen and not the gymnasiums and thus hardly prove society's confidence in classical education. As a result of Tolstoi's refusal to establish realschulen with ministerial funds alone, local sources in 1877 covered almost 30 percent of the realschule budget but only 11 percent of the gymnasium's! [57] Second, increased popular support of schools might indicate more a growing awareness of the importance of education than approval of specific institutions. If Russians wanted the benefits of education for their sons, they had little alternative but to aid the ministry's institutions. An imperfectly organized school was better than no school at all.

The amazing results at the gymnasium final examinations formed a less ambiguous part of the Tolstoi brief. Surprisingly enough, given the hostile reaction to the classics courses, the papers in Greek and Latin claimed no more victims than those in other subjects. Of the gymnasium graduates writing finals in 1877, 4.3 percent fell short in mathematics, 3.7 percent in Russian, 3.9 percent in Latin, and 2.9 percent in Greek. The differentiation had grown even smaller by 1880: 1.9, 1.8, 1.9, and 2.1 percent respectively. So well in fact did gymnasium students do in their exams that from 1876 to 1880 over 90 percent of those completing the course earned their school-leaving certificates, with a high of 96.5 percent in 1880.[58]

These percentages far surpass those recorded by the comparatively easier realschule or by the less-criticized Golovnin gymnasium. Between 1879 and 1881 only about 81 percent of realschule seniors wrote acceptable final tests. The incomplete data from the prereform period show that 50 to 75 percent of the 1866 and 1867 gymnasium graduating classes obtained their diplomas and that under Golovnin in 1864 just about 50 percent passed their finals.[59] The unprecedentedly low failure rate at the Tolstoi gymnasium was all the more striking since the professors present at the examinations reported that the commissions maintained high standards and often were overly severe.[60] The gymnasium program might have been dull, but at least it did provide its students with sufficient training to handle a series of exhaustive tests on their course of study. Neither its predecessors nor its competitors had enjoyed a comparable success.

Since the gymnasium remained Russia's major university preparatory school, the high proportion of its graduates continuing their education further justified the ministry's policies. According to official statistics, 1,133 of 1,310 certificate holders (or 86 percent) in 1876 planned to enter the university; by 1880 the number had risen to 2,145, a very impressive 94.5 percent. The 43 percent growth in university enrollment from 1877–78 to 1881 substantiates the above estimates.[61] Virtually doubling the quantity of university-bound graduates in only five years, the gymnasium certainly appeared to be doing its job.

Once again contemporary accounts challenged the ministry's optimistic conclusions. Not only did the state examinations violently disrupt a student's life, they did not always weed out the incompetent. So vital were these tests that the dread of failure caused many seniors to neglect their regular assignments and left a few severely traumatized. While probably apocryphal, the story of the pupil who, despite his father's sudden death, decided to finish his exams because the next set might be too difficult does indicate the psychological disturbances the gymnasium finals could produce.[62]

Strenuous though they were, these tests did not necessarily guarantee professors brighter classes. Instructors, motivated by compassion or by the fear that poor results would reflect on their teaching, trained their students specifically for the finals and, if unsupervised, gave easy orals. Rather than depend on the faculty's tentative assistance, some students devised elaborate schemes for acquiring advance copies of the examination. At Odessa, I. V. Gessen noted, pupils paid 10,000 rubles annually to a member of the curator's chancellery for the test questions. In Poltava, G. B. Sliozberg remembered, they bribed a post office employee to show them the examination when it arrived from the capital. The subterfuge worked so well that those who were not gymnasium graduates and hence were free to choose their place of testing flocked to Poltava for their finals.[63]

This widespread use of illegal means to avoid failure should not

startle anyone, for the excessive reliance on a particular examination like the gymnasium final to determine a person's future education and career encourages a dishonest attitude toward the entire process of testing. If the reader doubts this, let him recall the
careful preparation of American students for College Board Examinations, the cheating scandals during the mid-1960s at the
French baccalaureate exams in Marseilles, and the case reported
in the *New York Times* of 4 January 1970 of two Polish college
teachers smuggling answers to students writing an admissions test,
at a cost to the latter's parents of $1,440.

Even had all gymnasium graduates legitimately earned their
diplomas, Tolstoi's critics would not have been satisfied. For them
the extraordinary success rate at the finals did not compensate for
the large numbers of students who stayed back or never completed their course. Promotion at the ministry's schools did not
come easily: in one of Bogatinov's first-year classes at a Kiev gymnasium, twenty-six of forty pupils repeated the year; Beliavsky estimated that most Tver students took thirteen years to finish the
ten-year program (including the preparatory class). These were
not isolated complaints. Every year from 1874 to 1881 only about
two-thirds of each class advanced a grade. The average age of
gymnasium graduates, moreover, was high and rising. Students
normally entered grade 1 between ages ten and eleven and therefore should have finished, if not kept back, at the latest at age
nineteen. In 1876, however, 47 percent of those passing the final
examinations were twenty or over; in 1880 54 percent were.
Difficult promotion requirements thus prolonged the already
lengthy gymnasium course, making it still less attractive to families who could not afford the luxury of sending potential wage-
earners to school. Well aware of this result, Tolstoi nonetheless
warned against any lowering of standards, both because he
thought the gymnasium best suited to the needs of the upper
classes and because he rejoiced over the preponderance of mature
graduates.[64] Linking sobriety with age, the minister believed that
the older the student, the better able he would be to handle the
relatively free atmosphere of the university and the more likely he

would be to fulfill his obligations and resist distracting or dangerous influences.

The minister could not discover similar benefits in the fact that
few students lasted the full gymnasium course. Using ministry statistics, historians have substantiated contemporary reports of a
massive dropping out of school. If no one left early, if enrollment
remained stable, and if everyone graduated, the proportion of degree recipients to the total student body would have been 10 to
12½ percent; but in 1875 the percentage was a mere 2.3 percent.
While enrollment increases would account for a slight decrease in
the proportion of graduates to the entire student body, only a high
dropout rate could explain the 2.3-percent figure. As N. Antonov
calculated, 75 percent of all students from 1872 to 1889 did not
finish their gymnasium education.[65]

Most of Tolstoi's opponents blamed the demanding but boring
classical curriculum for this attrition and predicted disastrous
political consequences. Not content with bewailing the wasted resources embodied in the dropouts, they also wondered how backward Russia could reabsorb these failures into society. Unsuccessful gymnasium students, a university professor declared, "were
thrown right into the streets and became a contingent of dissatisfied, potential revolutionaries, the cannon fodder of anarchy." [66]

Although overly facile, V. Lebedev's remarks had their point.
Failure to complete his course could indeed threaten a student's
future. Having been educated for little else but further study
which would lead to a respectable career in the bureaucracy or in
one of the various professions, the dropout suddenly found himself
on his own without the degree necessary for his intended occupation and without the technical training necessary to take advantage of the limited opportunities available in Russia's underdeveloped trade and industry. For those who had a profitable family
business or estate to fall back on, expulsion was no tragedy; but it
was for those who had counted on their education to gain them a
secure position in Russia's relatively closed society. A few would
commit suicide; others, deprived by the system of the chance to
enter it, might eagerly follow the men who attacked the status

quo. Recognizing this possibility, the government in 1880 sought detailed information on dropouts and failures, particularly in the classics.[67]

Telling though these arguments might seem, they misrepresented the situation. In the first place, the ministry's critics made it appear that Tolstoi's classical program had produced a uniquely high dropout rate when in fact under Tolstoi both the amount and the proportion of dropouts declined, and tiny graduating classes and sizable attrition rates were common at that time to all secondary institutions in Russia and abroad. Despite the growth in enrollment from 41,714 to 65,671, the number of those not finishing the gymnasium tumbled from 10,788 to 8,136 between 1873 and 1881. This impressive fall in dropouts meant that by Tolstoi's last years his gymnasiums surpassed the Golovnin schools and the realschulen in the retention of students until graduation and almost reached Western European standards. During the school year 1877–78, of 53,072 gymnasium students 3,861 or 17 percent did not complete their course and 1,305 or 2.5 percent received their diplomas, while in 1864–65, 5,405 of 26,789 students or 20 percent had left early and 491 or 1.8 percent had graduated with the right to attend the university. Even the shorter, less rigorous realschule had a greater percentage of dropouts than the gymnasium: 19.7 percent to the gymnasium's 15.1 percent in 1879; 15 percent to 12.4 percent in 1881. Indeed, the gymnasium's results compared favorably with those achieved by its illustrious Prussian model which in 1877–78, according to the ministry, lost 15.3 percent and graduated 2.7 percent.[68]

In the second place, Tolstoi's enemies gave the impression that all who departed from a specific gymnasium were dropouts driven "into the streets" to thrive on revolutionary propaganda when in fact the majority of them either continued their education elsewhere or obtained respectable jobs. In 1875, 27.6 percent entered another gymnasium, 10.5 percent the realschule, 14.4 percent schools of different departments, and 14.7 percent found posts in government service or private industry. The 1877 figures reveal generally the same distribution: 47.9 percent to other schools and 13.8 percent to regular employment. Moreover, as Alston points

out, the lower classes because of the "shortage of more suitable facilities" often relied on the gymnasium to give their sons three to
four years of schooling and then withdrew them, thereby arti-
ficially sending up the dropout rate.[69]

In short, then, the dropout problem — given Russia's volatile
political climate and the inability of its economy to satisfy the career needs of ambitious but untrained gymnasium failures — was,
of course, dangerous because it did expand the ranks of the alienated; but the anti-Tolstoi forces had overdramatized conditions
and had falsely accused the minister of stimulating a crisis which
was actually abating during his term of office.

The one accomplishment that Tolstoi's detractors could not
question was the rapid spread of secondary education throughout
Russia. At his accession there were too few schools for all qualified
applicants. In 1867–68, for example, the gymnasiums had to turn
away about 700 good candidates. Tolstoi reacted promptly. He
requested 202,305 rubles in 1868 for twenty-three classical progymnasiums and 222,900 rubles in 1869 for fifteen realgymnasiums, but the Ministry of Finance twice denied him the funds.
Tolstoi, preoccupied with the impending gymnasium reforms and
growing ever more hostile to the realgymnasiums, did not pursue
the matter with his usual vigor.[70]

However, once he had given secondary education the direction
he wanted, he launched a triumphant campaign for more schools.
Where just before the 1871 reforms the ministry had 111 classical
gymnasiums, 22 classical progymnasiums, 12 realgymnasiums,
and 1 real progymnasium for a total of 146, by 1877–78 it could
report 129 gymnasiums, 77 progymnasiums, and 67 realschulen
for a total of 273. In seven years the ministry had nearly doubled
its schools and had even raised the percentage of nonclassical
schools in its system from 10 percent to the 25 percent recommended by Golovnin. Students flocked to the new institutions. In
contrast to the gradual 31.6-percent increase from 1857 to 1866,
enrollment shot up almost 100 percent from 35,356 to 65,765 during a similar ten-year period under Tolstoi, 1 January 1869 to 1
January 1878. By 1877–78 Russia had two and a half times the
secondary school students it had on the eve of Tolstoi's appoint-

ment.[71] The student body was growing much faster than the
population at large. The former had more than doubled its size in
thirteen years; the latter would take fifty years — from 1863 to
1913 — to accomplish this.

Another striking feature of the Tolstoi schools revealed by enrollment statistics but often neglected by the minister's critics was
the growing democratization of the student population. Table 1
shows that every group except the gentry and bureaucracy increased its share of secondary school places during the Tolstoi
ministry.

Table 1. Social origin of students at ministry schools.
Figures are given in percentages.

School year	Gentry and bureaucracy	Clergy	City residents	Villagers
Gymnasiums and Progymnasiums				
1864–65	69.7	3.6	20.7	3.9
1868–69	66.5	3.8	23.2	4.6
1872–73	57.9	5.7	28.6	6.3
1874–75	52.5	5.8	33.0	7.0
1877–78	50.2	5.4	35.2	8.9
1881–82	47.5	5.2	37.2	8.0
1894	56.4	3.4	31.6	6.0
Realschulen				
1877–78	44.7	2.7	38.7	11.0
1881–82	41.2	2.5	40.4	11.8
1894	37.4	0.8	43.8	11.5

SOURCE: Compiled from statistics contained in *Obzor 1862–64*, prilozhenie,
p. 275; *Obzor 1881–94*, pp. 258, 299; "Prilozhenie MNP 1868," *Zhurnal*,
CXLVII, otdel I, 155; "Prilozhenie MNP 1872," *Zhurnal*, CLXXV, otdel I,
39; "Prilozhenie MNP 1874," *Zhurnal*, CLXXXVIII (November 1876),
otdel I, 12; "Prilozhenie MNP 1877," *Zhurnal*, CCVI, otdel I, 92, 108; and
"Obzor 1879–81," *Zhurnal*, CCLIV, otdel I, 55–56, 81.

Most impressive was the middle classes' challenge to gentry
predominance at the gymnasium. Between 1864 and 1877 the
number of gentry there rose by a slim 14 percent from 18,660 to
21,290, whereas the middle-class student body nearly tripled,

going from 5,544 to 15,934, and accounted for much of the expansion in secondary school enrollment. Not until the 1880s when the government limited the admission of particular categories of pupils by setting quotas on Jews, by closing the easy-to-enter preparatory classes, and especially by issuing the famous "cook's circular" which specifically instructed curators to keep the lower classes out of the gymnasiums, did this trend reverse itself.[72]

Admittedly, Tolstoi did not intend his schools to serve as leveling agents, nor should one expect this from a conservative Russian bureaucrat at a time when elitist ideas about education prevailed in the more liberal nations of Europe and America. The English, so one historian has argued, did not systematically "provide a secondary education for the truly poor boy of working-class origin" before the twentieth century. In the United States, Richard Hofstadter noted, "the class system, . . . as in Europe was a primary determinant of the schooling children would get after the age of about thirteen or fourteen." [73] Indeed, an American businessman writing in 1885 sounded just like a member of Nicholas I's court. "Too much education of a certain sort . . . to a person of humble antecedents, is utterly demoralizing in nine cases out of ten, and is productive of an army of mean spirited 'gentlemen' who are above what is called a 'trade'." [74]

Tolstoi shared this general point of view. He too wanted to preserve the aristocracy's traditional supremacy in schooling and to prevent education from encouraging rapid social mobility. Hence he had established two differently oriented secondary schools in an effort to draw certain groups away from an education unsuited to their social background. Ideally, the gymnasium's prerogatives would attract the privileged classes while its lengthy, abstract course would push the lower orders into the shorter, more practical realschule.

As Table 1 indicates, Tolstoi's plan had failed. The urban classes poured into the gymnasiums. In fact, by 1877 three and a half times more townspeople attended the gymnasium than the realschule. That same year the gentry's majority at the gymnasium was threatened for the first time since it began attending state schools in large numbers.[75] These statistics reflect in part both the decline in noble fortunes after the emancipation and the increasing urbanization of Russia. With their landholdings falling 25.8 percent from 1861 to 1892, the impoverished nobility residing on their shrinking estates could less and less afford the expense of sending their children away to the gymnasium. To make matters worse, the network of privately supported, exclusive dormitories or pensions *(pansiony)* established under Nicholas I at more than half the gymnasiums to provide the gentry "living in the provinces with a means of bringing up their children properly and cheaply" was collapsing. Realizing that the gentry could no longer finance these institutions, Golovnin in 1864 supplied government funds; in return he changed the pension from an elite residence for the privileged into an open dormitory for no more than eighty students in grades 1 to 4. Even with state aid the pensions numbered only forty-one by 1870, or one for every three and one-half secondary schools.[76] While hurting the rural gentry, the location of most gymnasiums in the larger cities was certainly convenient for the nonnoble urban classes. Since Russia's town population was rising almost twice as fast as the overall population during the period 1863 to 1897,[77] it was natural that the former would start filling up the gymnasiums.

Under such conditions and in the face of society's growing demand for education, Tolstoi could keep the gymnasium an upperclass preserve only by placing artificial class restrictions on its enrollment. This Tolstoi, unlike his predecessors under Nicholas I and his successor Delianov, would not do. He did not even raise fees to deter the poor or build new pensions to attract the sons of the provincial gentry. His ministry left tuition charges to the local authorities, and they made few increases between 1863 and 1879. The fee scale for 1863 was 10 to 40 rubles in the Petersburg district, 15 to 30 in Moscow, and 10 to 30 in Kazan. Sixteen years later it was 15 to 50, 15 to 40, and 20 to 36 respectively.[78] Aside from urging marshals of the nobility to support the pensions and abolishing their admissions quotas set in 1864, Tolstoi gave these institutions little help. He certainly did not "revive" them, as Alexander Vucinich has recently claimed. In fact, the numbers and size of pensions fell from forty-three housing 3,354 in 1871 to forty-two housing 2,901 in 1877. The upswing in pension construction would not begin until 1883.[79]

Not only did Tolstoi avoid these obvious measures to alter enrollment patterns in the gentry's favor, at times it seemed as if he were actually contributing to the growth of middle- and lower-class applications. The rapid expansion of schools and the creation of the easily accessible preparatory classes gave the townspeople a better opportunity than ever to enter the gymnasiums. Moreover, those that might have preferred to go elsewhere sometimes had no choice but to attend the gymnasiums because the ministry's concentration on classical schools meant that other forms of education were neglected. To Tolstoi's credit, then, his department did not let its gentry bias impede its search for talent. As he told the people of Kherson in 1875, the gymnasiums are for aristocrats, but only aristocrats "of intellect . . . knowledge and hard work." [80]

Caught in the crossfire between the ministry's impressive statistical success and the students' personal complaints, the historian who must evaluate Tolstoi's policies faces a difficult chore. Certainly he did much to promote secondary education. He sought to guarantee minimum academic standards throughout his country by instituting centrally compiled examinations and teaching programs; and, more important, he left Russia with far more students, instructors, and schools than it had when he became minister. Russia benefited from these measures. The universities received ever-larger contingents of trained applicants from the gymnasiums; businessmen and industrialists had in the realschulen their first state-wide source of the technicians they needed. Marring this delightful picture was the actual nature of the education given in the classroom. Pupils suffered through dull, exhausting lessons which drove some to cheating and others to dropping out. Instructors experienced undue limitations against all forms of faculty initiative which prevented them from adopting anything but a mechanical, uninspiring approach to teaching.

The Gymnasiums and Political Discontent

Like so many contemporary schemes of education, Tolstoi's was more a quantitative than a qualitative success, but in the minister's case at least there were plausible reasons for the negative aspects of his system. Charged with strengthening Russian education, he also had to nullify the school's potentially revolutionary role in developing an intelligentsia which would attack the establishment Tolstoi had sworn to protect. It was this latter obligation that led Tolstoi to introduce procedures which incensed student and teacher and hindered the creation of optimum pedagogical conditions. Too unadventurous a bureaucrat to devise new ways of ensuring the loyalty of the student body, but too sensible a civil servant to rely on his predecessors' short-sighted policy of restricting the spread of learning, Tolstoi had adopted the two remaining traditional means of counteracting education's latent threat to autocracy: the use of extensive ministerial controls and the insistence on a grammar-dominated, apolitical curriculum. The question is, were these tactics sufficiently successful to make up for the hostility they aroused?

At first glance it appeared that the ministry's plan was working, for the gymnasium had not become a hotbed of radical teaching. Most students found their instructors all too faithful to the ministry's proscriptive programs. Their classes were dull, taxing, and definitely not politically relevant. Naturally, exceptions did exist like the populist lectures at Poltava and the evening meetings in Orenburg on Belinsky, Chernyshevsky, and Herzen.[81] However, gymnasium pupils usually did not pick up subversive ideas from their teachers, but rather acquired them from professional agitators, university students, relatives, or from their own observations on Russian conditions. In Lev Deich's words, the Tolstoi gymnasium "barely influenced the pupil's intellectual development — the major influences were one's family circle and one's environment." [82]

These external threats complicated the ministry's task. The measures it employed to keep dangerous thoughts out of the classroom would not necessarily protect students during their many hours outside of school. True, the ministry hoped the gymnasium's curriculum would be so demanding that pupils would have little leisure or interest for much else, but this was wishful thinking. Despite the pressures of the classical gymnasium, few adolescents would devote all their energies to schoolwork.

More practical were Tolstoi's two other defenses to shield students from revolutionary propaganda and its proponents — the regulation of student activity after school and the foundation of special accommodations for out-of-town pupils — but such devices proved difficult to implement. Those primarily responsible for student supervision (the director, inspector, and class preceptors) still had to perform their regular teaching and administrative duties. Hence they would not have the time to check on students after class. They could not even rely on the family for help, both because few parents upheld the school and because so many pupils did not live at home. In fact, most of those coming from out of town were left totally on their own, for the increase in ministry-controlled student apartments had not kept pace with the rise in enrollment. Although these residences did grow in size and number from 508 with 2,749 occupants in 1871 to 970 with 5,173 occupants six years later, the ministry had concentrated 90 percent of this total in the western districts of Warsaw, Vilna, and Kiev, the three districts it considered least stable because of their large Polish population. Only one hundred such apartments averaging five students apiece remained for the rest of Russia,[83] hardly an impressive number.

The inadequacies of the above efforts made Tolstoi's neglect of the school's propaganda potential all the more serious. If the ministry could not at the very least limit its charges' contact with pernicious forces outside the classroom, then it would have to strengthen the student's commitment to his country so that he could withstand the blandishments of those who challenged the regime. However, a curriculum stressing grammar and mathematics, while exercising the mind, would not instill the desired ideological orthodoxy necessary to counter the persuasive arguments of the radicals. The intensification of the revolutionary movement during the early 1870s, which culminated in the "going-to-the-people" episode of 1873–1874, and particularly the predominance of students in this illegal activity, finally demonstrated to Tolstoi the weakness of his defensive strategy. On 24 May 1875 he insisted that teachers meet the "political fanaticism" of youth head on by preparing "truly loyal people . . . who would conscientiously support the government and would . . . oppose every absurd doctrine no matter what its origin." [84]

Yet Tolstoi did not remodel the gymnasium program in accordance with its new task of political indoctrination. The revisions of 1877 left the emphasis just where it had been, on language study and math. Not until 1879 when terrorists again threatened the emperor's life did Tolstoi specifically encourage the faculty to ignore existing conspectuses in its fight against subversion. Admitting the increase of "pernicious" influences over the students, he underlined the faculty's obligation to inoculate its pupils against the "noxious infection of the anarchists' harmful teachings" and this time urged that instructors in the senior grades spend some class time exposing the stupidities of socialist views.[85] But this order was a temporary expedient in response to a crisis situation and not the start of the sophisticated use of propaganda in the schools.

Like his academic reforms, Tolstoi's strivings to prevent students from utilizing their recently acquired knowledge against the tsar achieved no more than partial success. Although secondary school students did not flock into the revolutionary movement as had their older brothers, especially those at the Medical-Surgical Academy and the technical institutes, they did comprise 5 to 10 percent of the recorded antigovernment forces during the 1870s.[86] Despite its focus on secondary education, the ministry had not cut off the flow of gymnasium students into the ranks of the disaffected.

It can be argued in Tolstoi's behalf that no educational system alone could have checked the spread of radical activity, that this required the transformation of Russia's administrative and economic structure. The shortcomings of the Russian state — the absence of political freedom, the venality of officials, the arbitrariness of the autocracy, the oppression of the lower classes, the persecution of the intellectuals — would alienate much of the student population no matter what they learned from their instructors. However, this type of plea does not vindicate the minister, for his enemies have contended that his major offense was not that he failed to counteract the appeal of revolutionary teachings but that he actually aroused subversive feelings in the students. According to them, the secondary school statutes endangered the state instead of serving it.

While most contemporaries agreed on the harm the Tolstoi ministry had done, they offered conflicting and oversimplified reasons for its failure. Some blamed the study of Greek and Latin for the prevalence of republican ideas,[87] but they ignored the overwhelmingly philological content of classics lessons. Others, like the panslav Ia. P. Polonsky, took the opposite tack. He complained: "Count Tolstoi had succeeded in making education so tedious and colorless . . . that our students accepted every foolish concept as fascinating truth." [88] Polonsky may have been right about this disturbing by-product of a dull course, but he did not consider the dangerous effects of animating the school's program. As present-day experience has so vividly revealed, an interesting curriculum usually implies a relevant one; and this might mean that those "foolish concepts" Polonsky attacked would become major topics of discussion in the classroom. Given the conditions of Russia in the 1870s, radical views would not seem so silly to young idealists as they did to Polonsky.

More telling were the criticisms levied against the sizable proportion of dropouts. Embittered by their failure which had interrupted their career plans and limited the number of good jobs available to them, these former students appeared especially vulnerable to "seditious" propaganda. Loris-Melikov, one of the prime advocates of this theory, told Alexander II, "These young people who have not finished school are thrown into the world still unfit for work and they thus seek an escape in illegal action and become followers of social heresies." At first glance the findings of the Third Section seem to confirm Melikov's accusations. Of the 525 individuals prosecuted for subversive activity between 1873 and 1877, 103 or 20 percent were dropouts and over

65 percent of them were unemployed. But on closer inspection this evidence is not so conclusive. Gymnasium dropouts accounted for only 18 of the dropout total and for a low 3 percent of all those arrested.[89] Few of the large contingent leaving the gymnasium had no alternative except revolt as Melikov intimates; most either transferred to other schools or entered government service. Also in Tolstoi's defense it must be noted that his policies, by weeding out the scholastically unprepared or unqualified, pleased thoughtful men like Valuev who felt that weak or lazy pupils comprised the most potentially disruptive element at institutes of higher learning.[90] Finally, one should remember that Tolstoi did not introduce the large dropout rate to Russia; it had been even higher before his appointment. In sum, then, the above theories may explain isolated instances of student disaffection, but they do not fully illumine the underlying dangers of the Tolstoi system.

V. V. Rozanov hit closest to the mark when he wrote: "If one wishes to preserve our youth for the state, keep them away from the state." [91] This Tolstoi had not done. His gymnasium had become an object of derision and hate: the Kadet V. A. Maklakov could not describe his years there impartially, so miserable had they been; an alumnus of the Moscow Third Gymnasium declared, "Long after finishing the gymnasium, I could not keep myself from spitting if passing its building"; and other contemporary reports fortify these impressions.[92]

Had the school been an autonomous institution, the student would have had just his teachers or their immediate superiors to blame for his unhappy experiences because they usually determined his course. In Russia, however, there was another guilty party. After 1871 the state, personified by the Ministry of Education itself, carefully defined all aspects of gymnasium life. Students could legitimately accuse the government, not the school, of causing their grievances and direct their anger accordingly. Since the Russian autocracy by the 1870s had betrayed its earlier reforming zeal, thereby further destroying youth's confidence in the regime's ability to improve itself, the slightest provocation could turn these personal complaints about the classical gymnasium into a general attack on the evils of tsarist rule.

By rigidly enforcing his unpopular school legislation, Tolstoi gave the student body first-hand evidence of what appeared to be the government's arrogant disregard of its subjects' needs. In this way the minister, despite his positive contributions to Russian education, actually stimulated the phenomenon he wished to combat, the growth of antistate sentiment among the students.

While the creation of a productive yet politically safe system of secondary and higher education posed considerable difficulties for Tolstoi, nothing would equal the enormous task of bringing elementary schooling to the people. The major problem was numbers. Because of their entrance requirements, demanding curricula, and substantial tuition, the gymnasiums and universities would have a limited clientele. On the other hand, cheap, unrestricted primary education in a country where by the mid-1860s roughly 94 percent of the population was illiterate[1] might attract millions of pupils. To complicate matters further, elementary education was the least developed sector of the Russian school system. Where Tolstoi's immediate predecessors inherited a well-established network of secondary and higher institutions, they would receive no similarly useful bequest at the primary level. The state, with the bulk of its subjects in bondage, had left the responsibility for their enlightenment to the church or the landlord. Once the autocracy liberated the serfs in 1861, however, it had an immense new segment of the population to educate. Realizing that without education the masses would be unable to fulfill their obligations as freemen or overcome their economic disadvantages, the compilers of the Emancipation Act stressed the peasants' right to enroll their children in state schools. No longer could the government ignore the educational needs of the lower classes.

Tolstoi quickly accepted the challenge, for he correctly considered elementary schools a major basis of public well-being *(blagoustroenie obshchestvennoe)* and a "solid guarantee of the illustrious future of our vast country." [2] Without widespread literacy industry would not have the trained workers; agriculture, the progressive farmers; the zemstvos, the educated constituencies; and the legal system, the competent jurors they needed for their success. Most important, illiteracy threatened the effectiveness of the Russian army and hence the very security of the state, because unschooled soldiers often could not understand the sophisticated techniques of modern warfare. Like others of his day, Tolstoi adjudged Prussia's compulsory education law and her nearly 100-percent literacy rate vital factors in that nation's easy victory over Austria in 1866.

The benefits a vigorous program in elementary education would produce did not obscure for Tolstoi the potential dangers of such a policy. The more educated the masses became, the better they would grasp the inequities of their situation, and the more responsive they might be to radical propaganda. Thus Tolstoi would again link his support of elementary education to the establishment of strong ministerial controls over schools.

Urban Elementary Education

The diversity of primary schooling available in Russia impedes any analysis of the ministry's efforts in this field. To keep from sinking into a morass of details, it is necessary to treat separately two broad categories of primary institutions, the urban and the rural. This is what the ministry itself did, for it realized that the town with its dense population, its comparative wealth, and its extensive employment opportunities needed and could afford a more advanced elementary school than the village with its dispersed, poverty-stricken inhabitants. This attempt to give the cities their own comprehensive primary institutions will first receive our attention.

At Tolstoi's accession in 1866 the only lower school entirely under his control was the anachronistic, unpopular county school. Unchanged since 1828, this institution had lost its usefulness. While insisting on stiffer entrance requirements than the gymnasium, the county school offered a six-year course of elementary and secondary education which merely prepared students for optional supplementary applied classes, not for the university, or even for transfer to the classical gymnasium. Such a program satisfied few, and the result was empty senior classes. Golovnin's solution was simple, but for an allegedly liberal minister rather surprising. Seemingly advocating the Nicholaian policy of assigning each class its own school, he proposed converting county institutions into two-grade parish schools "where a significant majority of the students belonged to the burgher or peasant classes which did not need a gymnasium education" or into gymnasiums "where there were numerous students from gentry, civil servant, or prosperous merchant and manufacturing families." [3] As so frequently with Golovnin's decisions, the minister's abrupt departure from office prevented their implementation.

Ignoring his predecessor's conservative advice, Tolstoi entrusted the pedagogue N. Kh. Vessel' with devising a much-needed system of urban primary education as a viable alternative for the county school.[4] His project, first published by the ministry in May 1869 in a rare attempt to solicit public opinion, then submitted in a modified version in 1871 to Stroganov's special conference, introduced a new type of institution called the municipal school (*gorodskoe uchilishche*). Unlike the county one, this school would ready its pupils for both further education and a practical career, since its six-year course imparted an "elementary intellectual and religio-moral education" and "the necessary technical knowledge . . . for practical activity." General subjects including the three

R's, religion, Church Slavonic, geometry, Russian geography, and history prevailed in the first four years; applied courses geared to local business interests in the last two.

This varied curriculum opened up numerous possibilities to the student. After four years he could automatically enter grade 1 of the ministry's secondary schools. After six he acquired the lowest service rank and could transfer to the gymnasium's second or third classes, not directly as Alston claims, but only provided he passed an examination on the extra subjects taught at the gymnasium. Its multipurpose character combined with its negligible fees, tuition exemptions for the poor, and the absence of admissions tests for those entering grade 1 would make the municipal school far more attractive and useful than its outdated precursor.[5]

To ensure that the municipal schools performed their manifold tasks properly, the ministry sought greater control over them than it currently exercised over most elementary schools. Centrally appointed elementary school inspectors — not the special boards Golovnin established to direct primary education or the recently created organs of city government, the dumas, which Tolstoi expected to support his schools — "personally managed" the new institutions. Subject only to the curator's authority, they selected teachers, nominated school principals, and settled tuition rates. In curricular matters the ministry reigned supreme. Its unalterable, compulsory academic plans predetermined the content of every municipal school course.[6] Even at the elementary level, where the rudimentary nature of the curriculum and the immaturity of the student body offered the professional agitator little scope, the ministry still distrusted independent action by either the faculty or community leaders.

This reform of the county schools, Tolstoi told the special conference, would strengthen secondary and technical as well as elementary education. Not only would it give Russia's towns their first custom-designed primary schools, but it would furnish local societies with an excellent model for their own elementary institutions. In addition, trade schools would benefit from the numerous well-trained candidates the municipal schools with their combination of utilitarian and general programs would supply. This increase in the quality and quantity of applicants, the minister theorized, would encourage the founding of more intermediate professional institutions, and they in turn might attract the weaker students from the gymnasium, thereby reducing the dropout rate.[7] Less hypothetical would be the municipal school's assistance in easing the pressure on the gymnasium's lower classes. It could draw off those students who simply wanted an advanced elementary education, but who attended the gymnasium because the city's primary and county schools were inadequate. Lest some dismiss his arguments as mere conjecture, Tolstoi again cited the Prussian experience for support. The acclaim won by the Prussian elementary school, he implied, would soon come to his proposed municipal schools since, except for a two-year shorter course, they generally corresponded to their most successful Prussian counterparts. Each taught applied subjects, and each prepared its pupils for secondary education, normal schools, or practical activity. If his projects became law, the minister concluded, Russia would soon have a "truly European network" of schools.[8]

While basically approving Tolstoi's legislation, the Stroganov committee did question the municipal school's most exciting feature, its great versatility. In its opinion neither the preparation of students for gymnasium classes above the first grade nor the teaching of technical subjects was an appropriate task for the municipal school: the former because its academic standards were too low, the latter because the urban school must remain an institution of general education; besides, the government could not afford the cost of a trade teacher at every school. The conference thus eliminated the clause opening the gymnasium's second and third classes to municipal school graduates and struck out all references to the school's professional character. Despite Tolstoi's assurances that he never intended these institutions to be trade schools and that "the imparting of applied knowledge" meant nothing more than "a method of teaching in which examples, explanations [and] . . . exercises were taken from the student's everyday life," the conference continued adamant in its aversion to technical education in ministry schools, an aversion it had already displayed during its discussions of the realschulen. The committee's only concession was to permit local societies to hire their own vocational instructor if they wished.[9]

These revisions were short-sighted, for they could produce that wasteful phenomenon, the empty senior class, which had so plagued the county school. His last two years might seem superfluous to the municipal school student since they did not help him get into a higher gymnasium grade and gave him no practical training. Nevertheless, Tolstoi, worn out by his recent battles over secondary education, accepted the conference's alterations; the reworked statute gained imperial confirmation on 31 May 1872.

Deprived of its vocational bias, the municipal school had the modest aim of developing the child's "understanding of the nature and life about him and of instilling in him . . . the proper religio-moral concepts and convictions." As at the gymnasium, a ministerial circular which exhaustively delineated each subject for each grade told faculty how to achieve the desired goals. But this decree was less restrictive in several ways than those issued for secondary schools. In the first place, it did not repeat their explicit prohibitions against exceeding the officially prescribed course content. All it did was sensibly caution teachers about adopting too sophisticated an approach or overburdening their students with superfluous information. Second, it gave the Russian and history courses a more important part to play in a pupil's moral education. Historians were to focus on the lessons, not the facts, of the past; Russian teachers were to choose readings that would inculcate patriotic feelings and respect for others as well as inspire a love of labor because "hard work is the best protection against . . . all transgressions." Third, it promulgated valuable pedagogical techniques. For instance, the ministry advocated the constant use of examples from the child's personal experience to illuminate the general principles of the various disciplines, a method long espoused by Russia's most famous pedagogue, K. D. Ushinsky. Hence geography classes concentrated on the neighboring environment; natural science courses, on domestic animals and beneficial and noxious plants; mathematics lessons, on matters relating to local industry and trade. This linking of classwork with the familiar objects of the pupil's surroundings would make his studies far more meaningful to him.[10]

Even a carefully devised syllabus needed competent faculty to carry it out, and finding such instructors, always a problem in Russia, was particularly difficult for the municipal schools. Their logical candidates, the teachers from the phased-out county schools, could not easily adjust from teaching a single subject to all classes, as they did at their former schools, to teaching all subjects to a single class, as required at the municipal school. This new method, while reducing the amount of faculty necessary, unfortunately ruled out most available instructors. Foreseeing the staffing crisis which might result from his reforms, Tolstoi won government approval for the creation along with the city schools of several teachers' institutes devoted solely to the preparation of municipal school instructors.[11] Having faced continual teacher shortages in elementary and secondary education, Tolstoi had wisely decided against establishing an additional network of schools before guaranteeing them a reliable source of faculty.

Like Russia's two other normal schools, the philological institute and the rural teachers' seminary, the teachers' institute had a twofold purpose. It could not just develop its students' pedagogical abilities but also had to ensure their political orthodoxy, for Tolstoi never forgot the potential dangers of education, especially when entrusted to disloyal or revolutionary-minded instructors. Although it would not be a simple task to organize the institute so that it could fulfill both its pedagogical and its political obligations, it was a vital one if the municipal schools were to thrive and yet not contribute to the growing instability of the Russian state. The ministry therefore insisted on determining the institute's structure and programs itself. It designated the school's director, set examination rules, issued detailed course conspectuses, and meticulously defined the duties of students, teachers, and administrators. The faculty, like their colleagues at the ministry's other institutions, had few opportunities for independent activity. They could not even modify classroom procedures, student regulations, or subject outlines without the curator's approval.[12]

Taking its philological institute for a model, the ministry decided on a boarding school with a modest, vocationally oriented curriculum and a comprehensive scheme of moral instruction and student controls as the best means of producing the skilled and faithful municipal schoolteachers it required. The institute's three-year course perfectly conformed to Tolstoi's dictum that "the future instructor must thoroughly master only . . . that knowledge essential for teaching" at the elementary level. Not only did the ministry limit the school's offerings, except for pedagogy, to those subjects given at the municipal school, it also warned the faculty against adding material which the students would not actually have to teach once they graduated. The ministry even tried to prevent spontaneous classroom discussions, which it felt were too time-consuming, by ordering instructors to adopt a dogmatic stance and permit questions for review purposes alone.

While restricting the institute's scholastic program, the ministry improved the more technical aspects of teacher training. It founded an elementary school at every institute so that students could conveniently gain experience in the schoolroom. Moreover, it urged that faculty stress such utilitarian topics as methodology, the use of visual aids, and the state of the textbook literature in their fields. In pedagogy class too, practical lessons on hygiene, the maintenance of discipline, and contemporary school legislation became prominent features of the course.[13]

The institute, it seemed, should furnish its students with the requisite information and pedagogical techniques but not widen their intellectual horizons. Yet one should not automatically condemn Tolstoi for curtailing the institute's academic pretensions. Admittedly, he did so in part because — as always — he feared a sophisticated course of study might easily introduce prospective teachers to the wrong ideas, but there were other, more generally acceptable reasons for his actions. The institute's low admissions requirements — a municipal school education or its equivalent — ruled out too advanced a program. Besides, the example of the country with the most successful system of elementary education argued against setting high standards. "The object of the training college," so the Prussian statute read, "is not to provide an education . . . but to equip the teacher with such knowledge and skills as are necessary for keeping an ordinary elementary school." [14] If hardly an ideal philosophy for modern industrial societies, it did conform to Russia's meager educational resources. With too few schools and teachers for its burgeoning urban population, Russia could not afford the time and money necessary to prepare the scholarly educator. It needed hordes of professionally trained technicians, and it needed them quickly. For this task the institute's course appeared admirably suited.

In contrast to its circumscribed curriculum, the institute's system of student guidance was quite elaborate. For Tolstoi the future teacher's character was as important as his mind, because the latter's personal example and actions would influence his pupils no less than their actual classwork. To ensure that Russia's prospective instructors would develop the proper traits, the ministry made the institute a closed boarding school with one of the most carefully supervised and tightly regulated student bodies in the empire. Its student code supplemented the usual statements on orderly conduct, compulsory church attendance, and faithful completion of assignments with a rigid schedule for all students that left them a minimal two to three hours of leisure time per day. Realizing that these rules would have little effect without adequate surveillance, Tolstoi had institute faculty take turns being monitors from nine in the morning until nine at night. While on duty, they were to preserve discipline, maintain hygienic standards, and record every absence, infraction, and punishment. To be more than just watchmen, they were also to instill in their charges Christian sentiments, patriotic feelings, and pride in the teaching profession. Such a program, the ministry claimed, would greatly benefit the students. Not only would it help inculcate the desired values and discourage frivolity, it would also assist in transforming the institute into a "model of that humble and arduous existence which awaited future elementary school teachers so that this life . . . becomes second nature for . . . the institute's students." [15]

Tolstoi also had a less publicized but equally important reason for his emphasis on regimentation and moral instruction. Frightened by the growing revolutionary movement, particularly the campaign in the 1870s to subvert the masses, the minister would do everything possible to guarantee that those he sent out to bring literacy to the people would not aid the radicals in their "pernicious" tasks. So easy a target for the agitator's poisonous barbs did he consider the immature institute student that instead of depending solely on the traditional shields of constant supervision and informal indoctrination, he decided to move the quarry out of range. He located the institutes at rural or secluded sites, permitted leaves only between four and five-thirty in the afternoon, limited visiting days to Tuesdays and Fridays, and insisted on the scrupulous checking of all guests and unscheduled departures. To reinforce the student's separation from the intellectual world around him, the ministry forbade possession of illicit literature, membership in unauthorized organizations, participation in group discussions without prior consent from school officials, and attendance at meetings not sanctioned by the government no matter what their purpose. For ignoring these prohibitions, a student could be expelled, placed under perpetual surveillance, and deprived of the right to further education.[16]

It was thus at the teachers' institute that the ministry's defense against the radicalization of students reached its apogee. To the stringent rules of the gymnasium and the oppressive boarding school atmosphere of the philological institute, the ministry had added the tactic of student isolation. However, since it usually did not employ the more aggressive strategy of direct propaganda attacks on the enemy's position, its graduates might still fall victim to an ambush once they left their institute fortress.

Of course, not even so careful a plan as Tolstoi's to resolve the teacher shortage without introducing disloyal elements into state schools could succeed if Russia did not have enough normal schools or if these institutions lacked students. Recognizing this danger, Tolstoi badgered the Minister of Finance for funds until in 1879 he finally achieved the desired ratio of one institute per education district.[17] This gradual increase in institutes was in a sense opportune since the ministry found it difficult to attract qualified applicants committed to a teaching career.

The "humble and arduous existence" of the elementary instructor, hardly alleviated by his meager starting salary of 450 rubles annually or by the cumbersome directives restricting his pedagogical activity, discouraged many from entering the institute. The ministry's major response was to dangle the bait of a free education: twenty of the twenty-five places in each class carried with them full scholarships for which the state demanded six years service in return. Although these grants would not draw gymnasium students away from the path to the lucrative, prestigious occupations a university degree opened to them, they might appeal to the poorer classes attending the municipal school who would appreciate any secure vocation. Hence Tolstoi concentrated his recruitment efforts on these students. There was only one problem: pupils who began the municipal school at the usual age of seven or eight would finish the six-year course two to three years before they reached the minimum age requirement set by the institute. Tolstoi therefore encouraged the better graduates to spend these few years at the city school as paid teaching assistants and promised those who did a good job priority over all other institute candidates. It was a clever policy, for it would both provide the institute with competent, experienced students and give the municipal school teacher much-needed help. Unfortunately, it did not fill the institutes. From 1877 to 1881 their classrooms remained a third empty.[18]

These troubles at the teachers' institutes considerably retarded the spread of urban elementary education. Rather than search for other less controlled sources of municipal school faculty, Tolstoi would wait until the institutes could supply the needed instructors. A few excellent schools, he felt, were better than many inadequate ones; therefore he would not establish municipal institutes unless qualified faculty were available. The result of this policy was a slow conversion rate of county into municipal schools — with the Petersburg and Moscow districts, the only two where teachers' institutes had existed since 1872, getting the bulk of the new schools in the 1870s. By 1 January 1878 the outmoded county schools still predominated over the municipal, 337 to 99. These statistics did not greatly disturb Tolstoi, however, for the small group of municipal institutions was already attracting more students than the county schools and enjoying a lower dropout rate. His concentration on quality seemed to be bearing fruit. Besides, the completion of the teachers' institute network by 1879 would guarantee a rapid increase in city schools. Benefiting from the 372 institute graduates produced just in the years 1879 to 1881, the transformation of county into municipal schools speeded up so that by 1882 the latter for the first time outnumbered the former, 262 to 229.[19]

Despite its leisurely implementation, Tolstoi's city school statute did strengthen Russian education. A rationally organized, if conventional, institution had replaced an unpopular, anachronistic one. It offered townspeople an advanced form of primary education geared in part to local requirements. That 99 municipal schools enrolled more students than 337 county schools in 1877–78 demonstrates how well the former suited the urban population. The teachers' institutes too, regardless of their limited curriculum and constricted boarding school atmosphere, were an improvement over the previous haphazard methods of teacher preparation, for they guaranteed the city schools a steady source of trained instructors.

Unmoved by these achievements, some critics condemned the minister for creating schools which did not ready their pupils for additional education, which were a dead end, designed with the less privileged classes in mind.[20] Tolstoi, it is true, had not reintroduced the ladder system, but it is also true that the Stroganov commission, not the minister, removed the provisions for admitting municipal graduates into the gymnasium's second and third grades and that according to the 1872 legislation those who successfully completed four years at the municipal school could automatically enter the first class of ministry secondary institutions. These students would have already spent two more years in school than those who started the gymnasium in the preparatory class, but at least they escaped taking any admissions test. Although Tolstoi tailored the municipal school for the urban lower classes, he never turned it into an educational blind alley.

Rural Elementary Schooling: Its Major Needs

On Tolstoi's accession primary education presented an even more deplorable picture in the countryside than it did in the towns. While most urban centers had some sort of educational institution, many villages did not; and those rural schools that did exist made the worst-run county school look exemplary. Unqualified and apathetic teachers gave dull lessons in decrepit, ill-equipped buildings. Often nobody supervised their work or offered them advice. William Phelp's description of primary education in 1870 America could easily apply to Russia: "Poor schools and poor teachers are in a majority throughout the country. . . . They afford the sad spectacle of ignorance engaged in the stupendous fraud of self-perpetuation at the public expense." [21] Russia's village schools cried out for more and better instructors, adequate financing, and a competent inspection system.

Tolstoi would heed their plea, yet he realized his ministry could not rectify the situation alone. After centuries of neglect the task of educating the Russian peasants, scattered as they were over vast distances, was too immense for a single government department, especially when that department, because of its former chiefs' indifference to elementary schooling, had inherited neither a sizable budget nor direct authority over primary education. For example, in 1864 Golovnin spent just 216,000 rubles on the mere 1,846 elementary institutions under his jurisdiction; two years later the clergy in the thirty-three central provinces still governed almost twenty times as many primary schools as did the ministry. Under such circumstances, Tolstoi asserted, he must "act jointly with the Orthodox church, the zemstvos, and society" to promote rural elementary education.[22] Ideally, the clergy would provide the teachers, the zemstvos the money, and the ministry the guidance and control.

As one might expect from an education minister who was also Procurator of the Holy Synod, Tolstoi judged the priests superior to all other instructors of the people. In the West theirs had been a historic role in education. In Russia too they were the group most involved with primary schooling and best qualified to imbue it with the "spirit of religious truths." There were also practical reasons for Tolstoi's decision: the clergy could live on low salaries since teaching provided only a part of their income, and, as the class closest to the peasant, they would better understand his needs and more effectively communicate with his children. Finally, they would in the future be skilled instructors, for their seminaries were now offering lectures in pedagogy and didactics and opening Sunday schools where seminarians could gain classroom training. The pedagogue S. Miropol'sky, who taught at the Kharkov and Petersburg seminaries, claimed that his pupils taught their Sunday school classes so successfully that parents came personally to praise the student teachers. Impressed by this and numerous similar reports, Tolstoi budgeted ministry funds for the seminaries' pedagogical courses.[23]

Experience would soon destroy his hopes in the clergy. Seminary graduates frequently found elementary school teaching too humble a profession and resigned at the first opportunity. Many of the parish schools claimed by the synod turned out to be ephemeral, if not paper, creations — how else can one explain the startling fluctuation in their number: 4,820 in 1853; 2,270 in 1857; 9,283 in 1861; and 4,348 in 1880.[24] Most important, those church schools which did function inspired no one. Attacks against the clergy for hiring incompetent assistants, shirking their duties, or performing them badly were all too common. It was unrealistic for Tolstoi to expect the relatively untrained parish priest to conduct school in addition to his other obligations.

Unlike the church, the zemstvo was a new force in education. Comprised of deputies elected separately by three constituencies (the nobility, the peasantry, and the townspeople), this organ of local self-government acquired responsibility for most matters of public welfare, including education. The extent of its duties, however, was a subject of controversy. While the statute of 1 January 1864 had stressed fiscal obligations, men like retired Education Minister Kovalevsky and Baron M. A. Korf of the Second Section wanted the zemstvo to have charge of all, not just the financial, aspects of primary education. After prolonged debate in the State Council, the government in its 1864 elementary school reforms ruled against Kovalevsky and Korf. It established provincial and county school councils to manage primary institutions, with the zemstvos merely one of many groups represented on these boards. For Golovnin, zemstvos should improve the schools' economic position and discover ways to found new schools, but he did not "think it possible to entrust them with the entire administration of schools." Tolstoi shared this view. Zemstvos, he declared, should guarantee teachers higher salaries and the ministry's institutions adequate funds.[25]

At first many evaded their responsibilities. Of the 325 county zemstvos active in 1868, 109 — or more than one-third — allocated nothing for schools, another 40 gave minute sums, and only 24 exceeded 5,000 rubles. Six of 34 provincial zemstvos also refused to shoulder education costs. Such evidence led B. V. Veselovsky to conclude: "During the sixties zemstvo delegates regarded the question of education with almost complete indifference."[26]

Generous zemstvos caused the ministry as much trouble as their tight-fisted counterparts, because they began demanding greater control over how their money was being used. A few vainly sought additional representation on the school councils. Others actively participated in the running of primary institutions, appointing teachers, compiling course outlines, and sometimes creating special subcommissions to disperse grants. Leaving such matters to the county zemstvos, the richer provincial assemblies concentrated on the preparation of instructors. Usually they assisted the pedagogical courses at the seminaries and state schools or sponsored short-term refresher programs on teaching methods, but by 1870 many were considering setting up their own normal schools. In short, the zemstvos did not fulfill the ministry's expectations either. On the one hand, most of them neglected the primary schools in their area. On the other, the few who were committed to educating the masses rejected the limitations the ministry placed on their activities. They wanted to be a major — if not *the* major — force in elementary education.

Both public opinion and the ministry's weak position in the countryside encouraged this attitude. Defending zemstvo ambitions in elementary education, the liberal press constantly echoed Baron N. A. Korf's claim that zemstvo people should not simply be the schools' financiers.[27] These journals hailed the creation of the zemstvo as the first step in the long process of letting the Russian people run their own affairs. Hence they supported any attempt by this institution to expand its authority.

Such expansion would be easy in the field of elementary education since the 1864 statute allowed local bodies rather than the ministry to dominate primary school administration. Instead of vying with powerful agents from St. Petersburg, the zemstvo had only to compete with the loosely organized school councils on which it was well represented. The county board (with two deputies from the zemstvo assembly and one each from the Ministry of Education, the Ministry of the Interior, the Orthodox church, and other departments aiding primary education) supervised instruction, opened and closed schools, certified teachers, and distributed approved texts and teaching aids. Its provincial counterpart, whose membership included the bishop, the governor, the director of schools, and two zemstvo nominees, reviewed the lower board's proposals, allocated ministry funds, and removed unsuitable instructors. Despite their powers, the councils often constituted no check on zemstvo activities. Many, particularly at the provincial level, met rarely, if at all, and neglected their obligations; for example, most provincial boards did not even submit the required school reports each year.[28] Even properly functioning councils might fall under zemstvo control, for Golovnin made possible a sizable increase in the zemstvo delegation by permitting locally elected school trustees, many of whom served on the zemstvos, to participate with full rights in county council meetings.[29] Given the board's heterogeneous membership, any group that could form a bloc would wield considerable influence.

With just a single deputy on each school board, the ministry could do little to challenge the zemstvo's predominance. Indeed, in those regions where its usual delegate, the county school principal, was not available, the ministry would have no say whatsoever on the course of elementary education. As Tolstoi wrote in 1872: "Forty-six county school councils had absolutely no representative from the education department. The government in those counties thus played no part in elementary education—an unheard-of situation in any European country." [30] A minister like Tolstoi, who relied on state control to protect his schools from subversive elements, would not tolerate for long the existence of so many institutions only nominally under his jurisdiction.

Clearly, Tolstoi's division of responsibilities had not worked out as planned. The clergy did not become conscientious, skilled teachers; the zemstvos either disregarded their obligations or extended their authority beyond fiscal matters; and the school councils by their very composition often excluded the ministry from direct control over primary education. If Russia were to possess the extensive, centrally regulated elementary school network Tolstoi felt it needed, he would have to reformulate the entire problem of administering and staffing these schools.

Increased State Control over Rural Schools

Retaining confidence for a time in the priest-teacher, Tolstoi first challenged the competence of the school councils. In 1867 he requested a large force of primary school inspectors because, he insisted, only trained personnel, not dilatory and unqualified school boards, could furnish Russian elementary education with the proper uniformity and direction. After two years the State Council, with the student demonstrations of March 1869 fresh in its members' minds, finally concurred and allotted one inspector for the Bessarabia region and for each of the thirty-three provinces covered by the zemstvo statute.[31]

This new official acquired authority over all elementary institutions governed by the school board. He played two roles, inquisitor and benefactor: in the former guise he examined teachers, curricula, texts, and the school's physical plant; in the latter he assisted young instructors, distributed emergency funds, and persuaded local societies to augment their grants. Although not directly responsible to the inspector, the faculty had good reason to be nervous about his visits, for the ministry had placed them under the inspector's "surveillance in academic matters" and had empowered him to remove undesirable teachers temporarily. Lest the council on which he served inhibit the inspector's activity, Tolstoi made him subordinate to the ministry alone and ordered that major disagreements between the inspector and the council be resolved in Petersburg.[32] This last provision enabled the inspector to override council resistance to his measures and to block decisions which opposed his minister's wishes. The inspectorate thus endangered the school board's predominance in elementary school administration.

To calm those who correctly saw in the inspector a threat to local, collegiate control over elementary education, the ministry played down his managerial and police functions. The inspector, one department spokesman argued, was not an informer who spied on teachers but an educator who guided them. In theory, this official would improve primary education, for he would disseminate advanced pedagogical methods, remove incompetent instructors, brief new staff, maintain hygienic standards, and engender support for both teacher and school. But the school councils already performed such tasks, Tolstoi's adversaries contended. The ministry replied that inexperience and factional strife hampered the board's activity, that the inspector's autonomous position would permit him to operate more efficiently. Besides, it speciously concluded, the inspector would not replace the council but merely "supplement" it.[33]

This supplement soon became more important than the main text. In August 1872 Tolstoi demanded a substantial expansion of the inspectorate's numbers and powers. As many as 142 extra officials, more than 4 per province, would join the existing 34 inspectors who would be promoted to provincial directors of elementary schools. Giving up all pretense of preserving the school boards' independence, Tolstoi planned to replace their elected chairmen by these directors and inspectors and to enlarge his own department's delegation on the boards while restricting the other parties to their 1864 quotas. Instead of a single ministerial deputy, the provincial council would have three, the county council two. The zemstvos did retain two men on each council, but they could not count on help from the elementary school trustees, since the latter could no longer participate in most board sessions.[34] If these proposals gained acceptance, the ministry would dominate the school councils; the state, not local societies, would control primary education.

In defense of his project Tolstoi repeated the familiar and often justified criticisms of the school boards and cited the numerous precedents in Russia and abroad for his actions. After surveying the negative reports he continually received on council activity, the minister concluded: "Board members visit schools rarely or not at all and examine them quite cursorily. Therefore, with few exceptions, local communities and zemstvos have little confidence in the county councils, and this is extremely detrimental to our primary schools." As for the provincial councils, they never even furnished essential statistical data on the numbers of teachers and students.[35] Although Tolstoi may have exaggerated the board's inadequacies, he did have a legitimate complaint. With the majority of its personnel occupied with full-time jobs elsewhere, the council was not prepared for the arduous task of overseeing Russian elementary education.

Far preferable to these ineffectual collegiate bodies, the minister insisted, were the powerful state inspectorates employed in the Vilna district and in most European nations. Fearing the spread of anti-Russian sentiments through the schools during the Polish uprising of 1863, the ministry had placed its own officials in charge of elementary education in Vilna. No representative organ existed at the county level; the inspector was the single authority. By 1870 this district had thirty inspectors, just four less than the total allotted all central Russia. The generally acknowledged success of Vilna's primary schools, Tolstoi claimed, demonstrated "the importance of continuous and effective control by specialists." It also indicated, although Tolstoi did not mention this, the value of generous state grants. In 1879, for example, the government assigned 203,240 rubles, or 30.6 percent of its elementary school budget, to the Vilna district and only 10 percent, approximately 66,000 rubles, to the zemstvo provinces.[36]

Not content to depend on the Vilna example, the minister, as in every preceding reform, looked across Russia's borders for support. In the West, he argued, both liberal and conservative regimes closely supervised elementary education. Basically he was right: in Prussia, local commissions handled many school affairs, but the task of inspection "belonged to the government alone"; in Belgium and the Netherlands, the law required state inspectors to visit every school at least twice a year; and in Bavaria, the inspector possessed sole jurisdiction over moral and scholastic matters and together with police officials appointed teachers, opened schools, and reviewed the local board's activity. No longer, Tolstoi declared, could the ministry ignore these precedents, for the "education of the people, the future of Russia," was too crucial a concern to let "slip from its hands." [37]

Unconvinced by Tolstoi's exhortations, the administration dawdled until the start of the "going-to-the-people" movement in 1873 demonstrated the necessity for greater control over primary education. With the arrest that year of A. V. Dolgushin and his followers in the Group of Twenty-Two, the government had proof that the radicals intended to undermine the peasantry's historic faith in autocracy. Since March these young men had been distributing in the villages leaflets full of phrases like "all men are equal," "the time has come to escape from poverty and darkness," and "rise up against the regime of injustice." [38] They were just the forerunners of the thousands of young intelligentsia who would the next year flock "to the people" in the naive hope of rousing the masses to free themselves from oppression; but the danger of exposing his subjects to such propaganda was already obvious to the emperor. He now fully realized that the growth of literacy could as easily serve the rebellious pamphleteer as the state.

On 21 December 1873 he convened a special session of the Council of Ministers to devise a means of stopping the spread of the "most pernicious and criminal teachings" in the elementary schools. P. A. Shuvalov, head of the Third Section, suggested making the marshals of the nobility also responsible for school supervision. Pleased with any effort to tighten surveillance over education, Tolstoi joined Shuvalov, Valuev, and Foreign Minister Gorchakov in drafting a resolution which embodied Shuvalov's proposals and received Alexander's approval on 25 December 1873.[39]

Although reaffirming the need for an educated populace, this rescript warned that a badly run school could be "turned into a weapon to corrupt the people morally." Only the strictest control, the central authorities believed, would prevent this from happening; and to establish this system, the emperor called not on the zemstvos and school councils, the two representative organs of the reform era specifically charged with superintending elementary education, but on his traditional allies the gentry.

> Primary schooling based on religion and morality is so great and sacred a cause that not only the clergy but all educated people in the country must work to support and improve it. . . . The major responsibility for this belongs to the Russian gentry, who have always set an example of honor and devotion to civil duty. I summon my faithful gentry to defend the elementary schools from pernicious and dangerous influences . . . to promote personally the multiplication of these schools and their moral and physical well-being.[40]

Throughout January 1874 Tolstoi met with selected marshals of the nobility and important government officials to discuss ways of incorporating the rescript's orders into a general revision of elementary school administration. By 14 February 1874 his plan was ready for the State Council.

The new statute offered a compromise between the previous emphasis on self-rule and Tolstoi's initial demands for total control over primary education. On the one hand, it furnished less opportunity for ministry domination than had the 1872 project. Not only would the education department's representation on the provincial board fall from three to two, but locally elected marshals of the nobility instead of centrally designated directors and inspectors would preside over school council sessions. Reflecting the rescript's concern for the political reliability of Russia's schools, the 1874 regulations also gave these gentry leaders the job of visiting primary institutions and investigating the faculty's moral qualities. If necessary, the provincial council could enlist reputable citizens to assist the marshals in this task.

On the other hand, the statute, despite these concessions to the emperor's misplaced trust in the gentry, retained earlier provisions which reduced both the autonomy and the powers of the school boards. In every zemstvo province the supervision of primary school teaching was transferred from the board to the director of elementary schools and his "immediate subordinates, the inspectors," the former appointed by the minister, the latter by the curator. True, the law nominally entrusted the council with "the satisfaction of the population's needs in elementary schooling" and the moral direction of education, but the inspector was responsible for most important decisions. He certified applications for faculty positions and, together with the council chairman, removed suspect teachers and temporarily closed institutions where "disorder and harmful methods of instruction" prevailed. Previously, the council had handled these matters; now it merely confirmed the inspector's actions. So dependent had the county board in fact become that it could no longer conduct any business without a ministry deputy present.[41]

The State Council accepted this project more readily than most of Tolstoi's, but it did insist on two substantial changes. Ironically, it chided the civil head of the Orthodox church for neglecting the clergy's vital role in education. Although the council's only specific modification was to make the school's "religious and moral" direction the special concern of the bishop as well as the parish priest, it warned that primary education could not succeed without the clergy's cooperation. Tolstoi thus received a sharp reminder that the government was not ready for the completely secular school system he envisioned. More serious yet was the state's inability to fund the vast inspectorate Tolstoi wanted. Where he had requested 142 new inspectors, the council allowed him just 68. This was, of course, still double the existing contingent of 34 inspectors, now promoted to provincial primary school directors.[42]

Even with these revisions the statute of 25 May 1874 greatly extended the ministry's control over elementary education. Unable to transform the council into his obedient instrument, Tolstoi had sought instead to undermine its influence so that it could not compete with the ministry's agents in determining school policy. He therefore eliminated its authority over classroom instruction and drastically restricted its initiative in such essential matters as the hiring and firing of teachers or the opening and closing of schools. Over a hundred government directors and inspectors had supplanted the school councils as chief administrators of the following institutions: church parish schools, ministry elementary schools, and locally supported rural schools of all types. The ministry had finally become the major force in primary education.

A dearth of inspectors, however, prevented the ministry from fully exercising its authority. In 1876 Tolstoi informed the State Council that its economy move to limit his department to two inspectors per province was depriving Russia's primary schools of necessary guidance. According to curator reports, each inspector, during a normal school year of 132 days, on the average had to visit more than 218 institutions and cover some 15,000 square miles in addition to attending school council sessions, compiling annual reports, and supervising pedagogical courses for elementary teachers. Ideally, the marshal of the nobility and the provincial director should have taken up the slack, but neither of these could offer much aid; the former because he lacked the power and training to review academic affairs, the latter because his administrative obligations as head of elementary schools in the province allowed little time for inspection tours. Under such conditions adequate control over education was impossible — an intolerable situation, Tolstoi argued; for education, if not properly directed, could actually harm the state. Never before was this danger so evident. The escapades of the populists in the "mad summer" of 1874, while failing to stimulate revolt, had demonstrated the ease with which subversive doctrines could penetrate Russia's villages. To protect his schools from these ideas, Tolstoi demanded more inspectors since they were "best qualified to watch out for the appearance of . . . propaganda at elementary institutions." Optimally, the ministry should triple their number so that the central provinces would have the same ratio of one inspector for every seventy schools as the Vilna district, but in view of the treasury's low reserves Tolstoi requested only seventy-four additional inspectors by 1 January 1877, thereby reducing the inspector-school ratio from 1 to 218 to 1 to 100. On 27 April 1876 the State Council approved the minister's petition but spread the funds over a three-year period.[43] As usual, the autocracy's straitened finances obstructed Tolstoi's plans.

Unexpected assistance came from the zemstvos. They first sought their own deputy inspectors, but the Senate, endorsing the ministry's narrow interpretation of zemstvo responsibilities in education, ruled by 1872 that zemstvos should concern themselves with economic matters alone and merely pay for additional inspectors chosen by the education department. Some zemstvos still felt these men worth their 1,500-ruble salary, for by 1877 they supported 19, or 17 percent, of Russia's 112 inspectors.[44]

Yet isolated zemstvo contributions could not offset the state's incapacity to underwrite the sizable inspectorate the ministry wanted. In 1876 Tolstoi had estimated that Russia needed 192 to 204 inspectors for each school to be seen briefly once a year. Despite the rapid increase in schools, the ministry could employ only 167 invigilators by 1882, well below the number required six years earlier.[45] Tolstoi's control apparatus was thus by no means perfect; too many schools could escape inspection each year.

Historians have customarily condemned the 1874 regulations as one more sterile, bureaucratic solution to Russia's educational problems. Fundamentally opposed to autocratic government, these scholars believed that liberal institutions like the zemstvos could only benefit Russia and that attempts to curtail their powers were by definition retrogressive. Judging developments in elementary education in this light, they credited all successes to local societies, particularly the zemstvos, and accused Tolstoi of impeding rather than encouraging their activity. For these critics the zemstvos were the major fount of pedagogical wisdom, the inspectors merely ministry policemen who had usurped functions rightfully belonging to private initiative.[46]

This interpretation needs modification. In the first place, a representative, locally elected assembly offers no automatic guarantee of a successful school program. Indeed, so many zemstvos disregarded their fiscal responsibilities in education that B. V. Veselovsky concluded: "It is necessary to analyze, not idealize, and then we will discover that the first zemstvo delegates did not begin their labors as some sort of fabled heroes but as landlords who had not yet forgotten the traditions of serfdom, who firmly retained their class privileges and prejudices." Only in the 1890s did the zemstvos generally accept their obligation to provide elementary schooling for everyone.[47] When zemstvos did generously allot support, there was still no assurance they would use these funds wisely — especially since the establishment of elementary institutions was for them a new and complex business. True, they had guides like Korf's excellent manual on the primary school, which in little over a year had sold 12,500 copies;[48] however, few of the more than 400 county zemstvos had qualified educators on their staff and almost none were of Baron Korf's stature. As a matter of fact, the gentry did not even reelect Korf to the Aleksandrovsk zemstvo in 1872. In Golovnin's scheme the school councils were to have supplied whatever guidance the zemstvos needed, but in practice many of them barely functioned.

Secondly, state control does not inevitably harm education. In fact, Tolstoi's centralizing policies had potential advantages which have frequently been overlooked. He made elementary schooling the responsibility of those officials who were supposedly best equipped to handle its special problems. Possessing either a higher education or considerable teaching experience, the directors and inspectors were not only more competent judges of academic matters than the average zemstvo delegate or council member but were also ideal carriers of advanced pedagogical techniques to the provinces. While some inspectors admittedly acted as spies, no ministerial circular restricted them to invigilation alone. On the contrary, the ministry proclaimed their primary task to be the assistance and instruction of faculty, a task well suited to their small numbers. The curriculum reforms, the improvements in teacher training, the increase in schools, achieved by men like V. P. Vakhterov in Smolensk and V. I. Lenin's father in Simbirsk, demonstrated how much good a committed inspector might do.[49] Furthermore, the significant percentage of inspectors supported by zemstvos suggests that even the inspectors' chief competitors in primary education valued the services of these men.

The Search for Teachers

Although Russia's rural schools needed a reliable source of instructors no less than an effective system of guidance, Tolstoi at first left staffing problems for the clergy to resolve. His reasons were political. As procurator, he had already opposed the hiring of too many lay elementary teachers because of their susceptibility to radical ideas. The Karakozov assassination attempt and the accompanying reports of widespread subversive activity reinforced his fears of dangerous elements using his schools for their own "nefarious" designs. He therefore withdrew his predecessor's proposals for teachers' seminaries, arguing, one ministry official claimed, that such institutions would "educate teachers as atheists, materialists and anarchists." The money for teachers' seminaries, Tolstoi urged, "ought to be transferred to the theological seminaries." [50] From 1866 to 1870 the ministry thus confined its own teacher training programs to the pedagogical courses set up by Golovnin at eleven county schools as a stopgap measure before the introduction of teachers' seminaries. These courses normally provided no more than a sketchy survey of teaching methods, superimposed on the regular county school curriculum.

Both the increasing demand for qualified instructors and the desire to control teacher training soon compelled Tolstoi to reverse his stand on the teachers' seminaries. As he admitted in his 1868 report, the existing means of teacher preparation — the supplementary classes at the theological seminaries and the loosely organized pedagogical courses — were not turning out instructors in anywhere near the quantity or quality required.[51]

What disturbed Tolstoi as much as this inability to eliminate the teacher shortage was the fact that his failure had encouraged local groups, particularly the zemstvos, to establish their own normal schools. Although Tolstoi agreed with Katkov that one no

longer "had to counter every attempt to introduce teachers' seminaries because one justifiably feared that the senseless nihilism
which so perniciously infects other spheres of education would
have dominated elementary school instructions," he warned that
"only teachers' seminaries which remain completely within the
jurisdiction of the education department can produce . . . experienced and capable instructors." Since poorly prepared faculty
would hinder intellectual development and "what is worse might
. . . harm society and the state," Tolstoi concluded his ministry
must control teacher training. His arguments convinced the State
Council. On 24 May 1871 it endorsed his plan for replacing the
eleven pedagogical courses by five teachers' seminaries, one each
in the Moscow, St. Petersburg, Kharkov, Kazan, and Odessa districts, and seven months later approved an additional five seminaries for the same districts.[52]

Tolstoi's familiar formula for the organization of normal
schools dominated the teachers' seminaries as well. For the minister, only centrally regulated, technically oriented training colleges
with extensive programs in character development could supply
loyal yet competent instructors. The seminaries would fit this pattern perfectly. Like the other normal schools, they fell totally
under the education department's control. In addition to confirm-
ing all staff and curriculum changes, the ministry also had the
power to define in a general instruction the nature of student life,
scholastic offerings, teaching methods, and internal administration at the seminary.[53]

This instruction, which appeared in July 1875, gave the seminary the same humble academic goals and ambitious plans of
moral training and student supervision that characterized all Tolstoi's normal schools. So limited was the seminary's program that
history and geography classes barely touched on European developments, Russian courses stressed syntax and composition (with
literary works used mainly for illustrating grammatical problems), and lessons in drawing and penmanship occupied the
greatest amount of class time. To deter teachers from expanding
their courses' scope, the ministerial circular explicitly warned
them against adding excessive or extraneous details or adopting

the more exciting catechistic methods of instruction. The proper approach, the decree declared, was the dogmatic; teachers should tell their students what they should know, but not encourage questions or discussions.

While rarely stimulating the future instructor's intellect, the seminary curriculum did prepare him in a practical way for his chosen career. In addition to his considerable time as observer and student teacher at the special primary schools set up under the seminary, he gained valuable help in readying himself for life outside the classroom. His pedagogy course, if superficial, did cover the typical problems he would face in Russia's backward villages; and more important, the seminary — alone of Russia's teacher preparatory institutes — offered a variety of trade subjects. Its pupils studied surveying, gardening, and handicraft because such knowledge, the ministry felt, would provide them with a much-needed source of income and bring them closer to their peasant students.[54] The ministry gave the prospective instructor's practical training higher priority than his overall mental development. This policy, a feature of all Russian normal schools, appears most justified at the seminary. The poor quality of its applicants, many of whom had no more than an elementary education,[55] the overwhelming primary school teacher shortage, and the rudimentary nature of the subjects the seminary graduate would teach made a more sophisticated, prolonged course impractical if not unnecessary.

For Tolstoi, of course, the training of teachers did not stop with giving them the necessary technical proficiency. Indeed, he considered the seminary's primary duty to be the development of character, not of mind. This task would be especially difficult for the seminaries because the minister, in view of the number of seminaries needed (five times the combined total of the two other normal schools), could not afford the expense of making them boarding schools. With most of their students residing in private rooms or apartments, the seminaries could not create that regimented atmosphere which the ministry had relied on elsewhere to mold its future teachers into loyal state servitors. Recognizing this, Tolstoi did not burden seminary officials with a long list of unenforceable student restrictions, but rather limited himself to a few specific suggestions: he merely required attendance at religious services, outlawed "reprehensible" pastimes like nights at the tavern, and urged the establishment of dormitories and the organization of extracurricular functions to protect students against the "unfortunate results" of unsupervised inactivity.

While thus not meticulously regulating the seminary pupils' lives, the ministry did want them carefully watched. Its 1875 circular ordered both faculty advisers and teacher monitors to check on student behavior by visiting their charges periodically in their rooms and by reporting any infraction of school rules. Since these men would have little influence once pupils left school for their various domiciles, sites far from the corruption of the city were even more essential for the seminary than for the institute. Tolstoi set up almost all his seminaries in small towns and discouraged unsanctioned excursions of any kind. In fact, students could not even return home during vacations without the director's permission.[56]

Despite these extensive precautions, seminary students, given the day-school character of their institution, had comparatively greater freedom than their peers at the other teacher academies. Such freedom would appear particularly dangerous to the ministry after the "going-to-the-people" movement had demonstrated that even the villages were not safe from the radicals. Realizing how easily a seminary pupil could acquire bad habits or subversive ideas during his many hours away from his teachers' vigilant eyes, Tolstoi recommended a broad program of indoctrination to counter whatever dangerous elements the student might meet when on his own.

According to the 1875 instruction a "general patriotic and moral purpose" should dominate every course, and faculty should inculcate feelings of "piety, devotion to throne and fatherland, respect for their profession." The historian, for instance, should "arouse . . . love of country and devotion to the emperor"; the religious teacher should encourage the faithful observance of ritual and cultivate "love of God and the Holy Church." The instructor's obligations did not end when he left the classroom; after all, his charges would "later be entrusted with one of the state's most essential tasks, the education of the people." Consequently, he must always set an example of the conscientious, obedient, and well-intentioned pedagogue. More important, each teacher acted as a sort of moral tutor to small groups of students. He saw them after school, talked with their family and friends, and in general strove to produce "those moral and intellectual qualities necessary for the future elementary instructor." [57] For the first time, the ministry attempted to exploit fully the propaganda potential of one of its schools.

If Tolstoi, by his curbing of normal school programs and by his emphasis on student control and indoctrination, betrayed his fear of subversive elements infiltrating his institutions, he never let this fear deter him from giving Russia the teachers' seminaries it needed. During his last decade in office, he vigorously campaigned for more seminaries, arguing that the teacher shortage had reached calamitous proportions. In 1873, for example, 3,700 of the 11,000 village schools in the five central districts either lacked instructors or suffered under incompetent ones. So irresistible were Tolstoi's demands on the usually niggardly Russian treasury that in just eight years, 1870 to 1877, he more than quadrupled the number of state seminaries, from eleven to forty-nine.[58]

This increase in schools further complicated the task of assuring them a steady supply of able and committed students. The unattractive life of a village school instructor would lure few to the seminary: these teachers seldom earned over 200 rubles a year, frequently worked without the basic instructional aids, and enjoyed a social position little above that of the peasants they taught. In view of these recruitment difficulties, the ministry could not afford a stringent admissions policy. Almost anyone sixteen or older could attend the seminary, for tuition was free and its entrance examination merely covered the rural primary school's abecedarian curriculum. Furthermore, the ministry awarded numerous stipends which, while binding the recipient to four years of state service, did guarantee him preference in teaching assignments. Such an indiscriminate approach had disappointing side effects. Many seminary graduates, especially the transfers from secondary schools, were so ill-suited for the hardships of country life that they left their posts at the first opportunity. These resignations convinced Tolstoi that normal school candidates should come from that environment in which they would have to live and work; that is, they should be peasant children educated in rural elementary schools. It was a sensible conclusion not only because the poor peasant would be least likely to scorn the meager benefits of an elementary school job, but also because, coming from the same milieu as most of his pupils, he would be best able to communicate with them.[59]

Implementation of this conclusion, however, proved troublesome. Like their municipal school counterparts, village school students generally could not meet the seminary's minimum age requirements immediately upon graduation. Consequently, Tolstoi had to adopt the city school practice of dispersing small grants (3 to 5 rubles a month) to those graduates who remained at their school until old enough for the seminary. Still discouraged by the quality and quantity of peasant applicants, the minister established between 1875 and 1879 for this group alone eleven preparatory classes at selected seminaries. The results pleased Tolstoi: by 1877 peasants comprised 51 percent of all seminary students and by 1881, 58 percent.[60]

The teachers' seminaries join the other normal schools as one of Tolstoi's most successful attempts to resolve his ministry's perpetual dilemma — how to promote education without thereby stimulating subversive elements. The seminaries' utilitarian curriculum, their restrictions on student freedom and faculty initiative, their use of propaganda both in and outside the classroom, while not foolproof devices, did in part shield students from radical influences and hence helped preserve the loyalty of Russia's future teachers. Of the thousands suspected of revolutionary activity in the 1870s, Tolstoi claimed that only three were seminary products.[61]

At the same time the seminaries, because of their practical course, intelligent recruitment programs, and especially their ever-increasing numbers, greatly contributed to Russian educational progress. This does not mean that the ministry's policies did not produce some harmful results (for the seminaries' narrow curriculum impaired their effectiveness as pedagogical institutions), but rather that Tolstoi's efforts raised the level of teacher training and created the dependable source of primary teachers Russia had lacked for so long. By Tolstoi's last year in office, the forty-nine state seminaries were averaging over 700 graduates annually, and they had yet to reach their full capacities.[62]

Impressive though their achievements were, the state seminaries could not by themselves resolve the teacher shortage, for there were far too few of them. Where Prussia, the European success story in elementary education, had one seminary for every 218,000 inhabitants in 1875, Russia two years later had only one for every 950,000. That year Tolstoi was still sixteen short of the desired ratio of one seminary per province.[63] Emergency measures were necessary, but Tolstoi warned against the indiscriminate hiring of people to fill vacancies. If the ministry did not insist on pedagogical competence and particularly political reliability, its primary schools, he feared, might become educational disasters and, worse, propaganda platforms for the radicals. Hence he advised the appointment of retired noncommissioned officers of good character and devoted to church, emperor, and country, but discouraged the employment of gymnasium and university dropouts, for they "had demonstrated their untrustworthiness" by not finishing their studies. After 1874 only those dropouts personally recommended by their gymnasium principal or university rector could receive elementary school posts. The high proportion of ex-students involved in the revolutionary plotting of the late 1870s forced Tolstoi to be ever more wary of bringing dropouts into his primary institutions. By 1880 the curator could not assign them to teaching positions until he had consulted the local governor as well as the director of the candidate's previous school.[64]

Zemstvo efforts to prepare teachers presented Tolstoi with a much thornier problem than the scattered instances of unqualified or suspect individuals applying for elementary school jobs. While he needed the instructors the zemstvos could supply, he did not want to entrust the training of such influential public figures as teachers to organizations he could not control, especially those with the antiautocratic tendencies of many zemstvos. His solution was simple: place the zemstvos' activity in teacher preparation under close ministerial surveillance.

In August 1875 the ministry brought the zemstvo refresher courses for teachers wholly within its jurisdiction. The elementary school inspector screened all participants; ministry, not zemstvo officials, selected the personnel in charge; and the department representative who personally supervised these meetings could on his own initiative remove disruptive delegates and suspend the session. Although deprived of their former authority over the courses, the zemstvos were still expected to cover all costs. Even with the above safeguards the ministry worried that these teacher conferences would serve other than instructional purposes. Putting political over pedagogical considerations, it refused at least one zemstvo's request for such sessions because it found them "superfluous" and potentially "harmful" since the "elementary teacher's low level of education" made him extremely susceptible to those agitators it felt the teachers' meetings would inevitably draw. As a result of the ministry's uncooperative attitude, the number of refresher courses sharply declined after 1875.[65]

The ministry's dealings with zemstvo normal schools were more conciliatory. Where it questioned the usefulness and feared the political consequences of the short-term pedagogical courses, it acknowledged the value of zemstvo-funded teachers' seminaries patterned after ministry schools. Any oppressive action which might close these institutions would be self-defeating. Tolstoi thus attempted a little bribery. In December 1871 he offered to extend the pension and service rights of state seminaries to zemstvo schools, provided that ministry rather than zemstvo officials appointed the faculty and supervised all school matters but the budget.[66] The zemstvos must sacrifice independence for privilege. Russia had then two types of zemstvo normal school; one supported by the zemstvo but controlled by the ministry, the other supported and controlled by the zemstvo.

Not satisfied with this arrangement, Tolstoi wanted all seminaries subordinate to his ministry. Each year he attacked zemstvo boards for mismanaging their teacher preparatory institutions, for hiring unqualified instructors, for allowing extraneous material into the curriculum; and each year he used these alleged shortcomings to back up his demands for state regulation of zemstvo seminaries. No such legislation resulted, but the ministry did make gains. The Moscow and Tver zemstvos transferred their normal schools to the ministry, apparently for financial reasons; the Riazan zemstvo retained jurisdiction over its school but reorganized it to meet the ministry's criticisms; however, the Chernigov zemstvo, one liberal journal claimed, shut its school rather than accept ministerial authority.[67] Despite Tolstoi's assaults, a majority of normal schools (six out of eleven) escaped ministry interference. With the eleven zemstvo institutes in 1877 graduating 206 elementary instructors, or 27.6 percent of the total from all state and private seminaries, any restrictions on their autonomy which could jeopardize their existence were unwise and impractical.[68]

Eager to control as well as improve education, the ministry worked hard, but with little regard for public participation, to remedy two major weaknesses of its elementary school system: its inadequate supervisory apparatus and its teacher shortage. Tolstoi had concentrated on these failings because for him the organization which inspected schools, regulated faculty appointments, and trained instructors would dominate primary education, and this body had to be his ministry. Only then could he be certain that Russia's elementary schools would serve not undermine the state. Such an attitude did not mean that Tolstoi would repudiate all society's efforts to educate the masses — this would have been foolhardy considering the government's straitened circumstances — only that he would oppose measures which challenged his authority. Hence he emasculated the school councils, attacked zemstvo seminaries, but solicited public assistance in resolving the one remaining problem plaguing Russian elementary education, the lack of funds to support the huge school network required. Whether society would readily accept this circumscribed yet onerous role in primary education was, of course, another matter.

Financing an Expanding School System

Both the immensity of the task of supplying the thousands of schools Russia needed and the ministry's unwillingness to use much of its budget to construct village schools made private subventions vital. During the 1870s Russia had probably the worst school-to-population ratio in Europe. In 1877, for example, less than 9 percent of all Russian children between the ages of seven and fourteen attended school, yet even a modest increase in enrollment would overtax existing institutions.[69] The ministry's major contribution toward rectifying the situation was to establish by 1879 a network of 1,009 model schools which it hoped would not only exemplify the proper "religious and moral organization" of education but would also by their accomplishments "arouse in the people a desire to create new schools." [70]

Otherwise the ministry did little to subsidize elementary institutions. As late as 1877, of 7,229,590 rubles spent on them, 992,482 rubles or 13.7 percent came from the government. This constituted about 6 percent of ministry expenditures. That same year the ministry covered 64.5 percent of gymnasium and 69.5 percent of teachers' seminary costs. It was a sensible order of priorities, given the heavy demands on the ministry's meager resources. Classical secondary education, after all, formed the cornerstone of Tolstoi's program, the gateway to the university and state service, while the preparation of teachers was the essential prerequisite for an expanding school system. Moreover, unlike the gymnasiums or normal schools, elementary institutions were cheap enough for small communities to afford; indeed, their funding was by law the responsibility of the zemstvo and the city duma. The ministry did assume a greater portion of school expenses in territories lacking zemstvos, but nationalistic considerations rather than the area's wants often determined this distribution. Thus Eastern Siberia, with only 2.1 percent of its school-age children in the classroom, obtained less than 14 percent of its funds from the state, in comparison with the $33\frac{1}{3}$ percent given the Vilna district — no doubt because in Vilna elementary education might counteract Polish influences.[71] In the zemstvo provinces the ministry provided only 382,069 rubles, or 8.2 percent of the 4,647,313 rubles assigned primary education there in 1877. Relying on the zemstvos to finance the schools, Tolstoi reserved ministry money for strengthening his inspection forces. In fact, he granted as much for the administration and supervision of elementary institutions in zemstvo districts as he did for their upkeep and support.[72]

At a glance it appears that Russia's new organs of local government were conscientiously fulfilling their obligations. Where the ministry by 1877 supplied 8.2 percent of elementary school costs in the five central districts, the dumas furnished 20.8 percent and the zemstvos 44.9 percent. Although the zemstvos and dumas accounted for 65.7 percent of the sums expended, one must not exaggerate their contribution. In the first place, these figures do not include funds for teacher preparation or school administration, the two areas where the ministry bore the heaviest charges. Furthermore, if one looks at the proportion of zemstvo and duma budgets assigned elementary schools rather than at the absolute amounts spent, a different picture emerges. In 1876 city governments earmarked just under 6 percent of their revenue for education, compared to Frankfurt's 25 percent, Breslau's 23 percent, and San Francisco's 15 percent. Partly to increase the pressure on duma treasuries, Tolstoi on 26 December 1876 approved special school boards for Russia's three largest municipalities — Moscow, St. Petersburg, and Odessa. Formerly the county councils had managed these cities' schools.[73] The frequently praised zemstvos were hardly more generous. From a total income of 31,845,000 rubles in 1877 they allotted primary schools 2,461,042 rubles or 7.7 percent, not much above the 6 percent share elementary institutions received from the ministry's budget.[74]

Thus during Tolstoi's tenure society, like the ministry, did not unstintingly finance primary education. While Tolstoi's insistence on central control may have discouraged contributions from those groups who wanted to direct the institutions they funded, one should not blame the ministry alone for the modest outlay of zemstvos and dumas. One can as easily fault these institutions' limited tax base, which could not provide sufficient income for all the services they were expected to perform, and the many zemstvo delegates who, as Veselovsky has stressed, had not yet realized the urgency of educating the masses.

Despite limited support from both the ministry and the public, a significant expansion of elementary institutions did occur. The average annual increment of new schools in the early 1860s was 648; by the 1870s it had passed 1,000. Between 1871 and 1877 the number of schools rose 48.4 percent from 16,379 to 24,853 and the number of students 57.8 percent from 675,317 to 1,065,889.[75] There was, however, a long way to go before Russia could bring literacy to all its people. In 1877 one out of every seventy-seven Russians was a student, an extremely poor showing when contrasted with the one-in-six ratio Prussia had achieved seven years previously. With so few of its people in school, Russia's literacy rate remained embarrassingly low. No detailed statistics on Russian literacy exist prior to the 1897 census, but from scattered surveys, from marriage records, and especially from the comprehensive information on army recruits after 1874, it is clear that during the seventies and eighties, except in the larger cities, less than 30 percent of all Russians could either read or write and a much smaller proportion could do both.[76]

Under such circumstances every school had to be wholly utilized; Russia could afford no half-empty classrooms. Even before Tolstoi became minister, zemstvos had inquired about compulsory schooling, and this time they found the new ministry receptive to their ideas. Tolstoi too wanted the greatest possible number of people educated. In 1874 a *Zhurnal* editorial supported obligatory attendance at schools with at least a 300-ruble annual budget, a properly certified teacher, and a course of study corresponding to the 1874 statute. The next year the ministry introduced a form of compulsory schooling by insisting upon regular attendance at the model schools.[77]

After the death in 1875 of A. S. Voronov, the ministry's major proponent of obligatory schooling, Tolstoi himself pushed the matter forward. Public apathy, he declared, was paralyzing elementary education. Since parents either did not send their children to school or withdrew them prematurely, "our school's fundamental and supreme task, the strengthening of the people's religious and moral feelings and the spread of useful knowledge, cannot be realized." [78] Believing compulsory schooling the solution, Tolstoi conducted Russia's first full-scale survey on the feasibility of obligatory elementary education. The replies of his primary school directors, which the ministry published in 1880, were discouraging. They revealed, as has our previous discussion on the state of elementary education, that Tolstoi's proposals were premature, that Russia could not yet supply the necessary teachers and institutions. [79] Not until 1908 would it have sufficient schools and faculty for the government to issue legislation on compulsory attendance.

Unfortunately for Russian education, many tsarist ministers did not share Tolstoi's desire to improve and extend the primary school network. The outbreak of terrorism and peasant unrest of 1878–1879, which culminated in an attempt on the emperor's life on 2 April 1879, blinded them to all but the political dangers of education even at the primary level. Declaring secularly trained teachers unreliable, these officials insisted that priests once more dominate primary education. For men like Third Section Head A. R. Drentel'n and Finance Minister S. A. Greig normal schools were superfluous, because primary teaching required no advanced pedagogical techniques, and dangerous, because their products would soon despise their humble situation and hence be most susceptible to radical propaganda.

Intent on saving his schools from the incompetent priest, Tolstoi refuted the reactionary contentions of Greig and Drentel'n. Proper teaching methods, he maintained, were more essential at the elementary school than at any other; yet the clergy knew nothing of these. Furthermore, the clergy, distracted as they were by their religious duties, could not give enough time to their classroom obligations. As for the aspersions on the seminary graduates' loyalty, Tolstoi pointed out that from 1871 to 1879 only three had been accused of state crimes.

It was a convincing performance, but the Committee of Ministers seemed too panicked by the threat of rebellion to heed reasoned argument. While not abolishing the teachers' seminaries, it warned them against attracting by "artificial means people belonging to the lower classes, primarily the peasantry," thus contradicting the minister's sensible recruitment policy. More disturbing still, the committee, although it admitted "the practical difficulties" its implementation would entail, did approve the principle of clergy predominance in primary education.[80] In the next decade K. P. Pobedonostsev would transform this retrogressive principle into an unhappy reality.

It is ironical that Tolstoi, who entered the education department an advocate of the priest-teacher, should end his career as Procurator of the Holy Synod and Minister of Education by defending the secularization of elementary schools. This shift in attitude provides a further indication of the minister's commitment to the advancement of Russian primary education. He established a fairly rational and rapidly expanding system of rural and urban elementary schools with their own teacher training institutions and government inspectors. Unlike some conservatives, Tolstoi recognized the urgency of his country's need for a literate population and worked conscientiously to fill this demand.

He also recognized the threat an independent education system posed for autocracy. Increased centralization of decision-making, extensive state surveillance, and strict control over teacher preparation formed his bulwark against the danger. As he told the emperor in his 1877 report, "I have continually tried to make the elementary school a properly functioning academic institution under the direct supervision and guidance of the Ministry of Education." [81] Tolstoi had again attempted a compromise between restriction and promotion. Both the right and the left attacked his solution, but Russian primary education clearly benefited.

"We are liberated," wrote Stasiulevich on 19 April 1880. "Tolstoi was dismissed yesterday." [1] The minister's fall should not have surprised his contemporaries, for he had been under attack since the early 1870s and had few backers to counter this assault. Vilified in liberal and radical journals, opposed by his own colleagues in the administration, and ill equipped personally to create a following of his own, Tolstoi had to rely too much on the emperor for the implementation of his policies. For example, only Alexander's unconditional support saved the secondary school legislation from drastic and unacceptable revisions. Unfortunately, the tsar was not always a consistent ally, as the education ministry's failure to gain a much larger share of the imperial budget or to undermine the war department's control over military schools demonstrated.

Tolstoi's position grew even less secure after 1874. His chief defender in the press, Katkov, began to harass him for not reforming the universities quickly enough; his bitterest enemy in the bureaucracy, the War Minister Miliutin, greatly increased his influence over Alexander II, particularly during the preparations for and conduct of the Russo-Turkish War of 1877–1878; and worst of all, his most powerful confederate, Count P. A. Shuvalov, relinquished his authority over the Third Section in 1874. Many considered Shuvalov the ablest leader the conservative faction had; with his departure Tolstoi lost an irreplaceable associate and a persuasive voice at court.

Despite his deepening isolation within the government, the minister would have tenaciously held onto his post had not the intensification of revolutionary activity in the late 1870s forcefully called his program into question. The special imperial conference set up to investigate the unprecedented wave of terrorism that began with Zasulich's shooting of Petersburg Police Chief Trepov in January 1878 and would not end until the assassination of Alexander II three years later, challenged Tolstoi's actions in all branches of education.

There was good cause for concern. A Third Section report stressed the high proportion of students involved in subversive agitation; recent Soviet research has confirmed these claims. "Students (or former students)," V. S. Antonov has argued, "played leading parts in almost all revolutionary circles in the 1860s and 1870s." Of the 5,664 people implicated in the radical movements of the seventies, 433 were teachers, 644 came from elementary or secondary schools, 266 from clerical seminaries, 37 from military gymnasiums, and 2,023 from institutes of higher learning: a total of 3,403 or 61.6 percent.[2]

Instead of watering down the fermenting spirits of Russia's students, Tolstoi had, according to many officials, actually added yeast to the dangerously bubbling mixture. Some, like Greig, blamed Tolstoi's progressive achievements, such as the rapid expansion in enrollment or the emasculation of the clergy's role in elementary education, for the troubles; others, like Loris-Melikov, singled out the ministry's repressive measures as the major factors in the alienation of the young. "Count Tolstoi," Melikov asserted, "undoubtedly deserves most of the credit for the loathsome direction Russian nihilism . . . has taken." [3] Whatever the reasons, the conclusion remained the same: Tolstoi was at fault.

Not only did the spread of revolutionary violence give Tolstoi's foes the evidence they needed to discredit his policies, it also brought to power the man primarily responsible for his downfall. One week after the dynamiting of the Winter Palace on 5 February 1880, the tsar named Count M. T. Loris-Melikov chairman of the newly formed Supreme Executive Commission. Having all departments, including the military, "unconditionally" subordinate to his commission and empowered "to undertake any action necessary to preserve state security and public tranquility," Loris-Melikov became virtual dictator of Russia.

His basic task was the familiar one of destroying the radical movement and of restoring stability; but Melikov, unlike many ministers, saw this assignment in terms broader than merely devising more effective police tactics. Realizing that the state would have to regain society's confidence to survive, he supplemented his attacks on subversives with a program of cautious concessions to public opinion, a program which might even include some form of representative assembly as long as this body did not inhibit autocratic prerogatives. One of Melikov's most famous conciliatory gestures to society would be the dismissal of Russia's detested Minister of Education. No sooner had he taken office than he started to challenge Tolstoi's position, and by 1 March 1880 he could boast to Valuev: "Tolstoi's days are numbered." [4]

Although Tolstoi's educational policies supplied the pretext, Melikov carried out his anti-Tolstoi campaign not in hopes of liberalizing the school system but for reasons of political expediency. Indeed, Melikov shared many of Tolstoi's ideas on education. He too wanted professional institutions for the poorer classes and the concentration of all schools under a single department. If anything, his views were more conservative than the minister's. While governor-general of Kharkov, he had joined the ranks of the education reactionaries by proclaiming the clergy the most appropriate primary school teachers and by proposing the elimination of gymnasium preparatory classes because these "attract an unmanageable *(neudobnyi)* contingent of students who then overcrowd the gymnasiums and universities." These two measures, it must be stressed, never received Tolstoi's approval, for he rightly considered them pedagogically unsound.[5]

However, his predilection for a restrictive education program did not prevent Melikov from demanding Tolstoi's resignation. The minister, though not necessarily his system, must go. The dictator's report of 11 April 1880 explained why:

> *Without, of course, changing its basic principles,* the education department must regain the confidence . . . of all classes and strata of society. I report to your Majesty without hesitation that the changes in the administrative personnel essential for this [the rehabilitation of public trust] will be greeted most sympathetically throughout Russia. Without these changes the success of measures already undertaken will be threatened.

In Melikov's opinion Tolstoi's continued presence in the administration endangered the autocracy. The latter's "harsh methods" and perpetual flaunting of public opinion had so increased his unpopularity that it had "begun to transfer itself from the minister to the government."[6] An astute politician, Loris-Melikov saw a twofold advantage in removing Tolstoi. He would earn the populace's gratitude by tossing out a hated minister and at the same time would dramatically disassociate his regime from the reactionary past personified by Tolstoi and thereby help restore society's faith in the state.

It was a clever scheme, but the emperor procrastinated until Tolstoi's own irascibility and tactlessness finally destroyed whatever backing he had once enjoyed at court. Exhibiting the same self-righteousness that had clouded his lyceum days, Tolstoi on 8 April 1880 condemned interior minister L. S. Makov's request for an Old Believer's church in Moscow and insinuated privately that the schismatics had bribed certain officials to endorse the project. A bitter quarrel ensued between Tolstoi and Makov, with Loris-Melikov and most ministers on Makov's side. Already the object of censure, Tolstoi had foolishly created a new scandal which further alienated his Petersburg colleagues. Loris-Melikov could now accuse him both of indirectly contributing to those subversive movements which imperiled the emperor's person and throne and of senselessly provoking a crisis within the government at a time when solidarity was vital. Alexander II reluctantly supported Melikov and asked for Tolstoi's resignation on 18 April. Melikov had won, and his plan seemed to be working. Contemporaries praised Melikov's action, for they thought it presaged the defeat of Tolstoi's policies. Even N. K. Mikhailovsky, the leading populist theorist, had to admit: "The dictator [Loris-Melikov] has performed a real service by retiring this Minister of Public Darkness (*pomrachenie*)." [7] Yet as he left the ministry, Tolstoi predicted his successors would not alter the system.[8] He proved the truer prophet.

An assassination attempt had catapulted Tolstoi to power; fourteen years later another such attempt brought him down. Like Uvarov, Tolstoi had hoped to improve and expand his country's educational system while averting the dangers this policy might create for autocracy. The result was a series of compromises that advanced Russian education, yet antagonized much of literate society and still did not prevent the elite the state so carefully trained from flowing in ever-increasing numbers into the revolutionary movement. Tolstoi, like his predecessors, could not resolve the dilemma facing Russia's education ministers.

The reasons for this failure can in part be found in the strategy Tolstoi adopted to prevent his school system from serving radical aims. He could not employ the two most effective measures available to him, the curtailment of educational opportunities or the liberalization of autocracy—the former because Russia urgently needed a skilled, literate populace, the latter because Tolstoi, even if he had the power (which he did not) to bring about such a change in government, wanted no fundamental revision of the Russian status quo. With both the most reactionary and the most progressive tactics ruled out, the task of devising a defense plan would become still more difficult. The minister had three major alternatives left: the preservation of secondary and higher education for those classes closest to the emperor, the encouragement of student loyalty through concessions and propaganda, and the introduction of rigorous state control over faculty and students. Although he would use all three, only the last truly appealed to Tolstoi.

For a man so often associated with the gentry party, Tolstoi did surprisingly little to transform his higher schools into exclusive institutions. True, he patterned the Russian gymnasium, the gateway to the university and hence to government service, after its European equivalent — partly in the belief that its long, classics-dominated course would, as in the West, discourage candidates from the poorer segments of society. He also created practically oriented, less prestigious schools like the realschulen and municipal schools to attract the urban commercial and laboring classes away from the gymnasium.

Yet these actions hardly constituted a vigorous campaign to make advanced schooling an aristocratic preserve. As Delianov discovered, only enrollment quotas could thwart the lower orders' desire for further education; but Tolstoi was too committed to his search for talent to interfere directly with admissions policies. He kept ministry schools open for all groups, defended the gymnasiums' easily accessible preparatory classes, left tuition rates to the local authorities, and did not challenge the universities' generous scholarship programs until the crisis years of the late 1870s. Consequently, the percentage of upper-class students at the gymnasiums and universities steadily declined between 1866 and 1881.

Equally ineffectual were the ministry's attempts to draw the student body to the regime. It had two different ploys at its disposal, cajolery and indoctrination. The former seemed best suited for the university population, whose relative sophistication lessened its susceptibility to propaganda. Indeed a sympathetic handling of legitimate complaints by university students might well have caused many to look more favorably on the existing system, but Tolstoi refused all concessions. They were, in his view, an unpardonable sign of weakness.

While not considering the indoctrination of students nearly so distasteful as yielding to their demands, Tolstoi never fully exploited his schools' propaganda potential. Of the ministry's institutions only the normal schools concentrated on the development of state-approved attitudes. Elsewhere the programs of political education were quite circumscribed. At the elementary level Tolstoi did instruct municipal school faculty to stress the homiletic aspects of subjects like history and Russian, but he actually diminished the village schools' religious-moral influence by removing them from the clergy's jurisdiction. Although the secondary school appeared the logical place for indoctrination work because its course was broader than the elementary school's and more closely regulated than the university's, the ministry still preferred to protect gymnasium students from subversive ideas than to inculcate the desired beliefs and values. It therefore wanted these students absorbed not in conversations about the importance of Orthodoxy, autocracy, and nationality but in lessons on languages and mathematics, those subjects least conducive to propaganda but most likely to engross the students in matters devoid of political content. A man with more faith in repression than in concession, in intellectual discipline than in psychological indoctrination, Tolstoi ignored the university student's grievances and forced upon the gymnasium pupil a dull, abstract program which exercised his mind without necessarily stimulating it. As a result of this narrow outlook, Tolstoi's schools would, if anything, alienate Russia's students instead of winning them over to the government.

Not admissions restrictions nor indoctrination nor conciliation but extensive bureaucratic controls served as the ministry's major guarantee that the educational system would aid rather than undermine the autocracy. Administrative centralization became the leitmotiv of the Tolstoi era. If the ministry could determine who taught, what was taught, and how it was taught, then, it argued, the chances of subversive elements infiltrating the schools would greatly diminish. Tolstoi therefore deprived the university assemblies, secondary school pedagogical councils, and local school boards of their former independence and initiative. Sacrificing the possible pedagogical benefits of educational freedom for the political security of tighter state controls, the ministry itself not only exhaustively defined every school's organization, academic plans, and programs of moral instruction, it also prohibited individual institutions from unilaterally taking any important action not covered by ministerial decree.

This power to dictate school policy would have little value, however, unless the ministry could count on the faithful acceptance of its rulings. It therefore checked classroom performances through state-directed final examinations and reinforced its supervisory apparatus by enlarging the district inspection team and by creating a network of elementary school inspectors. Despite these efforts Tolstoi could not afford to hire sufficient personnel to police his widely scattered schools effectively and thus assure the implementation of his elaborate statutes. Russia's vast distances and meager resources stymied his campaign for total domination over the ministry's schools.

In Tolstoi's scheme it was not enough to regulate what the students learned in class; the ministry must somehow govern their activity after school, for they could just as easily encounter pernicious doctrines outside the classroom as in. The boarding school appeared the ideal solution. Its residents could rarely leave the grounds and thus remained constantly under the eye of the authorities. Obviously, the minister could not convert all Russia's institutions into such schools, but he did establish them for those upon whose political reliability the whole educational system depended: the prospective elementary and secondary school faculty. All students at the historical-philological and teachers' institutes lived in, and day students at the teachers' seminaries found life at these secluded institutions rigidly controlled.

While unable to house all secondary school pupils in pensions or gymnasium-administered apartments, the ministry still sought to bring the boarding school's constrictive atmosphere to secondary education. It more than doubled the supervisory force at each institution, suggested pupils follow an inflexible daily regimen, and severely proscribed their extracurricular pursuits. University life was comparatively freer until the disturbances of the late 1870s provoked stern countermeasures. The university's lenient collegiate bodies relinquished their jurisdiction over disciplinary matters to a greatly strengthened inspectorate now directly subordinate to the ministry, and petty, often annoying, conduct rules soon resulted.

This policy of increased control over students and faculty had four main defects. First, it was based on the erroneous assumption that the causes of unrest and disaffection were primarily to be found in the youthful ego's susceptibility to the blandishments of professional agitators and not in existing conditions in Russia or in the nature of the educational system. Second, it could detract from the quality of education. No matter how good they were, the ministry's exhaustive course outlines would encourage a mechanical approach to teaching, deter instructors from searching for better classroom methods, and drive some unconventional but talented individuals away from a pedagogical career. Third, it could backfire on its proponents. As both the history of nineteenth-century Russia and our own experience with young dissidents reveal, repression can as easily turn people against the state as force them to support it. Fourth, the ministry's program of regimentation, while applied vigorously enough to antagonize those involved, could not be implemented fully. Tolstoi had too few inspectors and no truly effective means of supervising students outside the schoolroom. These shortcomings were especially harmful since control works best when the threat of its being exercised is always present — a situation which exists in modern totalitarian states, but which imperial Russia lacked the necessary techniques, resources, and probably even the will to bring about.

Under such circumstances the ministry could only make its authority universally felt with help from society; yet it did little to win its assistance. Quite the contrary, it often disregarded the public's demands and introduced legislation that alienated influential elements within the community. Although Tolstoi justifiably defended his statutes by stressing their beneficial aspects and their resemblance to plans widely accepted in the West, his arguments convinced few. Tolstoi had chosen to ignore the fact that for many the ministry's activities marked the first serious attempt to undo the reforms of the sixties and thus symbolized the government's repudiation of its liberal past. To aid the ministry was to aid reaction.

These failings and drawbacks of the ministry's efforts at centralization and restriction should not, as they so frequently have done, obscure the considerable accomplishments of the Tolstoi ministry. Tolstoi drove himself to provide Russia with an education system which could satisfy the demands of a rapidly modernizing country, for he recognized that his state could not emerge from its backwardness to compete successfully with the industrialized nations of the West without a skilled professional elite and a literate population. A publishing scholar in his own right, he strove to raise the level of Russian higher education. Not only did he tighten university admissions requirements and academic standards, he also encouraged scientific research by assisting academic meetings and associations and by strengthening Russia's laboratories, libraries, observatories, and Academy of Sciences.

Since there was little point in reinforcing the top rungs of the education ladder if the bottom and middle ones remained weak, Tolstoi devoted most of his energies to elementary and secondary schools. He converted anachronistic or redundant institutions into more functional ones. The multipurpose municipal primary school replaced the county school, whose combination of elementary and secondary course offerings had attracted few pupils; the technically oriented, adaptable realschulen supplanted the realgymnasiums, whose general curriculum in science and modern languages had prepared graduates for neither the university nor practical activity.

More laudable yet were the ministry's efforts to guarantee its schools abler teachers. Tolstoi was the only Russian minister in the nineteenth century to handle the problem of teacher training effectively. Dissatisfied with his predecessor's ad hoc remedies and with the clergy's blunderings in primary education, he founded special government-supported and administered institutions for the preparation of secondary and elementary instructors. Once appointed, the instructor continued to receive the ministry's careful attention. Although admittedly part of its control apparatus, the visits by the inspector, the articles on teaching in the *Zhurnal*, and especially the centrally compiled lesson plans and textbook lists had pedagogical benefits as well, for they supplied useful and often much-needed guidance to Russia's teachers.

Given the empire's tiny network of schools at Tolstoi's accession, such qualitative advances were futile unless accompanied by a tremendous quantitative increase in educational institutions. And it is in this area, the expansion of the Russian school system, that the Tolstoi ministry achieved its greatest successes. While many would question the wisdom behind some of Tolstoi's measures to improve education (like the extreme practical bias in normal school courses or the introduction of applied subjects into municipal school and realschule curricula), few could deny the value of his struggle to alleviate his country's critical shortage of schools and faculty.

In higher education he set up three new institutions, reinvigorated seven faltering ones, and initiated plans for a university in Siberia. Empty professorial chairs, a common predicament in underdeveloped countries with a comparatively small educated class, remained to plague the universities, but an extensive fellowship program for prospective instructors did decrease vacancies from 196 at six universities in 1868 to 154 at eight universities in 1877.

As the keystone of the Tolstoi system and the recipient of the largest share of the ministry's budget, secondary education registered far more impressive gains. Between 1871 and 1878 the number of gymnasiums and realschulen virtually doubled (from 146 to 273). Despite this unprecedented proliferation of schools, the ministry managed to reduce staffing problems by creating two historical-philological institutes and by introducing a wide variety of emergency teacher training programs.

The information on elementary schools is sketchy, but existing statistics indicate the ministry accomplished much in this branch of education too. During the 1870s regular primary schools grew in number from 16,379 to 24,583, one- and two-class model schools from 166 to 1,009, and municipal schools from none to over 100. This expansion of elementary institutions reflected in part the commendable performance of the ministry's recently established normal schools, which were graduating over 800 certified teachers a year by the end of the decade. With so many more schools and teachers available, the government could begin to answer its subjects' increasing demands for education. Secondary school enrollment rose 86 percent between 1869 and 1878, primary school enrollment 58 percent between 1871 and 1878. Thus in numerous respects the Tolstoi ministry was an era of substantial progress in Russian education.

Tolstoi had clearly succeeded more in improving the school system than in neutralizing the political awareness of its products. Despite his justifiable fears of education's latent threat to the regime he had sworn to uphold, he energetically promoted the spread of education throughout Russia; and for this he deserves praise too often denied him. Less fortunate were his efforts at preventing students and teachers from questioning and turning against the status quo. Quite possibly no program could have accomplished this, could have nullified the dangerous aspects of the dilemma of education, but Tolstoi's methods were definitely shortsighted. While he was not so myopic as to block the development of education, neither was he sufficiently sharp-sighted to employ the subtler, positive devices of concession and indoctrination in his campaign to render the school system safe for autocracy. Instead, he risked antagonizing Russia's students still further by adopting almost entirely negative tactics: the curtailment of local initiative, the greater regulation of faculty and students, the isolation of pupils from harmful outside influences, and the exclusion of politically relevant material from the curriculum.

Tolstoi was committed to strengthening his state, but only through bureaucratic solutions. Distrusting public opinion and the radical ideas it espoused, Tolstoi personified the failings of the Russian government during the latter half of the nineteenth century. Like the autocracy in general, his attempts to modernize his country helped create the very elements that might destroy the existing regime. Hence, like the autocracy, he was always on the defensive, fighting a rearguard action with the outmoded weapons of his predecessors — a strategy that would delay but not defeat the forces of change.

Abbreviations Used in the Notes

Notes   Bibliography   Index

Abbreviations Used in the Notes

MV   *Sobranie peredovykh statei "Moskovskikh vedomostei"*
PSZ   *Polnoe sobranie zakonov Rossiiskoi Imperii*
SP   *Sbornik postanovlenii po Ministerstvu Narodnogo Prosveshcheniia*
SR   *Sbornik rasporiazhenii po Ministerstvu Narodnogo Prosveshcheniia*

Notes

PREFACE

1. Patrick L. Alston, *Education and the State in Tsarist Russia* (Stanford, 1969), p. 295.

2. See, for example, N. V. Chekhov, *Narodnoe obrazovanie v Rossii s 60-kh godov XIX veka* (Moscow, 1912); P. F. Kapterev, *Istoriia russkoi pedagogii* (St. Petersburg, n.d.); V. I. Charnolusky, "Nachal'noe obrazovanie vo vtoroi poloviny XIX stoletiia," in *Istoriia Rossii v XIX veke* (St. Petersburg, 191?), VII, 106–169; Sh. I. Ganelin, *Ocherki po istorii srednei shkoly v Rossii vtoroi poloviny XIX veka* (2nd ed. rev.; Moscow, 1959); E. N. Medynsky, *Istoriia russkoi pedagogiki do velikoi oktiabr'skoi sotsialisticheskoi revoliutsii* (2nd ed. rev.; Moscow, 1938); V. Z. Smirnov, *Reforma nachal'noi i srednei shkoly v 60-kh godakh XIXv* (Moscow, 1954).

3. Nicholas Hans, *History of Russian Educational Policy (1701–1917)* (London, 1931), pp. 110–139.

CHAPTER 1   The Dilemma of Education, and Ministerial Solutions to 1866

1. S. S. Tatishchev, *Imperator Aleksandr II: ego zhizn' i tsarstvovanie* (St. Petersburg, 1903), II, 237.

2. "Mery i predpolozheniia otnositel'no gimnazii i nachal'nogo narodnogo obrazovaniia" (Measures and proposals relating to the gymnasiums and elementary education), in Russia, Ministerstvo Narodnogo Prosveshcheniia, *Zhurnal Ministerstva Narodnogo Prosveshcheniia*, CXXXIII (January 1867), otdel III, 1. Cited hereafter in notes and text as *Zhurnal*.

3. The best work on Russian education in the eighteenth century is M. I. Demkov, *Istoriia russkoi pedagogiki*, pt. II: *Russkaia pedagogika (XVIII vek)* (2nd ed. rev.; Moscow, 1910). See also S. V. Rozhdestvensky, *Ocherki po istorii sistem narodnogo prosveshcheniia v Rossii v XVIII–XIX vekakh*, vol. I (St. Petersburg, 1912).

4. S. V. Rozhdestvensky, *Istoricheskii obzor deiatel'nosti Ministerstva Narodnogo Prosveshcheniia 1802–1902* (St. Petersburg, 1902), p. 44.

5. Russia, Ministerstvo Narodnogo Prosveshcheniia, *Sbornik postanovlenii po Ministerstvu Narodnogo Prosveshcheniia*, vol. I: *1802–1825* (2nd ed., 1875), no. 63, 5 November 1804, cols. 295, 297–299, 304–309, 326. Cited hereafter as *SP*. By 1804 there were five universities in Russia, at Dorpat, Vilna, Moscow, Kharkov, and Kazan. Only the last three were covered by the 1804 regulations, which like most subsequent major educational acts did not apply in the non-Russian borderlands.

6. Ibid., cols. 326–329; no. 64, 5 November 1804, cols. 348, 356.

7. Ibid., no. 64, col. 341.

8. Hans, *History,* pp. 43–45, 46–49; *SP*, I, no. 64, cols. 334, 353, 360.

9. *SP*, I, no. 64, cols. 331–332, 352, 359.

10. Ibid., no. 1, 8 September 1802, col. 1.

11. Ibid., no. 64, col. 366.

12. Richard Pipes, *Karamzin's Memoir on Ancient and Modern Russia: A Translation and Analysis* (Cambridge, Mass., 1959), pp. 158–159.

13. On the problems involved in carrying out Alexander's early educational reforms, see, for example, Rozhdestvensky, *Istoricheskii obzor*, pp. 31–104; [T. Darlington], *Education in Russia* (London, 1909), pp. 36–53; E. K. Schmid, ed. and tran., *Istoriia srednikh uchebnykh zavedenii v Rossii* (published as appendixes to the *Zhurnal* 1877–1878 and bound as a single volume by Yale University Library), pp. 1–115; James T. Flynn, "The Universities, the Gentry and the Russian Imperial Services, 1815–1825," *Canadian Slavic Studies*, 2:486–503 (winter 1968).

14. See L. Pearce Williams, "Science, Education and Napoleon I," *Isis*, 47:369–382 (1956).

15. *SP*, I, no. 376, 24 October 1817, col. 1058.

16. Rozhdestvensky, *Istoricheskii obzor*, pp. 118–119.

17. Ibid., p. 116. The entire instruction can be found in *SP*, I, no. 461, cols. 1317–1337.

18. Quoted in Rozhdestvensky, *Istoricheskii obzor*, p. 124. The best account of the campaign against the universities is that of M. I. Sukhomlinov, *Issledovaniia i stat'i*, vol. I: *Materialy dlia istorii obrazovaniia v Rossii v tsarstvovanie Imperatora Aleksandra I* (St. Petersburg, 1889).

19. Quoted in Schmid, p. 87. See also Russia, Ministerstvo Narodnogo Prosveshcheniia, *Sbornik rasporiazhenii po Ministerstvu Narodnogo Prosveshcheniia*, vol. I: *1802–1834* (1866), no. 174, 5 June 1819, cols. 386–387. Cited hereafter as *SR*.

20. *SP*, I, no. 425, cols. 1258–1263.

21. *SR*, I, no. 251, 11 September 1824, col. 529. Shishkov directed only educational policy, for Alexander I had abolished the joint Ministry of Spiritual Affairs and Education when he dismissed Golitsyn.

22. Ibid., cols. 528–529.

23. Quoted in N. K. Shil'der, *Imperator Nikolai Pervyi: ego zhizn' i tsarstvovanie* (St. Petersburg, 1903), I, 705.

24. J.-A. Chaptal, *Rapport et projet de loi sur l'instruction publique* (Paris, 1801), p. 20, as quoted in Williams, *Isis*, 47:371; *SP*, vol. II, pt. I: *1825–1839* (2nd ed., 1875), no. 41, 19 August 1827, col. 71; *SR*, I, no. 251, col. 529.

25. *SP*, II, pt. I, no. 41, cols. 71–73; no. 84, 8 December 1828, cols. 200, 202, 204, 206, 211, 213–215, 225, 227–228; *SR*, I, no. 96, 18 September 1813, cols. 223–224.

26. *SP*, II, pt. I, no. 411, cols. 955–961.

27. Ibid., no. 417, 26 July 1835, cols. 970, 974, 975–977, 978–981.

28. *SR*, I, no. 433, 22 May 1833, col. 864.

29. Ibid., col. 866; *SP*, II, pt. I, no. 276, 5 December 1833, cols. 661–666; no. 417, col. 979; no. 540, 8 April 1837, cols. 1245–1247; Iu. N. Egorov, "Reaktsionnaia politika tsarizma v voprosakh universitetskogo obrazovaniia v 30-50-kh gg. XIX v.," *Nauchnye doklady vysshei shkoly: istoricheskie nauki*, no. 3 (1960), 68.

30. *SP*, II, pt. I, prilozhenie to no. 84, col. 9.

31. *SR*, vol. II: *1835–1849* (1866), no. 684, 17 November 1844, cols. 776–777; no. 812, 9 January 1847, cols. 924–925.

32. Ibid., no. 436, 31 December 1840, cols. 494–496; *SP*, II, pt. II: *1840–1855* (2nd ed., 1876), no. 304, cols. 629–631; no. 305, cols. 632–634; Alston, pp. 35–36.

33. "Materialy dlia istorii i statistiki nashikh gimnazii" (Materials for the history and statistics of our gymnasiums), *Zhurnal*, CXXI (February 1864), otdel II, 376–377.

34. Rozhdestvensky, *Istoricheskii obzor*, p. 733.

35. Ibid., p. 249; *SP*, II, pt. I, prilozhenie to no. 84, cols. 2–5; prilozhenie to no. 417, cols. 34–38; nos. 78–79, 30 September 1828, cols. 157–189; *SR*, II, no. 672, 10 October 1844, cols. 768–770.

36. N. Kh. Vessel', "Nasha sredniaia obshcheobrazovatel'naia shkola," *Russkii vestnik*, February 1903, p. 586. Vessel', however, did gloss over the inadequacy of the gymnasium courses in science. Cf. Alexander Vucinich, *Science in Russian Culture*, vol. I: *A History to 1860* (Stanford, 1963), pp. 253–254.

37. Hans, *History*, p. 235; Alston, p. 36.

38. Quoted in Shil'der, II, 629.

39. Rozhdestvensky, *Istoricheskii obzor*, pp. 226–227.

40. See, for example, Alston, pp. 39–40; Hugh Seton-Watson, *The Russian Empire 1801–1917* (Oxford, 1967), pp. 276–278.

41. Rozhdestvensky, *Istoricheskii obzor*, p. 260; *SR*, II, no. 865, 11 March 1848, cols. 994–996; *SP*, II, pt. II, no. 480, col. 1066.

42. *SP*, II, pt. II, no. 517, cols. 1135–1138.

43. Quoted in Alston, p. 40.

44. *SP*, II, pt. II, no. 494, 11 October 1849, cols. 1104–1105; no. 578, cols. 1242–1248; no. 498, 7 November 1849, cols. 1116–1118; *SR*, vol. III: *1850–1864* (1867), no. 38, 23 January 1851, cols. 42–43; A. F. Andriashev, "Vospominaniia starogo pedagoga," *Russkaia starina*, CXLVI (April 1911), 98–99.

45. *SP*, II, pt. II, no. 476, 21 March 1849, cols. 1051–1063; prilozhenie to no. 476, cols. 62–63.

46. Ibid., no. 624, 3 October 1851, col. 1313; no. 625, cols. 1314–1316; *SR*, III, no. 101, 14 May 1852, col. 88; prilozhenie to no. 101, cols. 6–19.

47. Quoted in Rozhdestvensky, *Istoricheskii obzor*, p. 271.

48. Tatishchev, II, 237.

49. A. S. Norov (1854–1858), E. P. Kovalevsky (1858–1861), E. V. Putiatin (June-December 1861) and A. V. Golovnin (1862–1866).

50. Chekhov, p. 10.

51. N. I. Pirogov, "Voprosy zhizni" (Vital questions), *Zhurnal*, XLI (September 1856), otdel II, 339–380. An analysis of Russian pedagogical thought lies beyond the scope of this study. For a brief discussion of these developments, see the following fairly recent but rather disappointing works: V. Z. Smirnov, *Ocherki po istorii progressivnoi russkoi pedagogiki XIX veka* (Moscow, 1963), pp. 163–232; Nicholas Hans, *The Russian Tradition in Education* (London, 1963), pp. 45–106, 129–149.

52. N. I. Pirogov, *Sochineniia N. I. Pirogova* (2nd ed.; St. Petersburg, 1900), I, 271–279, 345–391; N. D. Bogatinov, "Vospominaniia N. D. Bogatinova," *Russkii arkhiv*, bk. II (1899), 439, 530, 531, 538; Andriashev, *Russkaia starina*, CXLVIII (November-December 1911), 345–352, 619–624; Chekhov, pp. 12–19.

53. For a discussion of the Sunday schools, see Ia. V. Abramov, *Nashi voskresnye shkoly: ikh proshloe i nastoiashchee* (St. Petersburg, 1900), pp. 1–77; Reginald E. Zelnik, "The Sunday School Movement in Russia, 1859–1862," *Journal of Modern History*, 37:151–170 (June 1965).

54. *SP*, III, no. 28, 23 November 1855, col. 64; no. 250, 22 February 1860, cols. 510–515; no. 218, 2 September 1859, cols. 440–441; no. 347, col. 734; Rozhdestvensky, *Istoricheskii obzor*, p. 357.

55. See, for example, L. F. Panteleev, *Iz vospominanii proshlogo*, S. A. Reiser, ed. (Moscow-Leningrad, 1934), pp. 72–74; R. Vydrin, *Osnovnye momenty studencheskogo dvizheniia v Rossii* (Moscow, 1908), pp. 13–16; V. Ostrogorsky, *Iz istorii moego uchitel'stva, kak ia sdelalsia uchitelem (1851–1864 gg.)* (St. Petersburg, 1895), pp. 45–51.

56. A full account of the student movement can be found in Thomas J. Hegarty, "Student Movements in Russian Universities 1855–1861," (Ph.D. diss., Harvard University, 1965). On the Moscow and Petersburg universities alone, see William L. Mathes, "The Origins of Confrontation Politics in Russian Universities: Student Activism, 1855–1861," *Canadian Slavic Studies*, 2:28–45 (spring 1968).

57. *SP*, III, no. 355, cols. 732–736. For an account of these discussions on university organization, see G. Dzhanshiev, *Epokha velikikh reform: istoricheskie spravki* (7th ed. rev.; Moscow, 1898), pp. 281–314.

58. Vydrin, p. 15; V. V. Mavrodin, ed., *Leningradskii universitet v vospominaniiakh sovremennikov*, vol. I: *Peterburgskii universitet 1819–1895* (Leningrad, 1963), p. 266, n. 13.

59. Quoted in Franco Venturi, *Roots of Revolution: A History of the Populist and Socialist Movements in Nineteenth Century Russia*, tran. by Francis Haskell (London, 1960), p. 226.

60. On the Petersburg disorders, see V. I. Orlov, *Studencheskoe dvizhenie moskovskogo universiteta v XIX stoletii* (Moscow, 1934), pp. 142–166; Hegarty, pp. 104–141; *Materialy dlia istorii goneniia studentov pri Aleksandre II* (4th ed.; Leipzig, 1902); Mavrodin, I, 66–108. Alston (p. 50) mistakenly claims that all Russian universities were shut down.

61. See, for example, Terence Emmons, "The Peasant and the Emancipation," in *The Peasant in Nineteenth Century Russia*, Wayne S. Vucinich, ed. (Stanford, 1968), pp. 54–62.

62. [M. I. Semevsky], "Aleksandr Vasil'evich Golovnin," *Russkaia starina*, LIII (March 1887), 778.

63. The hypercritical Chicherin (in *Vospominaniia Borisa Nikolaevicha Chicherina*, vol. IV: *Moskovskii universitet*, S. V. Bakhrushin and M. A. Tsiavlovsky, eds. [Moscow, 1929], p. 55) described Golovnin as an "honorable man of small intellect," an allegation at variance with most contemporary accounts (cf. A. I. Del'vig, *Polveka russkoi zhizni; vospominaniia A. I. Del'viga 1820–1870*, S. Ia. Shtraikh, ed. [Moscow-Leningrad, 1920], II, 490–491) and belied by Golovnin's brilliant success at the Tsarskoe Selo Lyceum, where he graduated at the top of his class.

64. F. I. Buslaev, *Moi vospominaniia* (Moscow, 1897), p. 358; E. M. Feoktistov, *Vospominaniia E. M. Feoktistova: za kulisami politiki i literatury 1848–96*, Iu. G. Oksman, ed. (Leningrad, 1929), pp. 131–132.

65. For a brief but cogent analysis of these discussions, see Alston, pp. 51–57, 71–74; also the recent article by William L. Mathes, "N. I. Pirogov and the Reform of University Government, 1856–1866," *Slavic Review*, 31:34–49 (March 1972).

66. Only a quick summary of Golovnin's program will be given here, for it will receive close attention during the discussion of Tolstoi's efforts to undo it.

67. Russia, Ministerstvo Narodnogo Prosveshcheniia, *Obzor deiatel'nosti Ministerstva Narodnogo Prosveshcheniia i povedomstvennykh emu uchrezhdenii v 1862, 63 i 64 godakh* (St. Petersburg, 1865), p. 317. Cited hereafter as *Obzor 1862–64*.

68. The 1863 university statute set tuition rates of 50 rubles a year at Moscow and Petersburg universities and 40 a year in the provinces. *SP*, III, no. 517, col. 1065. The projects of 1862 had advocated without success a ladder system of education and a university open to graduates of the classical and regular gymnasiums, the latter offering only Latin and stressing mathematics and the natural sciences. See I. Aleshintsev, *Istoriia gimnazicheskogo obrazovaniia v Rossii (XVIII i XIX vek)* (St. Petersburg, 1912), pp. 217–250.

69. *SP*, III, no. 517, cols. 1041–1045; Rozhdestvensky, *Istoricheskii obzor*, pp. 419, 423; Alexander Vucinich, *Science in Russian Culture*, vol. II: *1861–1917* (Stanford, 1970), pp. 48–50.

70. V. I., "Po voprosu o prigotovlenii uchitelei dlia gimnazii i progimnazii" (On the question of preparing teachers for the gymnasium and progymnasium), *Zhurnal*, CXXXIV (April 1867), otdel II, 191–198; *SP*, vol. IV: *1865–1870* (1871), no. 23, 23 March 1865, cols. 149–152; Rozhdestvensky, *Istoricheskii obzor*, p. 733.

71. *SP*, III, no. 517, esp. cols. 1040–1056; A. I. Markevich, *Dvadtsatipiatiletie imperatorskogo novorossiiskogo universiteta* (Odessa, 1890), pp. 154–155.

72. *SP*, III, no. 631, esp. cols. 1422–1426, 1433–1435; no. 610, 14 July 1864, cols. 1342–1350.

CHAPTER 2   The Shaping of a Bureaucrat

1. D. Samarine, ed., *Correspondance de G. Samarine avec La Baronne de Rahden 1861–1876* (2nd ed.; Moscow, 1894), p. 39.

2. On Golovnin's fall see, for example, Del'vig, II, 267, 293–296; M. K. Lemke, ed., *M. M. Stasiulevich i ego sovremenniki v ikh perepiske* (St. Petersburg, 1911–1913), I, 131, 164–166; P. Gurevich, ed., "Nezabvennye mysli nezabvennykh liudei (Iz istorii reaktsii 60-kh godov)," *Byloe*, January 1907, pp. 236–239; Tatishchev, II, 4–8.

3. Quoted in Tatishchev, II, 259–261.

4. Quoted in Ibid., pp. 8–10.

5. *SR*, vol. IV: *1865–1870* (1874), no. 84, 1 June 1866, cols. 333–334.

6. For a detailed description of the lyceum's early history, see K. Ia. Grot, *Pushkinskii litsei (1811–1817): bumagi I-go kursa* (St. Petersburg, 1911); [N. Golitsyn], *Blagorodnyi pansion imperatorskogo tsarskosel'skogo litseia 1814–1829* (St. Petersburg, 1869): I. Seleznev, *Istoricheskii ocherk imperatorskogo byvshego tsarskosel'skogo nyne aleksandrovskogo litseia za pervoe ego piatidesiatiletie s 1811 po 1861 god* (St. Petersburg, 1861), pp. 29 ff.

7. Charles and Barbara Jelavich, eds., *The Education of a Russian Statesman: The Memoirs of Nicholas Karlovich Giers* (Berkeley, 1962), p. 51. On student medical care, see Ia. Grot, *Pushkin, ego litseiskie tovarishchi i nastavniki* (St. Petersburg, 1887), p. 54; K. S. Veselovsky, "Vospominaniia o tsarsko-sel'skom litsee, 1832–1838 gg.," *Russkaia starina*, CIV (October 1900), 17–18. On fees see Seleznev, p. 190.

8. Seleznev, pp. 263, 283, 286, 329–330, 351–352, 360, 378–379; Russia, *Polnoe sobranie zakonov Rossiiskoi Imperii*, 2nd series, vol. IX (1834), sect. II, no. 7391, 12 September 1834, p. 25. Cited hereafter as *PSZ*.

9. A. M. Unkovsky, "Zapiski," *Russkaia mysl'*, XXVII (June 1906), 185.

10. K. Grot, p. 422; "Predislovie," *Pamiatnaia knizhka imperatorskogo aleksandrovskogo litseia na 1880 god*, pp. V–VI; A. N. Iakhontov, "Vospominaniia tsarskosel'skogo litseista, 1832–1838 gg.," *Russkaia starina*, LX (October 1888), 112–115; Veselovsky, *Russkaia starina*, CIV, 9–15; V. A. Desnitsky, ed., *Delo petrashevtsev* (Moscow-Leningrad, 1937–1951), II, 319; N. Grot, ed., *Ia. K. Grot: neskol'ko dannykh k ego biografii i kharakteristike* (St. Petersburg, 1895), pp. 7–16.

11. Iakhontov, *Russkaia starina*, LX, 111–112; Veselovsky, *Russkaia starina*, CIV, 8, 20; Seleznev, pp. 394–398.

12. Seleznev, pp. 326, 381–382; A. A. Kharitonov, *Iz vospominanii A. A. Kharitonova (1824–1854)* (St. Petersburg, 1894), p. 12.

13. Jelavich, p. 53; Seleznev, pp. 328–329, 350, 359, 392–394; Veselovsky, *Russkaia starina*, CIV, 22–23.

14. Seleznev, pp. 225–227, 392–398; Iakhontov, *Russkaia starina*, LX, 111–112; Veselovsky, *Russkaia starina*, CIV, 20.

15. P. P. Semenov-Tian-Shansky, *Memuary*, vol. I: *Detstvo i iunost' (1827–1855)* (Petrograd, 1917), p. 129. M. M. Stasiulevich even used this story in a pamphlet attacking Tolstoi's appointment as Minister of the Interior in 1882 (Lemke, III, 763).

16. See M. V. Nechkina, *Dvizhenie dekabristov* (Moscow, 1955), I, pp. 107 ff.

17. Iakhontov, *Russkaia starina*, LX, 108–109; Veselovsky, *Russkaia starina*, CIV, 7–8, 16; Unkovsky, *Russkaia mysl'*, XXVII, 186–187.

18. Sidney Monas, *The Third Section: Police and Society in Russia under Nicholas I* (Cambridge, Mass., 1961), p. 249; Desnitsky, II; V. I. Semevsky, *Sobranie sochinenii*, vol. II: *M. V. Butashevich-Petrashevsky i petrashevtsy*, V. Vo-

dovozov, ed. (Moscow, 1922), pt. I, 25–29; K. S. Veselovsky, "Vospominaniia o nekotorykh litseiskikh tovarishchakh, Mikhail Vasil'evich Butashevich-Petrashevsky," *Russkaia starina*, CIII (September 1900), 449–452.

19. D. Kobeko, *Imperatorskoi tsarskosel'skii litsei: nastavniki i pitomtsy 1811–1843* (St. Petersburg, 1911), p. 478.

20. *Piatidesiatiletnyi iubilei imperatorskogo aleksandrovskogo litseia 19 oktiabria 1861 goda* (St. Petersburg, 1861), p. 19.

21. Jelavich, p. 93; *PSZ*, vol. XXXIV (1817), no. 26913, 7 June 1817, p. 379.

22. Rozhdestvensky, *Istoricheskii obzor*, pp. 394, 480. There are other striking parallels in the careers of Tolstoi and Golovnin. Both left the Fourth Section for the Ministry of the Interior; both aided Grand Duke Constantine Nikolaevich in his reorganization of the Naval Ministry, and both were members of the Central School Board before becoming Minister of Education. It is interesting to speculate that an intense rivalry sprang up between these two men and that this partially explains Tolstoi's animosity toward Golovnin and his policies.

23. On Tolstoi's early career, see Ibid., p. 480; "Konchina grafa Dmitriia Andreevicha Tolstogo" (The death of Count Dmitry Andreevich Tolstoi), *Zhurnal*, CCLXIII (May 1889), otdel IV, 2–3; O. Boratynskaia, "A. K. Kazembek," *Russkii arkhiv*, bk. IV (1893), 546–547; M. F. Shugurov, "Istoriia Evreev v Rossii," *Russkii arkhiv*, bk. I (1894), 500; D. A. Tolstoi, *Rimskii katolitsizm v Rossii* (St. Petersburg, 1876), I, v; N. Barsukov, *Zhizn' i trudy M. P. Pogodina* (St. Petersburg, 1888–1910), XI, 485–486, 499–500; XII, 407. Biographical details on Tolstoi's activities before 1866 are scarce. Even scholars with access to Soviet archives have discovered surprisingly little about his life. Cf. P. A. Zaionchkovsky, *Rossiiskoe samoderzhavie v kontse XIX stoletiia* (Moscow, 1970), pp. 60–65; James Cobb Mills, Jr., "Dmitrii Tolstoi as Minister of Education in Russia, 1866–1880" (Ph.D. diss., Indiana University, 1967).

24. V. P. Meshchersky, *Moi vospominaniia* (St. Petersburg, 1897–1898), I, 99.

25. S. F. Ogorodnikov, *Istoricheskii obzor razvitiia i deiatel'nosti Morskogo Ministerstva za sto let ego sushchestvovaniia (1802–1902 gg.)* (St. Petersburg, 1902), pp. 138–140.

26. Ibid., pp. 136–151; K. A. Mann, ed., *Obzor deiatel'nosti morskogo upravleniia v Rossii v pervoe dvadtsatipiatiletie blagopoluchnogo tsarstvovaniia Gosudariia Imperatora Aleksandra Nikolaevicha 1855–1880* (St. Petersburg, 1880), II, 906–955; Tatishchev, II, 159.

27. Mann, I, 373–374; II, 671–672, 908–909, 944, 950–951; A. F. Koni, *Na zhiznennom puti*, vol. II (St. Petersburg, 1912), pp. 360, 369; Dzhanshiev, *Epokha*, pp. 660–686.

28. Mann, II, 930–931; Ogorodnikov, p. 139; D. A. Tolstoi, "O pervo-

nachal'nom uchrezhdenii i posledovavshikh izmeneniiakh v ustroistve admiralteistv-kollegii," *Morskii sbornik*, XVI (June 1855), otdel IV, 203–227.

29. Feoktistov, p. 163; M. D. Buturlin, "Zapiski grafa Mikhaila Dmitrievicha Buturlina," *Russkii arkhiv*, bk. II (1897), 344; bk. I (1898), 156. Details of the elder Tolstoi's influence on his young relative are lacking. Count Dmitry Nikolaevich's memoirs unfortunately do not cover the period of his ward's childhood and youth. See D. N. Tolstoi, "Zapiski grafa Dmitriia Nikolaevicha Tolstogo," *Russkii arkhiv*, bk. II (1885), 5–70.

30. D. A. Tolstoi, *Istoriia finansovykh uchrezhdenii Rossii so vremeni osnovaniia gosudarstva do konchiny Imperatritsy Ekateriny II* (St. Petersburg, 1848), especially pp. 23, 31–34, 46, 61–62, 75, 95, 118, 202, 252, 258.

31. Feoktistov, pp. 163–164; A. N. Pleshcheev, *Izbrannye stikhotvoreniia, proza*, N. M. Gaidenkov and V. I. Korovin, eds. (Moscow, 1960), pp. 4–5, 65.

32. Barsukov, XI, 49, 499; XII, 407; Chicherin, IV, 194; I. M. Snegirev, "Dnevnik Ivana Mikhailovicha Snegireva," *Russkii arkhiv*, bk. III (1903), 103. Some of Tolstoi's educational policies would correspond to the views held by Uvarov, but how much of this is directly attributable to their meetings in the early 1850s is impossible to ascertain.

33. Chicherin, IV, 193–194; Feoktistov, p. 169. In his impressionistic study of Katkov, Grégoire Liwoff attributed to Tolstoi a pamphlet which appeared in Brussels in 1859 and argued for constitutional democracy, but I have found nothing to substantiate this dubious claim. Grégoire Liwoff, *Michel Katkoff et son époque: quelques pages d'histoire contemporaine en Russie 1855–1887* (Paris, 1897), p. 311. Kornilov claimed that Tolstoi, while director of the Department of Spiritual Affairs, severely oppressed the Catholics, but Kornilov's only source is D. P. Khrushchov, who, according to Chicherin, despised Tolstoi because he believed Tolstoi had stolen his (Khrushchov's) material for his own study on the Catholics. A. A. Kornilov, *Obshchestvennoe dvizhenie pri Aleksandre II (1855–81): istoricheskie ocherki* (Moscow, 1909), p. 178; Chicherin, IV, 193. Varadinov's detailed account of the Spiritual Department's activities provides no evidence of anti-Catholic policies during Tolstoi's tenure. See N. Varadinov, *Istoriia Ministerstva Vnutrennikh Del* (St. Petersburg, 1858–1863), pt. III, bk. III, 404–405, 527–529, 720–721; bk. IV, 98–101.

34. [D. P. Khrushchov, ed.,] *Materialy dlia istorii uprazdneniia krepostnogo sostoianiia pomeshchichikh krest'ian v Rossii v tsarstvovanie Imperatora Aleksandra II*, vol. III: *1860–1861* (Berlin, 1862), pp. 142–143. In this instance Khrushchov was correct, for scholars have recently discovered Tolstoi's memorandum with Alexander's comments on it. See Mills, pp. 29–32; Zaionchkovsky, *Rossiiskoe*, p. 61.

35. I. S. Listovsky, ed., "Pis'mo grafa D. A. Tolstogo k ego diade grafu D. N. Tolstomu," *Russkii arkhiv*, bk. I (1908), 688. On Tolstoi's quarrels

with his peasants see Zaionchkovsky, *Rossiiskoe*, pp. 61–62; G. Dzhanshiev, *A. M. Unkovsky i osvobozhdenie krest'ian* (Moscow, 1894), pp. 166–167, who bases his version on the not-too-accurate account in *Otechestvennye zapiski*, no. 11 (1862).

36. V. A. Mukhanov, "Iz dnevnykh zapisok V. A. Mukhanova," *Russkii arkhiv*, bk. I (1897), 55; P. A. Valuev, *Dnevnik P. A. Valueva Ministra Vnutrennikh Del*, P. A. Zaionchkovsky, ed. (Moscow, 1961), I, 131.

37. Rozhdestvensky, *Istoricheskii obzor*, p. 481.

38. Tolstoi, *Rimskii katolitsizm*, I, 72, 125; II, 265–266, 321, 433, 436–437.

39. Ibid., I, 2, 3, 60–61, 94.

40. Ibid., 156; II, 120, 227–228.

41. Ibid., II, 367.

42. Alston, p. 81.

43. Only a few Katkov supporters belittled Tolstoi's willpower (see pp. 143, 168). Many historians, without mentioning the feud between the two men, have merely repeated Chicherin's bilious description of Tolstoi as "a bureaucrat to the core hating . . . every appearance of freedom . . . deceitful, greedy, evil, vindictive, insidious, ready to do anything to achieve his personal aims which usually pleased tsars but which aroused loathing in all respectable people" (Chicherin, IV, 192–193).

44. Meshchersky, II, 129–130. See also Feoktistov, pp. 174–175; A. I. Georgievsky, "Pamiati grafa D. A. Tolstogo," *Russkii vestnik*, July 1889, pp. 263–264.

45. Georgievsky in *Russkii vestnik*, July 1889, p. 265; Feoktistov, p. 179; B. Modzalevsky, ed., *Perepiska L. N. Tolstogo s N. N. Strakhovym* (St. Petersburg, 1913), p. 123; D. A. Tolstoi, "Rechi proiznesennye grafom D. A. Tolstym vo vremia poseshcheniia im odesskogo okruga v avguste i sentiabre 1867 goda" (Speeches delivered by Count D. A. Tolstoi during his visit to the Odessa educational district in August and September 1867), *Zhurnal*, CXXXVI (October 1867), otdel III, 9. Tolstoi even boasted about his unpopularity when Alexander III approached him for the position of Minister of the Interior in 1882. See E. A. Peretts, *Dnevnik E. A. Perettsa (1880–1883)*, A. A. Sergeev, ed. (Moscow-Leningrad, 1927), p. 138; Hans Lothar von Schweinitz, *Denkwurdigkeiten des Botschafters General v. Schweinitz*, Wilhelm v. Schweinitz, ed. (Berlin, 1927), II, 200.

46. D. A. Tolstoi, "Rech', proiznesennaia grafom D. A. Tolstym v Moskve, 21-go avgusta 1869 goda, na obede po sluchaiu vtorogo s'ezda russkikh estestvoispytatelei" (Speech delivered by Count D. A. Tolstoi in Moscow, 21 August 1869, at a dinner on the occasion of the Second Congress of Russian Naturalists), *Zhurnal*, CXLV (September 1869), otdel IV, 2. For a list of Tolstoi's scholarly studies see the Bibliography or S. S. Trubachev, "Uchenye trudy grafa D. A. Tolstogo," *Istoricheskii vestnik*, June 1889, pp. 656–657.

47. On Tolstoi's library and bibliophile inclinations see A. V. Bogdanovich, *Tri poslednikh samoderzhtsa: dnevnik A. V. Bogdanovich* (Moscow-Leningrad, 1924), p. 94; S. F. Librovich, *Na knizhnom postu — vospominaniia i zapiski i dokumenty* (Petrograd–Moscow, [1916]), pp. 285, 289–290; H., Review of *Bibliothèque de Comte D. A. Tolstoi: catalogue des livres étrangères*, *Russische Revue*, XVII, no. 3 (1888), 386–387.

CHAPTER 3   The Ministry of Education: Its Structure and Authority

1. *SR*, IV, no. 84, 13 May 1866, cols. 333–334.

2. The other organs of the ministry — the Department of Education and the Archaeological Commission — took no part in determining policy: the former served as the ministry's chancellery, the latter collected and published important historical documents and was virtually independent of the ministry. See *SP*, III, no. 515, 18 June 1863, cols. 998–999, 1000–1002, 1033–1037.

3. Ibid., cols. 996–1000, 1007–1010, 1021–1022, 1034, 1036; Rozhdestvensky, *Istoricheskii obzor*, pp. 402–403.

4. S. M. Sukhotin, "Iz pamiatnykh tetradei S. M. Sukhotina," *Russkii arkhiv*, bk. I (1894), 430. Tolstoi's activities as procurator, except when they relate directly to the education ministry's policies, lie beyond the scope of this study.

5. Bogdanovich, pp. 94, 97. See also Meshchersky, II, 470–471; Feoktistov, pp. 169–170; *K. P. Pobedonostsev i ego korrespondenty: pis'ma i zapiski* (Moscow-Petrograd, 1923), I, 230–231.

6. *SP*, vol. VI: *1874–1876* (1878), no. 503, 19 November 1876, cols. 1692–1693; Rozhdestvensky, *Istoricheskii obzor*, p. 400; *Obzor 1862–64*, pp. 4–5.

7. Since no complete listing of ministry personnel was available to me, I have had to rely on the not-always-accurate reports of personnel changes in the first section of each issue of the *Zhurnal*.

8. D. A. Miliutin, *Dnevnik D. A. Miliutina*, P. A. Zaionchkovsky, ed. (Moscow, 1947–1950), IV, 130; S. Iu. Witte, *Vospominaniia: detstvo, tsarstvovaniia Aleksandra II i Aleksandra III (1849–1894)* (Berlin, 1923), p. 281; Peretts, p. 6.

9. Feoktistov, pp. 173–174; A. I. Georgievsky, "Moi vospominaniia i razmyshleniia," *Russkaia starina*, CLXIII (September 1915), 417–423; CLXIV (November 1915), 253; CLXV (March 1916), 455–459. Unfortunately, Georgievsky's memoirs only go as far as 1850.

10. A. I. Georgievsky, *Predpolozhennaia reforma nashei srednei shkoly* (St. Petersburg, 1901), p. 1.

11. *SP*, IV, no 19, 23 March 1865, cols. 142–144; *SR*, IV, no. 23, May 1865, cols. 68–93.

12. Modzalevsky, p. 151. For a brief outline of the committee's activities, see the detailed abstracts of Tolstoi's annual reports printed in the *Zhurnal* each year from 1868 to 1879.

13. A. I. Georgievsky, "K istorii uchenogo komiteta Ministerstva Narodnogo Prosveshcheniia" (Toward a history of the Academic Committee of the Ministry of Education), *Zhurnal*, CCCXXXI (October 1900), otdel III, 53–54, 58–60; CCCXXXII (December 1900), otdel III, 100–101. Academic Committee member N. S. Leskov claimed that books recommended by his committee could sell 30,000 copies. See N. S. Leskov, *Sobranie sochinenii v odinnadtsati tomakh*, B. G. Bazanov et al., eds. (Moscow, 1956–1958), X, 386.

14. *Zhurnal*, CCVI (December 1879), otdel I, 147–149; A. Sopotsinsky, ed., *Ukazatel' knigam, odobrennym uchenym komitetom Ministerstva Narodnogo Prosveshcheniia v period vremeni s 1856 po 1885 god* (2nd ed. rev.; Kiev, 1887), pp. i–ii; Georgievsky, "K istorii," *Zhurnal*, CCCXXXII, otdel III, 103–104; *SP*, V, no. 83, col. 451.

15. Valuev, *Dnevnik*, II, 254; Georgievsky, "K istorii," *Zhurnal*, CCCXXXII, otdel III, 50–51, 53–54; CCCXL (February 1902), otdel III, 33; *SP*, IV, no. 413, cols. 1140–1143.

16. *SP*, IV, no. 144, 30 January 1867, cols. 436–439.

17. Sopotsinsky, pp. iv–v; Georgievsky, "K istorii," *Zhurnal*, CCCXXXII, otdel III, 87; Leskov, X, 376. These statistics were tabulated from information provided in the ministry's annual reports published in the *Zhurnal*.

18. Georgievsky, "K istorii," *Zhurnal*, CCCXXXII, otdel III, 51, 74–84; *SP*, V, no. 376, 15 May 1873, cols. 2006–2019.

19. *SP*, III, no. 515, cols. 1001–1002; no. 586, 27 February 1864, cols. 1263–1265.

20. Ibid., IV, no. 148, 21 October 1866, cols. 353–355.

21. "Izvlechenie iz vsepoddaneishego otcheta Ministra Narodnogo Prosveshcheniia za 1867 god" (Abstract of the report to the emperor by the Minister of Education for the year 1867) (cited hereafter as "Izvlechenie MNP" followed by year of report), *Zhurnal*, CXLII (March 1869), otdel I, 95–96.

22. "Ob izdanii otdela klassicheskoi filologii v vide prilozheniia k *Zhurnalu Ministerstva Narodnogo Prosveshcheniia*" (Concerning the publication of a section on classical philology as an appendix to the *Journal of the Ministry of Education*), *Zhurnal*, CLXIX (October 1873), otdel V, 3–9.

23. *SP*, III, no. 258, 20 March 1860, cols. 555–558; *SR*, III, no. 483, 3 January 1862, col. 453; no. 516, 9 June 1862, cols. 493–499; *SP*, III, no. 520, 24 June 1863, cols. 1113–1118.

24. *SP*, III, no. 517, cols. 1051, 1054; no. 631, cols. 1423, 1428, 1433, 1434, 1435; no. 610, cols. 1346, 1347, 1349.

25. Evidence of these extensive shifts in personnel can be found in

Rozhdestvensky, *Istoricheskii obzor*, p. 482; *Zhurnal*, CXXXII (November 1866), otdel I, 23; CXXXIV (June 1867), otdel I, 90; CXXXV (July 1867), otdel I, 22; CXXXVII (March 1868), otdel I, 114; CXLVI (November 1869), otdel I, 1.

26. Tolstoi, "Rechi," *Zhurnal*, CXXXVI, otdel III, 6–7; M. N. Katkov, *Sobranie peredovykh statei "Moskovskikh vedomostei," 1867* (Moscow, 1897), no. 200, pp. 512–515. Cited hereafter as *MV* followed by the year covered in the volume. For contemporary accounts of Tolstoi on tour see, for example, P. Iudin, "Iz istorii uchebnoi reformy 60-kh godov (Otryvki iz vospominanii)," *Russkaia starina*, CXXI (March 1905), 689–691; N. A. Malevsky-Malevich, "Iz vospominanii N. A. Malevskogo-Malevicha," *Russkii arkhiv*, bk. I (1912), 298–299; S. Manassein, "Graf D. A. Tolstoi v Kazani (Po lichnym vospominaniiam i rasskazam starozhilov)," *Russkaia starina*, CXXII (June 1905), 573–574.

27. N. Bekkarevich, "Orenburgskaia gimnaziia starogo vremeni," *Russkaia starina*, CXVI (November 1903), 409–410; V. Smorodinov, "Gody sluzhby moei v varshavskom uchebnom okruge: epizody uchebnogo byta," *Russkaia starina*, CLV (July 1913), 186; Markevich, p. 582.

28. *SR*, IV, no. 84, cols. 333–334. See also Ibid., vol. V: *1871–1873* (1881), no. 135, 6 March 1872, cols. 384–386.

29. Ibid., V, no. 38, 8 May 1871, cols. 82–97; no. 135, cols. 384–386.

30. *SP*, vol. VII: *1877–1881* (1883), no. 907, 27 January 1881, cols. 2061, 2065–2068, 2151; IV, no. 181, 11 February 1867, cols. 425–426.

31. The above ratios were compiled from statistics in Ibid., VI, no. 66, cols. 191–192; VII, no. 907, cols. 2143–2146. All intermediate and secondary schools, male and female, public and private, fell within the inspector's authority.

32. Ibid., III, no. 501, 23 March 1863, cols. 968–969; VII, no. 907, cols. 2159–2170.

33. Ibid., VI, no. 66, cols. 174–175, 179–180; V, no. 320, 27 February 1873, cols. 1749–1750.

34. Michael T. Florinsky, *Russia: A History and an Interpretation* (New York, 1958), II, 934; Bekkarevich, *Russkaia starina*, CXVI, 409.

35. *SP*, VII, no. 907, cols. 2161–2163; VI, no. 66, col. 188; *SR*, V, no. 135, cols. 384–386.

36. *SP*, VII, no. 907, col. 2121. See also Bogatinov, *Russkii arkhiv*, bk. III (1899), 112–113.

37. "Ob ispytaniiakh zrelosti v gimnaziiakh i podobnykh im uchebnykh zavedeniiakh vedomstva Ministerstva Narodnogo Prosveshcheniia v 1874 god" (Concerning the graduation examinations of 1874 at gymnasiums and similar educational institutions under the Ministry of Education) (cited hereafter as "Ob ispytaniiakh" followed by the year of the examination), *Zhurnal*, CLXXX (April 1875), otdel IV, 159–161; *SP*, VII, no. 907, cols. 2161–2164; IV, no. 298, 22 April 1868, cols. 761–786.

38. *SR*, vol. VI: *1874–1876* (1901), no. 144, 5 August 1875, cols. 733–740; *SP*, VI, no. 90, 13 August 1874, cols. 487–489: VII, no. 907, cols. 2047–2048.

39. Marc Szeftel, "The Form of Government of the Russian Empire Prior to the Constitutional Reforms of 1905–1906," in *Essays in Russian and Soviet History in Honor of Geroid Tanquary Robinson*, John Shelton Curtiss, ed. (New York, 1963), pp. 107–110; Valuev, *Dnevnik*, II, 157–158.

40. *SP*, IV, no. 304, 22 April 1868, cols. 810–812; VI, no. 223, April 1875, cols. 981–982; *SR*, VI, no. 97, 10 May 1875, cols. 593–594.

41. This was not surprising, for two of Obolensky's three fellow commissioners, recently retired Assistant Minister Delianov and Fourth Section Head Prince P. G. Ol'denburgsky, were strong adherents of the classical system.

42. S. M. Seredonin, *Istoricheskii obzor deiatel'nosti Komiteta Ministrov*, vol. III: *Komitet Ministrov v tsarstvovanie Imperatora Aleksandra Vtorogo* (St. Petersburg, 1902), pt. II, 187; Miliutin, I, 134, 192; Del'vig, II, 558–560. Del'vig mistakenly refers to the ministry's report for 1873 as the one which produced this furor.

43. Russia, Ministerstvo Finansov, *Ministerstvo Finansov 1802–1902*, pt. I (St. Petersburg, 1902), pp. 636–639. The total of 8,507,000 rubles for 1867 given in these tables is clearly a misprint. Cf. I. S. Bliokh, *Finansy Rossii XIX stoletiia: istoriia — statistika*, vol. IV (St. Petersburg, 1882), p. 84.

44. Bliokh, IV, 239–241.

45. "Interesy narodnogo prosveshcheniia v Rossii i russkaia zhurnalistika" (The interests of public education in Russia and Russian journalism), *Zhurnal*, CXXXIII (March 1867), otdel III, 299–300, 318.

46. M. M. [Stasiulevich], "Po povodu polemiki o real'nom obrazovanii" (Concerning the polemic on nonclassical education), *Vestnik Evropy*, VI (May 1871), 488–489; "Interesy," *Zhurnal*, CXXXIII, otdel III, 318.

47. Alston, p. 92; Mills, p. 157.

48. *SP*, VI, no. 123, 13 November 1874, cols. 556–557; no. 187, 18 March 1875, col. 851; Del'vig, II, 544–549.

49. Seredonin, III, pt. II, 207; Miliutin, III, 193; V. G. Serebrennikova, "Demokraticheskaia zhurnalistika perioda vtoroi revoliutsionnoi situatsii," in *Obshchestvennoe dvizhenie v poreformennoi Rossii*, E. S. Vilenskaia et al., eds. (Moscow, 1965), p. 346.

50. *SP*, IV, no. 208, 15 May 1867, cols. 463–469; no. 260, 18 November 1867, cols. 577–581. The above apparatus, copied from that in Western Siberia, was hardly sufficient to direct education in all of Eastern Siberia, but the governor-general's request in 1878 for substantial additional funds and an assistant chief inspector went unheeded. See A. P. Panchukov, *Istoriia nachal'noi i srednei shkoly vostochnoi Sibiri* (Ulan Ude, 1959), pp. 236–237.

51. Richard A. Pierce, *Russian Central Asia 1867–1917: A Study in Colonial*

Rule (Berkeley and Los Angeles, 1960), pp. 46–91, 214; K. E. Bendrikov, *Ocherki po istorii narodnogo obrazovaniia v Turkestane (1865–1924 gody)* (Moscow, 1960), pp. 62, 88; *SP*, VI, no. 232, 17 May 1875, cols. 1018–1021, 1028. The Caucasus district, until it came under the ministry in 1881, sometimes served as a refuge for educators who disagreed with Tolstoi's policies.

52. N. A. Konstantinov and V. Ia. Struminsky, *Ocherki po istorii nachal'nogo obrazovaniia v Rossii* (Moscow, 1949), p. 112; *PSZ*, 2nd series, vol. XLII, sect. I, no. 44240, 11 February 1867, pp. 132–133; N. M. Druzhinin, *Gosudarstvennye krest'iane i reforma P. D. Kiseleva*, vol. II: *Realizatsiia i posledstviia reformy* (Moscow, 1958), p. 250.

53. *SP*, VI, no. 125, 20 November 1874, cols. 585–586, 589–591, 596; no. 66, cols. 174–175.

54. On Khudiakov's pedagogic activities and his connection with the Karakozov assassination attempt, see Venturi, pp. 338–350.

55. *SP*, IV, no. 413, 19 May 1869, col. 1140; Georgievsky, "K istorii," *Zhurnal*, CCCXXXII, otdel III, 19–22, 26–35, 38–43.

56. Miliutin, I, 32; III, 139–140. In an effort to reconcile these progressive views with his continued service in a reactionary administration, Miliutin explained: "I would be like Don Quixote if I decided to follow views completely antithetical to those dominating that sphere in which I move. These views would have made my official position impossible and would not have benefited anything."

57. Quoted in A. V. Fedorov, *Russkaia armiia v 50-70-kh godakh XIX veka, ocherki* (Leningrad, 1959), p. 236.

58. Valuev, *Dnevnik*, II, 54.

59. Bliokh, IV, 144, 150, 152; P. A. Zaionchkovsky, *Voennye reformy 1860–1870 godov v Rossii* (Moscow, 1952), pp. 55–56, 225–227; *MV 1873*, no. 301, 28 November 1873, p. 865. For a detailed treatment of the military schools during this period, see Forrestt A. Miller, *Dmitrii Miliutin and the Reform Era in Russia* ([Nashville], 1968), pp. 88–141.

60. Miller, pp. 207–208.

61. On the Tolstoi-Miliutin conflict over the Medical-Surgical Academy see Miliutin, I, 98, 109, 112–113, 128–129, 135–136, 141, 144, 151, 155–156, 170–171, 198–203; Valuev, *Dnevnik*, II, 285, 310; Seredonin, III, pt. II, 229–230.

CHAPTER 4   Controlling Higher Education

1. In 1880 the ministry had jurisdiction over eight universities (two of which—Dorpat and Warsaw—had their own separate regulations), four veterinary schools, four teacher preparatory institutes, and five special schools: the Archaeological Institute, the Demidov Juridical Lyceum, the

Lazarev Institute of Eastern Languages, the Institute of Agriculture and Forestry, and the Lyceum of the Tsarevich Nicholas.

2. D. A. Tolstoi, "Rech'," *Zhurnal*, CXLV, otdel IV, 2.

3. Quoted in Georgievsky, *Predpolozhennaia reforma*, p. 3.

4. Statistics based on figures in "Izvestiia o deiatel'nosti i sostoianii nashikh uchebnykh zavedenii" (News on the state and activity of our educational institutions) (cited hereafter as "Izvestiia"), *Zhurnal*, CXXXVIII (June 1868), otdel III, 289–297.

5. "Izvlechenie MNP 1866," *Zhurnal*, CXXXVII (January 1868), otdel I, 13; "Spisok litsam, otpravlennym ot Ministerstva Narodnogo Prosveshcheniia za granitsu dlia prigotovleniia k professorskomu zvaniiu" (The list of people sent abroad by the Ministry of Education to prepare for a professorial career), *Zhurnal*, CXXXIV (May 1867), otdel III, 283–292; Chicherin, IV, 56.

6. *SR*, IV, no. 110, 15 October 1866, cols. 371–372; *SP*, IV, no. 194, 27 March 1867, cols. 445–447; no. 242, 5 October 1867, cols. 540–541.

7. "Spisok litsam," *Zhurnal*, CXXXIV, otdel III, 283–292; "Izvlechenie MNP 1870," *Zhurnal*, CLX, otdel I, 3; "Izvlechenie MNP 1877," *Zhurnal*, CCV (September 1879), otdel I, 3.

8. "Izvlechenie MNP 1875," *Zhurnal*, CXCII, otdel I, 186; "Izvlechenie MNP 1876," *Zhurnal*, CXCVIII (August 1878), otdel I, 33; "Izvlechenie MNP 1877," *Zhurnal*, CCV, otdel I, 3.

9. *SP*, IV, no. 297, 22 April 1868, cols. 759–760; no. 184, 27 March 1867, cols. 427–429; *SR*, IV, no. 231, 16 August 1868, cols. 589–590, 599–601; VI, no. 138, 10 August 1874, cols. 276–277.

10. "Universitetskii vopros" (The university question), *Zhurnal*, CLXXXVII (October 1876), otdel IV, 148–151.

11. "Spisok vysshikh i srednikh uchebnykh zavedenii Ministerstva Narodnogo Prosveshcheniia" (A list of the higher and secondary academic institutions of the Ministry of Education), *Zhurnal*, CLXXXV (May 1876), otdel IV, 1–5; "Vnutrennee obozrenie" (Internal review), *Vestnik Evropy*, XI (July 1876), 357–360.

12. *SP*, VI, no. 153, 25 December 1874, cols. 722–735, 747; prilozhenie to no. 153, cols. 30–31; IV, no. 317, 3 July 1868, cols. 360–372; "Otchet po iaroslavskomu demidovskomu litseiu" (Report on the Iaroslav Demidov Lyceum), *Zhurnal*, CXXXII (October 1866), otdel II, 54, 64.

13. *SP*, VI, no. 409, 24 April 1876, cols. 1471–1472.

14. Ibid., col. 1473; VII, no. 70, 16 May 1877, cols. 155–157, 172, 193–195, 206–207, 212–213; no. 232, 16 May 1878, cols. 528–529, 537–545; no. 271, 4 October 1878, col. 618; no. 293, 4 November 1878, col. 694; no. 330, 10 January 1879, col. 807; no. 443, 4 July 1879, col. 1146.

15. *SP*, VII, no. 604, 26 February 1880, col. 1542; no. 615, 14 March 1880, cols. 1566–1575. On the difficulties of planning the Siberian university, see V. M. Florinsky, "Zapiski i vospominaniia V. M. Florin-

skogo," *Russkaia starina*, CXXV–CXXVI (January–June 1906), 75–109, 288–311, 564–594; 109–156, 280–323, 596–621.

16. *SP*, V, no. 289, 12 December 1872, cols. 1589–1597; no. 107, 27 October 1871, cols. 497–511; VI, no. 77, 3 July 1874, cols. 438–440; IV, no. 395, 31 March 1869, cols. 1084–1086.

17. *SP*, IV, no. 558, 12 May 1870, cols. 1590–1602; no. 206, 8 May 1867, cols. 458–460; no. 419, 28 May 1869, cols. 1224–1226; VI, no. 68, 25 May 1874, cols. 216–220; no. 42, March 1874, col. 117.

18. *SP*, IV, no. 608, 13 October 1870, col. 1706; VII, no. 12, 14 February 1877, cols. 29–30.

19. Ibid., IV, no. 207, 12 May 1867, col. 460.

20. Ibid., VI, no. 183, 28 February 1875, cols. 840–849; *SR*, VI, no. 59, 15 March 1875, cols. 497–498; *SP*, V, no. 6, 15 January 1871, col. 18; no. 347, 30 March 1873, cols. 1816–1817, 1819–1820.

21. On the achievements of the Russian academic community during this period, see Vucinich, II, 66–179.

22. P. D. Shestakov, "Tiazhelye dni kazanskogo universiteta," *Russkaia starina*, LXXXVIII (December 1896), 519.

23. Venturi, pp. 501–502; V. S. Antonov, "K voprosu o sotsial'nom sostave i chislennosti revoliutsionerov 70-kh godov," in *Obshchestvennoe dvizhenie v poreformennoi Rossii*, E. S. Vilenskaia et al., eds. (Moscow, 1965), p. 338.

24. On student political apathy see, for example, P. B. Aksel'rod, *Perezhitoe i peredumannoe*, bk. I (Berlin, 1923), pp. 83–85; N. V. Davydov, *Iz proshlogo* (Moscow, 1913), pp. 98–100; I. M. Grevs, "V gody iunosti," *Byloe*, June 1918, pp. 45–46.

25. Russia Ministerstvo Narodnogo Prosveshcheniia, *Materialy sobrannye otdelom vysochaishe uchrezhdennoi komissii dlia peresmotra obshchego ustava rossiiskikh universitetov* (St. Petersburg, 1876), I, 27 (cited hereafter as *Materialy*); Mavrodin, I, 198.

26. On student supervision see *SP*, III, no. 517, cols. 1049–1051, 1053–1054, 1056–1057, 1062–1064.

27. Markevich, p. 698; *SR*, III, no. 702, cols. 853–855, 858–859; no. 703, cols. 871–874; no. 704, cols. 893–896, 898; no. 705, cols. 913–917; no. 706, cols. 943–946.

28. *SP*, IV, no. 211, cols. 473–475.

29. An account of these disturbances can be found in S. Chudnovsky, "Iz dal'nikh let (Otryvki iz vospominanii)," *Byloe*, September 1907, pp. 286–294.

30. *SP*, IV, no. 453, 8 July 1869, cols. 1391–1394, 1397–1400.

31. Ibid., cols. 1391–1392.

32. *MV 1874*, no. 321, 21 December 1874, p. 793; *SR*, V, no. 140, 15 March 1872, cols. 391–393; *Materialy*, I, 74–86.

33. Seredonin, III, pt. II, 182; *SR*, III, no. 702, cols. 855–858; no. 704,

cols. 886–887; no. 705, cols. 908–910; no. 706, cols. 930–932; *SP*, IV, no. 212, 26 May 1867, cols. 475–476.

34. *Obzor 1862–64*, prilozhenie, p. 230; "Izvlechenie MNP 1877," *Zhurnal*, CCV, otdel I, 8.

35. *SP*, III, no. 517, cols. 1061–1062; no. 631, col. 1444; "O poverochnykh ispytaniiakh v universitetakh" (On university entrance examinations), *Zhurnal*, CXXXVIII (June 1868), otdel III, 278–279, 282–283, 286.

36. *SP*, IV, no. 453, cols. 1392–1394, 1396–1397.

37. *SR*, V, no. 111, 13 November 1871, cols. 357–358; no. 245, 8 December 1872, col. 874; *SP*, V, no. 385, 16 May 1873, cols. 2045–2047.

38. *SR*, V, no. 271, 17 January 1873, cols. 932–935; "Vnutrennee obozrenie," *Vestnik Evropy*, XI (April 1876), 808–812; *SP*, VII, no. 343, 23 January 1879, cols. 817–827.

39. Markevich, pp. 678–679.

40. "Izvlechenie MNP 1871," *Zhurnal*, CLXV (February 1873), otdel I, 101; "Izvlechenie MNP 1874," *Zhurnal*, CLXXXV (June 1876), otdel I, 52; "Izvlechenie MNP 1877," *Zhurnal*, CCV, otdel I, 8; *SR*, V, no. 61, 26 June 1871, cols. 161–162; Russia, Ministerstvo Narodnogo Prosveshcheniia, *Obzor deiatel'nosti vedomstva Ministerstva Narodnogo Prosveshcheniia za vremia tsarstvovaniia Imperatora Aleksandra III* (St. Petersburg, 1901), p. 161. Cited hereafter as *Obzor 1881–94*.

41. *Materialy*, I, 10, 12–13; "Izvlechenie MNP 1872," *Zhurnal*, CLXXIII (June 1874), otdel I, 74; "Izvlechenie MNP 1877," *Zhurnal*, CCV, otdel I, 12.

42. *Obzor 1862–64*, prilozhenie, p. 230; *Obzor 1881–94*, p. 161. Unfortunately, the ministry did not provide a breakdown of classes within each faculty, for universities like Moscow did not begin to supply such statistics until as late as 1881. *Otchet o sostoianii i deistviiakh imperatorskogo moskovskogo universiteta za 1880 god* (Moscow, 1881), pp. 102–103.

43. "Obozrenie deistvii Ministerstva Narodnogo Prosveshcheniia za 1871 god" (A review of the activity of the Ministry of Education for 1871) (cited hereafter as "Obozrenie MNP" followed by the year under review), *Zhurnal*, CLIX (February 1872), otdel IV, 144; "Izvlechenie MNP 1874," *Zhurnal*, CLXXXVI (July 1876), otdel I, 5; "Izvlechenie MNP 1875," *Zhurnal*, CXCII, otdel I, 192–193; "Izvlechenie MNP 1877," *Zhurnal*, CCV, otdel I, 11–12.

44. *Materialy*, I, 30, 43–44; "Izvlechenie MNP 1875," *Zhurnal*, CXCII, otdel I, 193.

45. "Izvlechenie MNP 1877," *Zhurnal*, CCV, otdel I, 11; *Materialy*, I, 38; V. Veresaev, *Sobranie sochinenii*, vol. V: *Vospominaniia*, Iu. U. Babushkin and V. M. Nol'de, eds. (Moscow, 1961), p. 206.

46. Mavrodin, I, 199; V. S. Chevazhevsky, "Iz proshlogo kievskogo universiteta i studencheskoi zhizni (1870–1875 gg.)," *Russkaia starina*, CL (June 1912), 56–63.

47. *SP*, IV, no. 477, 23 October 1869, cols. 1446–1449; no. 512, 4 February 1870, cols. 1503–1504; V, no. 39, 28 April 1871, cols. 81–83; Russia, Ministerstvo Narodnogo Prosveshcheniia, *[Zhurnaly zasedanii vysochaishe uchrezhdennoi 21 aprelia 1875 g. komissii po peresmotru universitetskogo ustava]* (St. Petersburg, n.d.), no. 5, 23 September 1876, pp. 4–5 (cited hereafter as *Zhurnaly zasedanii*); *Materialy*, I, 33–36; Markevich, pp. 719–722.

48. *SR*, IV, no. 390, 15 October 1870, cols. 946–949.

49. A. I. Georgievsky, *Materialy po universitetskomu voprosu*, P. Struve, ed. (Stuttgart, 1902), pp. 4–5.

50. Venturi, p. 568.

51. *Zhurnaly zasedanii*, no. 1, 16 September 1876, pp. 4, 7–9.

52. Ibid., no. 2, 18 September 1876, pp. 1–3; no. 3, 19 September 1876, pp. 1–3; no. 4, 21 September 1876, pp. 1–9; no. 5, 23 September 1876, pp. 1–5; no. 13, 5 October 1876, pp. 4–5; no. 17, 10 October 1876, pp. 37–39; no. 7, 25 September 1876, pp. 1–5; no. 8, 26 September 1876, pp. 2–3.

53. Ibid., no. 2, pp. 4–6; no. 3, pp. 3–5; no. 6, 24 September 1876, p. 6; Georgievsky, *Materialy po*, pp. 7–10; I. M. Sechenov, *Avtobiograficheskie zapiski Ivana Mikhailovicha Sechenova*, Kh. S. Koshtoiants, ed. ([Moscow], 1945), pp. 146–147.

54. Tatishchev, II, 595.

55. Miliutin, III, 106, 122, 172; Georgievsky, *Materialy po*, pp. 12–14; Orlov, pp. 177–178.

56. P. A. Zaionchkovsky, *Krizis samoderzhaviia na rubezhe 1870–1880 godov* (Moscow, 1964), pp. 98–106; P. A. Valuev, *Graf P. A. Valuev — dnevnik 1877–84*, V. Ia. Iakovlev-Bogucharsky and P. E. Shchegolev, eds. (Petrograd, 1919), p. 35.

57. Tatishchev, II, 608–609, 612–614; Seredonin, III, pt. II, 184–185; Georgievsky, *Materialy po*, pp. 15–16; *SP*, VII, no. 453, 2 August 1879, cols. 1172–1173.

58. *SP*, VII, no. 453, cols. 1169–1172, 1175–1178.

59. Georgievsky, *Materialy po*, pp. 16, 20; Venturi, p. 633; Tatishchev, II, 604–605.

60. *SP*, VII, no. 453, cols. 1175–1176; Georgievsky, *Materialy po*, pp. 17–19; Zaionchkovsky, *Krizis*, p. 121.

61. Georgievsky, *Materialy po*, pp. 18–20; Zaionchkovsky, *Krizis*, pp. 120–121.

62. Quoted in Georgievsky, *Materialy po*, p. 19. Italics added.

63. Quoted in Tatishchev, II, 606.

64. M. N. Tikhomirov et al., eds. *Istoriia moskovskogo universiteta* (Moscow, 1955), I, 271; Georgievsky, *Materialy po*, pp. 21, 22; Markevich, p. 660.

65. Miliutin, IV, 12–15, 160–161; Zaionchkovsky, *Krizis*, pp. 269–283.

66. "Priem g. Ministrom Narodnogo Prosveshcheniia gg. professorov i prepodavatelei kharkovskogo universiteta" (Reception by the Minister of Education for the professors and instructors of Kharkov University), *Zhurnal*, CLI (October 1870), otdel IV, 135; P. D. Shestakov, "Graf Dmitry Andreevich Tolstoi kak Ministr Narodnogo Prosveshcheniia," *Russkaia starina*, LXX (April 1891), 193–194.

67. *SP*, III, no. 517, col. 1061; IV, no. 332, cols. 977–980; no. 396, 31 March 1869, cols. 1086–1096; "Po povodu naznacheniia ot Ministerstva nekotorykh professorov v universitete Sv. Vladimira" (Concerning the appointment by the ministry of several professors at St. Vladimir University), *Zhurnal*, CXLI (January 1869), otdel IV, 24–26.

68. Chicherin, IV, 176–192, 196–227; *SP*, IV, no. 331, 20 September 1868, cols. 974–977.

69. *SP*, IV, no. 396, 31 March 1869, col. 1095; "Ezhemesiachnaia khronika" (Monthly chronicle), *Vestnik Evropy*, III (September 1868), 442–444.

70. "Vozhd' reaktsii 60-80-kh godov (Pis'ma Katkova Aleksandru II i Aleksandru III)," *Byloe*, October 1917, p. 9; Alston, pp. 111–112. Despite the persuasiveness of Alston's arguments, the lack of a clear chronology and any documentation makes them difficult to accept.

71. Feoktistov, pp. 177, 184; Mills, pp. 183–184, 213–216.

72. Rozhdestvensky, *Istoricheskii obzor*, p. 503.

73. See, for example, N. A. Liubimov, "Po povodu predstoiashchego peresmotra universitetskogo ustava" (Concerning the impending revision of the university statute), *Russkii vestnik*, February 1873, pp. 886–903; V. I. Ger'e (Guerrier), "Universitetskii vopros — po povodu mneniia pr. Liubimova o peresmotre universitetskogo ustava v *Rus. vestn.* 1873 fevral" (The university question — concerning Prof. Liubimov's opinion in the *Russian Herald* [February 1873] on the revision of the university statute), *Vestnik Evropy*, VIII (April 1873), 818–836, and the numerous follow-up articles in the 1875 and 1876 issues of *Russkii vestnik* and *Vestnik Evropy*.

74. Miliutin, I, 175; Georgievsky, *Materialy po*, pp. 4–5; *SP*, VI, no. 203, col. 898.

75. "Obozrenie MNP 1874," *Zhurnal*, CLXXVII (February 1875), otdel IV, 28; *Materialy*, I, 6–7.

76. *Materialy*, I, 1–6; "Universitetskii vopros," *Zhurnal*, CLXXXVII, otdel IV, 131–132; Georgievsky, *Materialy po*, p. 6.

77. Florinsky, *Russkaia starina*, CXXV (January 1906), 90–93; V. N., "Voprosnye punkty po povodu peresmotra universitetskogo ustava" (Points in question about the revision of the university statute), *Vestnik Evropy*, XI (January 1876), 269–304. (Because of an error in pagination, pages 278–301 do not exist.)

78. *Zhurnaly zasedanii*, no. 1, p. 1; Chicherin, IV, 248; Alston, p. 112; A.

V. Romanovich-Slavatinsky, "Moia zhizn' i akademicheskaia deiatel'-nost', 1832–1884 gg.," *Vestnik Evropy*, XXXVIII (June 1903), 502.

79. *SP*, III, no. 517, cols. 1041–1045, 1046, 1052, 1061; *Zhurnaly zasedanii*, no. 9, 28 September 1876, pp. 11–12; no. 12, 2/3 October 1876, p. 4; "Universitetskii vopros," *Zhurnal*, CLXXXVII, otdel IV, 151–152, 157–158.

80. *Zhurnaly zasedanii*, no. 9, pp. 9–11; no. 12, pp. 1–2; no. 13, 6 October 1876, pp. 1–2.

81. *SR*, III, no. 619, 4 January 1864, cols. 636–643; *Materialy*, I, 399–409; *Zhurnaly zasedanii*, no. 15, 7 October 1876, p. 3; no. 17, 10 October 1876, pp. 37–79; Friedrich Paulsen, *The German Universities and University Study*, tran. by Frank Thilly and William W. Elwang (New York, 1906), pp. 335–340.

82. Sheldon Rothblatt, *The Revolution of the Dons: Cambridge and Society in Victorian England* (New York, 1968), pp. 182–183.

83. *Materialy*, I, 426.

84. Ibid., II, 37, 40–46, 69 ff.; *Zhurnaly zasedanii*, no. 26, pp. 1–2; no. 24, 21/22 October 1876, pp. 6–7; no. 29, 2/3 November 1876, pp. 9–11.

85. *Zhurnaly zasedanii*, no. 9, attached report, pp. 1–5; no. 17, pp. 2–9; no. 35, pp. 1–6; no. 29, pp. 3–8.

86. Quoted in Tikhomirov et al., I, 270. Despite the censure of his colleagues and his reputation as a most "ungifted" teacher, Liubimov with backing from both Tolstoi and the curator gained Alexander's official support in his battle with the Moscow council, and this prompted the resignation of S. M. Solov'ev as rector. See P. F. Filatov, "Iunye gody: vospominaniia o meditsinskom fakul'tete (1868–73 gg.) moskovskogo universiteta," *Russkaia starina*, CLIV (April 1913), 144; M. Kovalevsky, "Moskovskii universitet v kontse 70-kh i nachale 80-kh godov proshlogo veka (Lichnye vospominaniia)," *Vestnik Evropy*, XLV (May 1910), 186.

87. G. I. Shchetinina, "Podgotovka universitetskogo ustava 1884 g.," *Nauchnye doklady vysshei shkoly: istoricheskie nauki*, no. 1 (1961), 45–48; Venturi, p. 691; Tatishchev, II, 635.

88. On the debates in the government about the new legislation and on Tolstoi's activity in its behalf, see A. A. Polovtsov, *Dnevnik gosudarstvennogo sekretaria A. A. Polovtsova v dvukh tomakh*, P. A. Zaionchkovsky, ed. (Moscow, 1966), I, 135–242, *passim*; Shchetinina, *Nauchnye doklady*, no. 1 (1961), 49–56; Zaionchkovsky, *Rossiiskoe*, pp. 318–328.

89. *MV 1884*, no. 239, 28 August 1884, p. 448.

90. *Obzor 1881–94*, pp. 118, 133–134; *SP*, III, no. 517, cols. 1042, 1047–1048, 1054, 1056–1057; IX, no. 135, cols. 985–989, 996, 999, 1000.

91. *SP*, III, no. 517, cols. 1046, 1051, 1061; IX, no. 135, cols. 994–995, 1006–1008, 1013; *Obzor 1881–94*, p. 120.

92. *SP*, IX, no. 135, cols. 989–990, 992, 996–999; III, no. 517, cols. 1050, 1051–1052, 1055.

93. *Obzor 1881–94*, pp. 124, 126–127, 130; *MV 1884*, no. 239, p. 498; *SP*, III, no. 517, cols. 1049–1052; IX, no. 135, cols. 991–992, 993–995.

94. *SP*, IX, no. 135, cols. 1005, 1010; Paulsen, *The German Universities*, pp. 87–92.

95. *SP*, IX, no. 135, cols. 1010–1011, 1014–1015, 1016; *Obzor 1881–94*, p. 121.

96. *SP*, IX, no. 135, cols. 1008, 1019, 1020; *Obzor 1881–94*, p. 121.

97. R. Freeman Butts, *A Cultural History of Education: Reassessing Our Educational Traditions* (New York, 1947), p. 433. However, just as Russia's universities were losing their independence, France's universities were gaining theirs. See Louis Liard, *L'enseignement supérieure en France 1789–1893*, vol. II (Paris, 1894), pp. 125–333.

98. Paulsen, *The German Universities*, pp. 76–79, 83–86, 335–340; Matthew Arnold, *The Complete Prose Works of Matthew Arnold*, vol. IV: *Schools and Universities on the Continent*, R. H. Super, ed. (Ann Arbor, Mich., 1964), pp. 256, 258, 261–264.

99. V. A. Maklakov, *Iz vospominanii* (New York, 1954), p. 59. Some, however, were not so enthusiastic. Cf. B. A. Shchetinin, "Pervye shagi (Iz nedavnego proshlogo)," *Istoricheskii vestnik*, XXVI, February 1905, pp. 502–504.

CHAPTER 5   The Entrenchment of the Classical System in Secondary Education

1. Alston, p. 86.

2. "Poezdka g. Ministra Narodnogo Prosveshcheniia po odesskomu uchebnomu okrugu" (The tour of the Minister of Education through the Odessa educational district), *Zhurnal*, CLXXXII (December 1875), otdel IV, 67; *SP*, V, no. 74, 19 June/1 July 1871, cols. 269–271. Italics added.

3. Butts, p. 429.

4. Arnold, IV, 298.

5. *SP*, V, no. 74, cols. 249–252; Ernst von Sallwürk, "Die höhere Bildungswesen in Frankreich von 1789–1899," in *Geschichte der Erziehung von Anfang bis auf unsere Zeit*, K. A. Schmid, ed. (Stuttgart-Berlin, 1901), V, pt. II, 126, 131–134; Fritz K. Ringer, "Higher Education in Germany in the Nineteenth Century," in *Education and Social Structure in the Twentieth Century*, Walter Laqueur and George L. Mosse, eds. (New York, 1967), pp. 128–131; Michael E. Sadler, "The Unrest in Secondary Education in Germany and Elsewhere," in *Education in Germany*, Michael E. Sadler, ed. (London, 1902), pp. 67, 173.

6. Percentages calculated from weekly lesson schedules in *SP*, V, no. 74, cols. 284, 287–289.

7. "Mery," *Zhurnal*, CXXXIII, otdel III, 6–8, 13–15.

8. *SP*, III, prilozhenie to no. 631, cols. 79–80.

9. K. D. Ushinsky, *Izbrannye pedagogicheskie sochineniia*, V. Ia. Struminsky, ed., vol. II (Moscow, 1954), pp. 272, 276, 278, 282. On Ushinsky's achievements, see especially V. Ia. Struminsky, *K. D. Ushinsky, ocherk zhizni i deiatel'nosti* (Moscow, 1960).

10. Smirnov, *Reforma*, pp. 299–303; "Vnutrennee obozrenie," *Vestnik Evropy*, IV (May 1869), 370–373; Ganelin, pp. 62–63.

11. *SP*, III, no. 631, cols. 1428, 1433, 1434; *SR*, IV, no. 11, 12 March 1865, cols. 32–53.

12. *SR*, IV, no. 43, September 1865, col. 191.

13. Ibid., no. 114, 12 November 1866, cols. 381–383.

14. Mills, p. 102.

15. "Mneniia i soobrazheniia popechitelei i popechitel'skikh sovetov uchebnykh okrugov o primenenii ustava gimnazii i progimnazii 19-go noiabria 1864 goda" (The opinions and considerations of the curators and the curators' councils of the educational districts on the implementation of the gymnasium and progymnasium statute of 19 November 1864), *Zhurnal*, CXXXIV (April 1867), otdel III, 1, 2–11, 14–20, 28–31, 48–50; "Izvlechenie MNP 1867," *Zhurnal*, CXLII, otdel I, 26–34.

16. *SR*, IV, no. 155, cols. 478–479; no. 199, 30 January 1868, col. 547; no. 228, 3 August 1868, cols. 583–584; *SP*, IV, no. 288, 13 March 1868, cols. 696–697.

17. A Kriukovsky, ed., *Alfavitnyi sbornik postanovlenii i rasporiazhenii po s-peterburgskomu uchebnomu okrugu za 1858–1876 g.* (St. Petersburg, 1876), p. 316.

18. E. V. Beliavsky, *Pedagogicheskie vospominaniia 1861–1902* (Moscow, 1905), p. 58.

19. Kriukovsky, pp. 511–513; "Izvestiia," *Zhurnal*, CXXXV (September 1867), otdel III, 317–331; CXLIV (July 1869), otdel IV, 41–42, 44–49; CXLV (September–October 1869), otdel IV, 69–72, 238–243; CXLVII (January 1870), otdel IV, 53–55, 56–58; Beliavsky, pp. 40–42.

20. *SP*, III, no. 631, col. 1428; *SR*, IV, no. 107, 21 September 1866, cols. 362–363; Kriukovsky, pp. 45–56; "Izvestiia," *Zhurnal*, CXXXIII (February 1867), otdel III, 174–177; CXXXVIII (May–June 1869), otdel IV, 98–108, 231–233; CXLIV (August 1869), otdel IV, 985–990.

21. *SP*, III, no. 631, cols. 1424–1426, 1432; V. Z. Smirnov, "O merakh podderzhaniia distsipliny uchashchikhsia gimnazii i progimnazii (1864–1874 gg.)," *Sovetskaia pedagogika*, X (August–September 1946), 52–58.

22. Smirnov, *Sovetskaia pedagogika*, X, 59; "Izvestiia," *Zhurnal*, CXL (October–December 1868), otdel III, 106–107, 111–112, 315–316; CXXXVII (January 1868), otdel III, 36; CXLIII (June 1869), otdel IV, 225; CXLII (April 1869), otdel IV, 134; CXLVIII (March 1870), otdel IV, 45.

23. *SP*, III, no. 631, col. 1424; IV, no. 545, 21 April 1870, cols. 1576–

1577; no. 570, 29 May 1870, cols. 1650–1652; nos. 584–586, 24 July 1870, cols. 1683–1688.

24. See, for example, "Izvestiia," *Zhurnal*, CXXXVIII (April, June 1868), otdel III, 94–96, 318–319; CXL (October 1868), otdel III, 107–109; "Izvlechenie MNP 1867," *Zhurnal*, CXLII, otdel I, 30–31.

25. Rozhdestvensky, *Istoricheskii obzor*, p. 517; Smirnov, *Reforma*, pp. 306–308.

26. Vessel', in *Russkii vestnik*, February 1903, pp. 599–600; *SP*, V, no. 196, cols. 947–948; Mills, pp. 126, 129–130.

27. *SP*, IV, no. 536, col. 1551; V, no. 74, col. 282; M. Briksman and M. Aronson, eds., "Tekushchaia khronika i osobye proisshestviia: dnevnik V. F. Odoevskogo 1859–1869 gg.," *Literaturnoe nasledstvo*, XXII–XXIV (1935), 140; Mills, p. 120.

28. Feoktistov, pp. 162–178. Feoktistov's adulation of Katkov hardly makes him a fair witness. Cf. Ibid., pp. 87–117; G. K. Gradovsky, "Iz minuvshego (Vospominaniia i vpechatleniia literatora 1865–1897 g.)," *Russkaia starina*, CXXXIII (January 1908), 82.

29. M. M. [Stasiulevich], "Po povodu," *Vestnik Evropy*, VI, 488–489; *MV 1871*, no. 66, 26 March 1871, p. 197.

30. Alston, p. 92; Mills, p. 157.

31. *SP*, V, no. 74, cols. 263–264.

32. Ibid., cols. 269–271. For a summary of Katkov's views on classicism's role in combating nihilist tendencies, see Martin Katz, *Mikhail N. Katkov: A Political Biography 1818–1887* (The Hague, 1966), pp. 142–164.

33. *SP*, V, no. 196, cols. 958–970.

34. Alston, p. 94. On the investigations leading up to the trial of the Nechaevtsy, see B. P. Koz'min, ed., *Nechaev i nechaevtsy; sbornik materialov* (Moscow-Leningrad, 1931), pp. 3–143.

35. *SP*, V, no. 25, cols. 67–69.

36. Tatishchev, II, 266; Mills, pp. 142–143, 146–147.

37. Quoted in Tatishchev, II, 269; *SP*, V, no. 196, col. 1127.

38. Tatishchev, II, 269–272; Aleshintsev, pp. 293–298; Del'vig, II, 554–555.

39. On these debates and the intrigues surrounding them, see Del'vig, II, 555–557; A. V. Nikitenko, *Dnevnik v trekh tomakh*, I. Ia. Aizenshtok, ed. (Moscow, 1955–1956), III, 207; Russia, Gosudarstvennyi Sovet, *Gosudarstvennyi Sovet 1801–1901* (St. Petersburg, 1901), pp. 118–119; Feoktistov, pp. 115–116; Aleshintsev, p. 301.

40. *SP*, V, no. 74, cols. 246, 256.

41. Mills, pp. 161–163.

42. Aleshintsev, p. 302; *SP*, V, no. 74, cols. 244–245.

43. *SP*, V, no. 74, cols. 334–335, 336; III, no. 631, col. 1427. All percentages are calculated from tables in Ibid., V, no. 74, cols. 289–293 and prilozhenie to no. 74, cols. 8–9.

44. *SR*, V, no. 61, 26 June 1871, col. 175.

45. *SP*, V, no. 74, cols. 340, 342.

46. Ibid., cols. 352–357.

47. Ibid., cols. 330–331; VI, no. 229, 13 May 1875, cols. 1010–1015; "Obozrenie MNP 1873," *Zhurnal*, CLXXI (February 1874), otdel IV, 77.

48. *SP*, III, no. 631, col. 1431; V, no. 74, cols. 317–322; no. 83, cols. 437–438; *SR*, V, no. 61, cols. 143–148.

49. *SP*, V, no. 74, cols. 383–391; no. 83, cols. 434, 435, 441, 451–452; III, no. 631, col. 1434.

50. Ibid., V, no. 74, col. 393; no. 83, cols. 441, 450–453. Cf. Ibid., III, no. 631, cols. 1432, 1433.

51. Ibid., V, no. 83, cols. 447–449; no. 74, cols. 367–368; James E. Russell, *German Higher Schools: The History, Organization and Methods of Secondary Education in Germany* (New York, 1899), pp. 163–164.

52. *SR*, V, no. 61, col. 169.

53. F. Struve, "Nashi klassicheskie gimnazii" (Our classical gymnasiums), *Zhurnal*, CXLIX (May 1870), otdel III, 11–12; *SP*, III, prilozhenie to no. 631, cols. 80–83; V, no. 83, cols. 440, 442, 447; no. 74, cols. 371–374; prilozhenie to no. 74, col. 4.

54. *SP*, V, no. 74, cols. 362–364, 393–394; no. 83, cols. 443–445; III, no. 631, col. 1423.

55. Ibid., prilozhenie to no. 631, col. 80; V, prilozhenie to no. 74, col. 4.

56. Ibid., III, no. 631, cols. 1435–1436; V, no. 83, cols. 454–455; no. 74, col. 398.

57. Ibid., III, no. 631, cols. 1430–1432; V, no. 83, cols. 437, 439–441, 455, 457, 458; Arnold, IV, 245–246.

58. *SR*, V, no. 61, cols. 162, 179–180.

59. *SP*, V, no. 196, col. 1111.

60. M. M. Stasiulevich, "Vysshaia real'naia shkola v Germanii" (The higher realschule in Germany), *Vestnik Evropy*, VI (October, December 1871), 583–628, 761–796; Lemke, III, 251–254. See also "Vnutrennee obozrenie," *Vestnik Evropy*, VI (November 1871), 395.

61. A. I. Georgievsky, "O real'nom obrazovanii v Prussii, Saksonii, Avstrii, Bavarii i Shveitsarii" (On nonclassical education in Prussia, Saxony, Austria, Bavaria, and Switzerland), *Zhurnal*, CLXVIII (December 1871), otdel III, 234–237; I. Shteinman, "Mneniia inostrannykh pedagogov v severnoi Germanii, Badene, Virtemberge, i Bel'gii o proekte ustava real'nykh uchilishch v Rossii" (The opinions of foreign pedagogues from northern Germany, Baden, Württemberg, and Belgium on the projected statute for realschulen in Russia), *Zhurnal*, CLIX (January 1872), otdel III, 95–115.

62. *SP*, V, no. 196, cols. 1117–1124, 1126.

63. Ibid., cols. 1126–1130. For a more balanced view of the *Realschule* debate, see Friedrich Paulsen, *Geschichte des gelehrten Unterrichts auf den deut-*

schen Schulen und Universitäten von Ausgang des Mittelalters bis zum Gegenwart, vol. II (2nd ed. rev.; Leipzig, 1897), pp. 556–565.

64. *SP*, V, no. 196, cols. 995–996, 1132–1135.

65. Ibid., cols. 1067, 1093, 1097–1098, 1111, 1135–1146.

66. Rozhdestvensky, *Istoricheskii obzor*, p. 526; Mills, pp. 177–181; *SP*, V, no. 196, cols. 910, 938–939, 954–956.

67. *SP*, V, no. 196, cols. 910–911, 933, 1053; prilozhenie to no. 196, cols. 17–18; no. 83, col. 431; III, no. 631, cols. 1420, 1444.

68. *SP*, V, no. 196, cols. 930–931, 1054. Alston (pp. 96–97, 110–111) places great emphasis on local influence over the realschule, on what he calls the school's "public" character, especially until 1875. However, one should not carry this interpretation too far; the ministry, not the public, determined in detail the realschule's curriculum, examination procedures, and rules for students — with its first regulations, the academic plans, appearing in May 1873. See *SR*, V, no. 312, cols. 1036–1154.

69. *SP*, V, no. 196, cols. 911, 915–916, 953.

70. *SR*, V, no. 205, 31 July 1872, cols. 538, 542; *SP*, V, no. 196, cols. 1025, 1143; prilozhenie to no. 196, col. 18.

71. *SR*, V, no. 205, col. 543.

72. Friedrich Paulsen, *German Education, Past and Present,* tran. by T. Lorenz (New York, 1908), p. 180.

73. V. V. Rozanov, *Sumerki prosveshcheniia: sbornik statei po voprosam obrazovaniia* (St. Petersburg, 1899), p. 223. On the Prussian gymnasium and *Realschule*, see *SP*, V, no. 74, col. 292; no. 196, cols. 1124–1125; Herman Bender, "Geschichte des Gelehrtenschulwesens in Deutschland seit der Reformation," in *Geschichte der Erziehung von Anfang bis auf unsere Zeit,* K. A. Schmid, ed. (Stuttgart, 1901), V, pt. I, 317–337.

74. D. A. Tolstoi, "Vzgliad na uchebnuiu chast' v Rossii v XVIII stoletii do 1782 goda," *Zapiski Imperatorskoi Akademii Nauk,* XLVII (1884), prilozhenie no. 2, pp. 12–13.

75. *SP*, V, no. 196, col. 1126.

76. Ibid., II, pt. I, no. 84, cols. 230, 237.

77. M. N. Kovalensky, "Sredniaia shkola," in *Istoriia Rossii v XIX vek* (St. Petersburg, 191?), VII, 171–172; Ganelin, p. 60; Katz, pp. 155–157.

78. N. P. Meshchersky, "Vospominaniia o M. N. Katkove," *Russkii vestnik,* August 1897, p. 25; Nikitenko, III, 51, 239–240. For similar accounts see, of course, Feoktistov, pp. 176–181 and, for example, D. Ilovaisky, "M. N. Katkov: istoricheskaia pominka," *Russkii arkhiv,* bk. I (1897), 120–121, 125.

79. "Vozhd'," in *Byloe,* October 1917, p. 23; Feoktistov, p. 212; Gradovsky, *Russkaia starina,* CXXXIII, 84.

80. *MV 1870,* no. 279, 24 December 1870, pp. 799–802; no. 126, 12 June 1870, pp. 369–371; *MV 1866,* no. 201, 13 September 1866, p. 426; *MV 1869,* no. 82, 12 April 1869, p. 219. See also Katz, pp. 143–149.

81. *MV 1872*, no. 321, 18 December 1872, p. 807. For Katkov's ideas on the gymnasium, see his editorials in *Moskovskie vedomosti*, 1864–1871; many of these were reprinted in M. N. Katkov, "Nasha uchebnaia reforma," *Russkii vestnik*, June 1879, pp. 826–926.

82. *MV 1872*, no. 43, 15 February 1872, p. 113.

83. B. V. Titlinov, *Dukhovnaia shkola v Rossii v XIX stoletie*, vol. II: *Protasovshaia epokha i reformy 60-kh godov* (Vilna, 1909), pp. 335, 344–347.

84. Gradovsky, *Russkaia starina*, CXXXIII, 78. On Tolstoi's support of *Moskovskie vedomosti* see, for example, Lemke, III, 745, 766; Sukhotin, *Russkii arkhiv*, bk. I (1894), 422, 426–427, 429.

CHAPTER 6   The Classical System in Practice

1. "Obozrenie MNP 1872," *Zhurnal*, CLXV (January 1873), otdel IV, 14.

2. *SR*, V, no. 206, cols. 550–555.

3. Ibid., cols. 575, 650–696, 714.

4. Ibid., cols. 597, 602–603, 619–634, 711–716; no. 264, 7 January 1873, col. 913.

5. *SP*, V, prilozhenie to no. 83, col. 8. For the full 1890 program, see V. Isaenkov, ed., *Sbornik postanovlenii i rasporiazhenii po gimnaziiam i progimnaziiam moskovskogo uchebnogo okruga za 1871–1895 gody* (2nd ed. rev.; Moscow, 1895), pp. 404–535.

6. *SR*, V, no. 312, cols. 1037–1039, 1040–1069, 1078, 1081–1096, 1123.

7. Ibid., no. 244, 2 December 1872 cols. 837, 843–844, 847; no. 263, 7 January 1873, cols. 907–908.

8. Ibid., no. 244, col. 860. The German examination included an essay, four problems in mathematics, and translations into Latin and from the Greek and the French (Russell, pp. 182–185).

9. *SR*, V, no. 244, cols. 863–865, 867, 868–871, 873.

10. Ibid., cols. 850, 854–857.

11. Ibid., VI, no. 78, 20 April 1875, cols. 522–563.

12. *SP*, V, no. 83, col. 441; *SR*, VI, no. 160, 7 September 1874, col. 339; *Zhurnal*, CLXXV (October 1874), otdel I, 163. These rules can be found in *SR*, VI, no. 83, cols. 149–165.

13. *SR*, VI, no. 83, cols. 165–173; no. 96, 15 May 1874, cols. 209–210.

14. Ibid., V, no. 244, col. 855.

15. Alston (p. 101) stresses this point. For him these 1874 rules contributed most "to convert the 'scholarly European school' of official intent into the 'bureaucratic police school' of public resentment."

16. *SR*, VI, no. 83, cols. 175–197.

17. Quoted in Tatishchev, II, 102.

18. "Prilozhenie ko vsepoddaneishemu otchetu Ministra Narodnogo

Prosveshcheniia za 1870 goda" (Appendix to the report to the emperor by the Minister of Education for 1870) (cited hereafter as "Prilozhenie MNP" followed by year of report), *Zhurnal*, CLXI (May 1872), otdel I, 65; "Izvlechenie MNP 1872," *Zhurnal*, CLXXIII, otdel I, 91, 96. The sections on teacher training in both this and the following chapter are in large part revised versions of my article, "Count Dmitrii Tolstoi and the Preparation of Russian School Teachers," *Canadian Slavic Studies*, 3:246–262 (summer 1969).

19. *SP*, IV, no. 22, 23 March 1865, cols. 147–149; no. 109, 18 March 1866, cols. 295–298.

20. Beliavsky, pp. 7–11, 17–20; Smorodinov, *Russkaia starina*, CLIV (June 1913), 563.

21. *SP*, IV, no. 221, cols. 490, 511–512; V. I., *Zhurnal*, CXXXIV (April, June 1867), otdel II, 214–217, 868–887; *MV 1867*, no. 106, 15 May 1867, pp. 247–251.

22. *SP*, IV, no. 221, cols. 490–495, 497, 520.

23. Ibid., cols. 493, 514–516; *SR*, VI, no. 98, 18 May 1874, col. 212; V. I. Modestov, *Shkolnyi vopros: pis'ma k redaktoru "Golos"* (St. Petersburg, 1880), pp. 83–84.

24. *SP*, IV, no. 221, cols. 490, 492, 516–519; *SR*, V, no. 63, 10 July 1871, col. 280; no. 230, 28 October 1872, cols. 790–791; no. 225, 7 October 1872, cols. 778–779; V. I., *Zhurnal*, CXXXIV, otdel II, 219.

25. *SP*, VI, no. 126, cols. 601, 605–608, 613–619, 654–656.

26. *SR*, VI, no. 52, 24 April 1876, cols. 944–960; no. 171, 13 November 1876, cols. 1281–1284; no. 39, 10 April 1876, cols. 923–930.

27. Ibid., V, no. 181, 7 June 1872, cols. 446–447; VI, no. 25, 16 February 1874, cols. 30–31; no. 174, 11 December 1876, cols. 1316–1318; no. 240, 4 June 1875, cols. 1063–1069; *Zhurnal*, CCIV (July 1879), otdel I, 19–20; "Obzor deiatel'nosti Ministerstva Narodnogo Prosveshcheniia za 1879, 1880, 1881" (A survey of the activity of the Ministry of Education for 1879, 1880, 1881) (cited hereafter as "Obzor 1879–81"), *Zhurnal*, CCLIII (October 1887), otdel I, 34–35, 37.

28. "Obzor 1879–81," *Zhurnal*, CCLIII–CCLIV (October–November 1887), otdel I, 34–35, 37, 101, 117; "Izvlechenie MNP 1877," *Zhurnal*, CCV, otdel I, 13. So few vacancies existed in history that the ministry closed the history section of the Petersburg institute in 1874 and never established one for the Bezborodko school.

29. Antonov, in *Obshchestvennoe dvizhenie*, p. 340.

30. *SR*, IV, no. 231, 16 August 1868, cols. 596–599.

31. *SP*, IV, no. 186, 27 March 1867, cols. 431–434; *SR*, IV, no. 150, 1 April 1867, cols. 444–449.

32. *SP*, IV, no. 221, col. 501; *SR*, IV, no. 367, 18 May 1870, cols. 888–889, 891–898; *SP*, IV, no. 298, 22 April 1868, cols. 781, 810–812.

33. *SP*, VII, no. 212, 26 April 1878, cols. 498–500.

34. On the philological seminary, see Ibid., V, no. 420, 14 August 1873, cols. 2142–2144; VI, no. 164, 4 February 1875, cols. 805–810; "Russkaia filologicheskaia seminariia pri leiptsigskom universitete s 1873 po 1877 god" (The Russian Philological Seminary at Leipzig University from 1873 to 1877), *Zhurnal*, CXCI (June 1877), otdel IV, 95–113; S. Zhebelev, "Iz universitetskikh vospominanii," *Annaly*, II (1923), 169.

35. "Izvlechenie MNP 1874," *Zhurnal*, CLXXXVI, otdel I, 10.

36. "Prilozhenie MNP 1873," *Zhurnal*, CLXXXI–CLXXXII (October–November 1875), otdel I, 150, 11; "Prilozhenie MNP 1877," *Zhurnal*, CCVI (December 1879), otdel I, 88, 99; "Obzor 1879–81," *Zhurnal*, CCLIII, otdel I, 35. These figures are not very reliable because some gymnasiums reported a vacancy whenever there was no salaried teacher for a subject, others only if the subject was not taught; and because new schools supplied very sketchy information. "O zameshchenii vakantnykh mest prepodavatelei v srednikh uchebnykh zavedeniiakh s 1871 po 1877 god vkliuchitel'no" (On the filling of teaching vacancies at secondary schools from 1871 to 1877), *Zhurnal*, CCIII (May 1879), otdel IV, 1–4.

37. "Izvlechenie MNP 1875," *Zhurnal*, CXCIII, otdel I, 4; "Prilozhenie MNP 1873," *Zhurnal*, CLXXXI–CLXXXII, otdel I, 152, 11; "Prilozhenie MNP 1877," *Zhurnal*, CCVI, otdel I, 106, 113. On these stipend programs see, for example, *SR*, VI, no. 48, 8 March 1875, cols. 482–483; *SP*, VI, no. 350, 27 January 1876, cols. 1378–1383.

38. "Izvlechenie MNP 1871," *Zhurnal*, CLXV, otdel I, 117, 120, 126; "Izvlechenie MNP 1872," *Zhurnal*, CLXXIII, otdel I, 88, 95; "Izvlechenie MNP 1875," *Zhurnal*, CXCII, otdel I, 214, 220; "Izvlechenie MNP 1876," *Zhurnal*, CXCVIII, otdel I, 49–51, 57, 58.

39. "Izvlechenie MNP 1877," *Zhurnal*, CCV, otdel I, 98, 114–115; "Obzor 1879–81," *Zhurnal*, CCLIV, otdel I, 78–79.

40. *SR*, VI, no. 193, 4 December 1876, cols. 1313–1316.

41. "Ob ispytaniiakh 1873," *Zhurnal*, CLXXIII, otdel IV, 5–10; *SR*, VI, no. 66, 6 April 1874, cols. 74–83; "Izvlechenie MNP 1875," *Zhurnal*, CXCII, otdel I, 229–230; "Ob ispytaniiakh 1877," *Zhurnal*, CC, otdel IV, 127–130.

42. "Izvlechenie MNP 1874," *Zhurnal*, CLXXXVI, otdel I, 12; *Zhurnal*, CXCIII (October 1877), otdel I, 110–117; "Izvlechenie MNP 1872," *Zhurnal*, CLXXIII, otdel I, 103–104; Panchukov, pp. 201–202.

43. "Izvlechenie MNP 1877," *Zhurnal*, CCV, otdel I, 28–31; "Obzor 1879–81," *Zhurnal*, CCLIV, otdel I, 52; Isaenkov, pp. 633–637.

44. "Izvlechenie MNP 1877," *Zhurnal*, CCV, otdel I, 28–29.

45. Ibid., 27–29; *SP*, VII, no. 678, April 1880, col. 1684.

46. N. Manuilovich, "O znachenii klassicheskogo obrazovaniia" (On the importance of a classical education), *Zhurnal*, CLXVIII (August 1873), otdel III, 44–70.

47. Bogatinov, *Russkii arkhiv*, bk. III (1899), 244; Modestov, pp. 51–54;

Isaenkov, pp. 329–330. On cheating and overwork at the gymnasium see Ganelin, p. 180; N. S. Rusanov, *Iz moikh vospominanii*, bk. I: *Detstvo i iunost' na rodine (1859–82)* (Berlin, 1923), pp. 69–70, 72; "Vnutrennee obozrenie," *Vestnik Evropy*, XII (June 1877), 799–802. 48. A. Samoilo, *Dve zhizni* (Moscow, 1958), p. 24; S. Kamensky, *Vek minuvshii (Vospominaniia)* (Paris, 1958), p. 16. The memoir literature of the period abounds with similar comments. See the Bibliography for further references.

49. Beliavsky, p. 221; Rozanov, pp. 171–173.

50. P. N. Miliukov, *Vospominaniia (1859–1917)*, M. M. Karpovich and B. I. El'kin, eds. (New York, 1955), I, 53; V. A. Posse, *Moi zhiznennyi put' i dorevoliutsionnyi period (1864–1917 gg.)*, B. P. Koz'min, ed. (Moscow-Leningrad, 1929), pp. 14–15.

51. Georgievsky, *Predpolozhennaia reforma*, pp. 69–71; Miliukov, I, 51; Bekkarevich, *Russkaia starina*, CXVI, 417; Beliavsky, pp. 62–64.

52. I. V. Gessen, *V dvukh vekakh: zhiznennyi otchet* ([Berlin], 1937), p. 22; M. P. Pogodin, "Obuchenie drevnim iazykam v Rossii (1875): pis'mo M. P. Pogodina k kniaziu A. I. Vasil'chikovu," *Russkii arkhiv*, bk. I (1902), 177. See also Rozanov, pp. 168, 176–178; Panteleev, p. 507; G. K. Gradovsky, *Itogi (1862–1907)* (Kiev, 1908), p. 60.

53. See, for example, John Holt, "To the Rescue," *New York Review of Books*, 13:27–36 (October 9, 1969).

54. Shestakov, "Graf," *Russkaia starina*, LXX (April 1891), 206–207; I. Matchenko, ed., "Pis'ma N. N. Strakhova k N. Ia. Danilevskomu," *Russkii vestnik*, January 1901, pp. 139–140.

55. "Raz'iasnenie (An explanation)," *Vestnik Evropy*, XIV (November 1879), 341.

56. "Izvlechenie MNP 1873," *Zhurnal*, CLXXX, otdel I, 210; "Obzor 1879–81," *Zhurnal*, CCLIV, otdel I, 47; "Spisok vysshikh," *Zhurnal*, CLXXXV, otdel IV, 6–12. These figures do not include schools in the Siberia, Warsaw, and Dorpat districts.

57. "Izvlechenie MNP 1877," *Zhurnal*, CCV, otdel I, 21–22, 93–94; *SP*, VI, no. 216, 23 April 1875, col. 941.

58. "Ob ispytaniiakh 1876," *Zhurnal*, CXCIII, otdel IV, prilozhenie after p. 130; "Ob ispytaniiakh 1877," *Zhurnal*, CC, otdel IV, 97, prilozhenie after p. 169; "Ob ispytaniiakh 1880," *Zhurnal*, CCXXI (May 1882), otdel IV, 6, 11.

59. "Obzor 1879–81," *Zhurnal*, CCLIV, otdel I, 86; "O rezul'tatakh ispytanii v gimnaziiakh s-peterburgskogo uchebnogo okruga v 1866 godu" (On the results of examinations at the gymnasiums of the St. Petersburg educational district in 1866), *Zhurnal*, CXXXI (August 1866), otdel II, 497; "Vedomosti o rezul'tatakh okonchatel'nykh ispytanii v gimnaziiakh v mae, iune, i avguste 1866" (Reports of the results of gymnasium final examinations in May, June, and August 1866), *Zhurnal*,

CXXXII (October–November 1866), otdel II, 128–131, 260–270; "Izvestiia," *Zhurnal*, CXXXV (August 1867), otdel III, 207–208; CXXXVI (November 1867), otdel III, 173–176; *Obzor 1862–64*, prilozhenie, pp. 266–278.

60. See, for example, "Ob ispytaniiakh 1877," *Zhurnal*, CC, otdel IV, 101–126; "Ob ispytaniiakh 1878," *Zhurnal*, CCIV, otdel IV, 95–110.

61. "Ob ispytaniiakh 1876," *Zhurnal*, CXCIII, otdel IV, 13; "Obzor 1879–81," *Zhurnal*, CCLIV, otdel I, 63–64.

62. Rozanov, pp. 96–97, 141; Malevsky-Malevich, *Russkii arkhiv*, bk. I (1912), 306–307; Rusanov, I, 71.

63. Beliavsky, pp. 74–75; Gessen, pp. 44–45; G. B. Sliozberg, *Dela minuvshikh dnei: zapiski russkogo evreia* (Paris, 1933), I, 108–110.

64. Bogatinov, *Russkii arkhiv*, bk. III (1899), 244–245; Beliavsky, pp. 116–117; "Izvlechenie MNP 1874," *Zhurnal*, CLXXXVI, otdel I, 24–25; "Izvlechenie MNP 1876," *Zhurnal*, CXCVIII, otdel I, 62; "Izvlechenie MNP 1877," *Zhurnal*, CCV, otdel I, 41–43; "Obzor 1879–81," *Zhurnal*, CCLIV, otdel I, 59.

65. Ganelin, p. 77; N. Antonov, "Klassitsizm v tsifrakh," in *Sbornik pedagogicheskikh statei v chest' redaktora zhurnala 'Pedagogicheskii sbornik' N. Ostrogorskogo* (St. Petersburg, 1907), p. 317.

66. V. Lebedev, "Uchebnye vospominaniia," *Russkaia starina*, CXXXI (July 1907), p. 147. See also "Vnutrennee obozrenie," *Vestnik Evropy*, XIV (September, November 1879), 389–390, 325, 327–328.

67. S. K. [S. N. Krivenko], "Ministerskaia polemika: iz literaturnykh vospominanii o gr. Dm. Andr. Tolstom," *Vestnik Evropy*, XLII (July 1907), 237–252; "Vozhd'," in *Byloe*, October 1917, p. 17.

68. "Prilozhenie MNP 1873," *Zhurnal*, CLXXXI, otdel I, 148, 150, 151; "Obzor 1879–81," *Zhurnal*, CCLIV, otdel I, 55, 68, 81, 90; "Prilozhenie MNP 1877," *Zhurnal*, CCVI, otdel I, 88, 90; *Obzor 1862–64*, prilozhenie, pp. 266–278; "Iz statistiki uchebnykh zavedenii" (From statistics on educational institutions), *Zhurnal*, CCIX (May 1880), otdel IV, 22.

69. "O raspredelenii uchashchikhsia po klassam i kursam v uchebnykh zavedeniiakh vedomstva Ministerstva Narodnogo Prosveshcheniia" (On the distribution of students according to class and course at educational institutions under the Ministry of Education), *Zhurnal*, CXC (April 1877), otdel IV, 87; "Iz statistiki," *Zhurnal*, CCIX, otdel IV, 18–19; Alston, pp. 123–133.

70. "Izvestiia," *Zhurnal*, CXXXVII (March 1868), otdel III, 321; "Izvlechenie MNP 1868," *Zhurnal*, CXLVII, otdel I, 20; "Obozrenie MNP 1869," *Zhurnal*, CXLVII (January 1870), otdel IV, 8.

71. "Izvlechenie MNP 1870," *Zhurnal*, CLX, otdel I, 28; "Prilozhenie MNP 1877," *Zhurnal*, CCVI, otdel I, 88, 90, 106–107; "Svedeniia o chisle uchashchikhsia v nashikh gimnaziiakh s 1857 po 1866" (Information on the number of students in our gymnasiums from 1857 to 1866), *Zhurnal*,

CXL (October 1868), otdel III, 24; "Prilozhenie MNP 1868," *Zhurnal*, CXLVII, otdel I, 151–152. The enrollment figures for 1868–69 include an estimated 7,700 students in the Warsaw district not mentioned in the official report.

72. "Prilozhenie MNP 1877," *Zhurnal*, CCVI, otdel I, 92, 108; *Obzor 1862–64*, prilozhenie, p. 275. For an interesting argument on the possible benefits to Russian education of these exclusion clauses see Alston, pp. 123–126, 128–133.

73. Rothblatt, p. 47; Richard Hofstadter, *Anti-Intellectualism in American Life* (New York, 1963), p. 324.

74. Edward Kirkland, *Dream and Thought in the Business Community, 1860–1900* (Ithaca, 1956), p. 101 as quoted in Hofstadter, pp. 257–258.

75. "Prilozhenie MNP 1877," *Zhurnal*, CCVI, otdel I, 92, 108; Hans, *History*, p. 236.

76. *SP*, II, pt. I, no. 84, col. 242; III, no. 631, cols. 1436–1438; "Izvlechenie MNP 1870," *Zhurnal*, CLX, otdel I, 31–33; "Prilozhenie MNP 1870," *Zhurnal*, CLXI, otdel I, 58–59.

77. A. G. Rashin, *Naselenie Rossii za 100 let (1811–1913 gg.): statisticheskie ocherki*, S. G. Strumilin, ed. (Moscow, 1956), pp. 87–97.

78. "Materialy," *Zhurnal*, CXXI, otdel II, 560–561; "Obzor 1879–81," *Zhurnal*, CCLIV, otdel I, 49.

79. "Prilozhenie MNP 1871," *Zhurnal*, CLXVI (April 1873), otdel I, 134; "Prilozhenie MNP 1877," *Zhurnal*, CCVI, otdel I, 93; Isaenkov, p. 668; Vucinich, II, 59.

80. "Poseshchenie Ministrom Narodnogo Prosveshcheniia odesskogo uchebnogo okruga" (The visit by the Minister of Education to the Odessa educational district), *Zhurnal*, CLXXXII (December 1875), otdel IV, 131–132; Alston, p. 128.

81. Bekkarevich, *Russkaia starina*, CXVI, 413–415; Sliozberg, I, 66–67.

82. L. Deich, *Za polveka* (Berlin, 1923), I, 32; Kamensky, p. 21; Rusanov, I, 63, 84–87, 105; A. O. Lukashevich, "V narod! (Iz vospominanii semidesiatnika)," *Byloe*, March 1907, pp. 1–3.

83. "Prilozhenie MNP 1871," *Zhurnal*, CLXVI, otdel I, 134; "Prilozhenie MNP 1877," *Zhurnal*, CCVI, otdel I, 93.

84. *SR*, VI, no. 105, col. 606.

85. *Zhurnal*, CCIII (June 1879), otdel I, 74–75.

86. Antonov, in *Obshchestvennoe dvizhenie*, pp. 336–343; N. I. Sidorov, ed., "Statisticheskie svedeniia o propagandistakh 70-kh godov v obrabotke III otdeleniia," *Katorga i ssylka*, no. 1 (38) (1928), 27–56.

87. Andriashev, *Russkaia starina*, CLIII (March 1913), 576; A. Vasil'chikov, *Pis'mo Ministru Narodnogo Prosveshcheniia grafu Tolstomu* (Berlin, 1875), pp. 11–13.

88. Ia. P. Polonsky, "Dnevnik — Rossiia v 1876 godu," *Na chuzhoi storone*, IV (1924), 94.

89. N. V. Golitsyn, "Konstitutsiia grafa Loris-Melikova: materialy dlia ee istorii," *Byloe*, April–May 1918, pp. 157–158; Sidorov, *Katorga i ssylka*, no. 1 (38), 34.

90. Tatishchev, II, 612–613; *MV 1879*, no. 136, 30 May 1879, pp. 267–268.

91. Rozanov, p. 40.

92. Maklakov, p. 37; L. N. Liubimov, "Iz zhizni inzhenera putei soobshcheniia," *Russkaia starina*, CLIV (April 1913), 90.

CHAPTER 7   Educating the Masses

1. Rashin, p. 289.

2. *SP*, IV, no. 436, 3 June 1869, col. 1257.

3. *Obzor 1862–64*, pp. 163–169; *SP*, II, pt. I, no. 84, cols. 214, 215.

4. Vessel', in *Russkii vestnik*, February 1903, pp. 597–598.

5. *SP*, V, no. 199, cols. 1284–1286, 1291–1293. I do not agree with Alston (p. 102) that the provision allowing entrance to the second and third gymnasium classes "restored the base of the democratic ladder," for the existence of admissions tests at the gymnasium in subjects not usually taught at the municipal school would prevent that ease of transfer essential to any truly democratic ladder system.

6. *SP*, V, no. 199, cols. 1284, 1286–1290.

7. Ibid., cols. 1275–1276.

8. Ibid., cols. 1237–1242, 1275.

9. Ibid., cols. 1175–1176, 1199–1201, 1204.

10. *Zhurnal*, CXC (March 1877), otdel I, 51, 62–67, 70, 82–93; *SP*, V, no. 199, cols. 1250–1251.

11. *SP*, V, no. 199, cols. 1175, 1246; A. Baranov, "K voprosu ob organizatsii uchebnoi chasti v gorodskikh uchilishchakh" (On the question of the organization of the academic sector at municipal schools), *Zhurnal*, CCV (October 1879), otdel III, 1–3.

12. *SP*, V, no. 199, cols. 1190, 1192–1197; *SR*, VI, no. 99, 1 June 1876, cols. 1021–1040; no. 152, 18 September 1876, cols. 1182–1186.

13. *SP*, V, no. 199, cols. 1188–1189, 1253; *SR*, VI, no. 168, 13 November 1876, cols. 1209–1270; no. 169, 13 November 1876, cols. 1272–1274.

14. Quoted in Paulsen, *German Education*, p. 248. However, in October 1872 the Prussian ministry removed many of its restrictions on the normal school program. Ibid., p. 252; von Sander, "Geschichte der Volksschule, besonders in Deutschland," in *Geschichte der Erziehung von Anfang bis auf unsere Zeit*, K. A. Schmid, ed. (Stuttgart-Berlin, 1902), V, pt. III, 224–226.

15. *SP*, V, no. 199, col. 1253; *SR*, VI, no. 99, cols. 1023, 1024, 1026–1027; no. 152, cols. 1182–1183, 1185–1186.

16. *SR*, VI, no. 152, cols. 1184–1185; M. Rodevich, "Neskol'ko slov o uchitel'skikh institutakh" (A few words on the teachers' institutes), *Zhurnal*, CLXXXII (December 1875), otdel III, 25; Russia, Ministerstvo Narodnogo Prosveshcheniia, *Uchebnye zavedeniia vedomstva Ministerstva Narodnogo Prosveshcheniia* (St. Petersburg, 1895), pp. 197–199.

17. "Obzor 1879–81," *Zhurnal*, CCLIV, otdel I, 100.

18. *SP*, V, no. 199, cols. 1185–1186, 1189, 1192, 1194; "Izvlechenie MNP 1877," *Zhurnal*, CCV, otdel I, 121; "Obzor 1879–81," *Zhurnal*, CCLIV, otdel I, 100; A. Razd — ky, "Tri goda v uchitel'skom institute," *Obrazovanie*, December 1900, p. 94.

19. "Prilozhenie MNP 1875," *Zhurnal*, CXCIV (November 1877), otdel I, 40; "Prilozhenie MNP 1877," *Zhurnal*, CCVI, otdel I, 116–117; "Obzor 1879–81," *Zhurnal*, CCLIV, otdel I, 101, 103, 128, 130.

20. See, for example, Chekhov, p. 88; Smirnov, *Reforma*, p. 160.

21. NEA, *Proceedings*, 1870, pp. 13, 17 as quoted in Hofstadter, p. 303. A convenient description of the Russian rural school of this period can be found in Jean Saussay, "La vie scolaire des compagnes à l'époque des reformes d'Alexandre II," *Cahiers du Monde russe et soviétique*, 9:392–413 (July–December 1969).

22. *Obzor 1862–64*, prilozhenie, pp. 320–327, 376; "Mery," *Zhurnal*, CXXXIII, otdel III, 17; "Izvlechenie MNP 1866," *Zhurnal*, CXXXVII, otdel I, 54. The sections in this chapter on rural primary education are in large part revised versions of my article, "Educating the Russian Peasantry: The Elementary School Reforms of Count Dmitrii Tolstoi," *Slavic Review*, 27:49–70 (March 1968).

23. "Izvlechenie MNP 1866," *Zhurnal*, CXXXVII, otdel I, 41–46; "Mery," *Zhurnal*, CXXXIII, otdel III, 15–18; S. Miropol'sky, "Voskresnaia shkola i pedagogicheskii kurs pri kharkovskoi seminarii" (The Sunday school and the pedagogical course at the Kharkov Seminary), *Zhurnal*, CXXXVIII (May 1868), otdel III, 217, 221, 223–243; "Izvestiia," *Zhurnal*, CXXXVIII (June 1868), otdel III, 330, 338–339; CXL (October 1868), otdel III, 135, 138–141. Ia. V. Abramov, however, concluded (pp. 85–90) that apart from those directed by Miropol'sky, most seminary Sunday schools achieved little.

24. Charnolusky, in *Istoriia Rossii v XIX vek*, VII, 127; *Nachal'nye narodnye uchilishcha i uchastie v nikh pravoslavnogo dukhovenstva* (St. Petersburg, 1865), p. 176.

25. *SP*, III, no. 610, 14 July 1864, cols. 1346, 1395–1396; "Izvlechenie MNP 1866," *Zhurnal*, CXXXVII, otdel I, 47–48.

26. B. V. Veselovsky, *Istoriia zemstva za sorok let*, vol. I (St. Petersburg, 1909), pp. 452–453, 459; I. Kornilov, "O summakh assignovannykh po smetam na 1868 god zemskimi uchrezhdeniiami na narodnoe obrazovanie" (On the sums zemstvo institutions assigned public education in their estimates for 1868), *Zhurnal*, CLXV (January 1873), otdel IV, 1–69.

27. N. A. Korf, "Russkoe narodnoe obrazovanie i zemstvo" (Russian public education and the zemstvo), *Vestnik Evropy*, VI (January 1871), 335.

28. *SP*, III, no. 610, cols. 1345–1350; E. S. Gordeenko, "Zemstvo i narodnye shkoly" (The zemstvo and primary schools), *Vestnik Evropy*, V (January 1870), 219; "Prilozhenie MNP 1867," *Zhurnal*, CXLIII, otdel I, 62–68; "Prilozhenie MNP 1869," *Zhurnal*, CLV, otdel I, 46–47.

29. On the elementary school trustee, see *SP*, III, no. 610, cols. 1344–1346; N. A. Korf, "Itogi obshchestvennoi deiatel'nosti po pol'zu narodnogo obrazovaniia v Rossii" (The results of community activity in behalf of public education in Russia), *Vestnik Evropy*, XI (June 1876), 906–907.

30. D. A. Tolstoi, *Rechi i stat'i grafa D. A. Tolstogo* (St. Petersburg, 1876), p. 191.

31. "Izvlechenie MNP 1869," *Zhurnal*, CLIV, otdel I, 35–38; *SP*, IV, no. 418, 26 May 1869, col. 1222; Rozhdestvensky, *Istoricheskii obzor*, p. 545.

32. *SP*, V, no. 110, 29 October 1871, cols. 530–532.

33. S. Miropol'sky, "Inspektsiia narodnykh shkol i ee zadachi" (The elementary school inspectorate and its tasks), *Zhurnal*, CLXI (May–June 1872), otdel III, 5–15, 24–46, 57–103; CLXII (July 1872), otdel III, 1–32.

34. *SP*, VI, no. 70, 25 May 1874, cols. 250–257, 317–318, 327–336; Tolstoi, *Rechi i stat'i*, pp. 184–185.

35. *SP*, VI, no. 70, cols. 248–250, 275–279.

36. Ibid., cols. 295–298; III, no. 501, 13 March 1863, cols. 968–971; "Izvlechenie MNP 1870," *Zhurnal*, CLX, otdel I, 53.

37. Tolstoi, *Rechi i stat'i*, p. 172. On European primary school sytems of the time, see P. A. Monthaye, *L'instruction populaire en Europe et aux Etats-Unis d'Amérique* (Bruges, 1876), I, 17, 45–49, 85–87; II, 11–12, 91–94, 182–184, 363–368, 373–374, 395, 410.

38. Venturi, pp. 497–500.

39. *SP*, VI, no. 70, col. 239; Valuev, *Dnevnik*, II, 285–286; Miliutin, I, 115–116.

40. Quoted in Tatishchev, II, 101–102.

41. *SP*, VI, no. 70, cols. 343–348; III, no. 610, cols. 1344–1348.

42. Ibid., VI, no. 70, cols. 221, 227, 231, 232, 236–237, 242–244, 257–258, 345, 348, 349.

43. Ibid., no. 411, cols. 1479–1497.

44. P. Annin, ed., *Svod glavneishikh zakonopolozhenii i rasporiazhenii o nachal'nykh narodnykh uchilishchakh i uchitel'skikh seminariiakh* (St. Petersburg, 1878–1879), I, 11–12; *SP*, VI, no. 320, 22 November 1875, cols. 1288–1295; "Izvlechenie MNP 1877," *Zhurnal*, CCV, otdel I, 141–142.

45. *SP*, VI, no. 411, col. 1485; "Obzor 1879–81," *Zhurnal*, CCLIV, otdel I, 133.

46. See, for example, William H. E. Johnson, *Russia's Educational Heri-*

tage (Pittsburgh, 1950), pp. 151–152; Charnolusky, in *Istoriia Rossii v XIX vek*, VII, 168–169; N. Karyshev, *Zemskie khodataistva 1865–1884gg.* (Moscow, 1900), pp. 62–66; A. Erzhov, "Narodnoe prosveshchenie i biurokratiia posle 1861 goda," *Obrazovanie*, June 1908, pp. 97, 102–104. Hans (*History*, pp. 131–138), while not censuring the inspectors, focuses primarily on zemstvo achievements. Medynsky (pp. 256–257, 318–320), on the other hand, criticizes both the zemstvos and the inspectors.

47. Veselovsky, I, 460, 586.

48. N. A. Korf, *Russkaia nachal'naia shkola: rukovodstvo dlia zemskikh glasnykh i uchitelei sel'skikh shkol* (4th ed. rev.; St. Petersburg, 1872), pp. ii, vi–viii. On Korf's career, see Smirnov, *Ocherki*, pp. 233–253.

49. *SP*, VI, no. 70, col. 228; "Raz'iasnenie," *Vestnik Evropy*, XIV (May 1879), 329–330; E. O. Vakhterova, *V. P. Vakhterov, ego zhizn' i rabota*, F. F. Korolev, ed. (Moscow, 1961), pp. 81–83; I. Ia. Iakovlev [Salembek], *Simbirskaia uchitel'skaia shkola i ee rol' v prosveshchenii chuvash* (Cheboksary, 1959), pp. 49–73.

50. Vessel', in *Russkii vestnik*, February 1903, p. 597; Smirnov, *Reforma*, p. 154.

51. "Izvlechenie MNP 1868," *Zhurnal*, CXLVII, otdel I, 35–36.

52. *MV 1868*, no. 22, 27 January 1868, p. 54; *SP*, V, no. 63, cols. 161–162, 165, 168; no. 136, 7 December 1871, cols. 598–600, 611.

53. *SR*, V, no. 145, 23 March 1872, cols. 398–400, 403.

54. Ibid., VI, no. 130, 4 July 1875, cols. 678–679, 684, 686–691, 696–697, 702–707; V, no. 145, cols. 398, 401, 402; "Izvlechenie MNP 1877," *Zhurnal*, CCV, otdel I, 133; A. Zabelin, "Opyt uchitel'skoi seminarii v severno-zapadnoi Rossii i ego ukazaniia" (The experiment of a teachers' seminary in northwest Russia and its lessons), *Zhurnal*, CXXXIII (February 1867), otdel II, 423–424.

55. Bogatinov, *Russkii arkhiv*, bk. III (1899), 378–383; A. Gurlady, "Poretskaia uchitel'skaia seminariia" (The Porets teachers' seminary), *Zhurnal*, CLXXXIV (March 1876), otdel III, 4–5.

56. *SR*, VI, no. 130, cols. 672–677; *Uchebnye zavedeniia*, pp. 200–211.

57. *SR*, VI, no. 130, cols. 661–663, 672–674, 684–685, 697–698.

58. "Obozrenie MNP 1871," *Zhurnal*, CLIX, otdel IV, 151; *SP*, V, no. 450, 11 November 1873, cols. 2188–2189; "Prilozhenie MNP 1877," *Zhurnal*, CCVI, otdel I, 118–123.

59. *SR*, V, no. 145, cols. 398, 401, 402; no. 254, 16 December 1872, cols. 886, 887.

60. Ibid., cols. 888–890; *SP*, VI, no. 302, 8 November 1875, cols. 1208–1209; "Obzor 1879–81," *Zhurnal*, CCLIV, otdel I, 116, 123–124; "Izvlechenie MNP 1877," *Zhurnal*, CCV, otdel I, 132.

61. Seredonin, III, pt. I, 151.

62. "Obzor 1879–81," *Zhurnal*, CCLIV, otdel I, 117. Information about the quality of normal school graduates is scarce, but it is clear that the

level of classroom instruction was not very high even after 1905. Cf. Alston, pp. 229–242.

63. "Izvlechenie MNP 1876," *Zhurnal*, CXCIX, otdel I, 4; "Izvlechenie MNP 1877," *Zhurnal*, CCV, otdel I, 127.

64. *SR*, VI, no. 100, 17 May 1875, cols. 597–598; no. 133, 28 July 1874, cols. 271–272; *Zhurnal*, CCVIII (March 1880), otdel I, 12.

65. *SR*, VI, no. 144, 5 August 1875, cols. 733–736, 740; Karyshev, p. 44; Veselovsky, I, 505; "Obzor 1879–81," *Zhurnal*, CCLIV, otdel I, 127.

66. *SP*, V, no. 143, 28 December 1871, cols. 625–627.

67. A. I. Koshelev, *Zapiski Aleksandra Ivanovicha Kosheleva 1812–1882 gody* (Berlin, 1884), pp. 208, 220–221, 330–331; "Prilozhenie MNP 1874," *Zhurnal*, CLXXXVIII, otdel I, 30; *SP*, VI, no. 245, 10 July 1875, cols. 1081–1086; Veselovsky, I, 503; "Vnutrennee obozrenie," *Vestnik Evropy*, XIII (April 1878), 843.

68. "Prilozhenie MNP 1877," *Zhurnal*, CCVI, otdel I, 122.

69. "Izvlechenie MNP 1877," *Zhurnal*, CCV, otdel I, 145; Monthaye, II, 418–422.

70. For a brief discussion of the model schools, see Sinel, *Slavic Review*, 27:67–68 (March 1968).

71. Percentages are calculated from tables in "Prilozhenie MNP 1877," *Zhurnal*, CCVI, otdel I, 100–105, 122–123, 126–129 and Rozhdestvensky, *Istoricheskii obzor*, p. 734.

72. By 1877 the state was spending 369,000 rubles a year for elementary school administration (*SP*, IV, no. 418, col. 1223; VI, no. 70, cols. 222–223; no. 411, col. 1479; "Prilozhenie MNP 1877," *Zhurnal*, CCVI, otdel I, 126–129).

73. "Prilozhenie MNP 1877," *Zhurnal*, CCVI, otdel I, 126–129; "Ob uchastii gorodskikh obshchestv v pozhertvovaniiakh na delo obrazovaniia" (On the participation of municipal societies in making donations for the cause of education), *Zhurnal*, CXCVI (April 1878), otdel IV, 191, 199; *SP*, VI, no. 549, cols. 1802–1807. On the later achievements of the St. Petersburg and Moscow boards, see *Dvadtsatipiatiletie nachal'nykh uchilishch goroda S-Peterburga 1877–1902: otchet gorodskoi komissii po narodnomu obrazovaniiu* (St. Petersburg, 1904); M. Shchepkin, "Upravlenie gorodskimi uchilishchami v Moskve: istoricheskii ocherk," *Russkaia mysl'*, XXVI (March 1905), 231–256.

74. "Prilozhenie MNP 1877," *Zhurnal*, CCVI, otdel I, 129; Veselovsky, I, 15, 452–453, 459–460, 586.

75. I. M. Bogdanov, *Gramotnost' i obrazovanie v dorevoliutsionnoi Rossii i v SSSR* (Moscow, 1964), p. 69; "Prilozhenie MNP 1871," *Zhurnal*, CLXVI, otdel I, 142–143; "Prilozhenie MNP 1877," *Zhurnal*, CCVI, otdel I, 124–125.

76. "Izvlechenie MNP 1877," *Zhurnal*, CCV, otdel I, 145; Bogdanov, pp. 20, 24–29, 51–52, 57.

77. "O vvedenii obiazatel'nogo obucheniia po khodataistvam nekotorykh zemskikh sobranii" (On the introduction of obligatory education in response to the petitions of several zemstvo assemblies), *Zhurnal*, CLXXV (December 1874), otdel IV, 117–130; *SR*, VI, no. 116, 4 June 1875, col. 630.

78. "Izvlechenie MNP 1875," *Zhurnal*, CXCIII, otdel I, 68–69.

79. "Izvlechenie MNP 1876," *Zhurnal*, CXCIX, otdel I, 29–30; K. K. Sent-Iler (Sainte-Hilaire) and Count Speransky, eds., *Materialy po voprosu o vvedenii obiazatel'nogo obucheniia v Rossii*, vol. I (St. Petersburg, 1880).

80. Seredonin, III, pt. I, 150–152; pt. II, 191–194; Zaionchkovsky, *Krizis*, pp. 105–106, 111–112.

81. "Izvlechenie MNP 1877," *Zhurnal*, CCV, otdel I, 154.

CHAPTER 8   Conclusion

1. Lemke, II, 149.

2. Antonov, in *Obshchestvennoe dvizhenie*, pp. 338–339; Sidorov, *Katorga i ssylka*, no. 1 (38) (1928), 27–56.

3. Valuev, *Graf P. A. Valuev*, p. 58; S. Shpitser, ed., "Ispoved grafa Loris-Melikova," *Katorga i ssylka*, XV, no. 2 (1925), 122.

4. Valuev, *Graf P. A. Valuev*, p. 71; Shpitser, *Katorga i ssylka*, XV, no. 2 (1925), 122. On Melikov and the Supreme Executive Commission, see Zaionchkovsky, *Krizis*, pp. 148 ff.

5. Golitsyn, in *Byloe*, April–May 1918, p. 181; Zaionchkovsky, *Krizis*, pp. 116–119.

6. Golitsyn, in *Byloe*, April–May 1918, pp. 160–161; Shpitser, *Katorga i ssylka*, XV, no. 2 (1925), 122. Italics added.

7. Quoted in Zaionchkovsky, *Krizis*, p. 216. On the Makov affair, see Lemke, III, 762–764; Valuev, *Graf P. A. Valuev*, pp. 82–88; Feoktistov, pp. 185–186.

8. Matchenko, in *Russkii vestnik*, January 1901, p. 140; *MV 1880*, no. 212B, 2 May 1880, p. 246.

Bibliography

The emphasis of the present study on state action in education has naturally meant that the bulk of the material has been drawn from official, especially ministerial, sources. Fortunately for the historian, the Ministry of Education was an assiduous gatherer and publisher of information on Russian education. Of its numerous publications, the most important — and the ones on which this monograph relies most heavily — are the ministry's monthly journal, the *Zhurnal Ministerstva Narodnogo Prosveshcheniia*, and the two collections of its decrees, the *Sbornik postanovlenii po Ministerstvu Narodnogo Prosveshcheniia* and the *Sbornik rasporiazhenii po Ministerstvu Narodnogo Prosveshcheniia*.

The *Zhurnal*, one of the heftiest of Russian periodicals, consistently devoted over half its space to education. In addition to articles on pedagogy and reviews of teaching materials, it carried the ministry's annual reports, editorial comments on impending school legislation, descriptions of foreign educational policy, and contemporary accounts of local school development including excerpts from zemstvo sessions, university council meetings, and inspectors' reports. Like the *Zhurnal*, the *Sborniki* offer a great fund of material. In addition to publishing those decrees which issued directly from the ministry and those that required imperial confirmation, they also in the volumes covering the Tolstoi ministry added to each major piece of legislation the minister's detailed presentation to the State Council, a short summation of that body's deliberations, and an analysis of the statutes relating to the regulations under consideration.

Admittedly, any overwhelming reliance on official sources would produce a one-sided picture of Russian education. To prevent such a distortion from occurring, this study has utilized diaries, memoirs, letters, and memoranda of the period, with particular attention paid to the views of those who worked with Tolstoi or taught or studied in his schools. The vast amount of anti-Tolstoi literature — from the writings of contemporary pedagogues like K. D. Ushinsky or Baron N. A. Korf, to the caustic critiques of liberal journals like *Vestnik Evropy*, to the hostile conclusions of Soviet historians — also provides a useful antidote to a heavy dosage of ministerial claims.

The bibliography which follows is an abbreviated one. It does not include every work consulted, but primarily those cited in the text. Nor does it include separate references to each *Zhurnal* article quoted or to the numerous contemporary comments on education in journals like *Russkii vestnik* and *Vestnik Evropy*. The addition of such articles would have made the bibliography far too cumbersome. However, they are cited in full in the notes and the translation of their titles is given there.

Tolstoi's Works

Tolstoi, D. A. "Akademicheskaia gimnaziia v XVIII stoletii po rukopisnym dokumentam arkhiva Akademii Nauk" (The academy

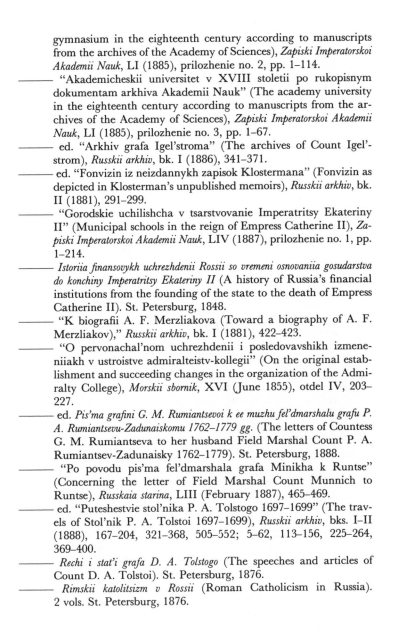

gymnasium in the eighteenth century according to manuscripts from the archives of the Academy of Sciences), *Zapiski Imperatorskoi Akademii Nauk*, LI (1885), prilozhenie no. 2, pp. 1–114.

———— "Akademicheskii universitet v XVIII stoletii po rukopisnym dokumentam arkhiva Akademii Nauk" (The academy university in the eighteenth century according to manuscripts from the archives of the Academy of Sciences), *Zapiski Imperatorskoi Akademii Nauk*, LI (1885), prilozhenie no. 3, pp. 1–67.

———— ed. "Arkhiv grafa Igel'stroma" (The archives of Count Igel'strom), *Russkii arkhiv*, bk. I (1886), 341–371.

———— ed. "Fonvizin iz neizdannykh zapisok Klostermana" (Fonvizin as depicted in Klosterman's unpublished memoirs), *Russkii arkhiv*, bk. II (1881), 291–299.

———— "Gorodskie uchilishcha v tsarstvovanie Imperatritsy Ekateriny II" (Municipal schools in the reign of Empress Catherine II), *Zapiski Imperatorskoi Akademii Nauk*, LIV (1887), prilozhenie no. 1, pp. 1–214.

———— *Istoriia finansovykh uchrezhdenii Rossii so vremeni osnovaniia gosudarstva do konchiny Imperatritsy Ekateriny II* (A history of Russia's financial institutions from the founding of the state to the death of Empress Catherine II). St. Petersburg, 1848.

———— "K biografii A. F. Merzliakova (Toward a biography of A. F. Merzliakov)," *Russkii arkhiv*, bk. I (1881), 422–423.

———— "O pervonachal'nom uchrezhdenii i posledovavshikh izmeneniiakh v ustroistve admiralteistv-kollegii" (On the original establishment and succeeding changes in the organization of the Admiralty College), *Morskii sbornik*, XVI (June 1855), otdel IV, 203–227.

———— ed. *Pis'ma grafini G. M. Rumiantsevoi k ee muzhu fel'dmarshalu grafu P. A. Rumiantsevu-Zadunaiskomu 1762–1779 gg.* (The letters of Countess G. M. Rumiantseva to her husband Field Marshal Count P. A. Rumiantsev-Zadunaisky 1762–1779). St. Petersburg, 1888.

———— "Po povodu pis'ma fel'dmarshala grafa Minikha k Runtse" (Concerning the letter of Field Marshal Count Munnich to Runtse), *Russkaia starina*, LIII (February 1887), 465–469.

———— ed. "Puteshestvie stol'nika P. A. Tolstogo 1697–1699" (The travels of Stol'nik P. A. Tolstoi 1697–1699), *Russkii arkhiv*, bks. I–II (1888), 167–204, 321–368, 505–552; 5–62, 113–156, 225–264, 369–400.

———— *Rechi i stat'i grafa D. A. Tolstogo* (The speeches and articles of Count D. A. Tolstoi). St. Petersburg, 1876.

———— *Rimskii katolitsizm v Rossii* (Roman Catholicism in Russia). 2 vols. St. Petersburg, 1876.

———— "Verel'skii mirnyi dogovor s Shvetsiiu 3-go avgusta 1790 goda (Po dokumentam iz arkhiva grafa Igel'stroma)" (The Verela Peace Treaty with Sweden of 3 August 1790 [According to documents from the archives of Count Igel'strom]), *Russkii arkhiv*, bk. III (1887), 457–520.

———— "Vzgliad na uchebnuiu chast' v Rossii v XVIII stoletii do 1782 goda" (A look at the education sector in Russia in the eighteenth century up to 1782), *Zapiski Imperatorskoi Akademii Nauk*, XLVII (1884), prilozhenie no. 2, pp. 1–100.

Public Documents: Official Publications and Histories, School Reports, and Surveys

Annin, P., ed. *Svod glavneishikh zakonopolozhenii i rasporiazhenii o nachal'nykh narodnykh uchilishchakh i uchitel'skikh seminariiakh* (A code of the principal statutes and decrees on elementary schools and teachers' seminaries). 3 vols. St. Petersburg, 1878–1879.

[Darlington, T.] *Education in Russia*. London: Wyman & Sons, 1909.

Dvadtsatipiatiletie nachal'nykh uchilishch goroda S-Peterburga 1877–1902: otchet gorodskoi komissii po narodnomu obrazovaniiu (Twenty-five years of elementary schools in the city of St. Petersburg 1877–1902: the report of the Municipal Commission on Public Education). St. Petersburg, 1904.

Dvadtsatipiatiletie s-peterburgskoi zemskoi uchitel'skoi shkoly s 1872 po 1897 gg. (The twenty-fifth anniversary of the St. Petersburg Zemstvo Teachers' School 1872–1897). St. Petersburg, 1897.

Isaenkov, V., ed. *Sbornik postanovlenii i rasporiazhenii po gimnaziiam i progimnaziiam moskovskogo uchebnogo okruga za 1871–1895 gody* (A collection of resolutions and decrees relating to the gymnasiums and progymnasiums of the Moscow educational district 1871–1895). 2nd ed. rev. Moscow, 1895.

Kriukovsky, A., ed. *Alfavitnyi sbornik postanovlenii i rasporiazhenii po s-peterburgskomu uchebnomu okrugu za 1858–1876 g.* (An alphabetical collection of resolutions and decrees relating to the St. Petersburg educational district 1858–1876). St. Petersburg, 1877.

Mann, K. A., ed. *Obzor deiatel'nosti morskogo upravleniia v Rossii v pervoe dvadtsatipiatiletie blagopoluchnogo tsarstvovaniia Gosudariia Imperatora Aleksandra Nikolaevicha 1855–1880* (A survey of the activity of the naval administration during the first twenty-five years of the prosperous reign of our sovereign the Emperor Alexander Nikolaevich 1855–1880). 2 vols. St. Petersburg, 1880.

Monthaye, P. A. *L'instruction populaire en Europe et aux Etats-Unis d'Amérique*. 2 vols. Bruges, 1876.

Moskovskii universitet. *Otchety o sostoianii i deistviiakh imperatorskogo mos-*

kovskogo universiteta za 1866–1874, 1876–1877, 1880 gody (Reports on the state and activities of the Imperial Moscow University for the years 1866–1874, 1876–1877, 1880). 11 vols. Moscow, 1868–1881.

Nachal'nye narodnye uchilishcha i uchastie v nikh pravoslavnogo dukhovenstva (Elementary schools and the Orthodox clergy's share in them). St. Petersburg, 1865.

Ogorodnikov, S. F. *Istoricheskii obzor razvitiia i deiatel'nosti Morskogo Ministerstva za sto let ego sushchestvovaniia (1802–1902 gg.)* (A historical survey of the development and activity of the Naval Ministry in its first hundred years of existence [1802–1902]). St. Petersburg, 1902.

PSZ. See Russia, *Polnoe sobranie zakonov Rossiiskoi Imperii.*

Rozhdestvensky, S. V. *Istoricheskii obzor deiatel'nosti Ministerstva Narodnogo Prosveshcheniia 1802–1902* (A historical survey of the activity of the Ministry of Education 1802–1902). St. Petersburg, 1902.

Russia. *Polnoe sobranie zakonov Rossiiskoi Imperii* (The complete collection of laws of the Russian Empire). St. Petersburg, 1830–1916.

Russia, Gosudarstvennyi Sovet. *Gosudarstvennyi Sovet 1801–1901* (The State Council 1801–1901). St. Petersburg, 1901.

Russia, Ministerstvo Finansov. *Ministerstvo Finansov 1802–1902* (The Ministry of Finance 1802–1902). 2 vols. St. Petersburg, 1902.

Russia, Ministerstvo Narodnogo Prosveshcheniia. *Materialy sobrannye otdelom vysochaishe uchrezhdennoi komissii dlia peresmotra obshchego ustava rossiiskikh universitetov* (Materials collected by a section of the commission established by the emperor to revise the general statute on Russian universities). St. Petersburg, 1876.

―――― *Obzor deiatel'nosti Ministerstva Narodnogo Prosveshcheniia i povedomstvennykh emu uchrezhdenii v 1862, 63, i 64 godakh* (A survey of the activity of the Ministry of Education and of the institutions subordinate to it in 1862, 63, and 64). St. Petersburg, 1865.

―――― *Obzor deiatel'nosti vedomstva Ministerstva Narodnogo Prosveshcheniia za vremia tsarstvovaniia Imperatora Aleksandra III* (A survey of the activity of the Ministry of Education during the reign of Emperor Alexander III). St. Petersburg, 1901.

―――― *Sbornik postanovlenii po Ministerstvu Narodnogo Prosveshcheniia* (A collection of resolutions relating to the Ministry of Education). Vols. I–III, 2nd ed., St. Petersburg, 1875–1876. Vols. IV–IX, St. Petersburg, 1871–1893.

―――― *Sbornik rasporiazhenii po Ministerstvu Narodnogo Prosveshcheniia* (A collection of decrees relating to the Ministry of Education). Vols. I–VI, St. Petersburg, 1866–1901.

―――― *Uchebnye zavedeniia vedomstva Ministerstva Narodnogo Prosveshcheniia* (Educational institutions under the Ministry of Education). St. Petersburg, 1895.

―――― *Zhurnal Ministerstva Narodnogo Prosveshcheniia* (The journal of the Ministry of Education). St. Petersburg, 1834–1917.

―――― *[Zhurnaly zasedanii vysochaishe uchrezhdennoi 21 aprelia 1875 g. komissii po peresmotru universitetskogo ustava]* (The journals of the meetings of the commission established by the emperor on 21 April 1875 to revise the university statute). St. Petersburg, n.d.

Sadler, Michael E., ed. *Education in Germany*. London: Wyman & Sons, 1902.

Sent-Iler (Sainte-Hilaire), K. K., and Count Speransky, eds. *Materialy po voprosu o vvedenii obiazatel'nogo obucheniia v Rossii* (Materials relating to the question of introducing obligatory education in Russia). Vol. I. St. Petersburg, 1880.

Seredonin, S. M. *Istoricheskii obzor deiatel'nosti Komiteta Ministrov* (A historical survey of the activity of the Committee of Ministers). Vol. III, pts. I–II: *Komitet Ministrov v tsarstvovanie Imperatora Aleksandra Vtorogo* (The Committee of Ministers in the reign of Alexander II). St. Petersburg, 1902.

Sopotsinsky, A., ed. *Ukazatel' knigam odobrennym uchenym komitetom Ministerstva Narodnogo Prosveshcheniia v period vremeni s 1856 po 1885* (A guide to the books approved by the Academic Committee of the Ministry of Education from 1856 to 1885). 2nd ed. rev. Kiev, 1887.

SP. See Russia, Ministerstvo Narodnogo Prosveshcheniia, *Sbornik postanovlenii po Ministerstvu Narodnogo Prosveshcheniia.*

SR. See Russia, Ministerstvo Narodnogo Prosveshcheniia, *Sbornik rasporiazhenii po Ministerstvu Narodnogo Prosveshcheniia.*

Varadinov, N. *Istoriia Ministerstva Vnutrennikh Del* (A history of the Ministry of the Interior). 8 vols. St. Petersburg, 1858–1863.

Diaries, Letters, Memoirs, Reminiscences, and Memoranda

Aksel'rod, P. B. *Perezhitoe i peredumannoe* (My past and thoughts). Bk. I. Berlin: Izdatel'stvo Z. I. Grzhebina, 1923.

Andriashev, A. F. "Vospominaniia starogo pedagoga" (The reminiscences of an old pedagogue), *Russkaia starina*, CXLV–CXLVI, CXLVIII (January, March–May, October–December 1911); CL (April 1912); CLIII, CLVI (February–March, October 1913), 184–194, 571–578; 94–101, 431–436; 151–158, 345–352, 619–624; 21–29; 367–375, 563–578; 142–148.

Bekkarevich, N. "Orenburgskaia gimnaziia starogo vremeni" (The Orenburg gymnasium of long ago), *Russkaia starina*, CXVI (November 1903), 401–417.

Beliavsky, E. V. *Pedagogicheskie vospominaniia 1861–1902* (Pedagogical reminiscences 1861–1902). Moscow, 1905.

Bogatinov, N. D. "Vospominaniia N. D. Bogatinova" (The reminiscences of N. D. Bogatinov), *Russkii arkhiv*, bks. I–III (1899), 281–303, 410–440, 661–673; 47–79, 245–270, 428–446, 515–548; 89–115, 225–255, 371–406, 556–569.

Bogdanovich, A. V. *Tri poslednikh samoderzhtsa: dnevnik A. V. Bogdanovich* (The three last autocrats: the diary of A. V. Bogdanovich). Moscow-Leningrad, 1924.

Bool', V. G. von. "Vospominaniia pedagoga" (The reminiscences of a pedagogue), *Russkaia starina*, CXVII–CXX (March–May, July–November 1904), 615–630; 111–123, 379–392; 213–227, 287–305, 578–593; 74–101, 300–348.

Briksman, M., and M. Aronson, eds. "Tekushchaia khronika i osobye proisshestviia: dnevnik V. F. Odoevskogo 1859–1869 gg." (A chronicle of routine and special events: the diary of V. F. Odoevsky 1859–1869), *Literaturnoe nasledstvo*, XXII–XXIV (1935), 79–308.

Buslaev, F. I. *Moi vospominaniia* (My reminiscences). Moscow, 1897.

Buturlin, M. D. "Zapiski grafa Mikhaila Dmitrievicha Buturlina" (The memoirs of Count Mikhail Dmitrievich Buturlin), *Russkii arkhiv*, bks. I–III (1897); bks. I–III (1898), 213–247, 396–444, 577–652; 5–74, 177–257, 337–439, 529–601; 33–106, 237–282, 313–367, 517–597; 125–164, 239–276, 388–424; 5–40, 303–331, 406–444, 522–589; 153–222.

Chevazhevsky, V. S. "Iz proshlogo kievskogo universiteta i studencheskoi zhizni (1870–1875 g.)" (Out of the past of Kiev University and student life [1870–1875]), *Russkaia starina*, CL–CLI (June–July 1912), 555–585; 127–133.

Chicherin, B. N. *Vospominaniia Borisa Nikolaevicha Chicherina* (The reminiscences of Boris Nikolaevich Chicherin). Vol. IV: *Moskovskii universitet* (Moscow University). S. V. Bakhrushin, ed. Moscow, 1929. Vol. V: *Zemstvo i moskovskaia duma* (The zemstvo and the Moscow duma). V. I. Nevsky, ed. Moscow, 1934.

———— "Zapiska po studencheskomu voprosu B. N. Chicherina" (A memorandum on the student question by B. N. Chicherin), *Byloe*, August 1907, pp. 79–83.

Chudnovsky, S. "Iz dal'nikh let (Otryvki iz vospominanii)" (From bygone years [Fragments from reminiscences]), *Byloe*, September–October 1907, pp. 278–295; 218–240.

Davydov, N. V. *Iz proshlogo* (Out of the past). Moscow, 1913.

Debogory-Mokrievich, V. *Vospominaniia* (Reminiscences). St. Petersburg, 1906.

Deich, L. *Za polveka* (After half a century). 2 vols. Berlin: Izdatel'stvo "Grani," 1923.

Del'vig, A. I. *Polveka russkoi zhizni: vospominaniia A. I. Del'viga 1820–70* (Half a century of Russian life: the reminiscences of A. I. Del'vig 1820–70). S. Ia. Shtraikh, ed. 2 vols. Moscow-Leningrad, 1930.

Feoktistov, E. M. *Vospominaniia E. M. Feoktistova: za kulisami politiki i literatury 1848–96* (The reminiscences of E. M. Feoktistov: behind the scenes of politics and literature 1848–96). Iu. G. Oksman, ed. Leningrad, 1929.

Filatov, P. F. "Iunye gody: vospominaniia o meditsinskom fakul'tete (1868–73 gg.) moskovskogo universiteta" (Years of youth: reminiscences about the medical faculty of Moscow University [1868–73]), *Russkaia starina*, CLIV (April–May 1913), 142–152, 281–300.

Florinsky, V. M. "Zametki i vospominaniia V. M. Florinskogo" (Notes and reminiscences of V. M. Florinsky), *Russkaia starina*, CXXV–CXXVI (January–June 1906), 75–109, 288–311, 564–596; 109–156, 280–323, 596–621.

Georgievsky, A. I. "Moi vospominaniia i razmyshleniia" (My reminiscences and reflections), *Russkaia starina*, CLXI–CLXIV (February, April–June, September–December 1915); CLXV–CLXVI (February–May 1916), 343–362; 72–89, 353–366, 453–471; 414–442; 80–90, 252–257, 431–440; 286–293, 454–459; 88–92, 282–292.

———— "Pamiati grafa D. A. Tolstogo" (Memories of Count D. A. Tolstoi), *Russkii vestnik*, July 1889, pp. 259–267.

Gessen, I. V. *V dvukh vekakh — zhiznennyi otchet* (In two centuries — a life account). [Berlin: Petropolis Verlag], 1937.

Golitsyn, N. V., ed. "Konstitutsiia grafa Loris-Melikova: materialy dlia ee istorii" (The constitution of Count Loris-Melikov: materials for its history), *Byloe*, April–May 1918, pp. 125–186.

Gradovsky, G. K. *Itogi (1862–1907)* (Results [1862–1907]). Kiev, 1908.

———— "Iz minuvshego (Vospominaniia i vpechatleniia literatora 1865–97 g.)" (Out of the past [Reminiscences and impressions of a writer 1865–97]), *Russkaia starina*, CXXXIII–CXXXIV, CXXXVI (January–February, April–May, October, December 1908); CXXXVIII (March 1909), 77–86, 323–330; 148–157, 293–302; 57–74, 553–562; 529–535.

Grevs, I. M. "V gody iunosti" (In the years of youth), *Byloe*, June 1918; no. 16 (1921), pp. 42–88; 137–166.

Gurevich, P., ed. "Nezabvennye mysli nezabvennykh liudei (Iz istorii reaktsii 60-kh godov)" (Unforgettable ideas of unforgettable people [From the history of the reaction of the 1860s]), *Byloe*, January 1907, pp. 236–242.

Iakhontov, A. N. "Vospominaniia tsarskosel'skogo litseista, 1832–1838 gg." (The reminiscences of a Tsarskoe Selo lyceist 1832–1838), *Russkaia starina*, LX (October 1888), 101–124.

Ilovaisky, D. "M. N. Katkov: istoricheskaia pominka" (M. N. Katkov: a historical note), *Russkii arkhiv*, bk. I (1897), 119–144.

Iudin, P. "Iz istorii uchebnoi reformy 60-kh godov (Otryvki iz vospominanii)" (From the history of the educational reform of the 1860s [Fragments from reminiscences]), *Russkaia starina*, CXXI (March 1905), 683–692.

Jelavich, Charles, and Barbara Jelavich, eds. *The Education of a Russian Statesman: The Memoirs of Nicholas Karlovich Giers*. Berkeley: University of California Press, 1962

K. P. Pobedonostsev i ego korrespondenty: pis'ma i zapiski (K. P. Pobedonostsev and his correspondents: letters and notes). 2 vols. Moscow–Petrograd, 1923.

Kamensky, S. *Vek minuvshii (Vospominaniia)* (The century gone by [Reminiscences]). Paris: n.p., 1958.

Kantor, R. M., ed. "Pis'ma K. P. Pobedonostseva k grafu N. P. Ignat'evu" (The letters of K. P. Pobedonostsev to Count N. P. Ignat'ev), *Byloe*, no. 27–28 (1924), 50–89.

Kharitonov, A. A. *Iz vospominanii A. A. Kharitonova (1824–1854)* (From the reminiscences of A. A. Kharitonov [1824–1854]). St. Petersburg, 1894.

Kizevetter, A. A. *Na rubezhe dvukh stoletii (Vospominaniia 1881–1914)* (At the crossroads of two centuries [Reminiscences 1881–1914]). Prague, Izdatel'stvo "Orbis," 1929.

Koni, A. F. *Na zhiznennom puti* (On life's path). Vol. II. St. Petersburg, 1912. Vol. III. Revet-Berlin: Izdatel'stvo "Bibliofil," 1922.

Koshelev, A. I. *Zapiski Aleksandra Ivanovicha Kosheleva (1812–1883 gody)* (The memoirs of Alexander Ivanovich Koshelev [1812–1883]). Berlin, 1884.

Kovalevsky, M. "Moskovskii universitet v kontse 70-kh i nachale 80-kh godov proshlogo veka (Lichnye vospominaniia)" (Moscow University at the end of the seventies and the beginning of the eighties of the last century [Personal reminiscences]), *Vestnik Evropy*, XLV (May 1910), 178–221.

Krashennikov, N. *Sobranie sochinenii* (Collected works). Vol. V: *Nevozvratnoe* (The irretrievable). 2nd. ed. Moscow, 1917.

[Krivenko, S. N.] "Ministerskaia polemika: iz literaturnykh vospominanii o gr. Dm. Andr. Tolstom" (A ministerial polemic: from literary reminiscences about Count D. A. Tolstoi), *Vestnik Evropy*, XLII (July 1907), 237–252.

Kropotkin, Peter. *Memoirs of a Revolutionist*. James Allen Rogers, ed. Garden City, N. Y.: Doubleday & Co., 1962.

Lebedev, V. "Uchebnye vospominaniia" (School reminiscences), *Russkaia starina*, CXXX–CXXXI (June–July 1907); CXXXV–CXXXVI (July–December 1908) 626–637; 133–148; 21–36, 241–255, 581–600; 245–264, 447–468, 721–733.

Lemke, M. K., ed. *M. M. Stasiulevich i ego sovremenniki v ikh perepiske* (M. M.

Stasiulevich and his contemporaries in correspondence). 5 vols. St. Petersburg, 1911–1913.

Leskov, N. S. *Sobranie sochinenii v odinnadtsati tomakh* (Collected works in eleven volumes). B. G. Bazanov et al., eds. Vol. X. Moscow, 1958.

Librovich, S. F. *Na knizhnom postu — vospominaniia i zapiski i dokumenty* (On the book beat — reminiscences, memoirs, and documents). Petrograd-Moscow, [1916].

Listovsky, I. S., ed. "Pis'mo grafa D. A. Tolstogo k ego diade grafu D. N. Tolstomu 30 aprelia 1861" (A letter of 30 April 1861 from Count D. A. Tolstoi to his uncle Count D. N. Tolstoi), *Russkii arkhiv*, bk. I (1905), 687–689.

Liubimov, L. N. "Iz zhizni inzhinera putei soobshcheniia" (From the life of an engineer in the means of communication), *Russkaia starina*, CLIV–CLVI (April–May, July–September, December 1913); CLVII (February–March 1914), 84–98, 390–397; 13–34, 217–253, 448–463, 651–679; 352–367, 582–605.

Lukashevich, A. O. "V narod! (Iz vospominanii semidesiatnika)" (To the people! [From the reminiscences of a man of the seventies]), *Byloe*, March 1907, pp. 1–45.

Maklakov, V. A. *Iz vospominanii* (From my reminiscences). New York: Izdatel'stvo imeni Chekhova, 1954.

Malevsky-Malevich, N. A. "Iz vospominanii N. A. Malevskogo-Malevicha" (From the reminiscences of N. A. Malevsky-Malevich), *Russkii arkhiv*, bk. II (1908); bk. II (1909); bk. II (1910); bk. III (1911); bk. I (1912), 82–100; 115–133; 585–603; 267–288; 290–308.

Manassein, S. "Graf D. A. Tolstoi v Kazani (Po lichnym vospominaniiam i rasskazam starozhilov)" (Count D. A. Tolstoi in Kazan [According to the personal recollections and accounts of the old residents]), *Russkaia starina*, CXXII (June 1905), 572–577.

Matchenko, I., ed. "Pis'ma N. N. Strakhova k N. Ia. Danilevskomu" (The letters of N. N. Strakhov to N. Ia. Danilevsky), *Russkii vestnik*, January–March 1901, pp. 127–142, 453–469, 125–141.

Matseevich, L. S., ed. "Pis'mo Ministra Narodnogo Prosveshcheniia grafa D. A. Tolstogo k popechiteliu odesskogo uchebnogo okruga S. P. Golubtsovu (1878 g.)" (A letter from the Minister of Education Count D. A. Tolstoi to the curator of the Odessa educational district S. P. Golubtsov [1878]), *Russkii arkhiv*, bk. II (1911), 457–458.

Mavrodin, V. V., ed. *Leningradskii universitet v vospominaniiakh sovremennikov* (Leningrad University in contemporary reminiscences). Vol. I: *Peterburgskii universitet 1819–1895* (Petersburg University 1819–1895). Leningrad, 1963.

Meshchersky, N. P. "Vospominaniia o M. N. Katkove" (Reminiscences about M. N. Katkov), *Russkii vestnik*, August 1897, pp. 1–49.

Meshchersky, V. P. *Moi vospominaniia* (My reminiscences). 2 vols. St. Petersburg, 1897–1898.

Miliukov, P. N. *Vospominaniia (1859–1917)* (Reminiscences [1859–1917]). M. M. Karpovich and B. I. El'kin, eds. 2 vols. New York: Izdatel'stvo imeni Chekhova, 1955.

Miliutin, D. A. *Dnevnik D. A. Miliutina* (The diary of D. A. Miliutin). P. A. Zaionchkovsky, ed. 4 vols. Moscow, 1947–1950.

Modzalevsky, B., ed. *Perepiska L. N. Tolstogo s N. N. Strakhovym* (The correspondence of L. N. Tolstoi with N. N. Strakhov). St. Petersburg, 1913.

Mukhanov, V. A. "Iz dnevnykh zapisok V. A. Mukhanova" (From the diaries of V. A. Mukhanov), *Russkii arkhiv*, bk. III (1896); bks. I–II (1897), 162–199, 327–336, 547–568; 45–109, 267–301; 75–94.

Naumov, A. N. *Iz utselevshikh vospominanii 1868–1917* (From memories that have survived 1868–1917). Vol. I. New York: Izdanie A. K. Naumovoi i O. A. Kusevitskoi, 1954.

Nikitenko, A. V. *Dnevnik v trekh tomakh* (A diary in three volumes). I. Ia. Aizenshtok, ed. 3 vols. [Moscow], 1955–1956.

Ostrogorsky, V. *Iz istorii moego uchitel'stva: kak ia sdelalsia uchitelem (1851–1864 gg.)* (From the history of my teaching career: how I became a teacher [1851–1864]). St. Petersburg, 1895.

Ovsiannikov, A. "Iz vospominanii starogo pedagoga" (From the reminiscences of an old pedagogue)," *Russkaia starina*, XCVIII–XCIX (May–July 1899); CI (January 1900), 417–434, 671–693; 133–144; 195–224.

Pahlen, K. I. "Zapiska Ministra Iustitsii grafa Palena: uspekhi revoliutsionnoi propagandy v Rossii (1875 g.)" (A memorandum of Justice Minister Pahlen: the successes of revolutionary propaganda in Russia [1875]), *Byloe*, September 1907, pp. 268–276.

Panteleev, L. F. *Iz vospominanii proshlogo* (From reminiscences of the past). S. A. Reiser, ed. Moscow-Leningrad, 1934.

Peretts, E. A. *Dnevnik E. A. Perettsa (1880–83)* (The diary of E. A. Peretts [1880–83]). A. A. Sergeev, ed. Moscow-Leningrad, 1927.

Pirogov, N. I. *Sevastopol'skie pis'ma i vospominaniia* (Sevastopol letters and reminiscences). S. Ia. Shtraikh, ed. [Moscow], 1950.

Pisnaia, V. N. "Studencheskie gody Zheliabova" (Zheliabov's student years), *Byloe*, no. 4 (32) (1925), pp. 171–195.

Polonsky, Ia. P. "Dnevnik — Rossiia v 1876 godu" (A diary — Russia in 1876), *Na chuzhoi storone*, IV (1924), 88–100.

Polovtsov, A. A. *Dnevnik gosudarstvennogo sekretaria A. A. Polovtsova v dvukh tomakh* (The diary of State Secretary A. A. Polovtsov in two volumes). P. A. Zaionchkovsky, ed. 2 vols. Moscow, 1966.

Posse, V. A. *Moi zhiznennyi put' i dorevoliutsionnyi period (1864–1917 gg.)* (My life and the prerevolutionary period [1864–1917]). B. P. Koz'min, ed. Moscow-Leningrad, 1929.

Razd—ky, A. "Tri goda v uchitel'skom institute" (Three years at a teachers' institute), *Obrazovanie*, December 1900, pp. 91–103.

Romanovich-Slavatinsky, A. V. "Moia zhizn' i akademicheskaia deiatel'nost' 1832–1884 gg." (My life and academic activity 1832–1884), *Vestnik Evropy*, XXXVIII (January–June 1903), 138–197, 606–650, 168–214, 527–566, 181–205, 499–508.

Rostovtsev, G. "Studencheskie volneniia v moskovskom universitete v 1887 g." (The student disturbances at Moscow University in 1887), *Russkaia starina*, CXXV (January 1906), 132–146.

Rusanov, N. S. *Iz moikh vospominanii* (From my reminiscences). Bk. I: *Detstvo i iunost' na rodine (1859–82)* (Childhood and youth in my native land [1859–82]). Berlin: Izdatel'stvo Z. I. Grzhebina, 1923.

Samarine, D., ed. *Correspondance de G. Samarine avec La Baronne de Rahden 1861–1876*. 2nd ed. Moscow, 1894.

Samoilo, A. *Dve zhizni* (Two lives). Moscow, 1958.

Schweinitz, Hans Lothar von. *Denkwurdigkeiten des Botschafters General v. Schweinitz*. Wilhelm v. Schweinitz, ed. 2 vols. Berlin: Verlag von Reimar Hobbing, 1927.

Sechenov, I. M. *Avtobiograficheskie zapiski Ivana Mikhailovicha Sechenova* (The autobiographical memoirs of Ivan Mikhailovich Sechenov). Kh. S. Koshtoiants, ed. [Moscow], 1945.

Semenov, D. D. "Pervoe desiatiletie s-peterb. gorodskikh nachal'nykh uchilishch v vedenii stolichnogo obshchestvennogo upravleniia" (The first decade of the St. Petersburg municipal elementary schools' being under the jurisdiction of the Metropolitan Community Board)," *Russkaia starina*, LV–LVI (September–October 1887), 667–703; 161–195.

Semenov-Tian-Shansky, P. P. *Memuary* (Memoirs). Vol. I: *Detstvo i iunost' (1827–1855)* (Childhood and youth [1827–1855]). Petrograd, 1917.

[Semevsky, M. I.] "Aleksandr Vasil'evich Golovnin (Alexander Vasil'evich Golovnin)," *Russkaia starina*, LIII (March 1887), 767–787.

Shchetinin, B. A. "Pervye shagi (Iz nedavnego proshlogo)" (First steps [From the recent past]), *Istoricheskii vestnik*, February 1905, pp. 501–514.

Shestakov, P. D. "Graf Dmitry Andreevich Tolstoi kak Ministr Narodnogo Prosveshcheniia" (Count Dmitry Andreevich Tolstoi as Minister of Education), *Russkaia starina*, LXIX–LXX (February, April 1891), 387–405; 183–210.

——— "Tiazhelye dni kazanskogo universiteta" (Gloomy days at Kazan University), *Russkaia starina*, LXXXVIII (December 1896); LXXXIX (January 1897), 519–539; 113–144.

Shpitser, S., ed. "Ispoved grafa Loris-Melikova" (The confession of Count Loris-Melikov), *Katorga i ssylka*, XV, no. 2 (1925), 118–125.

Sidorov, N. I., ed. "Statisticheskie svedeniia o propagandistakh 70-kh godov v obrabotke III otdeleniia" (Statistical information processed by the Third Section on the propagandists of the 1870s), *Katorga i ssylka*, no. 1 (38) (1928), 27–56.

Sliozberg, G. B. *Dela minuvshikh dnei: zapiski russkogo evreia* (The affairs of days gone by: the memoirs of a Russian Jew). 3 vols. Paris: Izdanie komiteta po chestvovaniiu 70-kh letnogo iubileia G. B. Sliozberga, 1933.

Smorodinov, V. "Gody sluzhby moei v varshavskom uchebnom okruge i epizody uchebnogo byta" (The years of my service in the Warsaw educational district and episodes from school life), *Russkaia starina*, CLIV–CLVI (June–October 1913), 552–570; 157–186, 297–302, 464–491; 181–196.

Snegirev, I. M. "Dnevnik Ivana Mikhailovicha Snegireva" (The diary of Ivan Mikhailovich Snegirev), *Russkii arkhiv*, bks. II–III (1902); bks. I–III (1903); bks. I–III (1904); bks. I–II (1905), 177–212, 369–435, 529–576; 5–65, 161–186, 306–320, 461–486; 95–111, 216–229, 369–388, 534–548; 82–95, 220–235, 445–457, 565–584; 86–108, 265–288, 433–456, 519–536; 98–114, 286–300, 449–464, 588–603; 37–59, 224–237, 427–446, 555–572; 60–75, 204–224, 382–403; 109–123, 295–305, 487–504, 647–661; 5–9.

Sukhotin, S. M. "Iz pamiatnykh tetradei S. M. Sukhotina" (From the notebooks of S. M. Sukhotin), *Russkii arkhiv*, bks. I–III (1894), 225–266, 417–436, 599–610; 139–149, 241–256, 433–447, 581–589; 51–68.

Tankov, A. "Ministr Narodnogo Prosveshcheniia graf D. A. Tolstoi i tserkovnye zapovedi (Nedavniaia starinka)" (The Minister of Education Count D. A. Tolstoi and church precepts [The recent past]), *Istoricheskii vestnik*, December 1910, pp. 878–884.

Tolstoi, D. N. "Zapiski grafa Dmitriia Nikolaevicha Tolstogo" (The memoirs of Count Dmitry Nikolaevich Tolstoi), *Russkii arkhiv*, bk. II (1885), 5–70.

Unkovsky, A. M. "Zapiski" (Memoirs), *Russkaia mysl'*, XXVII (June–July 1906), 184–196, 88–116.

Vakhterova, E. O. *V. P. Vakhterov, ego zhizn' i rabota* (V. P. Vakhterov, his life and work). F. F. Korolev, ed. Moscow, 1961.

Valuev, P. A. *Dnevnik P. A. Valueva Ministra Vnutrennikh Del* (The diary of P. A. Valuev Minister of the Interior). P. A. Zaionchkovsky, ed. 2 vols. Moscow, 1961.

———— *Graf P. A. Valuev — dnevnik 1877–84* (Count P. A. Valuev — diary 1877–84). V. Ia. Iakovlev-Bogucharsky and P. E. Shchegolev, eds. Petrograd, 1919.

Veresaev, V. *Sobranie sochinenii* (Collected works). Vol. V: *Vospominaniia* (Reminiscences). Iu. U. Babushkin and V. M. Nol'de, eds. Moscow, 1961.

Veselovsky, K. S. "Vospominaniia o nekotorykh litseiskikh tovar-ishchakh, Mikhail Vasil'evich Butashevich-Petrashevsky" (Remi-niscences about some lyceum companions, Mikhail Vasil'evich Butashevich-Petrashevsky), *Russkaia starina*, CIII (September 1900), 449–456.

——— "Vospominaniia o tsarsko-sel'skom litsee, 1832–1838 gg." (Remi-niscences about the Tsarskoe Selo Lyceum 1832–1838), *Russkaia starina*, CIV (October 1900), 3–29.

Vessel', N. Kh. "Nasha sredniaia obshcheobrazovatel'naia shkola" (Our general education secondary school), *Russkii vestnik*, February–March 1903, pp. 581–612, 193–228.

Vishniak, M. *Dan' proshlomu* (A tribute to the past). New York: Izda-tel'stvo imeni Chekhova, 1954.

Volkonsky, S. *Moi vospominaniia* (My reminiscences). Vol. III: *Rodina* (Na-tive land). [Munich]: Knigoizdatel'stvo Mednyi Vsadnik, [1923].

Voronov, A. "Vospominaniia byvshego studenta kharkovskogo universi-teta v 60-kh godov" (The reminiscences of a former student of Kharkov University in the 1860s), *Russkaia starina*, CLIV (June 1913), 571–595.

"Vozhd' reaktsii 60-80-kh godov (Pis'ma Katkova Aleksandru II i Alek-sandru III)" (The leader of the reaction from the 1860s to the 1880s [Katkov's letters to Alexander II and Alexander III]), *Byloe*, October 1917, pp. 3–32.

Witte, S. Iu. *Vospominaniia: detstvo, tsarstvovaniia Aleksandra II i Aleksandra III (1849–1894)* (Reminiscences: childhood, the reigns of Alexander II and Alexander III [1849–1894]). Berlin: Knigoizdatel'stvo "Slovo," 1923.

Zaionchkovsky, P. A., and A. N. Sokolov, eds. *Moskovskii universitet v vospo-minaniiakh sovremennikov* (Moscow University in contemporary rem-iniscences). Moscow, 1956.

Zhebelev, S. "Iz universitetskikh vospominanii" (From university remi-niscences), *Annaly*, II (1923), 168–187.

Periodicals, Pedagogical Writings, and Miscellaneous Primary Sources

Arnold, Matthew. *The Complete Prose Works of Matthew Arnold*. Vol. IV: *Schools and Universities on the Continent*. R. H. Super, ed. Ann Arbor, Mich.: University of Michigan Press, 1964.

Barsukov, N. *Zhizn' i trudy M. P. Pogodina* (The life and works of M. P. Po-godin). 22 vols. St. Petersburg, 1888–1910.

Desnitsky, V. A., ed. *Delo petrashevtsev* (The affair of the Petrashevtsy). 3 vols. Moscow-Leningrad, 1937–1951.

Georgievsky, A. I. *Predpolozhennaia reforma nashei srednei shkoly* (The pro-posed reform of our secondary school). St. Petersburg, 1901.

Grot, K. Ia. *Pushkinskii litsei (1811–1817): bumagi I-go kursa* (The Pushkin lyceum [1811–1817]: documents of the first course). St. Petersburg, 1911.

Grot, N., ed. *Ia. K. Grot: neskol'ko dannykh k ego biografii i kharakteristike* (Ia. K. Grot: some information toward a biography and character sketch). St. Petersburg, 1895.

Il'minsky, N. I. *Izbrannye mesta iz pedagogicheskikh sochinenii, nekotorye svedeniia o ego deiatel'nosti i o poslednikh dniakh ego zhizni* (Selected passages from his pedagogical works, some information on his activity and on the last days of his life). Kazan, 1892.

Katkov, M. N. "Nasha uchebnaia reforma" (Our educational reform), *Russkii vestnik*, June 1879, pp. 826–926.

—— *Sobranie peredovykh statei "Moskovskikh vedomostei" 1863–1887* (A collection of editorials from the "Moscow Gazette" 1863–1887). 25 vols. Moscow, 1897–1898.

[Khrushchov, D. P., ed.,] *Materialy dlia istorii uprazdneniia krepostnogo sostoianiia pomeshchichikh krest'ian v Rossii v tsarstvovanie Imperatora Aleksandra II* (Materials for a history of the abolition of the serfdom of the seigneurial peasants in Russia in the reign of Emperor Alexander II). Vol. III: *1860–1861*. Berlin, 1862.

Korf, N. A. *Russkaia nachal'naia shkola: rukovodstvo dlia zemskikh glasnykh i uchitelei sel'skikh shkol* (The Russian elementary school: a guide for zemstvo members and for teachers at rural schools). 4th ed. rev. St. Petersburg, 1872.

Koz'min, B. P., ed. *Nechaev i nechaevtsy: sbornik materialov* (Nechaev and the Nechaevtsy: collected materials). Moscow-Leningrad, 1931.

Materialy dlia istorii goneniia studentov pri Aleksandre II (Materials for a history of the persecution of students under Alexander II). 4th ed. Leipzig: E. L. Kasprowicz, 1902.

Mikhnevich, V. O., ed. *1863–1877 piatnadtsatiletie gazety "Golos"* (1863–1877 the fifteenth anniversary of the newspaper "The Voice"). St. Petersburg, 1878.

Modestov, V. I. *Shkolnyi vopros: pis'ma k redaktoru "Golos"* (The school question: letters to the editor of "The Voice"). St. Petersburg, 1880.

MV. See Katkov, *Sobranie peredovykh statei "Moskovskikh vedomostei" 1863–1887.*

Pamiatnaia knizhka imperatorskogo aleksandrovskogo litseia na 1880 god (The yearbook of the Imperial Alexander Lyceum for 1880). St. Petersburg, 1880.

Piatidesiatiletnyi iubilei imperatorskogo aleksandrovskogo litseia 19 oktiabria 1861 goda (The fiftieth anniversary jubilee of the Imperial Alexander Lyceum 19 October 1861). St. Petersburg, 1861.

Pipes, Richard. *Karamzin's Memoir on Ancient and Modern Russia: A Translation and Analysis.* Cambridge, Mass.: Harvard University Press, 1959.

Pirogov, N. I. *Sochineniia N. I. Pirogova* (The works of N. I. Pirogov). 2 vols. 2nd ed. St. Petersburg, 1900.

Pleshcheev, A. N. *Izbrannye stikhotvoreniia, proza* (Selected poems, prose). N. M. Gaidenkov and V. I. Korovin, eds. Moscow, 1960.

Pogodin, M. P. "Obuchenie drevnim iazykam v Rossii (1875): pis'mo M. P. Pogodina k kniaziu A. I. Vasil'chikovu" (The teaching of classical languages in Russia [1875]: a letter of M. P. Pogodin to Prince A. I. Vasil'chikov), *Russkii arkhiv*, bk. I (1902), 162–188.

Rachinsky, S. *Zametki o sel'skikh shkolakh* (Notes on rural schools). St. Petersburg, 1883.

Rozanov, V. V. *Sumerki prosveshcheniia: sbornik statei po voprosam obrazovaniia* (The twilight of enlightenment: collected articles on questions of education). St. Petersburg, 1899.

Russkii vestnik (The Russian Herald). Moscow and St. Petersburg, 1856–1906.

Ushinsky, K. D. *Izbrannye pedagogicheskie sochineniia* (Selected pedagogical works). V. Ia. Struminsky, ed. 2 vols. Moscow, 1952–1954.

Valk, S. N., ed. *Materialy po istorii leningradskogo universiteta 1819–1917* (Materials relating to the history of Leningrad University 1819–1917). Leningrad, 1961.

Vasil'chikov, A. I. *Pis'mo Ministru Narodnogo Prosveshcheniia grafu Tolstomu* (A letter to the Minister of Education Count Tolstoi). Berlin, 1875.

Vessel', N. Kh. *Ocherki ob obshchem obrazovanii i sisteme narodnogo obrazovaniia v Rossii* (Essays on general education and on the system of public education in Russia). V. Ia. Struminsky, ed. Moscow, 1959.

Vestnik Evropy (The Herald of Europe). St. Petersburg, 1866–1919.

Secondary Works

Abramov, Ia. V. *Nashi voskresnye shkoly: ikh proshloe i nastoiashchee* (Our Sunday schools: their past and present). St. Petersburg, 1900.

Aleshintsev, I. *Istoriia gimnazicheskogo obrazovaniia v Rossii (XVIII i XIX vek)* (A history of gymnasium education in Russia [The eighteenth and nineteenth centuries]). St. Petersburg, 1912.

Alston, Patrick L. *Education and the State in Tsarist Russia*. Stanford: Stanford University Press, 1969.

Antonov, N. "Klassitsizm v tsifrakh" (Classicism in figures), in *Sbornik pedagogicheskikh statei v chest' redaktora zhurnala "Pedagogicheskii sbornik" N. Ostrogorskogo* (A collection of pedagogical articles in honor of the editor of the journal "Pedagogical Miscellany" N. Ostrogorsky). St. Petersburg, 1907, pp. 307–320.

Antonov, V. S. "K voprosu o sotsial'nom sostave i chislennosti revoliutsionerov 70-kh godov" (On the question of the numbers and social composition of the revolutionaries of the 1870s), in *Obshchest-vennoe dvizhenie v poreformennoi Rossii* (Social movements in Russia after the reforms). E. S. Vilenskaia et al., eds. Moscow, 1965, pp. 336–343.

Belokonsky, I. "Krest'ianstvo i narodnoe obrazovanie" (The peasantry and public education), in *Velikaia reforma* (The great reform). A. K. Dzhibelegov, S. P. Mel'gunov, and V. I. Picheta, eds. Vol. VI. Moscow, 1911, pp. 288–302.

Bender, Hermann. "Geschichte des Gelehrtenschulwesens in Deutschland seit der Reformation," in *Geschichte der Erziehung von Anfang bis auf unsere Zeit*. K. A. Schmid, ed. Vol. V, pt. I. Stuttgart: F. G. Gotta'sche Buchhandlung, 1901, pp. 1–337.

Bendrikov, K. E. *Ocherki po istorii narodnogo obrazovaniia v Turkestane (1865–1924 gody)* (Outlines of the history of public education in Turkestan [1865–1924]). Moscow, 1960.

Bliokh, I. S. *Finansy Rossii XIX stoletiia: istoriia – statistika* (Russian finances in the nineteenth century: history — statistics). Vol. IV. St. Petersburg, 1882.

Bogdanov, I. M. *Gramotnost' i obrazovanie v dorevoliutsionnoi Rossii i v SSSR* (Literacy and education in prerevolutionary Russia and in the USSR). Moscow, 1964.

Boratynskaia, O. "A. K. Kazembek" (A. K. Kazembek), *Russkii arkhiv*, bk. IV (1893), 537–555.

Butts, R. Freeman. *A Cultural History of Education: Reassessing Our Educational Traditions*. New York: McGraw-Hill Book Company, Inc., 1947.

Charnolusky, V. I. "Nachal'noe obrazovanie vo vtoroi polovine XIX stoletiia" (Elementary education in the second half of the nineteenth century), in *Istoriia Rossii v XIX vek* (A history of Russia in the nineteenth century). Vol. VII. St. Petersburg, 191?, pp. 109–169.

Chekhov, N. V. *Narodnoe obrazovanie v Rossii s 60-kh godov XIX veka* (Public education in Russia since the sixties of the nineteenth century). Moscow, 1912.

Demkov, M. I. *Istoriia russkoi pedagogiki* (A history of Russian pedagogy). Pt. II: *Russkaia pedagogika (XVIII vek)* (Russian pedagogy [The eighteenth century]). 2nd ed. rev. Moscow, 1910.

Druzhinin, N. M. *Gosudarstvennye krest'iane i reforma P. D. Kiseleva* (The state peasants and the reform of P. D. Kiselev). Vol. II: *Realizatsiia i posledstviia reformy* (The realization and results of the reform). Moscow, 1958.

Dzhanshiev, G. *A. M. Unkovsky i osvobozhdenie krest'ian* (A. M. Unkovsky and the emancipation of the peasants). Moscow, 1894.

—— *Epokha velikikh reform: istoricheskie spravki* (The epoch of the great reforms: historical inquiries). 7th ed. rev. Moscow, 1898.

Egorov, Iu. N. "Reaktsionnaia politika tsarizma v voprosakh universitet-skogo obrazovaniia v 30–50-kh gg. XIXv." (The reactionary policy of tsarism in questions of university education from the thirties to the fifties of the nineteenth century), *Nauchnye doklady vysshei shkoly: istoricheskie nauki*, no. 3 (1960), 60–75.

Emmons, Terence. "The Peasant and the Emancipation," in *The Peasant in Nineteenth Century Russia*. Wayne S. Vucinich, ed. Stanford: Stanford University Press, 1968, pp. 41–71.

Erzhov, A. "Narodnoe prosveshchenie i biurokratiia posle 1861 goda" (Public education and the bureaucracy after 1861), *Obrazovanie*, XVII (April–June 1908), 1–39, 52–82, 71–116.

Fedorov, A. V. *Russkaia armiia v 50–70-kh godakh XIX veka, ocherki* (The Russian army from the fifties to the seventies of the nineteenth century, essays). Leningrad, 1959.

Ferliudin, P. *Istoricheskii obzor mer po vysshemu obrazovaniiu v Rossii* (A historical survey of measures relating to higher education in Russia). Vol. I: *Akademiia Nauk i universitety* (The Academy of Sciences and the universities). Saratov, 1894.

Florinsky, Michael T. *Russia: A History and an Interpretation*. 2 vols. New York: The Macmillan Company, 1958.

Flynn, James T. "The Universities, the Gentry and the Russian Imperial Services, 1815–1825," *Canadian Slavic Studies*, 2:486–503 (winter 1968).

Ganelin, Sh. I. *Ocherki po istorii srednei shkoly v Rossii vtoroi poloviny XIX veka* (Outlines of the history of the secondary school in Russia in the second half of the nineteenth century). 2nd ed. rev. Moscow, 1954.

Georgievsky, A. I. "K istorii uchenogo komiteta Ministerstva Narodnogo Prosveshcheniia" (Toward a history of the Academic Committee of the Ministry of Education), *Zhurnal Ministerstva Narodnogo Prosveshcheniia*, CCCXXXI–CCCXXXII (October–December 1900); CCCXL–CCCXLI (February–March 1902), otdel III, 25–61; 17–61, 74–121; 33–72; 21–56.

―――― *Materialy po universitetskomu voprosu* (Materials relating to the university question). P. Struve, ed. Stuttgart: Izdanie redaktsii "Osvobozhdeniia," 1902.

[Golitsyn, N.] *Blagorodnyi pansion imperatorskogo tsarskosel'skogo litseia 1814–1829* (The noble pension of the Imperial Tsarskoe Selo Lyceum 1814–1829). St. Petersburg, 1869.

Grigor'ev, V. V. *Istoricheskii ocherk russkoi shkoly* (A historical survey of the Russian school). Moscow, 1900.

Grot, Ia. *Pushkin, ego litseiskie tovarishchi i nastavniki* (Pushkin, his lyceum companions and teachers). St. Petersburg, 1887.

Hans, Nicholas. *History of Russian Educational Policy (1701–1917)*. London: P. S. King & Son Ltd., 1931.

———— *The Russian Tradition in Education*. London: Routledge & Kegan Paul, 1963.

Hegarty, Thomas J. "Student Movements in Russian Universities 1855–61," Ph.D. diss., Harvard University, 1965.

Hofstadter, Richard. *Anti-Intellectualism in American Life*. New York: Alfred A. Knopf, 1963.

Holt, John. "To the Rescue," *New York Review of Books*, 13:27–36 (October 9, 1969).

Iakhontov, A. N. *Istoricheskii ocherk imperatorskogo aleksandrovskogo (b. tsarskosel'skogo) litseia* (A historical survey of the Imperial Alexander [formerly Tsarskoe Selo] Lyceum). Paris: Izdanie ob'edineniia b. vospitannikov imperatorskogo aleksandrovskogo litseia, 1936.

Iakovlev, I. Ia. [Salembek]. *Simbirskaia uchitel'skaia shkola i ee rol' v prosveshchenii chuvash* (The Simbirsk teachers' school and its role in educating the Chuvash). Cheboksary, 1959.

Iakovlev-Bogucharsky, V. Ia. *Iz istorii politicheskoi bor'by v 70-kh i 80-kh gg. XIX veka: partiia "Narodnoi voli," ee proiskhozhdenie, sub'by i gibel'* (From the history of the political struggle in the seventies and eighties of the nineteenth century: the party "The People's Will," its origin, fortunes, and downfall). Moscow, 1912.

Ivanov, P. *Studenty v Moskve: byt', nravy, tipy (Ocherki)* (Students in Moscow: mode of life, customs, types [Essays]). Moscow, 1903.

Johnson, William H. E. *Russia's Educational Heritage*. Pittsburgh: Carnegie Press, 1950.

Kapterev, P. F. *Istoriia russkoi pedagogii* (A history of Russian pedagogy). St. Petersburg, n.d.

Karyshev, N. *Zemskie khodataistva 1865–1884 gg.* (Zemstvo petitions 1865–1884). Moscow, 1900.

Katz, Martin. *Mikhail N. Katkov: A Political Biography 1818–1887*. The Hague: Mouton & Co., 1966.

Kobeko, D. *Imperatorskii tsarskosel'skii litsei: nastavniki i pitomtsy 1811–1843* (The Imperial Tsarskoe Selo Lyceum: teachers and students 1811–1843). St. Petersburg, 1911.

Konstantinov, N. A. *Ocherki po istorii srednei shkoly* (Outlines of the history of the secondary school). Moscow, 1947.

———— and V. Ia. Struminsky. *Ocherki po istorii nachal'nogo obrazovaniia v Rossii* (Outlines of the history of elementary education in Russia). Moscow, 1949.

Kornilov, A. A. *Obshchestvennoe dvizhenie pri Aleksandre II (1855–81): istoricheskie ocherki* (Social movements under Alexander II [1855–81]: historical essays). Moscow, 1909.

Kovalensky, M. N. "Sredniaia shkola" (The secondary school), in *Istoriia Rossii v XIX vek*. Vol. VII. St. Petersburg, 191?, pp. 170–202.

Leontowitsch, Victor. *Geschichte des Liberalismus in Russland*. Frankfurt: Vittorio Klostermann, 1957.

Liard, Louis. *L'enseignement supérieure en France 1789–1893.* 2 vols. Paris, 1888–1894.

Likhacheva, E. *Materialy dlia istorii zhenskogo obrazovaniia v Rossii* (Materials for a history of female education in Russia). 2 vols. St. Petersburg, 1899–1901.

Liubimov, N. A. *Mikhail Nikiforovich Katkov i ego istoricheskaia zasluga* (Mikhail Nikiforovich Katkov and his historical service). St. Petersburg, 1889.

Liwoff, Grégoire. *Michel Katkoff et son époque: quelques pages d'histoire contemporaine en Russie 1855–1887.* Paris, 1897.

Markevich, A. I. *Dvadtsatipiatiletie imperatorskogo novorossiiskogo universiteta* (The twenty-fifth anniversary of the Imperial University of Novorossiia). Odessa, 1890.

Mathes, William L. "N. I. Pirogov and the Reform of University Government, 1856–1866," *Slavic Review,* 31:29–51 (March 1972).

———— "The Origins of Confrontation Politics in Russian Universities: Student Activism, 1855–1861," *Canadian Slavic Studies,* 2:28–45 (spring 1968).

Medynsky, E. N. *Istoriia russkoi pedagogiki do velikoi oktiabr'skoi sotsialisticheskoi revoliutsii* (A history of Russian pedagogy before the great October socialist revolution). 2nd ed. rev. Moscow, 1938.

Miliukov, P. N. *Ocherki po istorii russkoi kultury* (Outlines of the history of Russian culture). Pt. II: *Tserkov' i shkola* (Church and school). 3d ed. rev. St. Petersburg, 1902.

Miller, Forrestt A. *Dmitrii Miliutin and the Reform Era in Russia.* [Nashville]: Vanderbilt University Press, 1968.

Mills, James Cobb, Jr. "Dmitrii Tolstoi as Minister of Education in Russia, 1866–1880." Ph.D. diss., Indiana University, 1967.

Mintslov, S. P. *Obzor zapisok, dnevnikov, vospominanii, pisem i puteshestvii otnosiashchikhsia k istorii Rossii i napechatannykh na russkom iazyke* (A survey of memoirs, diaries, reminiscences, letters, and travel accounts relating to the history of Russia and printed in Russian). Novgorod, 1911–1912.

Monas, Sidney. *The Third Section: Police and Society in Russia under Nicholas I.* Cambridge, Mass.: Harvard University Press, 1961.

Mosse, W. E. *Alexander II and the Modernization of Russia.* London: The English Universities Press Ltd., 1958.

Nechkina, M. V. *Dvizhenie dekabristov* (The Decembrist movement). 2 vols. Moscow, 1955.

Nevedensky, S. *Katkov i ego vremia* (Katkov and his time). St. Petersburg, 1888.

Orlov, V. I. *Studencheskoe dvizhenie moskovskogo universiteta v XIX stoletii* (The student movement at Moscow University in the nineteenth century). Moscow, 1934.

Panchukov, A. P. *Istoriia nachal'noi i srednei shkoly vostochnoi sibiri* (A history of elementary and secondary schools in Eastern Siberia). Ulan-Ude, 1959.

Paulsen, Friedrich. *German Education Past and Present.* Tran. by T. Lorenz. New York: Charles Scribner's Sons, 1908.

——— *Geschichte des gelehrten Unterrichts auf den deutschen Schulen und Universitäten von Ausgang des Mittelalters bis zur Gegenwart.* Vol. II, 2nd ed. rev. Leipzig, 1897.

——— *The German Universities and University Study.* Tran. by Frank Thilly and William W. Elwang. New York: Charles Scribner's Sons, 1906.

Pierce, Richard A. *Russian Central Asia 1867–1917: A Study in Colonial Rule.* Berkeley and Los Angeles: University of California Press, 1960.

Protopopov, D. D. *Istoriia s-peterburgskogo komiteta gramotnosti (1861–1895 gg.)* (A history of the St. Petersburg Committee on Literacy [1861–1895]). St. Petersburg, 1898.

Rashin, A. G. *Naselenie Rossii za 100 let (1811–1913 gg.): statisticheskie ocherki* (The population of Russia over a one-hundred-year period [1811–1913]: statistical sketches). S. G. Strumilin, ed. Moscow, 1956.

Riasanovsky, Nicholas V. *Nicholas I and Official Nationality in Russia, 1825–1855.* Berkeley and Los Angeles: University of California Press, 1959.

Ringer, Fritz K. "Higher Education in Germany in the Nineteenth Century," in *Education and Social Structure in the Twentieth Century.* Walter Laqueur and George L. Mosse, eds. New York: Harper and Row, 1967, pp. 123–138.

Rothblatt, Sheldon. *The Revolution of the Dons: Cambridge and Society in Victorian England.* New York: Basic Books, 1968.

Rozhdestvensky, S. V. *Ocherki po istorii sistem narodnogo prosveshcheniia v Rossii v XVIII–XIX vekakh* (Outlines of the history of the systems of education in Russia in the eighteenth and nineteenth centuries). Vol. I. St. Petersburg, 1912.

Russell, James E. *German Higher Schools: The History, Organization and Methods of Secondary Education in Germany.* New York: Longmans, Green & Co., 1899.

Sallwürk, Ernst von. "Die höhere Bildungswesen in Frankreich von 1789–1899," in *Geschichte der Erziehung von Anfang bis auf unsere Zeit.* K. A. Schmid, ed. Vol. V, pt. II. Stuttgart-Berlin: F. A. Gotta'sche Buchhandlung, 1901, pp. 107–141.

Sander, von. "Geschichte der Volksschule, besonders in Deutschland," in *Geschichte der Erziehung von Anfang bis auf unsere Zeit.* K. A. Schmid, ed. Vol. V, pt. III. Stuttgart-Berlin: F. A. Gotta'sche Buchhandlung, 1902, pp. 1–291.

Saussay, Jean. "La vie scolaire des compagnes a l'époque des reformes d'Alexandre II," *Cahiers du Monde russe et soviétique*, 9:392–413 (July–December 1969).

Schmid, E. K., ed. and tran. *Istoriia srednikh uchebnykh zavedenii v Rossii* (A history of secondary schools in Russia). (Published as appendixes to the *Zhurnal Ministerstva Narodnogo Prosveshcheniia* 1877–1878 and bound as a single volume by the Yale University Library.)

Seleznev, I. *Istoricheskii ocherk imperatorskogo byvshego tsarskosel'skogo nyne aleksandrovskogo litseia za pervoe ego piatidesiatiletie s 1811 po 1861 god* (A historical survey of the Imperial, formerly Tsarskoe Selo and now Alexander, Lyceum for its first fifty years from 1811 to 1861). St. Petersburg, 1861.

Semevsky, V. I. *Sobranie sochinenii* (Collected works). Vol. II: *M. V. Butashevich-Petrashevsky i petrashevtsy* (M. V. Butashevich-Petrashevky and the Petrashevtsy). Pt. I. V. Vodovozov, ed. Moscow, 1922.

Serebrennikova, V. G. "Demokraticheskaia zhurnalistika perioda vtoroi revoliutsionnoi situatsii" (Democratic journalism of the period of the second revolutionary situation), in *Obshchestvennoe dvizhenie v poreformennoi Rossii*. E. S. Vilenskaia et al., eds. Moscow, 1965, pp. 344–365.

Seton-Watson, Hugh. *The Russian Empire 1801–1917.* Oxford: Oxford University Press, 1967.

Shchepkin, M. "Upravlenie gorodskimi uchilishchami v Moskve: istoricheskii ocherk" (The administration of municipal schools in Moscow: a historical survey), *Russkaia mysl'*, XXVI (March 1905), 231–256.

Shchetinina, G. I. "Klassifikatsiia i analiz osnovnykh istochnikov po istorii universitetskoi kontrreformy 1884 goda" (A classification and analysis of the principal sources relating to the history of the university counterreform of 1884), in *Maloissledovannye istochniki po istorii SSSR XIX–XXvv (Istochnikovedecheskii analiz)* (Little-explored sources for the history of the USSR in the nineteenth and twentieth centuries [A historiographical analysis]). N. A. Iunitsky et al., eds. Moscow, 1964, pp. 148–174.

———— "Podgotovka universitetskogo ustava 1884 g." (The preparation of the university statute of 1884), *Nauchnye doklady vysshei shkoly: istoricheskie nauki*, no. 1 (1961), 44–56.

Shil'der, N. K. *Imperator Nikolai Pervyi: ego zhizn' i tsarstvovanie* (Emperor Nicholas I: his life and reign). 2 vols. St. Petersburg, 1903.

Sinel, Allen. "Count Dmitrii Tolstoi and the Preparation of Russian School Teachers," *Canadian Slavic Studies*, 3:246–262 (summer 1969).

———— "Educating the Russian Peasantry: The Elementary School Reforms of Count Dmitrii Tolstoi," *Slavic Review*, 27:49–70 (March 1968).

Smirnov, V. Z. *Ocherki po istorii progressivnoi russkoi pedagogiki XIX veka* (Outlines of the history of progressive Russian pedagogy of the nineteenth century). Moscow, 1963.

―――― "O merakh podderzhaniia distsipliny uchashchikhsia gimnazii i progimnazii (1864–1874 gg.)" (On the measures for maintaining discipline among gymnasium and progymnasium students [1864–1874]), *Sovetskaia pedagogika*, X (August–September 1946), 52–63.

―――― *Reforma nachal'noi i srednei shkoly v 60-kh godakh XIXv.* (The reform of elementary and secondary schools in the sixties of the nineteenth century). Moscow, 1954.

Struminsky, V. Ia. *K. D. Ushinsky, ocherk zhizni i deiatel'nosti.* (K. D. Ushinsky, a survey of his life and activity). Moscow, 1960.

Sukhomlinov, M. I. *Issledovaniia i stat'i* (Papers and articles). Vol. I: *Materialy dlia istorii obrazovaniia v Rossii v tsarstvovanie Imperatora Aleksandra I* (Materials for the history of education in Russia in the reign of Emperor Alexander I). St. Petersburg, 1889.

Szeftel, Marc. "The Form of Government of the Russian Empire Prior to the Constitutional Reforms of 1905–06," in *Essays in Russian and Soviet History in Honor of Geroid Tanquary Robinson.* John Shelton Curtiss, ed. New York: Columbia University Press, 1961, pp. 105–119.

Tatishchev, S. S. *Imperator Aleksandr II: ego zhizn' i tsarstvovanie* (Emperor Alexander II: his life and reign). 2 vols. St. Petersburg, 1903.

Tazhibaev, T. T. *Prosveshchenie i shkoly Kazakhstana vo vtoroi polovine XIX veka* (Education and schools in Kazakhstan in the second half of the nineteenth century). Alma Ata, 1962.

Thaden, Edward C. *Conservative Nationalism in Nineteenth Century Russia.* Seattle: University of Washington Press, 1964.

Tikhomirov, M. N. et al., eds. *Istoriia moskovskogo universiteta* (A history of Moscow University). Vol. I. Moscow, 1955.

Titlinov, B. V. *Dukhovnaia shkola v Rossii v XIX stoletii* (The clerical school in Russia in the nineteenth century). Vol. II: *Protasovshaia epokha i reformy 60-kh godov* (The Protasov epoch and the reforms of the 1860s). Vilna, 1909.

Trubachev, S. S. "Uchenye trudy grafa D. A. Tolstogo" (The scholarly works of Count D. A. Tolstoi), *Istoricheskii vestnik*, June 1889, pp. 653–659.

Venturi, Franco. *Roots of Revolution: A History of the Populist and Socialist Movements in Nineteenth Century Russia.* Tran. by Francis Haskell. London: Weidenfeld and Nicolson, 1960.

Veselovsky, B. V. *Istoriia zemstva za sorok let* (A history of the zemstvo after forty years). Vol. I. St. Petersburg, 1909.

Vladimirsky-Budanov, M. F. *Istoriia imperatorskogo universiteta Sv. Vladimira* (A history of the Imperial University of St. Vladimir). Vol. I: *Universitet Sv. Vladimira v tsarstvovanie Imperatora Nikolaia Pavlovicha* (The

University of St. Vladimir in the reign of Emperor Nicholas Pavlovich). Kiev, 1884.

Vucinich, Alexander. *Science in Russian Culture.* Vol. I: *A History to 1860.* Stanford: Stanford University Press, 1963. Vol. II: *1861–1917.* Stanford: Stanford University Press, 1970.

Vydrin, R. *Osnovnye momenty studencheskogo dvizheniia v Rossii* (The principal features of the student movement in Russia). Moscow, 1908.

Williams, L. Pearce. "Science, Education and Napoleon I," *Isis*, 47:369–382 (1956).

Zaionchkovsky, P. A. *Krizis samoderzhaviia na rubezhe 1870–1880 godov* (The crisis of the autocracy in the late 1870s and early 1880s). Moscow, 1964.

———— *Rossiiskoe samoderzhavie v kontse XIX stoletiia* (The Russian autocracy at the end of the nineteenth century). Moscow, 1970.

———— *Voennye reformy 1860–1870 godov v Rossii* (The military reforms of the 1860s and 1870s in Russia). Moscow, 1952.

Zelnik, Reginald E. "The Sunday School Movement in Russia, 1859–1862," *Journal of Modern History*, 37:151–170 (June 1965).

Index

Russian Research Center Studies

12. *Terror and Progress USSR: Some Sources of Change and Stability in the Soviet Dictatorship*, by Barrington Moore, Jr.
13. *The Formation of the Soviet Union: Communism and Nationalism, 1917–1923*, by Richard Pipes. Revised edition
14. *Marxism: The Unity of Theory and Practice — A Critical Essay*, by Alfred G. Meyer. Reissued with a new introduction
15. *Soviet Industrial Production, 1928–1951*, by Donald R. Hodgman
16. *Soviet Taxation: The Fiscal and Monetary Problems of a Planned Economy*, by Franklyn D. Holzman*
17. *Soviet Military Law and Administration*, by Harold J. Berman and Miroslav Kerner*
18. *Documents on Soviet Military Law and Administration*, edited and translated by Harold J. Berman and Miroslav Kerner*
19. *The Russian Marxists and the Origins of Bolshevism*, by Leopold H. Haimson
20. *The Permanent Purge: Politics in Soviet Totalitarianism*, by Zbigniew K. Brzezinski*
21. *Belorussia: The Making of a Nation — A Case Study*, by Nicholas P. Vakar*
22. *A Bibliographical Guide to Belorussia*, by Nicholas P. Vakar*
23. *The Balkans in Our Time*, by Robert Lee Wolff (also American Foreign Policy Library)
24. *How the Soviet System Works: Cultural, Psychological, and Social Themes*, by Raymond A. Bauer, Alex Inkeles, and Clyde Kluckhohn †
25. *The Economics of Soviet Steel*, by M. Gardner Clark*
26. *Leninism*, by Alfred G. Meyer*
27. *Factory and Manager in the USSR*, by Joseph S. Berliner †
28. *Soviet Transportation Policy*, by Holland Hunter*
29. *Doctor and Patient in Soviet Russia*, by Mark G. Field †*
30. *Russian Liberalism: From Gentry to Intelligentsia*, by George Fischer
31. *Stalin's Failure in China, 1924–1927*, by Conrad Brandt
32. *The Communist Party of Poland: An Outline of History*, by M. K. Dziewanowski
33. *Karamzin's Memoir on Ancient and Modern Russia: A Translation and Analysis*, by Richard Pipes*
34. *A Memoir on Ancient and Modern Russia*, by N. M. Karamzin, the Russian text edited by Richard Pipes*
35. *The Soviet Citizen: Daily Life in a Totalitarian Society*, by Alex Inkeles and Raymond A. Bauer †*
36. *Pan-Turkism and Islam in Russia*, by Serge A. Zenkovsky

* Out of print.
† Publications of the Harvard Project on the Soviet Social System.